Poetry
for Students

Poetry for Students

Presenting Analysis, Context, and Criticism on Commonly Studied Poetry

Volume 10

Michael L. LaBlanc, Editor

Foreword by David Kelly, College of Lake County

GALE GROUP

Detroit
New York
San Francisco
London
Boston
Woodbridge, CT

Poetry for Students

Staff

Series Editor: Michael L. LaBlanc.

Contributing Editors: Elizabeth Bellalouna, Anne Marie Hacht, Kimberly Hazelmyer, Mark Milne, Jennifer Smith.

Managing Editor: Dwayne Hayes.

Research: Victoria B. Cariappa, *Research Manager*. Cheryl Warnock, *Research Specialists*. Tamara Nott, Tracie A. Richardson, *Research Associates*. Nicodemus Ford, Sarah Genik, Timothy Lehnerer, *Research Assistants*.

Permissions: Maria Franklin, *Permissions Manager*. Sarah Tomasek, *Permissions Associate*.

Manufacturing: Mary Beth Trimper, *Manager, Composition and Electronic Prepress*. Evi Seoud, *Assistant Manager, Composition Purchasing and Electronic Prepress*. Stacy Melson, *Buyer*.

Imaging and Multimedia Content Team: Barbara Yarrow, *Manager*. Randy Bassett, *Imaging Supervisor*. Robert Duncan, Dan Newell, *Imaging Specialists*. Pamela A. Reed, *Imaging Coordinator*. Leitha Etheridge-Sims, Mary Grimes, *Image Catalogers*. Robyn Young, *Project Manager*. Dean Dauphinais, *Senior Image Editors*. Kelly A. Quin, *Image Editor*.

Product Design Team: Kenn Zorn, *Product Design Manager*. Pamela A. E. Galbreath, *Senior Art Director*. Michael Logusz, *Graphic Artist*.

Copyright Notice

National Advisory Board

Table of Contents

Just a Few Lines on a Page

I have often thought that poets have the easiest job in the world. A poem, after all, is just a few lines on a page, usually not even extending margin to margin—how long would that take to write, about five minutes? Maybe ten at the most, if you wanted it to rhyme or have a repeating meter. Why, I could start in the morning and produce a book of poetry by dinnertime. But we all know that it isn't that easy. Anyone can come up with enough words, but the poet's job is about writing the *right* ones. The right words will change lives, making people see the world somewhat differently than they saw it just a few minutes earlier. The right words can make a reader who relies on the dictionary for meanings take a greater responsibility for his or her own personal understanding. A poem that is put on the page correctly can bear any amount of analysis, probing, defining, explaining, and interrogating, and something about it will still feel new the next time you read it.

It would be fine with me if I could talk about poetry without using the word "magical," because that word is overused these days to imply "a really good time," often with a certain sweetness about it, and a lot of poetry is neither of these. But if you stop and think about magic—whether it brings to mind sorcery, witchcraft, or bunnies pulled from top hats—it always seems to involve stretching reality to produce a result greater than the sum of its parts and pulling unexpected results out of thin air. This book provides ample cases where a few simple words conjure up whole worlds. We do not actually travel to different times and different cultures, but the poems get into our minds, they find what little we know about the places they are talking about, and then they make that little bit blossom into a bouquet of someone else's life. Poets make us think we are following simple, specific events, but then they leave ideas in our heads that cannot be found on the printed page. Abracadabra.

Sometimes when you finish a poem it doesn't feel as if it has left any supernatural effect on you, like it did not have any more to say beyond the actual words that it used. This happens to everybody, but most often to inexperienced readers: regardless of what is often said about young people's infinite capacity to be amazed, you have to understand what usually does happen, and what could have happened instead, if you are going to be moved by what someone has accomplished. In those cases in which you finish a poem with a "So what?" attitude, the information provided in *Poetry for Students* comes in handy. Readers can feel assured that the poems included here actually are potent magic, not just because a few (or a hundred or ten thousand) professors of literature say they are: they're significant because they can withstand close inspection and still amaze the very same people who have just finished taking them apart and seeing how they work. Turn them inside out, and they will still be able to come alive, again and again. *Poetry for Students* gives readers of any age good practice in feeling the ways poems relate to both the reality of the time and place the poet lived in and the reality of our emotions. Practice is just another word for being a student. The information given here helps you understand the way to read poetry; what to look for, what to expect.

With all of this in mind, I really don't think I would actually like to have a poet's job at all. There are too many skills involved, including precision, honesty, taste, courage, linguistics, passion, compassion, and the ability to keep all sorts of people entertained at once. And that is just what they do

with one hand, while the other hand pulls some sort of trick that most of us will never fully understand. I can't even pack all that I need for a weekend into one suitcase, so what would be my chances of stuffing so much life into a few lines? With all that *Poetry for Students* tells us about each poem, I am impressed that any poet can finish three or four poems a year. Read the inside stories of these poems, and you won't be able to approach any poem in the same way you did before.

David J. Kelly
College of Lake County

Introduction

Purpose of the Book

The purpose of *Poetry for Students* (*PfS*) is to provide readers with a guide to understanding, enjoying, and studying poems by giving them easy access to information about the work. Part of Gale's "For Students" Literature line, *PfS* is specifically designed to meet the curricular needs of high school and undergraduate college students and their teachers, as well as the interests of general readers and researchers considering specific poems. While each volume contains entries on "classic" poems frequently studied in classrooms, there are also entries containing hard-to-find information on contemporary poems, including works by multicultural, international, and women poets.

The information covered in each entry includes an introduction to the poem and the poem's author; the actual poem text; a poem summary, to help readers unravel and understand the meaning of the poem; analysis of important themes in the poem; and an explanation of important literary techniques and movements as they are demonstrated in the poem.

In addition to this material, which helps the readers analyze the poem itself, students are also provided with important information on the literary and historical background informing each work. This includes a historical context essay, a box comparing the time or place the poem was written to modern Western culture, a critical overview essay, and excerpts from critical essays on the poem, when available. A unique feature of *PfS* is a specially commissioned overview essay on each poem by an academic expert, targeted toward the student reader.

To further aid the student in studying and enjoying each poem, information on media adaptations is provided when available, as well as reading suggestions for works of fiction and nonfiction on similar themes and topics. Classroom aids include ideas for research papers and lists of critical sources that provide additional material on the poem.

Selection Criteria

The titles for each volume of *PfS* were selected by surveying numerous sources on teaching literature and analyzing course curricula for various school districts. Some of the sources surveyed included: literature anthologies; *Reading Lists for College-Bound Students: The Books Most Recommended by America's Top Colleges;* textbooks on teaching the poem; a College Board survey of poems commonly studied in high schools; and a National Council of Teachers of English (NCTE) survey of poems commonly studied in high schools.

Input was also solicited from our expert advisory board, as well as educators from various areas. From these discussions, it was determined that each volume should have a mix of "classic" poems (those works commonly taught in literature classes) and contemporary poems for which information is often hard to find. Because of the interest in expanding the canon of literature, an emphasis was also placed on including works by international, multicultural, and women authors. Our advisory board members—current high school and college teachers—helped pare down the list for each volume. If a work was not selected for the present volume, it was often noted as a possibility for a future volume. As always, the editor welcomes suggestions for titles to be included in future volumes.

How Each Entry Is Organized

Each entry, or chapter, in *PfS* focuses on one poem. Each entry heading lists the full name of the poem, the author's name, and the date of the poem's publication. The following elements are contained in each entry:

- **Introduction:** a brief overview of the poem which provides information about its first appearance, its literary standing, any controversies surrounding the work, and major conflicts or themes within the work.

- **Author Biography:** this section includes basic facts about the poet's life, and focuses on events and times in the author's life that inspired the poem in question.

- **Poem Text:** when permission has been granted, the poem is reprinted, allowing for quick reference when reading the explication of the following section.

- **Poem Summary:** a description of the major events in the poem, with interpretation of how these events help articulate the poem's themes. Summaries are broken down with subheads that indicate the lines being discussed.

- **Themes:** a thorough overview of how the major topics, themes, and issues are addressed within the poem. Each theme discussed appears in a separate subhead and is easily accessed through the boldface entries in the Subject/ Theme Index.

- **Style:** this section addresses important style elements of the poem, such as form, meter, and rhyme scheme; important literary devices used, such as imagery, foreshadowing, and symbolism; and, if applicable, genres to which the work might have belonged, such as Gothicism or Romanticism. Literary terms are explained within the entry, but can also be found in the Glossary.

- **Historical and Cultural Context:** This section outlines the social, political, and cultural climate *in which the author lived and the poem was created.* This section may include descriptions of related historical events, pertinent aspects of daily life in the culture, and the artistic and literary sensibilities of the time in which the work was written. If the poem is a historical work, information regarding the time in which the poem is set is also included. Each section is broken down with helpful subheads. (Works written after the late 1970s may not have this section.)

- **Critical Overview:** this section provides background on the critical reputation of the poem, including bannings or any other public controversies surrounding the work. For older works, this section includes a history of how poem was first received and how perceptions of it may have changed over the years; for more recent poems, direct quotes from early reviews may also be included.

- **Sources:** an alphabetical list of critical material quoted in the entry, with full bibliographical information.

- **For Further Study:** an alphabetical list of other critical sources which may prove useful for the student. Includes full bibliographical information and a brief annotation.

- **Criticism:** at least one essay commissioned by *PfS* which specifically deals with the poem and is written specifically for the student audience, as well as excerpts from previously published criticism on the work, when available.

In addition, most entries contain the following highlighted sections, set separately from the main text:

- **Media Adaptations:** a list of audio recordings as well as any film or television adaptations of the poem, including source information.

- **Compare and Contrast Box:** an "at-a-glance" comparison of the cultural and historical differences between the author's time and culture and late twentieth-century Western culture. This box includes pertinent parallels between the major scientific, political, and cultural movements of the time or place the poem was written, the time or place the poem was set (if a historical work), and modern Western culture. Works written after the mid-1970s may not have this box.

- **What Do I Read Next?:** a list of works that might complement the featured poem or serve as a contrast to it. This includes works by the same author and others, works of fiction and nonfiction, and works from various genres, cultures, and eras.

- **Study Questions:** a list of potential study questions or research topics dealing with the poem. This section includes questions related to other disciplines the student may be studying, such as American history, world history, science, math, government, business, geography, economics, psychology, etc.

Other Features

PfS includes a foreword by David J. Kelly, an instructor and cofounder of the creative writing periodical of Oakton Community College. This essay provides a straightforward, unpretentious explanation of why poetry should be marveled at and how *Poetry for Students* can help teachers show students how to enrich their own reading experiences.

A Cumulative Author/Title Index lists the authors and titles covered in each volume of the *PfS* series.

A Cumulative Nationality/Ethnicity Index breaks down the authors and titles covered in each volume of the *PfS* series by nationality and ethnicity.

A Subject/Theme Index, specific to each volume, provides easy reference for users who may be studying a particular subject or theme rather than a single work. Significant subjects from events to broad themes are included, and the entries pointing to the specific theme discussions in each entry are indicated in **boldface.**

Illustrations are included with entries when available, including photos of the author and other graphics related to the poem.

Citing **Poetry for Students**

When writing papers, students who quote directly from any volume of *Poetry for Students* may use the following general forms. These examples are based on MLA style; teachers may request that students adhere to a different style, so the following examples may be adapted as needed.

When citing text from *PfS* that is not attributed to a particular author (i.e., the Themes, Style,

Historical Context sections, etc.), the following format should be used in the bibliography section:

"Angle of Geese." *Poetry for Students.* Eds. Marie Napierkowski and Mary Ruby. Vol. 1. Detroit: Gale, 1997. 8–9.

When quoting the specially commissioned essay from *PfS* (usually the first piece under the "Criticism" subhead), the following format should be used:

Velie, Alan. Essay on "Angle of Geese." *Poetry for Students.* Eds. Marie Napierkowski and Mary Ruby. Vol. 1. Detroit: Gale, 1997. 8–9.

When quoting a journal or newspaper essay that is reprinted in a volume of *PfS*, the following form may be used:

Luscher, Robert M. "An Emersonian Context of Dickinson's 'The Soul Selects Her Own Society.'" *ESQ: A Journal of American Renaissance* 30, No. 2 (Second Quarterl, 1984), 111–16; excerpted and reprinted in *Poetry for Students,* Vol. 2, eds. Marie Napierkowski and Mary Ruby (Detroit: Gale, 1997), pp. 120–34.

When quoting material reprinted from a book that appears in a volume of *PfS*, the following form may be used:

Mootry, Maria K. "'Tell It Slant': Disguise and Discovery as Revisionist Poetic Discourse in 'The Bean Eaters,'" in *A Life Distilled: Gwendolyn Brroks, Her Poetry and Fiction,* edited by Maria K. Mootry and Gary Smith (University of Illinois Press, 1987, 177–80; excerpted and reprinted in *Poetry for Students,* Vol. 1, Eds. Marie Napierkowski and Mary Ruby (Detroit: Gale, 1997), pp. 59–61.

We Welcome Your Suggestions

The editors of *Poetry for Students* welcome your comments and ideas. Readers who wish to suggest poems to appear in future volumes, or who have other suggestions, are cordially invited to contact the editor. You may write to the editor at:

Editor, *Poetry for Students*
Gale Group
27500 Drake Rd.
Farmington Hills, MI 48331–3535

Literary Chronology

1830: Emily Dickinson is born in Amherst, Massachusetts, where she will live all her life.

1830: Christina Rossetti is born in London, England, the daughter of Italian exile Gabriele Rossetti and Frances Polidori Rossetti.

1862: Christina Rossetti publishes "A Birthday," first collected in *Goblin Market and Other Poems*.

1874: Robert W. Service is born on January 16 in Preston, Lancashire, England, to Robert and Emily (Parker) Service.

1874: Robert Frost is born in San Francisco.

1886: Emily Dickenson dies of Bright's disease, a kidney dysfunction, in May.

1890: "The Bustle in a House," is published as "Aftermath" in Emily Dickinson's posthumous first collection, *Poems by Emily Dickinson*.

1893: Wilfred Owen is born in Oswestry, Shropshire, England

1894: Christina Rossetti dies of cancer in January.

1902: Langston Hughes is born in Joplin, Missouri, to James Nathaniel and Carrie Mercer Langston Hughes.

1904: Pablo Neruda is born Ricardo Eliezer Neftali Reyes y Basoalto on July 12 in the agricultural region of Parral, Chile.

1905: Stanley Kunitz is born in Worcester, Massachusetts, the youngest of three children of

Russian-Jewish parents. His father commits suicide six weeks before Kunitz is born.

1907: Robert W. Service writes "The Cremation of Sam McGee" while working as a bank teller in the Yukon Territory.

1907: W. H. Auden is born on February 21 in York, England.

1913: Muriel Rukeyser is born in New York.

1916: Robert Frost publishes "Out, Out—."

1918: Wilfred Owen is killed in battle a week before the armistice that ends World War I.

1920: English poet Siegfried Sassoon publishes much of Wilfred Owen's work in a volume titled *Poems*.

1920: Howard Nemerov is born in New York City.

1921: Langston Hughes publishes his first poem, "The Negro Speaks of Rivers."

1923: Naomi Long Madgett is born on July 5 in Norfolk, Virginia.

1923: Alan Dugan is born on February 12 in Brooklyn, New York.

1924: Robert Frost wins the first of his four Pulitzer Prizes.

1924: Pablo Neruda publishes "Tonight I Can Write."

1930: Bruce Dawe is born in Geelong, Victoria, Australia.

1935: Charles Wright is born in Hardin County, Tennessee.

1936: W. H. Auden's poem, "Funeral Blues," first appears in *The Ascent of F6,* a play written with Auden's longtime collaborator Christopher Isherwood.

1942: Henry Taylor is born in Lincoln, Virginia.

1943: James Tate is born in Kansas City, Missouri.

1943: Michael Hartnett is born in Newcastle West in County Limerick, Ireland.

1948: W. H. Auden wins the Pulitzer Prize in Poetry for *The Age of Anxiety.*

1950: Howard Nemerov publishes "The Phoenix."

1951: Jorie Graham is born in New York City in May.

1956: Robert W. Service dies of a heart attack on September 11 and is buried in the Brittany region of France.

1956: Alan Dugan writes "How We Heard the Name," which appears in the multiple award-winning *Poems* in 1961.

1958: Stanley Kunitz's "The War Against the Trees" appears in *Selected Poems, 1928-1958.*

1962: Alan Dugan's *Poems* wins the Pulitzer Prize, the National Book Award, and the Prix de Rome (awarded by the American Academy of Arts and Letters).

1963: Robert Frost dies.

1965: Naomi Long Madgett publishes "Alabama Centennial" in her third book of poems, *Star by Star.*

1967: Langston Hughes dies in New York on May 22.

1970: James Tate publishes "Dear Reader."

1971: Pablo Neruda wins the Nobel Prize in Literature.

1973: Muriel Rukeyser writes "Ballad of Orange and Grape" toward the end of her long career.

1973: W. H. Auden dies and is buried in the Poet's Corner in Westminster Abbey.

1973: Pablo Neruda dies from heart failure on September 23.

1975: Michael Hartnett publishes "A Farewell to English."

1980: Muriel Rukeyser dies.

1983: Henry Taylor publishes "Landscape with Tractor."

1986: Henry Taylor wins the Pulitzer Prize for *The Flying Change,* which includes "Landscape with Tractor."

1988: Howard Nemerov is named Poet Laureate of the United States.

1989: Jorie Graham's "The Hiding Place" first appears in the May 22 issue of the *New Yorker.*

1991: Howard Nemerov dies.

1996: Jorie Graham's *Dream of the Unified Field: Selected Poems 1974-1994* wins the Pulitzer Prize for poetry.

1997: Charles Wright publishes "Black Zodiac."

1999: Bruce Dawe publishes "Drifters" in his first book of poetry, *No Fixed Address.*

1999: Michael Hartnett dies in Dublin on October 13.

Acknowledgments

The editors wish to thank the copyright holders of the excerpted criticism included in this volume and the permissions managers of many book and magazine publishing companies for assisting us in securing reproduction rights. We are also grateful to the staffs of the Detroit Public Library, the Library of Congress, the University of Detroit Mercy Library, Wayne State University Purdy/Kresge Library Complex, and the University of Michigan Libraries for making their resources available to us. Following is a list of the copyright holders who have granted us permission to reproduce material in this volume of *Poetry for Students* *(PFS)*. Every effort has been made to trace copyright, but if omissions have been made, please let us know.

COPYRIGHTED MATERIAL IN *PFS*, VOLUME 10, WERE REPRODUCED FROM THE FOLLOWING PERIODICALS:

Poetry, "Now We Heard the Name" by Alan Dugan. © by the Modern Poetry Association. Reproduced by permission of the Editor of *Poetry* and the author.

COPYRIGHTED MATERIAL IN *PFS*, VOLUME 10, WERE REPRODUCED FROM THE FOLLOWING BOOKS:

Auden, W. H. From *W. H. Auden: Collected Poems*. Random House, 1940. Reproduced by permission of Random House. In the UK by permission of Faber & Faber Ltd.—Graham, Jorie. From *Region of Unlikeness*. Ecco Press, 1991. Copyright © 1991 by Jorie Graham. Reprinted by permission of HarperCollins Publishers, Inc.—Madgett, Naomi Long. From *Star by Star*. Harlo Press, 1965, Evenill, Inc., 1970. Reproduced by permission.—Rukeyser, Muriel. From *Breaking Open*. Random House, 1973. Copyright © 1973 Random House. Reprinted by permission of International Creative Management, Inc.—Tate, James. From *The Oblivion Ha-Ha*. Little, Brown, 1970. Reproduced by permission of the Scott Meredith Literary Agency, Inc.—Taylor, Henry. From *The Flying Change*. Louisiana State University Press, 1985. Copyright © 1985 by Louisiana State University Press. Reproduced by permission.—Wright, Charles. From *Black Zodiac*. Farrar Straus & Giroux, 1997. Copyright © 1997 by Charles Wright. Reprinted by permission of Farrar, Straus and Giroux, LLC.

PHOTOGRAPHS AND ILLUSTRATIONS APPEARING IN *PFS*, VOLUME 10, WERE RECEIVED FROM THE FOLLOWING SOURCES:

American troops during World War I gas attack, 1918, France, photograph. Corbis-Bettmann. Reproduced by permission.—Federal troops escorting black students, Little Rock, Arkansas, photograph. Corbis-Bettmann. Reproduced by permission.—Alexander the Great, engraving. UPI/Corbis-Bettmann. Reproduced by permission.—Auden W. H., photograph. The Library of Congress.—Dickinson, Emily, photograph of a painting. The Library of Congress.—Dugan, Alan, photograph. The Library of Congress.—Frost, Robert, photograph. The Library of Congress.—Graham, Jorie, photograph. AP/Wide World Photos. Reproduced by permission.—Hughes, Langston, photograph. AP/Wide World Photos. Reproduced by permission.—Nemerov, Howard, photograph. Corbis-Bettmann/Oscar White. Reproduced by permission.—Owen, Wilfred with young boy, photograph. © Hulton-Duetsch Collection/ CORBIS. Reproduced by permission.—Rexroth, Kenneth, photograph. AP/Wide World Photos. Reproduced by permission.—Rossetti, Christina, portrait by James Collinson.—Rukeyser, Muriel, photograph. AP/Wide World Photos. Reproduced by permission.—Taylor, Henry, photograph. AP/ Wide World Photos. Reproduced by permission.

Contributors

Greg Barnhisel: Greg Barnhisel holds a Ph.D. in American Literture from the University of Texas at Austin. He has taught English as Assistant Professor at Southwestern University in Georgetown, Texas. He has published articles on Ezra Pound, and has worked as a freelance writer and editor. Entry on *The Phoenix*. Original essays on *Black Zodiac*, *The Hiding Place*, and *The Phoenix*.

Jonathan N. Barron: Jonathan N. Barron is associate professor of English at the University of Southern Mississippi. He has co-edited *Jewish American Poetry* (forthcoming from University Press of New England), *Robert Frost at the Millennium* (forthcoming from University of Missouri Press), as well as a forthcoming collection of essays on the poetic movement, New Formalism. Beginning in 2001, he will be the editor-in-chief of *The Robert Frost Review*. Original essay on *Landscape with Tractor*.

Greg R. Bernard: Bernard has an M.A. in English literature from Bemidji State University in Bemidji, MN, where he is also an English instructor. Entry on *Dulce et decorum est*.

Adrian Blevins: Adrian Blevins, a poet and essayist who has taught at Hollins University, Sweet Briar College, and in the Virginia Community College System, is the author of *The Man Who Went Out for Cigarettes*, a chapbook of poems, and has published poems, stories, and essays in many magazines, journals, and anthologies. Original essay on *Landscape with Tractor*.

Chloe Bolan: Bolan teaches English as an adjunct at Columbia College of Missouri extensions in Lake County and Crystal Lake, IL. She writes plays, short stories, poems and essays and is currently working on a novel. Original essay on *The Negro Speaks of Rivers*.

David Caplan: Caplan is a doctoral candidate at the University of Virginia, writing a dissertation on contemporary poetry. Original essay on *Black Zodiac*.

Jeanine Johnson: Johnson received her Ph.D. from Yale University and is currently visiting assistant professor of English at Wake Forest University. Original essays on *Dear Reader*, *Funeral Blues*, and *Phoenix*.

Elizabeth Judd: Judd is a freelance writer and book reviewer with an M.F.A. in English from the University of Michigan and a B.A. from Yale. Original essay on *A Birthday*.

David Kelly: David Kelly is an instructor of creative writing at several community colleges in Illinois, as well as a fiction writer and playwright. Entries on *Drifters* and *A Farewell to English*. Original essays on *Ballad of Orange and Grape*, *Drifters*, and *A Farewell to English*.

Judi Ketteler: Ketteler has taught Literature and English Composition and is currently a freelance writer based in Cincinnati, Ohio. Entry on *Alabama Centennial*. Original essay on *Alabama Centennial*.

Aviya Kushner: Aviya Kushner is the Contributing Editor in Poetry at *BarnesandNoble.com* and the Poetry Editor of *Neworld Magazine*. She is a graduate of the acclaimed creative writing program in poetry at Boston University, where she received the Fitzgerald Award in Translation. Her writing on poetry has appeared in *Harvard Review* and *The Boston Phoenix*, and she has served as Poetry Coordinator for *AGNI Magazine*. She has given readings of her own work throughout the United States, and she teaches at Massachusetts Communications College in Boston. Original essays on *Funeral Blues* and *Out, Out—*.

Michael Lake: Lake holds an MA in English and is a poet residing in California. Original essay on *The Bustle in theHouse*.

Kimberly Lutz: Lutz is an instructor at New York University and has written for a wide variety of educational publishers. Original essays on *A Birthday* and *Dulce et decorum est*.

Sarah Madsen-Hardy: Madsen Hardy has a doctorate in English literature and is a freelance writer and editor. Entry on *Ballad of Orange and Grape*. Original essays on *Ballad of Orange and Grape*, *The Bustle in the House*, and *The Negro Speaks of Rivers*.

Mary Mahony: Mary Mahony earned an M.A. in English from the University of Detroit and a M.L.S. from Wayne State University. She is an instructor of English at Wayne County Community College in Detroit, Michigan. Entry on *The Negro Speaks of Rivers*.

Tyrus Miller: Tyrus Miller is an assistant professor of comparative literature and English at Yale University, where he teaches twentieth-century literature and visual culture. He has published a book entitled *Late Modernism: Politics, Fiction, and the Arts Between the World Wars*. Original essay on *Dulce et decorum est*.

Katrinka Moore: Moore teaches writing at Long Island University in Brooklyn, New York, and is a poet whose work appears in anthologies and literary journals. Entry on *A Birthday*. Original essay on *A Birthday*.

Carl Mowery: Mowery has a Ph.D. in writing and literature from Southern Illinois University, Carbondale, IL. Original essay on *The Cremation of Sam McGee*.

Daniel Moran: Moran is a secondary-school teacher of English and American Literature. He has contributed several entries and essays to the Gale series *Drama for Students*. Entry on *Out, Out—*.

Original essays on *Dulce et decorum est* and *Out, Out—* .

Wendy Perkins: Perkins, an Associate Professor of English at Prince George's Community College in Maryland, has published articles on several twentieth-century authors. Entry on *Funeral Blues*. Original essay on *Funeral Blues*.

Elisabeth Piedmont-Marton: Piedmont-Marton teaches American literature and directs the writing center at a college in Texas. Entry on *The Bustle in the House*. Original essay on *The Bustle in the House*.

Dean Rader: Dean Rader is Assistant Professor of English at Texas Lutheran Univerity in Seguin, Texas. Entry on *The Hiding Place*. Original essays on *Black Zodiac*, *The Hiding Place*, and *The Negro Speaks of Rivers*.

Sean K. Robisch: Robisch is an assistant professor of ecological and American literature at Purdue University. Original essays on *Dear Reader* and *The Phoenix* .

Cliff Saunders: Saunders teaches writing and literature in the Myrtle Beach, South Carolina, area and has published six chapbooks of poetry. Original essay on *Dear Reader*.

Chris Semansky: Chris Semansky holds a Ph.D. in English from Stony Brook University and teaches writing and literature at Portland Community College in Portland, Oregon. His collection of poems *Death, But at a Good Price* received the Nicholas Roerich Poetry Prize for 1991 and was published by Story Line Press and the Nicholas Roerich Museum. Semansky's most recent collection, *Blindsided,* has been published by 26 Books of Portland, Oregon. Entry on *Landscape with Tractor*. Original essay on *Landscape with Tractor*.

Erica Smith: Smith is a writer and editor. Original essays on *Drifters* and *How We Heard the Name*.

Pamela Steed Hill: Pamela Steed Hill has had poems published in over 100 journals and has been nominated for a Pushcart Prize three times. Her first collection, *In Praise of Motels,* was published in 1999 by Blair Mountain Press. She is an associate editor for University Communications at Ohio State University. Entries on *Black Zodiac* and *Dear Reader*. Original essays on *The Hiding Place* and *How We Heard the Name*

Erika Taibl: Taibl has a master's degree in English writing and writes for a variety of educational publishers. Original essay on *Ballad of Orange and Grape*.

Karen D. Thompson: Thompson has done graduate work at the University of North Carolina, Greensboro, and has taught English at Asheboro High School (NC), Manor High School, Dripping Springs High School, and Dripping Springs Middle School (TX). Original essays on *Alabama Centennial* and *A Farewell to English.*

Bill Wiles: Wiles teaches and writes in the shadow of Vermont's Green Mountains. Entry on *The Cremation of Sam McGee.* Original essays on *The Cremation of Sam McGee* and *Out, Out—.*

Paul Witcover: Witcover is a novelist and editor in New York City with an M.A. in Creative Writing and Literature from the City University of New York. Entry on *How We Heard the Name.* Original essays on *Alabama Centennial* and *How We Heard the Name.*

Alabama Centennial

Naomi Long Madgett
1965

"Alabama Centennial" is a poem from Naomi Long Madgett's third book of poems, *Star by Star,* published in 1965. It is representative of one of the two general categories into which her poems are divided: the lyric poems of her youth (influenced by Romanticism), and the more directly political works which recognize and trumpet the importance of civil rights issues for African Americans in the 1950s and 1960s. Clearly, "Alabama Centennial" falls into the latter category as it is a rhetorical recounting of the protest slogans and activist experience in Montgomery, Alabama, and other places. The poem was the result of a conversation Madgett had with a visiting scholar from the Netherlands, Rosey E. Pool. They first met in Detroit, where Madgett was to live for most of her life, and then began a correspondence. Clearly the poem is a proclamation of the strength of African Americans in their fight for civil rights. By mentioning certain historical protests and marches, it also serves as a chronicle. Perhaps it is most vehement though as a demand, as with its recounting of the trials and suffering of African Americans it announces that "the chain of patient acquiescence" has broken and the time for equality and dignity is "Now!"

Author Biography

Madgett was born July 5, 1923, in Norfolk, Virginia. Her father Clarence Marcellus Long was a member of the clergy, and her mother Maude Long was a teacher. Madgett published her first volume of poetry, *Songs to a Phantom Nightingale*, in 1941. After graduating with honors from Virginia State College in 1945, Madgett took a job as a reporter for the *Michigan Chronicle*. In 1946 she married Julian Witherspoon and left the newspaper. She was divorced in 1949 and worked as a service representative for the Michigan Bell telephone company until 1954, the same year she married William Harold Madgett. For ten years, beginning in 1955, Madgett taught in the Detroit public school system. The following year she received a master's degree in education from Wayne State University. Madgett taught English at Eastern Michigan University from 1968 until she was named professor emeritus in 1984. She served as an editor at Lotus Press from 1974 to 1993, when she was named director. Madgett has contributed poetry to more than 100 anthologies and to numerous periodicals, in addition to publishing her own volumes of poetry.

Poem Text

They said, "Wait." Well, I waited.
For a hundred years I waited
In cotton fields, kitchens, balconies,
In bread lines, at back doors, on chain gangs,
In stinking "colored" toilets   5
And crowded ghettos,
Outside of schools and voting booths.
And some said, "Later."
And some said, "Never!"

Then a new wind blew, and a new voice   10
Rode its wings with quiet urgency,
Strong, determined, sure.
"No," it said. "Not 'never,' not 'later,'
Not even 'soon.'
Now.   15
Walk!"

And other voices echoed the freedom words,
"Walk together, children, don't get weary,"
Whispered them, sang them, prayed them, shouted
          them.
"Walk!"   20
And I walked the streets of Montgomery
Until a link in the chain of patient acquiescence
          broke.

Then again: Sit down!
And I sat down at the counters of Greensboro.
Ride! And I rode the bus for freedom.   25
Kneel! And I went down on my knees in prayer
          and faith.
March! And I'll march until the last chain falls
Singing, "We shall overcome."

Not all the dogs and hoses in Birmingham
Nor all the clubs and guns in Selma   30
Can turn this tide.
Not all the jails can hold these young black faces
From their destiny of manhood,
Of equality, of dignity,
Of the American Dream   35
A hundred years past due.
Now!

Poem Summary

Lines 1-2:

"Alabama Centennial" opens by establishing a very personal tone, the first person "I" in contrast with an anonymous "They." One could easily assume, given the title and subject of the poem that the "They" is the white American establishment whose racist views and policies kept African Americans in a state of inequality. The gravity of this is then emphasized by the second line which reminds the reader of the history behind such a situation, how long it has been the case.

Lines 3-7:

Here a list begins that adds historical context to the poem. "Cotton fields" and "kitchens" refer to times of slavery when these were the predominant places African Americans were forced to work. "Bread lines" and "chain gangs" then introduce the ideas of extreme poverty, most specifically during the Great Depression, and of jail, a very literal image of the bondage experienced by African Americans. Line 5 then offers one of the strongest of the list, a reference to segregated bathrooms. This line stands out, it seems, because of this word "stinking" which is sharp sounding relative to the words that surround it. It also evokes a particular sensory reaction, that of smell, which adds strength. "Crowded ghettos" then shifts the focus briefly to the inner city, the urban scene where though there are "Schools and voting booths," the speaker of the poem is left "Outside" of them. All of these images together provide an historical line of neglect and oppression.

It is worth noting as well how Madgett uses anaphora in lines 3, 4, and 5 to add rhythm and strength to the list. Anaphora is the repetition of a word or phrase at the beginning of the line, and here, with the repetition of the short, sharp word "In," it almost has the effect of hammering in a nail.

Lines 8-9:

Here Madgett closes the first stanza by referring back to the words of the opposition and in doing so adds some complexity to the situation by showing different extents of the opposition: some asking for more time before change, others saying forget it. Both, however, given the tone established in the opening of the poem, are unacceptable to the speaker.

Lines 10-12:

Then, with the beginning of the second stanza, a shift takes place. First the wind is offered as an image of change, and carried by that wind, a voice. Notice too the importance of the shift of that voice. In the first stanza, it was the anonymous "they" that spoke the words, while those oppressed said nothing. Here, now that it has been introduced, it is the voice of the neglected—"strong, determined, sure"—that is about to be heard.

Lines 13-16:

The voice here readdresses the oppressive shouts of the first stanza by negating them. The speaker is claiming them to be unacceptable, even in their milder forms of "soon" and "later." To continue the earlier idea that the anaphoric "In" in stanza one was like hammering in a nail, the repetition here has a similar effect. The word "not" being repeated drives home the idea of unacceptability, of resistance, and line 15, with its brevity and isolation, almost appears as a nail driven fully in: "Now." The poem then shifts from the theme of sound and speaking, to one of action, with an equally short and exclamatory line: "Walk!"

Lines 17-18:

Here a new stanza seems appropriate for the combining of the voices and action, as others join in both the speaking of the words and the walking in protest. It is interesting to note the use of the word "children" in line 18. This word, it could be argued, carries both the connotations of vulnerability, that a child is at the mercy of someone larger, and of hope, as children have almost their whole lives ahead of them. The emphasis then is on togetherness, which could offer strength in the face of weariness.

Lines 19-20:

Here we are given the variety of forms in which the voices offer themselves, from the very subtle, to the musical, to the religious, to the angry. All different forms of expressing oneself in the face of adversity. As these echo in the head of the reader, the command comes again with force in line 20: "Walk!"

Media Adaptations

- *Furious Flower: Conversations with African-American Poets* was released by California Newsreel in 1998.

- *A Poet's Voice: Poetry by Naomi Long Madgett from Octavia and Other Poems* was released by Vander Films in 1997.

- *Words Like Freedom: Sturdy Black Bridges,* recorded with permission from the Starz Channel, 1997.

- *Writers Live with Naomi Long Madgett* was released by Municipal Library Access Channel 9 in 1996.

- *A Poet's Voice* produced by Carousel Film and Video, 1990.

Lines 21-22:

At this point in the poem, specific reference to the speaker returns as the first person "I" tells of following the command and taking to the streets of Montgomery. This is a reference to the peaceful protest march that took place in Montgomery, Alabama, one of the centers of the Civil Rights Movement. And the walking continued until the "patient acquiescence," likened metaphorically here to a chain that has bound the marchers, is replaced by the more fervent demand of "Now" heard earlier in the poem.

Lines 23-24:

The fourth stanza begins what will be a list of demands for different kinds of action, and the speaker's response to them. From walking we now shift to sitting, no doubt a reference to the sit-in non-violent protests of segregated establishments held across the country during this time. In this case it is in Greensboro, North Carolina, which again, as with the previous mention of Montgomery, presents both a geographic and historical context for the poem. The specific detail of sitting at the counters also helps strengthen the image of the protest.

Line 25:

Here another activity that was central to the Civil Rights Movement is alluded to. In this case it is the Freedom Rides of the South which held as their goal the desegregation of buses.

Line 26:

With this command and the following one, Madgett introduces not a specific time or place, but the role of faith in the speaker's struggle. This mentioning of religion also broadens the scope of the poem as it now includes issues of morality, and not only justice.

Lines 27-28:

The fourth stanza then concludes with one final command, returning full circle to that which started the list, walking. Now though it has been altered, even transformed, into marching. This of course carries connotations of added strength, given that the word "marching" makes one think of greater numbers of people than "walking" does, and also brings in the idea of an army. The last line here then returns the poem full circle to the voice that is now singing one of the key protest songs of the entire Civil Rights Movement, "We Shall Overcome."

It is worth noting how this paragraph coheres in part because of the parallel structure employed by Madgett. This is when a similar rhetorical structure is used with different phrases, and an excellent example exists here in the fourth stanza as lines 25 to 27 all begin with a one-word exclamatory command, which is then followed by an affirmative sentence beginning with the phrase "And I ..." As well as implying the relatedness of these different acts, it also presents them in a smoother, almost musical way that mimics the singing about to come. In poetry, choice of rhetorical structure—where and how to place the words—is as important as which words are being used.

Lines 29-31:

With the action of the above stanzas well established and indefinite ("until the last chains fall") the poem now shifts toward its closing. It reaffirms the strength of the movement and protest by listing certain things that have been used to squash efforts in the past and stating that they will no longer work. These specific details help to sharpen the image of the confrontations as one can easily picture "dogs" and "clubs" and "guns." There is also reference again to actual places where protest and confrontation have occurred, Montgomery and Selma being key locations of non-violent protest and gathering during the Civil Rights Movement.

This line not only serves as another illustration of how the struggle for equality cannot be stopped, because, literally, there is not enough room or force to detain the people, but it also helps tie the poem together before its end by making reference to the physical restraint—the chain gang—of the first stanza.

Here the poem nears its end and finally comes out and tells what the goal of all the protest recounted has been. Clearly there is some idea throughout the poem, with all the historical references, but to summarize the poem speaks of the "destiny of manhood, / of equality, of dignity." The key word here in regards to the rest of the poem, it could be argued, is "destiny" as it implies that what is desired—the freedom and equality to grow and live one's life—is not only a right, but is a fundamental part of a larger plan. It is how it is suppose to be, the poem claims with this one word. This presents an opposing idea to that of Manifest Destiny which was used by Europeans founding America to justify whatever actions—slave-trading being only one of the horrific ones—they took.

Lines 36-37:

This second to the last line echoes the second line of the poem by stating the duration of the oppression, and it here sets up the final line, "Now!", which can be seen as yet another nail being driven home. The message of the poem, that the time has come, echoes in the reader's mind.

Themes

American Dream

The phrase "The American Dream" brings many things to mind: self-reliance, entrepreneurship, freedom, equality, and economic prosperity, to name a few. The early literature of the nation was very concerned with defining the American Dream. Thomas Jefferson dreamt of a nation of farmers, while Ralph Waldo Emerson rhapsodized about the importance of self-reliance. At the same time discussions of this American Dream were going on, a whole race of people were being systematically denied the tenets that make up the dream: freedom, the vote, economic independence, even the ownership of one's own body. Instead of owning homes, getting an education, farming land, and building towards a future, African-Americans were held "in bread lines, at back doors, on chain gangs / In stinking 'colored' toilets / And crowded ghettos, / Outside of schools and voting booths."

Economically disenfranchised during and after slavery, African-Americans were denied access into the places of society where the American Dream resides. But Madgett's message in "Alabama Centennial" is one of hope. Her generation is reclaiming that lost dream through protest. Civil disobedience was first enumerated in this country by transcendentalist essayist Henry David Thoreau. A few generations later, India's Mahatma Gandhi shaped civil disobedience into a fight for Indian independence from British rule. Then in the 1950s and 60s, the torch was passed to Martin Luther King. The Civil Rights Movement took as its foundation the principals of civil disobedience. In this way, black Americans were claiming their right to the American dream by practicing one of the most fundamental rights guaranteed by the Bill of Rights: civil protest. Madgett speaks of her people "riding," "marching," and "kneeling" for freedom in protests throughout the South. In this way, they claim the American Dream, as she says, "A hundred years past due."

Justice and Injustice

Madgett's "Alabama Centennial" takes as its premise that the past hundred years, and two hundred or so years before that were filled with injustice. She never mentions the word "slavery"—instead she conjures it up through potent images: "cotton fields, kitchens balconies." She envisions history as a struggle between the weight of justice and drag of injustice. In the poem, that struggle is initially represented through contrasting voices: "they," vs. "I," and eventually "we." "They" represents the negative forces of white America, with extremist groups such as the Ku Klux Klan and institutions such as Jim Crow laws. Madgett's single "I" is joined by the larger "we" to fight these injustices, and that "we" voice grows stronger throughout the poem, culminating with the song "We shall overcome" in the next-to-last stanza.

Madgett's vision of history is dynamic, with forces of injustice and justice always fighting each other. For every "never" white America sends down, the collective "we" speaker responds with a "no," "not never," "not later." There is movement and energy. To fight injustice, black Americans sit-in at lunchcounters, boycott buses, and march peacefully while chanting. Fighting injustice is marked in a physical way, with blood and sweat

Topics for Further Study

- Consider a social injustice that you think should be corrected and write a poem about how you think society could go about conquering it, centering your energies around specific exclamations, as this author does with "Walk!" "Ride!" "Kneel!" "March!" and "Now!"

- Langston Hughes's "Dreams" also addresses the problem of living with racial segregation in America, but his poem is much quieter, more understated. Which poem do you think would be more successful in affecting its readers? What does the fact that Hughes's poem is structured like blues music and Madgett's has no formal structure tell you about the point that each author is trying to make?

- This poem was published in 1965, at the height of the civil rights movement in America. Explain the author's use of the towns Montgomery, Greensboro, Birmingham, and Selma. What happened in these places? Is it a good idea for an author to refer to specific historical events, or does their meaning fade with time?

and bodies placed in jail. Madgett also speaks of the movement as having a life of its own: "Not all the dogs and horses in Birmingham / ... Can turn this tide."

Rites of Passage

Madgett doesn't speak of rites of passage in an overt way in "Alabama Centennial"; rather, it is implied. The topic of her poem—the Civil Rights Movement—was in many ways a youth movement, with groups such as the Student Nonviolent Coordinating Committee training hundreds of student civil rights workers on college campuses. In general, people speak of the decade of the sixties as a time of youth revolution.

While the collective "we" of the poem is meant to cut across the age divide, in many ways, Madgett is recounting a coming of age of an entire generation in lines such as, "Walk together, children, don't get weary." The movement towards freedom is also a movement towards adulthood. The tired bones of the older generation of black Americans who grew up in the earlier part of the twentieth century are "revived," in a way, by the eager, younger generation not content to accept legalized discrimination. She refers specifically to youth in the concluding stanza: "Not all the jails can hold these young black faces / From their destiny of manhood." In this way, "Alabama Centennial" is very forward-looking. Madgett focuses on what this next generation will achieve.

Style

"Alabama Centennial" is written in free verse. This means that there is not an established meter or rhyme, as in traditional poetic forms. It is probably fair to say that the content of this poem is what determines its form. Given that the poem is about breaking free from the binding forces of racism and inequality, the language itself breaks from older, traditionally European forms. This was not just happening for writers writing of racial oppression; a movement among American writers to break from traditional structure had begun decades earlier. In this case, though, the relationship between the idea of free verse, and the subject of the poem, seems clearly present.

If there is a formal consistency to the poem it is the use of lists, places or events, that recur throughout. This is heightened with the use of anaphora, which is the repetition of a word or phrase at the beginning of a line, and with the use of parallelism, which is a rhetorical device that uses similar phrasing to hold things together. A good example is line 13, which reads " 'No,' it said. 'Not 'never,' not 'later.' " The repetition of the word "not" not only binds the words, but creates a certain rhythm in the process.

Historical Context

When Madgett refers to the American Dream "one hundred years past due," she is situating the African-American struggle for civil rights in a century-long struggle for equality and respect. Madgett wrote "Alabama Centennial" in 1965—the middle of a tumultuous and sometimes violent decade. But it was also a decade of substantial progress for civil rights movements, with people such as Martin Luther King, Malcolm X, and Rosa Parks ushering in winds of change.

This poem was written exactly one hundred years after the Civil War ended and blacks were at last freed from slavery. But the residues of slavery would live long into the next century, spurred by such organizations as the Ku Klux Klan and institutions such as black codes and Jim Crow laws.

The South remained highly segregated long after reconstruction. There was little progress in easing racial tensions through the end of the nineteenth century and into the early twentieth century. In Alabama in 1901, a new state constitution was adopted, which had the effect of further disenfranchising black voters. In fact, total blacks registered in 14 counties in Alabama fell from 78,311 in 1900 to 1,081 in 1903.

Segregation was a way of life in the South, and in other regions of the country as well. Blacks and whites attended separate schools, drank from different water fountains and had different bathrooms. When riding the bus, blacks were forced to give up seats on the front of the bus for white people and had to move to the back of the bus. There were "white only" lunch counters, restaurants, parks, and theaters. The doctrine "separate but equal," derived from Plessy v. Ferguson (1896) was supposedly the guiding force behind segregation, but things were far from equal in terms of public facilities and distribution of wealth.

Things began to change in the 1950s and 60s when blacks and sympathetic whites rose up in civil protest. First, in 1954, the Supreme Court declared that separate educational facilities were "inherently unequal" in its landmark ruling in Brown v. Board of Education Topeka, Kansas. Still, things were slow to change until 1955, when Rosa Parks helped to spark a movement when she refused to move to the back of the bus in Montgomery, Alabama. Her act of defiance led to the Montgomery bus boycott, which lasted a year and was nearly 100% successful in ending segregation on the buses. The boycott was the beginning of massive civil rights demonstrations in Birmingham, Alabama (April 1963) and Selma, Alabama (March 1965). The protests consisted of nonviolent direct action—the philosophy preached by Baptist minister and leader of the movement Martin Luther King. Finally in 1964, Congress passed the Civil rights Act. This piece of legislation prohibited discrimination in employment and established the Equal Employment Opportunity Commission. This act also outlawed

Compare & Contrast

- **1950s:** Many public schools remained segregated into the 1950s, as established by the 1896 *Plessy v. Ferguson* ruling that declared "separate but equal" as the guiding standard for segregation. The "Separate but equal" standard was overturned in *Brown v. Board of Education* in 1954 when segregation of public schools was outlawed.

  1970s: Bussing, the practice of moving students to different districts to promote racial integration, becomes a means for integrating school districts that are predominantly white.

  Today: Public education continues to reflect economic status, with larger city schools facing financial issues compared with wealthier, suburban school districts.

- **1960s:** Strong and charismatic civil rights leaders emerge nationally. Martin Luther King proved integral in starting the nonviolent action movement, with peaceful sit-ins, marches, and protests aimed at change. Malcolm X was a leader in the Black Nationalist movement to empower African-Americans. The Black Panthers were a militant group for the rights of African-Americans.

  Today: No lone figure dominates as the spokesperson in the struggle for equality and justice.

---

discrimination in public accommodations linked to interstate commerce such as restaurants and hotels. In 1965, the Voting Rights Act was passed, prohibiting local governments or individuals from interfering with the right of blacks to register and vote.

Although King advocated non-violence, it was a bloody decade. Black churches were bombed, civil rights workers were killed, the police assaulted demonstrators, and riots broke out. Other movements also gained momentum in the 1960s, such as the women's movement, the gay rights movement, the Native American movement, and the Anti-War movement. It was a time of intense energy on the part of young people all across the country. College campuses became radical organizing grounds for protest movements. The desire to change society was felt in many social arenas, including politics. Many regarded president John F. Kennedy as a social reformer; but his presidency was cut short when he was assassinated in 1963. Lyndon Johnson was his successor. Johnson wanted to create the "great society"; he started many of the entitlement programs we still have today, such as welfare. As the decade wore on and the 1970s were ushered in, the activity in Vietnam continued to increase. Robert F. Kennedy, Martin

Luther King, and Malcolm X were all assassinated in the late sixties. The mood of optimism and energy slowly began to shift in the 1970s as inflation rose and veterans came back from Vietnam to find themselves outcasts. The fight for civil rights on part of African-Americans and other minorities continued, and still continues today.

Critical Overview

Madgett is often hailed as a teacher and publisher as much as she is celebrated as a poet. She taught in Detroit area schools for much of her life and has spent over twenty years as a professor of creative writing and African-American Literature at Eastern Michigan University in Ypsilanti, Michigan. In 1972 she began Lotus Press, which focused on publishing work by black writers who were rejected by white editors and publishers. Madgett's work in particular was often refused because it was either "not black enough" or "too black," which meant that it either wasn't direct enough about the sufferings of African Americans, or it was too angry and volatile. Her skill was apparent from the earliest days, and she was referred to by Saunders Red-

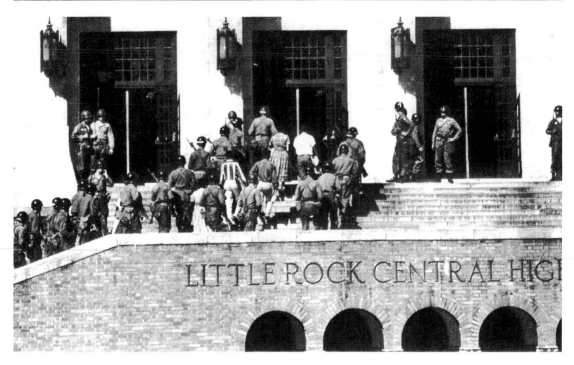

U. S. Federal Troops surround African American students as they enter Little Rock Central High School during the first days of integration.

ding in *Negro Digest* as "a natural poet." Redding also observed that "for all her metrical skill, her phrasing was weak" and that she used "shopworn images and vague 'poetic' terms like 'dreams.'" In stating such criticism, it was his hope that Madgett would soon develop a "more rigorous diction" to complement her "intelligence and prosodic ability."

Criticism

Judi Ketteler

Judi Ketteler has taught Literature and English Composition and is currently a freelance writer based in Cincinnati, Ohio. In this essay, Ketteler discusses the way in which Madgett uses language to make a political statement about racism and injustice in this country.

In "Alabama Centennial," Madgett creates a political poem through her elevated language and carefully chosen images and metaphors regarding the black experience in America. Madgett also takes special care to highlight shifting voices in the poem, illustrating the power struggle between the

white establishment and African-American activism in the 1950s and 1960s. "Alabama Centennial," is a testimony to the brutal century of racism and indignity suffered by black Americans. But Madgett moves beyond painting her people as victims; instead, she chooses images of strength in speaking about the Civil Rights Movement, underscoring the ways in which she and her fellow black Americans have fought, and in fact, have triumphed.

It is worth noting that Madgett wrote "Alabama Centennial," in 1965, in the midst of a decade filled with large scale civil rights protests. A very versatile poet, Madgett has also written a great deal of lyric and romantic poetry, using images from nature to address such topics as love, death, and spirituality. "Alabama Centennial" is part of the collection *Star by Star*, which contains both types of poems. Madgett has a deep appreciation for language, whether she is using it to raise her voice in political protest, or to celebrate the beauty of morning dew on a rose.

In "Alabama Centennial," Madgett uses language in a very personal way. She begins by situating a voice outside of herself with the opening stanza, "They said,"; this is then contrasted with "I waited." This juxtaposition of voice and perspective sets up the entire poem. The reader is introduced to a litany of images. The order of these images is important in that it serves as a historical chronicle, filling in the gaps left by traditional histories. Madgett recalls all the places blacks have inhabited throughout their history in America: "Cotton fields, kitchens, balconies" chronicles the days of slavery; the Reconstruction Era and the early twentieth century is represented "in bread lines, at back doors, in chain gangs"; then, her contemporary era is reflected "In stinking 'colored' toilets / And crowded ghettos / Outside of schools and voting booths." In each of these sets of images, Madgett highlights the exclusion of African-Americans. Literally speaking, they are excluded from the household, from school, from good jobs; figuratively, they are excluded from opportunity, and as Madgett points out later in the poem, from the American Dream.

If Madgett is acting as a chronicler of African-American history, she is also borrowing from the tradition of the "griot." Griots were storytellers in preindustrial African societies. Literary critic Eugene Redmond, author of *Drumvoices: The Mission of Afro-American Poetry,* explained that the "black poet, as creator and chronicler, evolves from these artisans—human oral recorders of family and national lore. Trained to recite without flaw the genealogy, eulogies, victories, and calamities of folk, griots (like the lead singers of spirituals) had to spice their narration with drama and excitement." Madgett certainly uses drama and excitement in her narration of the Civil Rights movement. Her language has energy. As the poem progresses, her voice grows louder, more forceful, more certain. She wants to preserve this moment in history for future generations. This too is another function of the griot. In *Racism 101,* African-American poet and essayist Nikki Giovanni commented, "There must always be griots … else how will we know who we are?".

Just as history is marked with the exclusion and with the blood and struggles of African-Americans, it is also marked with their resistance and dissenting voices. The voice introduced in the beginning—the all-consuming "they"—loses ground to the more powerful "we" and the image of a "strong, determined, sure" black presence. Madgett is creating an African-American identity of resistance. There is a sense of urgency in the second stanza of the poem, and it is an urgency long overdue. A powerful "No" in line 13, a refusal to stay subservient, then an echoing of that no reiterates

> " *Madgett has a deep appreciation for language, whether she is using it to raise her voice in political protest, or to celebrate the beauty of morning dew on a rose.* "

that refusal: "And other voices echoed the freedom words."

In creating this dialog of dissension, Madgett is invoking the call/response technique of traditional black spirituals. When blacks were held in slavery, they often used spirituals to communicate, to pass information about escape plans and to relay messages. It was a means of communicating subversively, or communicating subversive information within the bounds of what was acceptable and wouldn't raise suspicion. In *Drumvoices,* Redmond noted: "Through songs, aphorisms, fables, jokes, blues, and other enduring forms, Blacks capture severe hardships and tribulations, folk wisdom, joys and tragedies, and longings and hopes during and after slavery." Madgett calls upon this tradition as a means of delivering her people. Instead of fighting the slave master, she and her fellow black Americans are fighting a system of legalized bigotry. They are gathering strength through their words. The voices of protest that "whispered them, sang them, prayed them, shouted them" become stronger throughout the poem. The energy Madgett creates by recalling these voices of protest is another way in which language is of central importance in this struggle. It is what builds the sense of urgency; it multiples, as other voices "echo the freedom words." Language is what creates a space for agency, and Madgett draws on the oratory, a powerful mode of communication.

The oratory, or public speech, was extremely important in the nineteenth century, especially in the anti-slavery movement. Such leaders as William Lloyd Garrison and Wendell Phillips would organize anti-slavery conventions, inviting such powerful speakers as Frederick Douglass and Sojourner Truth, both of whom were ex-slaves.

What Do I Read Next?

- Poet, playwright, and novelist Ntozake Shange is an important voice in contemporary African-American poetry. Her *for colored girls who have considered suicide when the rainbow is enuf* is a long "choreopoem" that was also staged as a Broadway Play in 1976. Shange tackles issues such as racism, identity, and black womanhood in her poetry.

- Nobel Prize winner Toni Morrison has written several novels and essays. Her first novel, *The Bluest Eye,* set in the 1940s, tells the story of an eleven-year-old girl trying to come to terms with her own blackness in a world obsessed with white standards of beauty. Morrison addresses the inner struggle that many African-American writers consider, including Madgett.

- Nikki Giovanni was first widely published in the 1960s during the Civil Rights movement. *The Selected Poems of Nikki Giovanni* (1996) is both personal and political. Giovanni is an important voice in African-American culture and her poems are very accessible.

Madgett is borrowing from this rhetorical tradition in the way she chronicles the events of the Civil Rights movement. She speaks in first person: "And I sat at the counters of Greensboro. / Ride! And I rode the bus for freedom. / Kneel! And I went down on my knees in prayer and faith. / March! And I'll march until the last chain falls / Singing, 'We shall overcome.'" Just as ex-slaves would recount their experiences in slavery and their escapes, Madgett is recounting the modern day movement towards freedom, trying to inspire a mixture of emotions: anger, hope, pride, and excitement, to name a few.

Madgett's words act as a road map, locating the physical presence of black people in places all over the south: Montgomery, Greensboro, Birmingham, Selma. These were all sites of protest and revolution, marked with the sweat and tears of Madgett's people. These were also sites of white resistance to the black struggle for civil rights— police using fire hoses to spray the crowd, nightsticks flying, churches burned, Ku Klux Klan demonstrations. Leaders such as Martin Luther King, Jr., were jailed as a result of demonstrations. Madgett addresses this resistance in the final stanza: "Not all the dogs and hoses in Birmingham / Nor all the clubs and guns in Selma / Can turn this tide." The movement, the desire for freedom and opportunity, is stronger than the hatred and fear of white America.

As a black woman, Madgett is speaking from a doubly marginalized identity in 1960s American culture. The contemporary women's movement gained momentum later than the civil rights movement, picking up steam in the late 1960s and 1970s. It is interesting to consider Madgett's position in these two movements. As an African-American, she clearly identifies with the Civil Rights movement. In the final stanza, she chooses an interesting image to present: "Not all the jails can hold these young black faces / From their destiny of manhood." One imagines Martin Luther King writing his famous letter from a jail cell in Birmingham, Alabama, as well as the scores of other black men jailed. But the reader is left to wonder about the destiny of womanhood. Historian and critic Deborah Gray White, in *Too Heavy a Load: Black Women in Defense of Themselves, 1894–1994,* commented: "The masculine ethos of the era was certainly an impediment, but so was the Civil Rights movement's subsumption of gender and class issues. The movement was at once a black women's movement, a black movement, and a class-based movement, and it was not easy to define what was, and was not, a women's issue."

To throw gender into the mix complicates a reading of "Alabama Centennial." When historians speak of the Civil Rights movement, sometimes the male role in the movement is emphasized, with impassioned speeches from Martin Luther King. There is no doubt that the male leaders of the movement had tremendous impact in mobilizing an entire culture to protest. But black feminism also held—and still holds—great influence in the African-American community. Madgett does not outwardly identify with the burgeoning black feminism of the 1960s, nor does she dismiss it. We can only surmise that it is there as one of the many political forces shaping her work.

Certainly "Alabama Centennial" is a call to action. Madgett carefully constructs the poem to evoke both anger and empowerment. The anger and desire for freedom and full rights of American citizenship is what fuels the fight for equality. The empowerment is the net result that comes from years of protest and struggles to reeducate American society—a struggle that still resonates.

Source: Judi Ketteler, in an essay for *Poetry for Students,* Gale, 2001.

Paul Witcover

Paul Witcover is a novelist and editor in New York City with an M.A. in Creative Writing and Literature from The City University of New York. In the following essay, he discusses themes of racism and responsibility in Naomi Long Madgett's poem, "Alabama Centennial."

Naomi Long Madgett's poem, "Alabama Centennial," published in her 1965 collection *Star by Star,* is at once a stirring call to action and a moving record of psychological and social transformation. The poem works on a variety of levels to communicate its theme of the struggle for individual and collective emancipation. That struggle occurs within the confines of a culture of institutionalized racism that employs violence, fear, and habit to shape, consciously and unconsciously, every aspect of public life and private thought. Poems like this one, which rely upon a reader's familiarity with political and historical events, and which seek to move that reader toward a particular point of view by appeals to reason, conscience, and emotion, fall into the category of didactic poetry.

The title of Madgett's poem refers to a centennial, a word meaning the celebration of a one hundred anniversary. But what anniversary is referred to? Readers might naturally assume at first that it is the one hundred anniversary of Alabama's statehood, but in fact Madgett has a very different anniversary in mind. It is no coincidence that "Alabama Centennial." appeared in 1965, exactly one-hundred years after the end of the Civil War. That is the centennial to which Madgett's ironic but also hopeful title refers.

What was the status of African-Americans in the United States 100 years after the defeat of the Confederacy and the abolition of slavery? Despite Congressional passage of the Civil Rights Act of 1964, African-American men and women in 1965 were still treated as second-class citizens throughout much of the country. The legacy of institutionalized racism persisted. That legacy includes Jim Crow laws adopted by states to deny their non-white citizens full participation in, and access to,

> *Madgett has no interest in reducing the problems of segregation and racism to a black versus white, good versus evil, dichotomy. The reality she perceives is too complex for that."*

the government under which they lived, to which they paid taxes, and in whose armies they fought and died. The phrase "separate but equal" was the rallying cry used by those—like Alabama's governor, George Wallace—determined to protect white privilege and power at all costs. While Alabama's reputation as a bastion of racism made it a logical place for Madgett to set her poetic centennial, she is not writing about Alabama alone, but every state in the Union. When the reader recalls that the states of the Union are represented on the American flag by stars, the title of the collection in which "Alabama Centennial." appears, *Star by Star,* takes on a new significance.

The Jim Crow laws, and the philosophy of "separate but equal" used to rationalize them, came under increasing attack from the 1950s. Many historians date the beginning of the modern Civil Rights movement to 1955-1956, when Rosa Parks's brave refusal to give up her bus seat triggered the Montgomery, Alabama bus boycott, the event which catapulted a charismatic advocate of non-violent resistance, the Rev. Martin Luther King, Jr., to national prominence.

1965 would prove to be a turning point for the Civil Rights movement, as Dr. King's philosophy of non-violence was challenged by other African Americans impatient with the pace of change. In March of that year, Dr. King led more than 25,000 peaceful marchers into Montgomery, Alabama to press for passage of the Voting Rights Act. That triumphant march that serves as the occasion of Madgett's poem. But it is worth remembering that while President Lyndon B. Johnson signed the Voting Rights Act into law on August 6, 1965, racial tensions in the United States had grown so high by then that just five days later, on August 11, a routine traffic stop by white police officers in the Los Angeles neighborhood of Watts sparked one of the worst riots in American history.

This and subsequent events, such as the assassination of Dr. King in 1968 and the rioting that followed, cannot help but influence readers' reactions to "Alabama Centennial." Are readers wrong to bring knowledge unavailable to Madgett into their experience of her poem? Surely not. If a poem is to be more than a lifeless artifact entombed in language, it must grow and change with the wider world. At the same time, readers have a responsibility to remain rooted as much as possible in the language, rhythms, and images of the poem itself before looking beyond them.

Robert Sedlack, writing in the *Dictionary of Literary Biography,* states that the narrator of "Alabama Centennial" "assumes the collective voice of [civil rights] protestors." There is a progression from the "I" of the poem's first line—repeated no less than six times in the following lines—to the "we" of line 28. Not only that, but the poet almost immediately lets her readers know that the "I" is not just a single person; after all, it is unlikely that one individual could wait "for a hundred years" and in such a wide variety of places as those featured in lines 3-7. Just as the State of Alabama in the poem's title stands for both itself and all 50 states, so, too, does the "I" stand for both an individual person and a multitude of people. This is a common poetic device known as synecdoche: that is, the use of a part to mean the whole.

The poem opens with a simple sentence: "They said, 'Wait.'" But nothing in this poem is as simple as it appears. Who exactly are "they"? The first stanza continues in a list that includes cotton fields, chain gangs, "stinking 'colored' toilets" and the "outside of schools and voting booths." Each of these items powerfully evokes the narrow opportunities available to, and the humiliations and brutalities inflicted upon, generations of African Americans under the Jim Crow laws. The narrator speaks of waiting in these places, but for what? The answer isn't stated explicitly until the third stanza, line 17, where the word "freedom" appears. But even in the first stanza that answer is already clear, partly because of the poem's title and the historical ironies and associations embedded therein, and partly because of the list of places carefully selected by the poet to elicit specific reactions in her audience. The reader might therefore decide that "they,"

the ones who tell the narrator to wait, are white people, especially when the stanza goes on to conclude with the lines: "And some said, 'Later.' / And some said, 'Never!'"

The narrator is indeed referring to white people. But not only whites. The ambiguity of the words "they" and "some" allows the poet to cast a wider net. Madgett has no interest in reducing the problems of segregation and racism to a black versus white, good versus evil, dichotomy. The reality she perceives is too complex for that.

The second stanza introduces "a new voice." This voice answers the voices of the first stanza. "'No,' it said. 'Not "never," not "later," / Not even "soon." / Now. / Walk!'" The poem moves from the passivity of waiting to the action of walking: the peaceful protest marches that were among the most visible and successful tools of the civil rights movement. The reader would not be wrong to identify this "new voice" with that of Dr. King, and in fact, the sermon-like rhythms and even the language and images of the entire poem closely parallel Dr. King's famous "I Have A Dream" speech from 1963. But again, because the owner of the voice is never explicitly identified, it seems to issue from a multitude of throats in a force as fresh and pervasive as the wind with which it is compared: "Strong, determined, sure."

In the third stanza, other voices join in to echo "the freedom words." Up until now, all the voices in the poem have "said" their words. But suddenly the words are whispered, sung, prayed, and shouted. The explosive variety of verbs, contrasted with the flat repetition of "said," expresses the mounting passion and determination of those who walk "the streets of Montgomery." This stanza is the heart of the poem structurally; two stanzas precede it and two stanzas follow. It is also the heart of the poem in a figurative sense, the turning point where a dramatic change takes place. That change occurs in the final line of the stanza: "Until a link in the chain of patient acquiescence broke."

It is worth looking at this line closely, for it is the well-oiled hinge upon which the poem, like a hidden door, swings smoothly and unexpectedly open. The words "link" and "chain" suggest the bonds of slavery which have continued to shackle the supposedly free descendants of slaves even after a hundred years. But the chain the narrator refers to is one of "patient acquiescence." This is no iron chain imposed by force or trickery upon African Americans, nor is it even the more subtle but equally restrictive chain of oppressive laws. It is hard to see how those chains could be characterized as patient or acquiescent. No, this chain is an inner chain forged by fear and habit within the soul of the narrator, who, it should not be forgotten, speaks for multitudes. Freedom does not lie simply in breaking the chains imposed by racist white society. Those chains must certainly be broken, but the poet suggests more is necessary. Note that it is not enough to walk. Walking is only the beginning. The narrator walks until a link in the chain of patient acquiescence breaks. The narrator is that link. The chain is made up of many links, each an individual African American who must, like the narrator, decide to patiently acquiesce no more. In other words, the poet is stating that African Americans must wake to their own complicity in the racist status quo. Suddenly, with a shock, the reader realizes that the "they" of the first stanza is not made up of whites alone, but of African Americans as well. It is difficult to convey the hostility this message would have generated in the increasingly militant atmosphere of the civil rights movement of the mid-1960s. Indeed, it remains a controversial opinion nearly half a century later.

Once this inner awakening or liberation has occurred, real transformation of self and society can take place. This is what happens in the fourth and fifth stanzas. The "new voice" from the second stanza returns, demanding more of its listeners than mere walking. "Sit down!" it exhorts. "Ride!" "Kneel!" "March!" Each of these sharp commands evokes a protest tactic of the civil rights movement, from lunch counter sit-ins to freedom rider voter registration drives. The "I" of the poem, both individual and collective, vows to "march until the last chain falls." And now the chain refers to both the inner chain of patient acquiescence and the outer chain of racist society. This is a process that, once started, cannot be stopped. "Not all the jails can hold these young black faces / From their destiny of manhood, / Of equality, of dignity, / Of the American Dream / A hundred years past due. / Now!"

There are three things to note about these closing lines. First, the freedom the narrator claims for the "young black faces" is to be found within the American system of government, not outside it. Unlike such groups as the Black Panthers, the narrator does not wish to escape or overthrow the American Dream but rather to join in. Second, while the poem begins with the word "wait," it ends with "Now!" A transformation has taken place in the all-important line 22, an individual awakening

of political and social awareness that prompts a change of stance from passive acceptance to active engagement. Third, in a sharp historical irony, women are missing from the narrator's call for freedom, equality, and dignity. The destiny the narrator refers to is one of "manhood." This omission is a kind of blind spot, reflecting the reality of 1965, when the women's liberation movement, itself inspired by the civil rights struggle, had yet to emerge as a powerful force in its own right. So it is that even as the poem's triumphant last word rings in the reader's mind like the peal of a bell stirring a sleepy countryside to action, the echo of that bell down the years is somewhat attenuated and flattened due to the interpolation of events, of history, between "Alabama Centennial" as Madgett wrote it and the poem's contemporary reader.

Source: Paul Witcover, in an essay for *Poetry for Students,* Gale, 2001.

Karen D. Thompson

In this essay, Thompson discusses how Madgett's diction and structuring of "Alabama Centennial" contribute not only to the poem's pace, but also to its irony.

A title like "Alabama Centennial" conjures images of a parade winding its way down Main Street featuring the high school marching band; little children run out into the street, while parents caution them, and pick bright disks of candy from the hot asphalt where clowns riding ridiculously small tricycles have thrown it. Festive picnickers sate their holiday appetites with weightless biscuits that threaten to float away if they're not held onto, cold fried chicken that's still crispy and smells of grease, and peach cobbler heavy enough to bend a foil baking pan held by the edges.

This is a realistic picture of an Alabama Centennial, is it not? Centennial, after all, means celebration.

No.

Centennial *connotes,* but does not *denote* celebration. It means simply a period of one hundred years, or the marking of one hundred years. In Madgett's poem, the word "centennial," far from suggesting a celebration, evokes serious and sad retrospection. For in "Alabama Centennial" Madgett bemoans a hundred years of the failure of the United States to deliver the justice promised by the Civil War, and she mourns the tragedy of lost lives and the degradation endured in the charade of "separate but equal" living conditions.

> *This poem moves as justice moves: with stops and starts, fits and jerks.*"

The decade of the 1960s could have been a time for celebration. The United States could have seized upon the opportunity to commemorate the one-hundredth anniversary of the end of the Civil War and the Constitutional amendment that ended slavery. Instead the hundred years after the end of the Civil War was marked, or marred, by Jim Crow Laws and violence.

Naomi Madgett's choice of the word "centennial," with its celebratory connotation, as her poem's title presents a paradox. This paradox forces readers to identify her meaning and to scrutinize a poem they may otherwise skim because they've heard the story many times. Madgett continues to employ incongruity in the poem's message. This is a poem about a movement: in this case, the Civil Rights movement. The very word "movement" presents a paradox. Movement is not limited to a single direction, is often incremental rather than continuous, and is often deceptive. Likewise, the hundred-year pursuit of freedom from color prejudice moves forward as well as backward, and it also stops. Additionally, movement toward justice is deceptive. It cannot be seen as it happens, but only as one looks back at a landmark and measures the distance traveled.

So it is with movement, or change, in society. Madgett mimics society's erratic and sometimes imperceptible pace of change in this poem. Because it is free verse, the poem does not conform to a standard meter, which is one of the ways in which a poet achieves movement in a poem. The poem's free verse form contains no intentional rhyme. If Madgett had used end rhyme, her readers would have moved quickly through the poem, perhaps pausing momentarily at the end of a couplet or quatrain, but then hurrying on toward the completion of the next rhyme. Perhaps the strongest sense of movement in poetry is accomplished with internal rhyme, a device which Madgett used along with end rhyme to great effect in her poem "Midway": "I'm coming and I'm going / And I'm stretching and I'm growing / And I'll reap what I've been sowing or my skin's not black."

"Alabama Centennial" is devoid of rhyme and rhythm, and perhaps intentionally so. This poem moves as justice moves: with stops and starts, fits and jerks. Its appearance on the page is jagged and irregular with lines of varying length, many of which are interrupted with punctuation marks. The lack of regular pace is fitting. When the word pace is applied to a liberation movement, an oxymoron is created. A liberation movement has no real pace, only a perceived pace, which for the oppressed is always too slow, for the oppressors is unacceptable, and for the fearful fringes is too fast.

While it lacks recognizable pace, the poem manages to elicit a feeling of urgency. However, this is not the result of standard poetic devices, but the result of punctuation and sentence length. The exclamations—"Never!" and "Walk!" and "Now!" are shouts of urgency. They are also, as single-word utterances, indicative of commands that demand immediate response. The use of these commands and the actions they elicit produce more than a feeling of exigency, they also contribute to the poem's underlying irony. In line 10 "a new wind blew, and a new voice / rode its wings with quiet urgency." Only after a single voice called out for freedom did other voices join the cry, and they joined as echoes. This image presents a sad irony.

The tragic legacy of the oppressed is that they are often so scarred by captivity that they evolve into a group without a voice, and sometimes without a vision. When a strong voice does rise, as one did with Reverend King, the voices of the oppressed masses, when they finally join in, are raised as echoes—almost as involuntary responses. The voices that joined the Civil Rights movement joined, it seems in this poem, in response to orders, as their ancestors had done for centuries. "Walk!" the voice said, "And I walked the streets of Montgomery," and later, "Ride! And I rode the bus for freedom." This is in truth sad irony, for one hundred years after the Civil War no black person should have been testing the waters of freedom for the first time. No black person should have still been waiting for an order to exercise an inalienable right. Fortunately, as was the case with Dr. King, directives sometimes issue from a beneficent source, and following them allows the dependent to move toward independence. Yet oppression persists. It persists for persons of color, persons of creed, persons of sexuality, persons of age, persons of gender. The list is as long as the people who will make it.

That is why I find two of the most troubling lines of this poem to be these: "Not all the jails can hold these young black faces / From their destiny of manhood." Why did Madgett apparently exclude herself and all other females from the American Dream? Could a woman with a voice this strong, a mind this keen, and a vision this clear have been blind to the oppression of women? Could a woman so closely identified with her people that she used the pronoun "I" when referring to her entire race be intentionally exclusive of any of its members? Did she believe that civil rights was the destiny of black men and was to be led by black men? Was she careless? Was she a product of a generation not yet concerned with women's rights?

I choose to believe that she was not. Instead, I believe she understood that the fight for justice demands a united army and a focused offensive because it is a war, as all are, of life and death. I believe that as she finished this poem, Madgett was convinced that a later Alabama Centennial *would* celebrate one hundred years of freedom for her people; that as soon as she felt that freedom for black males was secured, or at least securely on the horizon, she would turn her attention to the quest for women's freedom; and that in her new fight she would willingly raise her voice first and loudest, providing the words that her sisters could echo.

Source: Karen D. Thompson, in an essay for *Poetry for Students,* Gale, 2001.

Sources

Randall, Dudley, *The Black Poets,* Bantam Books, 1971.

Giovanni, Nikki, *Racism 101,* William Morrow & Co., 1994.

Redding, Saunders, "Books Noted," in *Negro Digest,* September, 1966, pp. 51-52.

Redmond, Eugene B., *Drumvoices: The Mission of Afro-American Poetry,* Anchor Press, 1976.

Sedlack, Robert P., *Dictionary of Literary Biography, Volume 76: Afro-American Writers, 1940–1955,* edited by Trudier Harris, Gale, 1988.

White, Deborah Gray, *Too Heavy a Load: Black Women in Defense of Themselves, 1894–1994,* W. W. Norton & Co., 1999.

For Further Study

Redmond, Eugene B., *Drumvoices: The Mission of Afro-American Poetry,* Anchor Press, 1976.

A chronicle of African-American literature, including critical debates, a study of various African-American poets, background information, and a framework for studying African-American poetry.

Smith, Valerie, et al, *African American Writers: Profiles of Their Lives and Works from the 1700s to the Present,* Macmillan, 1991.

A study of African-American writers and the themes they explore in their work. An excellent resource book.

Walker, Alice, *In Search of our Mother's Gardens,* Harcourt Brace Jovanovich, 1984.

From essays about black writers such as Zora Neale Hurston and Jean Toomer to a tribute to Martin Luther King and a retrospective on the Civil Rights movement, this collection is a good companion to any study of African-American literature.

Ballad of Orange and Grape

Muriel Rukeyser

1973

Muriel Rukeyser wrote "Ballad of Orange and Grape" toward the end of her long career. The poem reflects one of the central concerns of her life and art—the power of language to shape the world's realities. Rukeyser was a pacifist and promoted many international social justice issues throughout her life. She always sought to express her political passions through her poetry, an attribute that made her stand out among women poets of her time.

"Ballad of Orange and Grape" takes the form of a ballad, telling a simple story in verse form. The speaker, a poet or thinker like the author, goes to a hot-dog stand in East Harlem at the end of a day's work. After passing through a scene of urban squalor, she arrives at the hot-dog stand and encounters the vendor refilling two drink machines—clearly labeled orange and grape respectively—with the wrong flavor of beverage. This provides the poem's central metaphor. Questioning such disregard for language, Rukeyser connects the vendor's indifference with the inability of people in the neighborhood to take action to change their violent and depressed environment.

The poem was published in Rukeyser's 1973 collection, *Breaking Open* and later appeared in several collections of her work. It is one of her better known poems. Critics are divided as to whether Rukeyser's writing will stand the test of time. Some see her poetry as hampered by a naive or propagandistic message, while others, particularly feminists, view her as a renegade whose contributions to American poetry have yet to be fully appreciated.

Author Biography

Rukeyser was born in New York in 1913 to Lawrence and Myra Rukeyser, a conservative and well-off Jewish couple. Her parents provided her with many privileges of wealth, including a chauffeur and a private education. However, her parents' unhappy marriage also contributed toward Rukeyser's incipient pacifism. "The memories of emotional violence which she retained from her childhood must have colored her lifelong commitment to nonviolence, as surely as the graphic images from the battlefields of the Great War (World War II)," wrote Kate Daniels in her introduction to *Out of Silence.*

By her late teens Rukeyser had completely rejected her parents' lifestyle, throwing herself into her writing and political commitments. She attended Vassar College for two years, then withdrew in 1932 in order to write full time. In 1933 she attended the trial of the Scottsboro Boys, an infamous case in which black men were falsely accused of raping a white woman. She was profoundly affected by the injustice she witnessed. She continued to travel as an advocate against injustice of all kinds, which took her from West Virginia, where she protested unsafe working conditions for miners, to Spain, where she protested the holding of the Olympic Games in Nazi Germany. She published her first, highly acclaimed volume of poetry, *Theory of Flight,* in 1935, which reflected many of these experiences. During the 1930s, when Rukeyser was in her twenties, she, like many other New York writers and intellectuals, joined the Communist party. By the end of the decade she had cut ties with the party, adopting politics of nonpartisan pacifism that is evident throughout her body of work.

Rukeyser wrote prolifically and successfully until single motherhood slowed her productivity. She had a very brief marriage and then, in 1947, became pregnant out of wedlock by a man whose identity she never disclosed. In order to support her son, she took a job teaching at Sarah Lawrence College. Her position there was threatened when, in the conservative tenor of the 1950s, her ties to the Communist party were investigated, but the college supported her and she was able to retain her post. In the 1960s, when her son was grown and the mood of the country had become more sympathetic to her political activism, her career had a renaissance. Rukeyser published more frequently and remained politically active. She was once jailed for her participation in a Vietnam War demonstration.

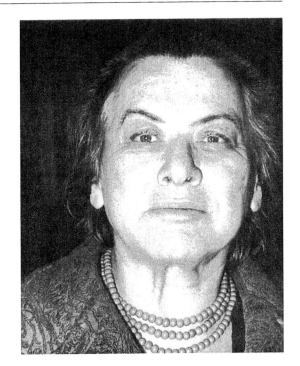

Muriel Rukeyser

In her sixties and in poor health, Rukeyser traveled to South Korea to protest the death sentence of a dissident poet. She based her last major poem, "The Gates," published in 1976, on this experience. Rukeyser died in 1980.

Poem Text

After you finish your work
after you do your day
after you've read your reading
after you've written your say—
you go down the street to the hot dog stand,   5
one block down and across the way.
On a blistering afternoon in East Harlem in the
      twentieth century.

Most of the windows are boarded up,
the rats run out of a sack —
sticking out of the crummy garage   10
one shiny long Cadillac;
at the glass door of the drug-addiction center,
a man who'd like to break your back.
But here's a brown woman with a little girl dressed
      in rose and pink, too.

Frankfurters frankfurters sizzle on the steel   15
where the hot-dog-man leans —
nothing else on the counter
but the usual two machines,

the grape one, empty, and the orange one, empty,
I face him in between.   20
A black boy comes along, looks at the hot dogs,
      goes on walking.

I watch the man as he stands and pours
in the familiar shape
bright purple in the one marked ORANGE
orange in the one marked GRAPE,   25
the grape drink in the machine marked ORANGE
and orange drink in the GRAPE.
Just the one word large and clear, unmistakable, on
      each machine.

I ask him: How can we go on reading
and make sense out of what we read? —   30
How can they write and believe what they're
      writing,
the young ones across the street,
while you go on pouring grape into ORANGE
and orange into the one marked GRAPE —?
(How are we going to believe what we read and we   35
      write and we hear and we say and we do?)

He looks at the two machines and he smiles
and he shrugs and smiles and pours again.
It could be violence and nonviolence
it could be white and black   women and men
it could be war and peace or any   40
binary system, love and hate, enemy, friend.
Yes and no, be and not-be, what we do and what
      we don't do.

On a corner in East Harlem
garbage, reading, a deep smile, rape,
forgetfulness, a hot street of murder,   45
misery, withered hope,
a man keeps pouring grape into ORANGE
and orange into the one marked GRAPE,
pouring orange into GRAPE and grape into
      ORANGE forever.

Poem Summary

Lines 1-7

Introducing the speaker, the opening stanza uses the second-person voice, describing the speaker as "you." This strategy aligns readers with the speaker and places them in the midst of the action of the poem. The stanza also introduces the brief story the poem will tell by situating it in time. "You" walk to a nearby hot-dog stand "after you finish your work, after you do your day." For this second-person speaker, work entails reading and writing, activities that are intellectual and solitary. Such work might well describe that of a poet like Rukeyser, and the speaker may be understood as loosely autobiographical.

The repetition of the word "after" in lines 1-4 emphasizes the contrast between such intellectual work and the visit to the hot-dog stand that is the main subject of the poem. While the speaker's work is described in general and abstract terms, Rukeyser is very concrete and specific in her description of the world the speaker enters as she sets out on her walk. In this opening stanza, Rukeyser describes the neighborhood in which the speaker lives in terms of its geographical location and its broad historical context: "East Harlem in the twentieth century." This contrast between the abstract and the concrete is only the first of a series of pairs of opposite terms, or binaries, that Rukeyser sets up throughout the poem. Thus she subtly introduces the poem's theme of difference. The fact that the unpaired last line of the stanza (line 7) breaks the *abcbdb* paired rhyme scheme, as it does in each stanza to follow, further underscores the idea of difference.

Lines 8-14

The poem's second stanza describes the cityscape that the speaker passes through on her way to the hotdog stand. It is a scene of urban squalor, suggesting poverty and other related social ills, such as substance abuse and violence. Most of the focus is on this threatening and depressing environment. But there is an implicit contrast between the speaker, who lives a life of the mind as she works all day, and the very tangible physical attributes of the street she walks—a contrast between the intellect and the world. The speaker herself is referred to only once, again in the second-person, in a vulnerable relation to a loitering man whom she passes "who'd like to break your back." The longer, unpaired last line of the stanza (line 14) again introduces contrast: "But here's a brown woman with a little girl dressed in rose and pink, too." They are not threatening or hopeless, as are the other images in this stanza. In this one line, three warm colors are mentioned. Through the woman and girl, the more positive and hopeful attributes of the environment are associated with femininity.

Lines 15-21

In this stanza the speaker arrives at the hot-dog stand. Here she encounters the vendor with whom she will engage in a kind of philosophical debate for the rest of the poem. It is significant that in this stanza the speaker shifts from a second-person to first-person voice. Rukeyser turns "you" into "I," reversing the terms of a binary opposition. This stanza is also pivotal because it introduces the poem's central metaphor: "the usual two machines" for dispensing drinks, "the grape one, empty, and the orange one, empty." Seen by the speaker in the most abstract way, these everyday items represent the distinctions made possible through the labels of language. Line 21, the last line of the stanza introduces the figure of a "black boy" who wanders through the scene. His racial labeling as "black" (as opposed to "brown" in the stanza above) is a concrete example of how language is used to make either/or distinctions that have real social significance.

Lines 22-28

In these lines the speaker describes the action that informs the central idea of the poem. She observes the hot-dog vendor refilling the drink machines. Paying no heed to the words on the machines that make a clear distinction between the two flavors, he puts the grape drink in the one marked orange, and vice versa. This stanza, through its repetition and capitalization of the words "orange" and "grape," emphasizes the relationship between language and reality. The words are "large and clear, unmistakable," but that does not mean that they reflect reality.

Lines 29-35

In this stanza the speaker interprets the events described in the preceding stanza in the form of a series of questions posed to the hot-dog vendor, interrogating his disregard for language. She asks him, how can we come to understand anything, "How can we go on reading and make sense of what we read," if people pay so little heed to so simple and clear a distinction as that between orange and grape? This refers back to her own work as a reader and writer. In the next question, she frames the issue more broadly, in terms of the children in the neighborhood and their ability to have faith in the knowledge that is communicated through language: "How can they write and believe what they're writing, / the young ones across the street?" In the stanza's closing lines she expands on her point about the faith in knowledge that comes from reading and writing to encompass "what we say" (another form of language) and also, crucially, "what we do." For Rukeyser, writing poetry is a political act that has real impact on the world; abstract concepts shape lived reality.

Lines 36-42

The hot-dog vendor's response to this series of questions is to shrug and smile. He is indifferent to

Media Adaptations

- A film concerning Rukeyser, *Three Women Artists: Anna Sokolow, Alice Neel, Muriel Rukeyser,* by Lucille Rhodes and Margaret Murphy, is available on a 1998 videotape distributed by Kultur.

her passionate attachment to the integrity of language and the distinctions it enables us to make. He doesn't seem to see her point. But his indifference toward the meaningful distinction between the categories of orange and grape could just as well be, she suggests, an indifference toward the distinction between the opposing terms in "any binary system," including "violence and nonviolence," "white and black," "women and men." These distinctions, as Rukeyser has subtly illustrated earlier in the poem, have a huge impact on life in East Harlem in the twentieth century. The ability to have faith in the meaning and integrity of language makes the difference between "what we do and what we don't do." Again, Rukeyser connects language to action.

Lines 43-49

Rukeyser closes the poem with a descriptive stanza that has a somewhat looser form than the previous ones. The rhyme scheme, which is always broken in the last line, is further attenuated in this stanza by the slant rhyme between "rape," "hope," and "GRAPE." This loosening of the rhyme scheme points up the chaos of the urban setting: "garbage, reading, a deep smile, rape, / forgetfulness, a hot street of murder, / misery, withered hope." These are the concrete human repercussions of people's indifference to language and its potential to effect change. The poem closes by reiterating the hot-dog vendor's central symbolic action, projecting him pouring grape into orange and orange into grape "forever." Thus, Rukeyser suggests that action and change are not possible until people—everyone, not just poets and intellectuals—understand and respect the integrity of language.

Topics for Further Study

- Why do you think Rukeyser starts the poem in a second-person voice and then shifts to the first-person?

- How are the rhymes important to the overall meaning of the poem? Why does Rukeyser choose not to rhyme certain lines?

- Do you think that it is true, as a general rule, that one should aim to accurately reflect reality when writing or speaking? Describe an instance when it is especially crucial to do so. Or describe an example of when playing with or distorting words' meaning is worthwhile or valid.

- Do some research to find out what the daily conditions of life were like for people living in East Harlem in the period when Rukeyser wrote. How effective a statement is the poem about these conditions?

- Idenitify the various political causes and movements with which Rukeyser was affiliated. Choose one that seems appropriate, research it, and explore how its tenets relate to the themes of "Ballad of Orange and Grape."

Themes

The poem tells a simple story about the speaker visiting a hot-dog stand in East Harlem. There the hot-dog vendor refills two drink dispensers with the wrong flavor beverages, putting grape in the one marked orange, and vice versa. Rukeyser uses this action as an example of indifference to language's power.

Difference

The central metaphor in the "Ballad of Orange and Grape" is the pair of dispensers that a vendor fills with the wrong flavor of drink. He disregards the "unmistakable" words that mark the difference between grape and orange, committing what the speaker sees as a blow against language's integrity and, therefore, our power to use language to shape

our world in constructive ways. The basic property that lends language its power is its ability to allow people to make distinctions and conceptualize differences. If people are indifferent to this power, Rukeyser suggests, impoverished and violent social conditions, like those that pertain in the environment she describes, will remain. If here, in the violent and economically depressed neighborhood where we live, we see orange drink in the machine marked grape and vice versa, she asks, how can we have faith in *any* words that we read or write, hear or say? How, therefore, can we make meaningful distinctions between the terms of far more crucial binaries, such as violence and nonviolence, war and peace, love and hate? And how can we make sense of the categories of difference that organize and stratify our society, such as men and women, black and white? Earlier in the poem, Rukeyser obliquely raises the issues of racial and gender difference in relation to the bleak conditions of the neighborhood. She also refers to the presence of violence in the lines "a man who'd like to break your back," "rape," and "a hot street of murder." She argues that respecting the difference between orange and grape is one step toward shaping reality and changing its ills and inequities.

Language and Meaning

Rukeyser sees language, properly used, as an important tool for understanding reality and also for shaping it and effecting change. The poem's speaker rails against the hot-dog vendor for his indifference toward the meaning of the words "grape" and "orange." Such indifference toward language's meaning has huge repercussions for Rukeyser. In stanzas five and six she describes how such indifference erodes everyday people's faith in language (she speaks as part of a collective "we") as an accurate reflection of the larger world's reality. "How can we go on reading / and make sense of what we read?" the speaker asks. "How can they write and believe what they're writing, / the young ones across the street?" If people see that, in its everyday use, orange really means grape, and vice versa, then maybe love really means hate and war really means peace. For Rukeyser such reversals undermine language's power as an instrument of political change. She goes on to claim that the integrity of language's meaning is necessary not only for knowledge, but also for the action that brings about change, "what we do and what we don't do." In the last stanza, she uses a list of nouns to describe the disorganized, powerless, and therefore nearly hopeless atmosphere of the East Harlem neighborhood. Its denizens are hampered from drawing meaningful distinctions by a disregard to language and its power as represented by the man pouring orange into grape and grape into orange "forever."

Order vs. Disorder

Order and disorder are often important ideas in poems with irregular rhyme and meter schemes, like the "Ballad of Orange and Grape." Rukeyser, who most often wrote in free verse (poetry that is not strictly structured), uses a fairly structured form of seven stanzas of seven lines each. The lines are in rhyming pairs, except for the longer, extra seventh line in each stanza that breaks the pattern, sounding irregular. This introduces an element of disorder. The poem's structure is, of course, integrally related to its content. Indeed, one of the poem's important themes relates the social disorder in East Harlem to the disorder or confusion between binary terms in language. When the vendor pours the wrong flavor drink into the two drink dispensers, he undermines language by breaking its order. The drinks are, one might say, disorganized. Rukeyser attributes great significance to this, using it as an example: once language's categories are violated, meaning is undermined and action and change are impossible. The poem's last stanza is its loosest, in terms of both grammar and rhyme. It takes the form of a list of varied but disorganized images. This stanza illustrates the disorder of a social world that has no faith in language and the paralysis that comes with it.

Style

As identified in its title, Rukeyser's "Ballad of Orange and Grape" takes its form from the musical and literary genre of the ballad. Arising in the late Middle Ages, ballads were originally short folk songs telling concise stories. The literary ballad, growing out of the musical form, borrows certain stylistic elements from song. For example, they often tell emotionally charged stories and repeat significant words or lines. Early literary ballads employed a specific form—four-line stanzas with iambic lines of seven accents in rhymed pairs (*abcb, defe,* etc.) In the twentieth century, with the growing domination of free verse, these formal features of literary ballads became less important. However, many modern ballads still employ some pattern of rhyme and repetition, in keeping with the

form's musical roots. Most ballads bear some resemblance to songs, and songwriters continue to employ the ballad form often as well.

"Ballad of Orange and Grape" is a typical modern ballad. It tells a short, compact story in verse form. Playing on the ballad's history of emotionally heightened narrative, the poem takes a seemingly mundane event—visiting a hot-dog stand—and places it as the center of the story, and endows it with great significance. While Rukeyser is known mostly as a free-verse poet, this poem has a clear structure and rhyme scheme that bears some relation to the ballad's heritage through its use of rhymed pairs. There are seven stanzas of seven lines in "Ballad of Orange and Grape", with the first six lines in rhymed pairs and with the last, non-rhyming line unpaired and longer than the rest (*abcbdbe*). The last line in each stanza stands out to the ear for this reason and suggests a contrast or shift. Though Rukeyser does not repeat any line at regular intervals, as in a traditional ballad, she does repeat phrases that describe the central action of the man pouring grape into orange and orange into grape in the fourth and seventh stanzas.

Historical Context

Idealism and Apathy in the 1970s

Critic Jascha Kessler stated that reading Rukeyser's *Collected Poems* is "like rereading the last forty years, not in terms of the arts or even history, but in terms of the events and issues that are most typical of the times." "Ballad of Orange and Grape" reflects the integrative sense of historical time for which Rukeyser is known, offering a representative event that reflects the larger spirit of the historical moment.

The poem is set in time generally, "in the twentieth century," suggesting that the poet's concern for language is not tied to a particular decade or period, but to the shifts represented by the whole century. However, the social and political climate at the particular time Rukeyser wrote doubtless shaped the vision of lost faith that she puts forth in the poem. When the poem was published in 1973, the legacy of the liberalizing political movements of 1960s continued, but with their idealism severely hampered in the wake of the assassinations of John F. Kennedy, Robert Kennedy, Martin Luther King, and Malcolm X. The politically active set of which Rukeyser was part struggled on, but with considerably less optimism than they had had in the years

Compare & Contrast

- **1973:** The last American troops are withdrawn from Vietnam, ending a period of great social unrest associated with anti-war activism.

  1990: Iraq invades Kuwait under the command of President Saddam Hussein. The U.S. responds by working through the United Nations and sending troops to Saudi Arabia. Amidst protest from other governments, the U.S. and allies attack Iraq and liberate Kuwait. Public sentiment in America is strongly in favor of the display of U.S. military might. Hussein remains in power.

- **1973:** In a decision known as *Roe v. Wade* the U.S. Supreme Court declares unconstitutional state laws that prohibit abortion up until the sixth month of pregnancy. Feminists hail the decision as one of the most significant strides for women's rights of the century.

  1990s: After decades of being legal, abortion remains one of the most controversial and divisive issues in American politics. In some parts of the country there are no health care providers who will perform abortions. The number of abortions performed is in decline.

- **1973:** President Richard Nixon denies any knowledge of the illegal events surrounding the Watergate scandal, in which members of his administration have been indicted. Televised hearings rivet public attention. A year later, among calls for his impeachment, Nixon resigns.

  1999: President Bill Clinton, after initially denying an extra-marital affair with a young intern, admits to some sexual contact with her. Because he stated in a separate case that they had had no sexual relations, he is impeached by Congress for lying under oath. Impeachment means to accuse and try a government official. Clinton undergoes an impeachment trial in the U.S. Senate, but the charges fail to achieve the necessary two-thirds majority of votes needed to remove the president from office.

- **1973:** Already facing economic troubles, Americans confront an energy crisis that leads to high prices and rationing. Combined cutbacks in gas, home heating, and transportation fuel lead to the loss of an additional 100,000 U.S. jobs.

  2000: Amidst a period of unprecedented economic prosperity in the United States, the price of petroleum products surges. Home heating fuel and gasoline prices nearly double in some parts of the country.

---

before. Public cynicism was generally high, with the fiasco of the Vietnam War and the Watergate scandal in the White House undermining faith in government. In a 1975 survey, 69% of Americans said they believed that over the past decade leaders had consistently lied to the people.

The 1970s were, furthermore, a time of severe economic problems for the United States. This brought a conservative backlash as well as urban riots and white flight to the suburbs. While the struggles of the civil rights movement of the 1960s had led to significant legislative changes, it failed to translate into greater economic equality for people of color in the 1970s. Feminism was perhaps the most vital social movement of the decade, but it too failed to bring economic equality for women. In the 1970s, the American underclass was increasingly black and female.

East Harlem

In contrast to its general historical setting, the poem is set in a very particular geographical place, East Harlem. At the time when Rukeyser wrote the poem she was working with the Writers' and Teachers' Collaborative, which was located in East Harlem. The poem is likely based on an autobiographical anecdote. Rukeyser was born in New York and never ranged far from her hometown.

"Ballad of Orange and Grape" reflects her intimacy with the city's geography and social history.

East Harlem is adjacent to but distinct from the better known neighborhood of Harlem. In the 1880s cheap apartments sprang up in the formerly rural area to house an influx of immigrants. It has remained a poor immigrant neighborhood, though its ethnic makeup has changed. In the first decades of the twentieth century East Harlem was known as a Jewish ghetto. Along with the neighboring Harlem, it formed the second-largest Jewish community in the United States. Puerto Ricans began to move into East Harlem over the next few decades, and white immigrants slowly moved out. Because of its Latino population, it is now sometimes known as "El Barrio." However, reflecting the racial diversity of the United States, East Harlem has been home to many blacks and Italians as well as Latinos in recent decades. As a poor immigrant neighborhood, East Harlem has borne more than its share of social ills. Poor housing, unemployment, and poverty have long been associated with this struggling, but vital neighborhood.

Critical Overview

Rukeyser earned early praise as a poet, winning a Yale Younger Poet's Prize for her first volume, *Theory of Flight,* published when she was only twenty-two, followed by a series of other awards and honors in the 1940s. Known as an outspoken activist in the words of *Poetry* magazine's Linda Gregerson, led a "lifelong campaign against the conventional partitioning of thought and action," her poetry is often evaluated through the lens of politics, and her critical reputation has risen and fallen accordingly. While her career flourished in the 1940s, it faded during the conservative 1950s, rose in the radical 1960s, and fell again after her 1980 death. Some signs of a critical reevaluation of Rukeyser's place in American letters are taking place, as evidenced in new collections of her poetry published in the 1990s as well as a laudatory collection of essays on her work, *How Shall We Tell Each Other of the Poet?* published in 1999.

Breaking Open, the 1973 volume in which "Ballad of Orange and Grape" first appeared, received generally positive reviews, though some critics had reservations. Peter Meinka of the *New Republic* interprets the collection's title: "What Rukeyser is breaking open are the living moments of her life, our lives, a conscious affirmation of the

meaning and energy that our best poetry has always given us." He goes on to call the volume "a testament to human toughness and compassion, even against overwhelming odds." J. J. McGann of *Poetry* likes the collection but is less effusive, writing that "*Breaking Open* shows no diminishment of her early [technical] mastery.... Yet the book is decidedly uneven." Though *Breaking Open* is not one of Rukeyser's most frequently discussed collections, "Ballad of Orange and Grape" has appeared in all of the major anthologies reviewing her career, identifying it as one of the volume's strongest poems. It has also been included in a number of poetry anthologies and other collections.

Some critics find Rukeyser's political messages too heavy-handed or not sufficiently timeless to be the substance of great poetry. Some of her lines "appear politically naive at this distance from the turbulent times in which they were written," stated a *Publisher's Weekly* critic in a 1992 review of her *Collected Poems*. She has been embraced by feminist critics, who sometimes claim that she has been under-credited for her talent because she exceeded certain boundaries set for the female poet. "Rukeyser's desire to transform herself from a silenced member of an oppressed group into a powerful spokesperson for herself and other women led her to break many of the barriers and taboos that impeded the development of women's writing earlier in the century," writes editor Kate Daniels in her introduction to the Rukeyser collection *Out of Silence*.

Many scholars and critics have connected Rukeyser's poetic vision with that of Walt Whitman. In a 1974 retrospective article on her career in *American Poetry Review* Virginia R. Terris placed Rukeyser in the tradition of nineteenth-century American Transcendentalism, a literary movement of which Whitman was part. "Her reliance on primary rather than on literary experience as the source of truth," according to Terris, ties Rukeyser "to her forebears in the nineteenth century." Terris added: "At the same time, through her highly personal contemporary voice, they project her into our era" and secure her a place as "one of its most important figures." Terris explored the connections between Whitman and Rukeyser in what was then her most recent collection, *Breaking Open,* arguing that "both poets recognize the variety within unity. For each, the self is the One but also the Many, all mankind is joined mystically and is thus one, and each human being partakes of the life of every other human being, living and dead and yet unborn, in all cultures and in all lands." In another comparison to Whitman, a *Library Journal* reviewer summed up Rukeyser's career in a way that reflects on the meaning and method of "Ballad of Orange and Grape": "Her muse demanded that she pay as much attention to the shared, literal world as the world of literature, so, like Whitman, she personalized the public events of her time."

Criticism

Sarah Madsen Hardy

Madsen Hardy has a doctorate in English literature and is a freelance writer and editor. In the following essay, she discusses Rukeyser's ideas about the relationship between language, power, and morality in "Ballad of Orange and Grape."

In "Ballad of Orange and Grape," Muriel Rukeyser suggests that a hot dog vendor's indifference to language when he pours an orange drink into a machine labeled "grape" and grape drink into a machine labeled "orange" is part of a larger moral problem. For her, social ills in the East Harlem neighborhood of which she writes can be attributed to people's lack of faith in the meaning of language. In this atmosphere of lost faith, morally loaded categories that should be distinct, such as "war and peace" and "love and hate," start to blur. Without going so far as to *compare* the two acts, Rukeyser *connects* them using the wrong word to connote acts of physical violence. The prevalence of real, physical violence named in the poem's last stanza, "rape, forgetfulness, a hot street of murder," can be related to the casual, everyday 'violence' that people like the hot dog vendor do to language. This seems like a polemical claim, perhaps even a hyperbolic one. This essay explores and questions the ideas about language, power, and morality that Rukeyser voices in "Ballad of Orange and Grape."

Rukeyser, who was born during World War I and came of age during World War II, was sensitive to violence in all its forms. Her life spanned much of the century and she saw herself as a spokesperson of causes surrounding its crises. In another work entitled "Poem" dated from the 1940s she states, "I lived in the century of world war." Rukeyser was a well-known pacifist, and her strong leftist political views grew out of a sense of outrage at the violence of the times in which she lived. Though "Ballad"'s setting is portrayed in specific detail and can be connected to specific biographical facts of her life, Rukeyser describes the events

of the poem in sweeping terms as taking place "in the twentieth century." The shocking violence of the World Wars of Rukeyser's childhood and youth—experienced by her and other Americans at an arm's length, mediated by press reports—shaped her view of morality and her understanding of the power of language. It is through this lens that she observes East Harlem of the 1970s in "Ballad."

Rukeyser saw her lifelong commitment to pacifism as inextricable from her work as a poet. Though Rukeyser was affiliated with Marxism and the Proletariat School of Poetry in the earliest part of her career, she soon broke off from any specific school of political thought or poetic style to exhort readers in her own individualistic voice. Louise Kertesz, who wrote *The Poetic Vision of Muriel Rukeyser* (1980), one of the first book-length studies of her work, describes how Rukeyser bucked all of the dominant trends in modern poetry—irony, alienation, and an increasing interest in form—to write out of a highly personal mission of meaning, hope, and social change. Kertesz quotes Rukeyser, writing in the wake of the discovery of the concentration camps at the end of World War II, describing the poet's role on the world stage: "The war for those concerned with life, the truth which is open to all, is still ahead. It is a struggle in which poetry also lives and fights."

This vision of the poet as a fighter is one that, Kertesz argues, "explains the remarkable thrust of her work to the present." As a pacifist, Rukeyser participates in the century's wars with a pen rather than a sword. In "Poem," Rukeyser goes on to describe the poet's task in this century of world war. She has a heroic vision of her vocation that can be traced back to Whitman—a belief that the poet belongs in the public sphere, speaking and writing in an emphatic voice that people can understand and to which they respond more emotionally and morally than intellectually or aesthetically. "In the day I would be reminded of those men and women / Brave, setting up signals across vast distances, / Considering a nameless way of living, of almost unimagined values," she writes in "Poem." It is the poet's job, according to Rukeyser, to use language in a way that fosters meaning and creates new possibilities for change and hope—or, as she writes in the same poem, "to construct peace, to make love." To do less—to use language in a way that nullifies meaning—is a form of destruction that colludes with the forces of violence and exploitation. And for Rukeyser, such forces are always readily and clearly identifiable, as "unmistakable" as the labels on the two drink machines in "Ballad."

But the context and the tone of 1973's "Ballad" are radically different from those of "Poem." The poem takes place here in the United States, in a neighborhood the poet/speaker inhabits. Rukeyser attempts to apply the moral vision forged by her abhorrence of the World Wars to a more subtle and intimate local situation—a poor neighborhood in which the speaker works. Though the poem is, in some ways, a exhortation typical of her earlier style, an older and perhaps wearier Rukeyser recognizes that the poet's work of making meaning and therefore bringing about social change is in many ways ineffectual, even in a modest local context. She wrote the poem while she was involved with the Writers' and Teachers' Collaborative in East Harlem, an effort through which Rukeyser expressed her commitment to pass along a sense of poetic mission to the underprivileged. Thus, when the speaker asks the vendor "How can we go on reading / and make sense out of what we read?— / How can they write and believe what they're writing, / the young ones across the street?" she sees him as a force eroding the values of empowerment through language that Rukeyser tried to foster among the East Harlem youth.

If Rukeyser's vision of the poet is that of a valiant fighter, what is the speaker fighting for in "Ballad"? She fights for faith—belief in language as a system of signs that is intrinsically moral. If the word orange can really mean grape and vice versa, then humanity has no way to sort out right from wrong, to recognize moral truths. Without being able to make clear moral distinctions, action and change are impossible. Thus, the poem concludes, the dilapidated neighborhood will continue on its entropic course. With black-and-white language distinctions muddied by the hot dog vendor's mixing of orange and grape, what is left to stop the young ones across the street from continuing on the course of deprivation, addiction, and crime that they see around them? The threatening atmosphere that stanza two describes—boarded-up windows, a Cadillac sticking out of a "crummy garage," a menacing drug addict "who'd like to break your back," all contrasted with the hopeful, vulnerable image of a woman and girl dressed in rose and pink—is interpreted in stanza five as the result of a paralysis in moral distinctions brought about by indifference to language. If we can't distinguish the orange from the grape, the purity from the garbage, the good from the bad, "How are we

> *She has ... a belief that the poet belongs in the public sphere, speaking and writing in an emphatic voice that people can understand and to which they respond more emotionally and morally than intellectually ..."*

going to believe what we read and we write and we hear and we say and we do?" Ignorant of or indifferent to language's meaning-making power and, therefore, to its moral implications, the hot dog vendor indirectly perpetuates the cycle of violence and exploitation in the neighborhood. The last stanza creates a depressing picture of the neighborhood's fate illustrated through the melding of contrasting categories. In this unwholesome place, "a deep smile" is followed by "rape." Rukeyser's last word, "forever," is a bitter one for this poet of hope.

The question for Rukeyser is not related to her view of language as intrinsically moral, but to her valuation of the binary nature of language. She rejects the vendor's shrug toward the difference between orange and grape as the equivalent of his dismissal of any binary or "two-part" system, such as that which allows people to say *either* yes *or* no, to *either* act *or* not act on a community's behalf. While irony—a literary trend that Rukeyser bucked for her entire career—has often been associated with a politics of apathy, it does point toward a more complex, multiple view of meaning in language—a "third part" to meaning, that hovers between yes and no, either and or. In the high literary modernism of the 1940s against which Rukeyser reacted, irony may have been largely apolitical, but this is not the case with the popular culture of the 1970s, a context far more relevant to the East Harlemites of whom Rukeyser writes. Suppose the vendor is not being indifferent, but ironic? Ironic reversals in meaning are a common feature of the vernacular of oppressed groups. In this case, the vendor's undermining of the distinction be-

What Do I Read Next?

- Readers wishing to get a sense of the breadth of Rukeyser's writing career should begin with *A Muriel Rukeyser Reader,* edited by Jan Heller Levi. This compilation includes highlights from Rukeyser's eleven volumes of poetry as well as a provocative array of her songs, lectures, and biographical writings.

- *Theory of Flight,* published when she was only twenty-two years old, was Rukeyser's daring and highly praised literary debut. It is still among her most frequently discussed collections of poetry.

- The poet to whom Rukeyser is most often compared is Walt Whitman, an impassioned voice of the democratic American spirit and an inventor of free verse. His classic collection *Leaves of Grass* was one of Rukeyser's strongest influences.

- *No More Masks!,* an anthology of feminist poetry edited by Florence House and Ellen Bass, takes its name from a line in a Rukeyser poem. This volume places Rukeyser in the context of an emerging tradition of feminist poets.

- Adrienne Rich shares with Rukeyser a strong belief in the political relevance of poetry. Rich's *The Dream of a Common Language* is a critically acclaimed collection of poetry addressing themes of oppression, feminism, sexuality, and motherhood.

tween orange and grape could be seen as a symbol of rebellion, a gesture toward undermining the categories that unequally divide the social world of East Harlem, "black and white, women and men."

Rukeyser saw her role as a poet globally. She wrote sweepingly, passionately, and personally of her century and her world, drawing daring parallels between the self and the universe in a Transcendentalist tradition. But there is a flip side to such heroically vast vision. It tends to obliterate the

diversity and complexity of the local. Thus it is, for me, as a poem of *place* that "Ballad" falters. Its speaker does not acknowledge that she is not really a member of the East Harlem community or admit that she may not be attuned to its own, particular brand of language use with its own unique and unappreciated powers.

Source: Sarah Madsen Hardy, in an essay for *Poetry for Students,* Gale, 2001.

Erika Taibl

Taibl has a master's degree in English writing and writes for a variety of educational publishers. In the following essay, she discusses the interplay of opposing words, such as good and evil, in "The Ballad of Orange and Grape," and how the poem questions and celebrates the complex meanings of words.

With *The Theory of Flight,* published in 1935, Muriel Rukeyser, at a mere twenty-one years-old, entered the poetry scene as a full blown "spokespoet." As a voice for women and the marginalized (those outside the mainstream) of society, Rukeyser strove from the very beginning to share her political and social visions of humanitarian action. The collection won her the Yale Younger Poets award and launched her career as a political poet. From the beginning, Rukeyser has melded her career and passion as a writer with her political activism. Separating life from politics, for Rukeyser, is like separating life from poetry, which she viewed as being impossible. Thirty-eight years after *Theory of Flight,* came *Breaking Open,* a continuation of Rukeyser's political convictions through powerful images. Critics have likened reading Rukeyser's work to reading the history of her times. She is stubborn in her loyalty to current social struggles and honest in her frustrations. She is a poet of witness, training her readers to be witnesses.

Her collection of essays and elegies, *Life of Poetry,* offers keen insight into the goals and struggles of the poet as an agent of culture and change. In the text, Rukeyser notices "how in our culture every quality is set against another quality." She discusses how good and evil, for example, are taken as opposites, not as two problems in their "interplay." "Ballad of Orange and Grape" is one of many poems that explore this theory of perceived opposites. Rukeyser stretches the language, and questions the meanings of words. Is orange really orange? What *is* orange exactly, and, more deeply, what does it mean and how did it get that way? Rukeyser explores the time after people discover that nothing is as it seems. The poem asks, "How are we going to believe what we read and we write and we hear and we say and we do?" Ultimately, "Ballad of Orange and Grape" leads readers not to the horrifying loss of meaning but to the possibility of things. She leads readers to make connections, at once horrifying and inspiring, in "Ballad of Orange and Grape."

"Ballad of Orange and Grape" requires the reader to encounter the rhythm of the ballad as it sweeps into a landscape of opposites. Rukeyser, who preferred writing in long, free-flowing, unrhymed verse, uses the ballad form, rhymed every other line, to create a feeling of walking. The narrator is going down the street after a day of work. It is the "twentieth century." These statements of setting in the first stanza place the reader in a time that is moving forward. The reader is "you," a collective you, a fellow witness. At the second stanza's "windows boarded up" the reader is already into another moment of the century, propelled by the rhythm of the text, which is a rhythm of discovery as the reader sees the windows, then the rats, the garage, and the Cadillac. The reader makes a steady path through the words and down the street, riding through the neighborhood as it reveals a raft of opposites: a rundown building and a Cadillac, an ominous "man who'd like to break your back" and a serene woman and child. There are things to be scared about and things to respect and desire.

In *The Life of Poetry,* Rukeyser wrote, "Outrage and possibility are in all the poems we know." The poem suggests that these opposing forces, outrage and possibility, are life itself. The words simultaneously travel the street of poverty, drug addiction, and violence and the possibility of beauty in children and future hope. The poem pushes the reader to confront and unravel opposing systems, or binaries, in a way that is not always natural or comfortable. Opposing forces within consciousness are also revealed and confronted, as the reader wrestles with the poem. He or she walks along and discovers that words in connection with their meanings are infinitely complex.

The shock of complexity stops the poem in its tracks. The rhythm continues in the third stanza with "Frankfurter frankfurter," but the repetition slows the thought. The emphasis implies uncertainty, as if asking, what is this name? What is a *frankfurter?* The ballad pushes the reader forward to the orange and grape soda machines, which are both empty. The reader will discover shortly that the words are also empty. They hold no meaning

> *What is orange exactly, and, more deeply, what does it mean and how did it get that way?"*

except that given to them through social construct. Orange soda is only made orange after it's given the name orange. Before that it could just as well be purple or blue or pink.

The "I" in the poem faces the hot dog man "in between" the two machines. The "I" is an "eye," seeing the emptiness of words, seeing words as containers for meaning for the first time and stuck between what is known and familiar and what is unknown and utterly mysterious. These words, and by default all words, are empty, just as the soda machines are empty.

The soda man fills the emptiness and propels the poem forward again, only to have it run circles around the words orange and grape. The wheels spin as he pours "in the familiar shape." The words are familiar to the witness. Orange is orange and grape is grape, yet the man pours the opposites into one another. He pours "the grape drink into the one marked ORANGE and orange drink into the one marked GRAPE." Perceptions fall apart. Even with the words grape and orange, "large and clear, unmistakable," the familiar becomes convoluted.

Jane Cooper, a critic and scholar of Rukeyser's work, wrote in the introduction to *The Life of Poetry* that Rukeyser, "liked to say that poems are meeting-places, and certainly as one composes a poem there is a sense of seeing farther than usual into the connection of things, and then of bringing intense pressure to bear on those connections, until they rise into full consciousness for oneself and others." The road to consciousness in the poem is accepting that orange has just been poured into grape and grape has just been poured into orange; for all the reader knows, this is the way it is really supposed to be. This is the moment of enlightenment, the moment when a horrifying truth is revealed: meanings do not mean in the ways the witness believed. The meanings themselves are empty.

The witness, the "I," enters the poem to rescue meaning, grasp after it, and question how a society can move forward without set constructs, set meanings for words, ideas and acts. The hot dog man shrugs his shoulders. He is not a witness to the revelation. It is not a big deal to him. His non-chalance fuels the "I," as the poem explores bina-ries, or opposites. The poem asks what the world would do if "war" bled into "peace" a little bit, or "love" slipped just a tiny bit into "hate." The "wit-ness" in the poem, the "I," is aggravated and maybe a bit afraid, as if saying there must be meaning we can all believe in. Rukeyser plays with the audi-ence, suggests the "interplay" of words, and revels in the fact that life offers this conundrum. "Love" *is* in "hate." "Violence" *is* in "non-violence." In-deed, how can there be one without the other? If the world defines words according to their coun-terparts, meanings *seep* over boundaries. Rukeyser has fun with the reader, seeming to suggest that it is time to lighten up. As she pokes at the "I," she is serious as well.

Rukeyser writes in *The Life of Poetry,* that through poetry, "we are brought face to face with our world and we plunge deeply into ourselves, to a place where we sense the full value of the mean-ings of emotions and ideas in their relations with each other, and understand, in the glimpse of a mo-ment, the freshness of things and their possibili-ties." In the sometimes ugly words of the penulti-mate stanza, Rukeyser implies that words are at play with and in each other. She lets the opposing ideas breathe into one another and offer, in their "interplay," another layer of meaning.

The whole concept of opposites breathing into each other is a source of great power for the mar-ginalized. With the outrage of lost voice, there must also be possibility. Rukeyser seems to offer herself, as marginalized poet, that gift as well. The critic Michele Ware, writes in "Opening the Gates: Muriel Rukeyser and the Poetry of Witness," that "Rukeyser's work has been relegated until very re-cently to a kind of critical back water reserved for women writers long dismissed by a Modernist male poetic sensibility." If Rukeyser harbors outrage at this neglect by a Western male dominated canon, she has also used it to discover her own possibil-ity. Ware claims that the general critical consensus before 1974 was that Rukeyser's work was too po-litical, that her first person "posturings," a word used frequently by the critic M.L. Rosenthal, were in love with themselves, and that the poems were full of exhortation and public promises. The tide changed after 1974, as Rukeyser's name was men-tioned in the ranks of female poets whose writing succeeded in propelling them into the ranks of

"myth makers." Her optimism, which was once so sharply criticized, became, as Michele Ware claimed, "a feminist denial of the Modernist male poetic system, a denial that attempts to defy limi-tation." Her writing is a ballad of orange and grape. She defies the limitation of containers and allows meanings to move through and reside within each other.

In the final stanza of the poem, the opposing words are gone. In their place is the moment de-scribed in extreme. The place is East Harlem. There is "garbage," "a deep smile," "rape." With every word and idea the reader is meant to feel or sense the opposite, because the opposite is always in the moment. There is possibility with outrage and out-rage with possibility. They keep pouring into each other, as orange is poured into grape. Rukeyser brings life to the relations of word and meaning and defines the poem through its opposites. In *The Life of Poetry,* she wrote, "I have attempted to suggest a dynamics of poetry, showing that a poem is not its words or its images, any more than a symphony is its notes or a river its drops of water. Poetry de-pends on the moving relations within itself. It is an art that lives in time expressing and evoking the moving relation between the individual conscious-ness and the world." There is truth in "interplay," and a chance at reformation and transformation. It is the experience of "Ballad of Orange and Grape," and an experience, Rukeyser seems to say, of a life lived in poetry.

Source: Erika Taibl, in an essay for *Poetry for Students,* Gale, 2001.

David Kelly

David Kelly is an instructor of Creative Writ-ing and Composition at two colleges in Illinois. In the following essay, he examines how the apparent weaknesses in a poem like "Ballad of Orange and Grape" can actually help enforce the poem's over-all message.

Relatively late in her long and illustrious life, in her second-to-last completed collection of po-etry, Muriel Rukeyser produced a poem, "Ballad of Orange and Grape," that was typical of her work. In this piece, like her best poems, Rukeyser slides effortlessly back and forth over the line that divides formal verse from informal thought. She escapes the categories that people rely on when they label serious art and seal it off somewhere, so that it won't become mixed up with the personal musings of someone who is just thinking with a pen in hand. Getting this near to casualness, I believe, accounts for the unevenness of Rukeyser's reputation since her death; she made poetry seem too easy.

A poem like "Ballad of Orange and Grape" seems to only touch on any sort of artistic design when it wants to, or when it remembers to, but not with a strong enough structure to make readers confident that the author is in control. As with all of Rukeyser's best work, her detractors can believe that those who like the poet's work are simple people able to vaguely recognize occasional rhythm and rhyme and think that nice thoughts are nice. Her supporters, on the other hand, are surprised to see how many people fail to understand that under the guise of simplicity Rukeyser was a wise old fox.

The best thing that can be said about any artistic work, and this poem in particular, is that it takes its own circumstances into account and includes the readers' feelings about the work into their understanding of it. This is a poem about division, about dichotomies, about those lines that humans mentally draw in order to understand, or to control, or to conquer. Any sense that it doesn't "belong" with serious poetry helps to draw attention to its point.

One thing often mentioned about Rukeyser's work is the way she used it to bring factions together. In the preface to her *Collected Poems,* she used a basic example of how surprising it might have seemed to some that her publisher, McGraw-Hill, would put out her book, when at the time their reputation rested on publishing scientific texts. This situation suited her fine, Rukeyser wrote, because "I care very much about that meeting-place, of science and poetry." The same wording appeared in Eileen Myles' review of the 1997 reissue of Rukeyser's *The Life of Poetry.* "Muriel Rukeyser," Myles wrote, "unspools one of the most passionate arguments I've ever seen for the notion that art creates meeting places, that poetry creates democracy." She went on to explain, "'Meeting-place' is her mantra, and it means linking the public to a cumulative privacy of people, to living."

The distinction between "cumulative privacy" and "the public" is that the first depends on seeing things (or even oneself) as an independent unit, separate from all others. The same goes for the concept of "meeting place." A place by itself can stand complete, as a concept, but when it becomes a meeting-place it brings together different, distinct elements that usually stand alone. At the meeting-place they stand alone in each other's presence.

The last two stanzas of "Ballad of Orange and Grape" bring together opposites. Rukeyser starts

> *This is a poem about seeing beyond form, and it has to break its form to fully make its point."*

out with sets of opposites that are contradictory just because of semantics. Our language is arranged in such a way that a word often has an opposite word, which leads us to think the things represented by these words actually are opposites. The words here represent binary systems, the areas where things can only be either one or the other. There are a whole lot of divisions of this kind that are real and truthful: you are either inside of a room or out, unless you are one of those rare cases that linger in the doorway; an event either did or did not take place, provided that you define it well enough to rule out the idea that it "sort of happened"; someone is either dead or alive. The first examples that Rukeyser gives—white and black, women and men, love and hate, enemy and friend, etc.—are binary pairings. But these are just the first ones. Then the logic of seeing things in this binary way falls apart.

The later things are not pairs that we usually see linked together: garbage and reading, a deep smile and rape, forgetfulness and a hot street of murder. Are they opposites? They can be, if you look at them as opposites. Are they different ways of saying the same thing? They can be.

It doesn't matter, one's the same as the other, there is no rule requiring that these concepts must be defined. That is the attitude of the poem's hot dog vendor, who ignores the labels on his drink machines and pours the wrong syrups into each. Apparently, he is not acting out of illiteracy, because once the mistake is pointed out he does nothing to fix it. It hardly seems that he is being completely subversive, either, as he would if he crossed them up on purpose just to contradict expectations and make people think. The shrug and the smile might be signs that this act is done as a joke, but he has no audience to play to. Most likely, this reversal was done out of laziness and carelessness, because he cannot see how it could make any difference to call one thing the other. The narrator does, though. Established as the sort of person who goes out for a hot dog only after the day's work is done, this is a person who appreciates order and worries over the disorder that brings the woman and the little girl together in the same place as the back-breaker and the addicts.

The speaker of the poem has limits as to how much she thinks we should, on the one hand, live by socially stifling divisions, but also, on the other hand, how much we ought to ignore them. Knowing this, it helps to step back and look at the broader dichotomies (pairings of different things) played out in Rukeyser's style. For instance, the first stanza talks about the poet in the second person, as "you," not as "I." As a poetic device to make readers feel involved in the poem, this technique has limits to its effectiveness. However, it picks up greater significance in the third stanza when the reference changes from "you" to "I." This is the sort of change within the poem that earned Rukeyser a reputation for being uneven, unable to stay with the pattern that she herself set out. It does, though, fit the poem's theme of sticking to labels (or not) perfectly. Many poems take readers to places they have never been before, making them live new situations that are dictated to them as "you," but this poem, as a meditation on differences, is in its rights to act as a meeting-place for one person's "you" and "I."

The poem's title identifies it as a ballad. Traditionally, a ballad is a folk tale about the exploits of some central character. This poem's weary reader-and-writer fits that profile. Since the ballad is an ancient form, we associate it with the opportunity they give to examine exotic cultures, which is certainly something that this ballad offers. But while this poem starts off like many ballads, with its main character setting off on a quest (in this case, for a frankfurter), the quest disappears somewhere in the telling. The story disappears. It starts with someone going somewhere, bringing readers into their physical world, but it dissolves in the last stanzas into a chant about opposites. At the same time that this is happening, the rhyme scheme falters; it is undeniably *bcbdbe* in the first three stanzas, but in the fourth the rhyme is worn out, matching the words *shape, GRAPE,* and then *GRAPE* again. From there on the rhymes are approximate, at best: *read / street / GRAPE, again / men / friend, rape / hope / grape.* The inconsistency from the beginning of the poem to the end might be taken as a weakness, but only by readers who are not paying enough attention to the poem's overall message.

I cannot say whether this harmony between subject matter and what appears to be clumsy execution is intentional. Since that pattern recurs time and again in Muriel Rukeyser's poetry, it is probably not accidental here. Regardless of how it happened, "Ballad of Orange and Grape" is doing what it a poem is supposed to. This is a poem about seeing beyond form, and it has to break its form to fully make its point. It is a poem about opposites, and it has to introduce the vendor's unclear thinking to balance out the poet's clarity. In the end, a poem about order needs to flirt with disorder, even if it means that some readers might feel that the poet is out of control.

Source: David Kelly, in an essay for *Poetry for Students,* Gale, 2001.

Sources

Cooper, Jane, *The Life of Poetry,* by Muriel Rukeyser, Paris Press, 1996.

Daniels, Kate, Introduction to *Out of Silence,* by Muriel Rukeyser, Northwestern University Press, 1997.

Gregerson, Linda, *Poetry,* Vol. 167, February 1996, pp. 292-97.

Kessler, Jascha, "The Collected Poems of Muriel Rukeyser," in *Gramercy Review,* Vol. 3, No. 4 and Vol. 4, No. 1, Autumn-Winter, 1979–80, pp. 27-9.

Library Journal, May 1, 1992.

McGann, J. J., *Poetry,* Vol. 125, October 1974, p. 44.

Meinka, Peter, *New Republic,* November 24, 1973, p. 25.

Myles, Eileen, "Fear of Poetry," in *The Nation,* April 14, 1997.

Publishers Weekly, March 23, 1993.

Rukeyser, Muriel, *The Life of Poetry,* Paris Press, 1996.

Terris, Virginia R., "Muriel Rukeyser: A Retrospective," in *American Poetry Review,* Vol. 3, No. 3, May-June, 1974, pp. 10-15.

Ware, Michele, "'Opening the Gates': Muriel Rukeyser and the Poetry of Witness," in *Women's Studies,* Vol. 22, No 3, June 1993, p. 297.

For Further Study

Herzog, Anne R. and Janet E. Kaufman, eds., *"How Shall We Tell Each Other of the Poet?": The Life and Writing of Muriel Rukeyser,* St. Martin's, 1999.
    A compilation of essays by nearly forty prominent poets and critics seeks to redress the neglect of Rukeyser's work since her death in 1980. Selections

include discussions of Rukeyser's poetry and tributes to her as a woman and artist.

Kertesz, Louise, *The Poetic Vision of Muriel Rukeyser,* Louisiana State Press, 1979.
    One of the few book-length treatments of Rukeyser, this study is appropriate for readers seeking a sustained, in-depth interpretation of Rukeyser's career. It includes detailed information on critical reception and influences and also offers interpretations of specific poems.

Rich, Adrienne, "Beginners," in *The Kenyon Review,* Vol. 15, No. 3, Summer 1993, p. 12.
    In this article Rich compares Rukeyser to two of the most highly esteemed American poets, Emily Dickinson and Walt Whitman. She suggests that, like Dickinson and Whitman, Rukeyser was too daring and innovative to be appreciated by critics in her own time.

Rukeyser, Muriel, *The Life of Poetry,* Current Books, 1949.
    Rukeyser's treatise on the meaning and purpose of poetry reflects her passionate commitment to both art and social justice. In this work she explains her motivations to write, as well as discussing the origins of American poetry and its social role.

A Birthday

Christina Rossetti

1862

While nearly all of Christina Rossetti's other love poems focus on themes of loss and isolation, "A Birthday," which was first collected in *Goblin Market and Other Poems* (1862), articulates the ecstasy of found love. In it, the speaker grasps joyously to identify those images and comparisons which might accurately express her exhilaration. She searches first in the realm of the natural, attempting to equate her emotions with a "singing bird," "an apple tree" heavy with fruit, and "a rainbow shell" in the sea. But none of these natural wonders can compare: in love, her heart "is gladder than all these." In the second stanza, the speaker abandons the search for the perfect simile, or comparison, and instead demands action. In honor of her figurative "birthday," she demands the construction of a lush dais replete with "silk and down," "doves" and "peacocks with a hundred eyes," gold and silver. Such a construction, ornamented with images from nature, can better represent her love because it is a lasting artifact, like poet John Keats' Grecian urn in his "Ode on a Grecian Urn." Unlike nature, which perishes, the dais will always mark the day in which "love has come" to the speaker.

Christina Rossetti's work is representative of the Pre-Raphaelite movement founded by her brother, Dante Gabriel Rossetti. The movement, which started in 1848 and influenced both poetry and painting, celebrated the devotional spirit found in Italian religious art of the pre-Renaissance. Some characteristics of the Pre-Raphaelite sensibility apparent in "A Birthday" include pictorial richness

and attention to detail, sensuousness, and a concern for symbolism.

Author Biography

Rossetti was born in London, England, in 1830 to Gabriele Rossetti and Frances Polidori Rossetti. Her father was an Italian exile who had moved to London some four years earlier. As a child Rossetti lived in Buckinghamshire in England's countryside and often visited her maternal grandfather, Gaetano Polidori, who lived nearby. These experiences gave her a lifelong love for nature and animals. In 1839 the Rossetti family moved to London where Christina was to spend her adolescent years. Her father taught Italian at King's College and tutored students privately as well. As his health declined, the family developed other sources of income. For a time Rossetti's mother became a governess and opened a small school in London. In 1853 the family moved to Somerset to run a school, but that effort ended a year later in failure. Rossetti's brother William, who worked for the Inland Revenue Office and wrote for newspapers, was to provide the bulk of the family's income. Rossetti demonstrated her poetic gifts early, writing sonnets in competition with her brothers William and Dante Gabriel. Her first published poem appeared in the *Athenaeum* magazine when she was eighteen. Dante Gabriel founded the journal *The Germ* in 1852, and Rossetti became a frequent contributor. Her book *Goblin Market and Other Poems* appeared in 1862 in an edition for which Dante Gabriel provided two illustrations. He also designed and provided woodcut illustrations for Rossetti's next book, *The Prince's Progress and Other Poems* (1866).

In 1848 Rossetti became engaged to a painter named James Collinson. Collinson was, with Dante Gabriel, a member of the group of young artists known as the Pre-Raphaelite Brotherhood, and he had exhibited his work at the Royal Academy. Religious differences finally pulled the couple apart; Rossetti, a strict Anglican, could not accept Collinson's conversion to Catholicism in 1850. During the 1860s Rossetti again came close to marriage, this time with Charles Cayley, a linguist and translator. Although religious differences again played a part in their eventual break-up (Cayley was not a Christian) the two remained friends.

Subsequently, Rossetti lived a quiet and sheltered life. She lived with her mother until her

Christina Rossetti

mother's death in 1886 and then took care of two elderly aunts until they passed away in the 1890s. Only twice did she travel outside England. In 1862 she went with her mother and her brother William to France; in 1865, the three visited northern Italy. During much of her life Rossetti suffered from various illnesses, including Grave's disease and bouts of what doctors at the time attributed to "religious mania," probably psychosomatic in origin. In the 1860s Rossetti served for a time at the House of Charity, an organization in Highgate working with prostitutes and unwed mothers. During the 1880s she began working with the Society for Promoting Christian Knowledge, publishing devotional books with them. In 1892 Rossetti was diagnosed with cancer, went through surgery, and died in January of 1894.

Poem Text

My heart is like a singing bird
   Whose nest is in a watered shoot;
My heart is like an apple tree
   Whose boughs are bent with thickset fruit;
My heart is like a rainbow shell   5
   That paddles in a halcyon sea;
My heart is gladder than all these
   Because my love is come to me.

Raise me a dais of silk and down;
    Hang it with vair and purple dyes;   10
Carve it in doves and pomegranates,
    And peacocks with a hundred eyes;
Work it in gold and silver grapes,
    In leaves and silver fleurs-de-lys;
Because the birthday of my life   15
    Is come, my love is come to me.

Poem Summary

Lines 1-2:

The speaker opens with a simile, or a figure of speech expressing the similarity between two seemingly unlike things. Here, she compares her heart with a "singing bird," which suggests pure happiness and energy, and herself to a "watered shoot" in which the bird has nested. A shoot is a young branch or leaf that develops from a bud. By using this simile the speaker implies she feels as if she were newly born, as the title figuratively suggests. But while a shoot is brought to life by water, the speaker has come alive with love.

Lines 3-6:

In these lines the speaker continues to search for the perfect simile to express her love. First she compares her heart to "an apple tree" whose branches are so heavy with sensuous, life-giving fruit that they are "bent." Next she compares it to "a rainbow shell," bright with color and paddling in the "halcyon," or peaceful, sea. Each of the similes in the first six lines tries to describe the speaker's emotion in a different way. This frenzied approach reveals the speaker's urgent need to express her joy. Yet the comparisons also share one quality: each is from nature, implying that love is above all a natural, and therefore innocent, wonder.

Lines 7-8:

In the last two lines of the first octave, the speaker decides that none of the similes in fact suffices. Though all are glad images, her "heart is gladder than all of these" because "love has come" to her.

Lines 9-10:

In the second octave, the speaker abandons her attempt to compare her love with the miracles of nature. Instead, she commands the listener build her a "dais," or a platform built in a hall to honor someone. She wants the dais to be lush, layered in "silk and down" and covered with "vair," or squirrel fur, and "purple dies." This ornate spectacle, we might

Media Adaptations

- The songs from a musical adaptation of *Goblin Market* can be heard on a CD put out by CDJay Records in 1996. The music is by Polly Pen.

- *Dante Gabriel Rossetti and the Pre-Raphaelite Brotherhood* (1969) is a BBC film on the life of Rossetti's brother and his circle of fellow artists (of whom Rossetti herself was a marginal member).

guess, is to celebrate her "birthday." Because her love has elevated her to such lofty heights, the splendid dais seems like one fit for royalty. Also notice the shift in voice from the declarative of the first stanza to the imperative, or command form, of the second stanza. The speaker is no longer tentative, no longer gropes for the proper images. She now knows what she wants and commands that it be done.

Lines 11-14:

In these lines the speaker describes exactly how she would like her dais to be built. It should be sculpted with "doves" and "peacocks with a hundred eyes," with "pomegranates," "gold and silver grapes" and "silver fleur-de-lys," or iris, the symbol of French royalty. In contrast with the first stanza, these images are not directly from nature but are "carved" representations of natural objects. Unlike phenomena of nature—like birds, apples, and shells—these carved renditions do not perish. Rather, they stand eternal, calling to mind the natural objects the way Keats' Grecian urn forever immortalizes youth long passed. Thus, the dais is a more fitting symbol of the speaker's love because it will not perish.

Lines 15-16:

In the final lines, the speaker confirms the meaning of the poem's title, which is a metaphor—or an implied, rather than directly stated, comparison between two things—for the way she feels. Though it might not be her chronological birthday, it seems to her that love has brought new life, or made her "reborn."

Themes

Love and Passion

"A Birthday" celebrates romantic love. The speaker expresses the joy of falling in love and knowing that she is loved in return. In the first stanza the poet describes the private emotion of realizing and recognizing love. The speaker seems to be treasuring her feelings, perhaps not ready to share them with the world. In the second stanza, though, she demands a public celebration, with elaborate decorations, of her happiness.

The poet begins by developing similes in which the heart is compared to something in nature. Each simile shows a different aspect of falling in love. In the first, the speaker is jubilant and wants to sing out. In the next simile (lines 3-4), her heart is full, like a tree with ripe fruit. The third comparison is slightly more complex: the speaker's heart is a beautiful shell on a halcyon, or calm, sea, as if she finds peace by being in love. However, halcyon also means carefree, so the poet may be showing that she no longer worries of whether or not she is loved in return.

As beautiful as these images are, they are not enough to express this feeling of love: the speaker must share her feelings with the world. In the second stanza the poet's images come from works of art, and the setting is public. Now love is honored with lush materials—the purple of royalty, designs in gold and silver. All of this decorative art commemorates the speaker's new life, which is brought on by love.

Nature and Its Meaning

Rossetti's nature imagery ranges widely in this short poem; she describes inanimate objects, plants, and animals. All these images reveal the poet's sensuous experience of the natural world. The singing bird connotes (suggests) ecstasy, providing a picture of a bird opening its beak and trilling with abandon. The images in lines two through four relate to growth and reproduction. The nest, the site of eggs or just-born birds, sits on a young branch of a tree that is watered and thus healthily growing. The apple tree is glutted with fruit, proof of its fertility. These descriptions of the nest and trees represent the happy development of love and imply sexuality and reproduction that may be a part of love. The love grows like plants and animals in

Topics for Further Study

- In a poem that has a distinct rhyme scheme, describe what you think would be the best possible celebration of your birthday?

- Read "Silent Noon," which was written by the author's brother Dante Gabriel Rossetti. What similar concerns do you see in the works of these two siblings? What is different in their styles? What is the same?

- What is the relationship between the nature imagery in the first stanza and the imagery in the second? Are they to be considered opposites? Or part of the same thing?

nature, and the lovers may experience ecstasy and fruit, or children of their own. The nature of human love is portrayed as something as beautiful and innocent as the seasonal rebirth that takes place in the natural world.

With the image of the "rainbow shell," the poet turns to a quieter aspect of nature—and of love. The shell is beautiful—many-colored, possibly shining—and it moves in a gentle sea. Here the inanimate object, which also represents the speaker's heart, "paddles" in the body of water, which symbolizes love. After the singing and growing of the earlier lines, this image describes peacefulness.

At the end of the stanza, Rossetti includes human nature in this scenario. Despite the beauty and joy of the natural world, the human speaker is more fortunate than all the images meant to express her joy. Love between people is a deeper emotion than can be expressed even by natural images of rapture and abundance.

Style

Aesthetics

Rossetti reveals her aesthetic sense, or her perception of what is beautiful, throughout this poem.

Her appreciation for nature, one aspect of this sense, is clear in the first stanza. In the second stanza the poet moves into the realm of artifacts, or human-made things. She describes ornate works of decorative art. The dais, or platform, seems designed for a queen, with its "silk," "purple dyes," and "fleurs-de-lys." Both the color purple and the fleurs-de-lys are traditional symbols of royalty. Much of the design, while artificial, is derived from nature. The speaker asks for representations of "doves," "pomegranates," and peacocks" to be carved into the dais, and for "gold and silver" "grapes" and "leaves" to be included. The natural objects are transformed into fanciful, elaborate works of art.

In these aesthetics, Rossetti shows what she shares with ideas of the Pre-Raphaelite Brotherhood (PRB), a movement of artists and poets that was founded by her brother, Dante Gabriel Rossetti. Members of the PRB promoted ideal representations of nature, often in a fantastic, dreamlike manner. Since Rossetti moves in "A Birthday" to the description of works of art in order to better express the speaker's feelings about love, we may assume that she gave the artistic a higher status than the natural. However, she makes it clear that the art has its basis in nature.

Rossetti's aesthetic sense includes her appreciation for the music of lyric poetry. The poem has a regular meter, or rhythm of lines, and a consistent rhyme scheme. She uses ordinary language, though she creates extraordinary pictures with it. "A Birthday" is an ideal lyric poem: it is song-like and it expresses the speaker's feelings.

Metrics/Prosody

"A Birthday" is written in two octaves, or stanzas of eight lines each. Rhetorically, the octaves parallel one another, each attempting to construct a way to express the speaker's love and each reaching a climax in the final two lines. By dividing the lines of the first stanza into feet, or units of rhythm, we can see that they are written in iambic tetrameter. This means that each line consists of four iambs, or two-syllable segments in which the first syllable is unstressed and the second is stressed. As an example of iambic tetrameter, consider the following line from the first stanza:

> My heart is like a singing bird

If we divide the four iambs from one another and mark the unstressed and stressed syllables, the line appears like this:

> Myheart / islike / a sing / ing bird.

The strongly accentuated syllables in each iamb give a rapid pace to the line and to the stanza, imitating the ecstatic energy of the speaker.

Historical Context

Economy

Christina Rossetti's life (1830-1894) closely coincides with the reign of Queen Victoria (from 1837 to 1901). The British Empire was at its height during this period: Britain's navy dominated the seas, enabling the country to expand its holdings around the globe, and the Industrial Revolution was well-advanced, making England the world leader in manufacturing and trade.

However, there were problems that accompanied this military power and economic success. Factory workers toiled long hours for little pay; and there were a million and a half people living in poverty at mid-century. *Laissez-faire* economics, which means no government intervention in the economy, was the prevailing policy, and it seemed to doom much of the population to dire circumstances.

Much of the blame for economic problems was placed on the rapidly growing middle class. This group included small businessmen and shopkeepers, but it also encompassed factory owners, bankers, and entrepreneurs. The high status of business interests and the predominance of materialism seemed to define the economic situation.

In response to a wide gap between the poor and those of moderate means, many people fought for reform during the Victorian Era. There were movements to allow more people the right to vote and to protect workers and children. Furthermore, some English citizens did not favor their country's overseas expansion, and they supported home rule for Ireland and attempts by India to win independence from Great Britain. Many Victorian writers and artists denounced the materialism of the business-oriented Empire.

As a writer and a member of the middle class, Rossetti was affected by the events of her day. In one of her poems, "Counterblast on Penny Trumpet," she praises a government minister who resigned his post in protest over a British attack on Egypt. Rossetti was opposed to war and violence; she volunteered as a social worker to help prostitutes and unmarried mothers; and she supported a movement to prevent child prostitution. After

Compare
&
Contrast

- **1867:** Women's suffrage societies are formed in England and the United States.

  Early 1970s: A new wave of feminism and women's movement begins. One outcome is a

renewed interest in literature by women.

1980s: The rise of feminist literary criticism contributes to an increase in scholarly studies of Rosetti's poetry and prose.

---

learning about vivisection, the practice of dissecting living animals for physiological research, she became an ardent antivivisectionist.

Women and Society

Despite her status in society and her popularity as a poet, Rossetti faced disadvantages as a woman artist. Although she had ambitions and apparently desired fame, she was constricted by the social taboo on women "displaying" themselves publicly. Even after publishing some well-received poems in magazines, she was unable to find a publisher for her first book and had to rely on her brother's assistance. Like other women writers, Rossetti was expected to limit her subjects to matters suitable for women. "A Birthday," like many of her lyric poems, was considered acceptable because it dealt with love, an approved theme.

Because of Rossetti's acceptance of these restrictions on women, modern readers may view her work with some reservations. However, she was rebellious in her own terms. She did not always bow to her brother's advice on artistic matters, and she resisted efforts by her publisher to have her simply continue writing on themes that had been well received by the public.

Science and Religion

During the Victorian Era, many people became less fervent in their religious beliefs. Part of the cause was the development of science, which challenged some fundamental religious teachings about life. Charles Darwin's *On the Origin of Species,* a treatise on evolution published in 1859, helped influence this change. Rossetti, however, remained a deeply devout Anglo-Catholic (as opposed to a Roman Catholic) throughout her life. She believed that

each person could have a direct relation with God, and thus had a duty to speak to Him.

Critical Overview

Christina Rossetti's work attracted many admirers during her time. After the 1890 publication of *Poems,* which contains "A Birthday," many critics remarked upon the spirited yet controlled pathos of the poem. Writing in 1896, Edward Gosse argues that "there is not a chord of a minor key in 'A Birthday,' and yet the impression which its cumulative ecstasy leaves upon the nerves is almost pathetic." He comments that few poets share Rossetti's "rare gift of song writing." Like other critics, he notes that the love poem is one of Rossetti's few "jubilant" ones. In an 1893 essay, Katherine Hinkson agrees that "Miss Rossetti's poetry has always been … melancholy with the half sweet trouble of a young imagination." Yet she argues that a melancholy spirit does not "always have to be sad." In "A Birthday," Hinkson writes, Rossetti shows an imagination "full of joy." It is this scope that compels Hinkson to place Rossetti's work at the pinnacle of Victorian literature: "As a mere personal judgment, I should rank the poetry of no other living poet beside Miss Rossetti's." More modern critics as well have noted the dualities in Rossetti's work. Theo Dombrowski, writing in 1976, comments that Rossetti's poems try to "resolve or control an underlying tension" by examining the "destructive conflict of opposites." As an example, he cites "A Birthday," "where the comparatively subtle shift from the inward-looking first stanza … to the imperative stance of the second … is central to the success of the poem."

Criticism

Katrinka Moore

Katrinka Moore teaches writing at Long Island University in Brooklyn, New York, and is a poet whose work appears in anthologies and literary journals. In this essay, she discusses "A Birthday" in light of Christina Rossetti's conflict between her passion for poetry and her life as a Victorian woman.

In an 1895 essay on the poetry of Christina Rossetti published in *The Westminster Review,* Alice Law compared Rossetti's lyrics to the "loosening of the imprisoned notes in a bird's throat," whose rich sounds "swell and fall, and burst upon one another in their hurry to be out." Law could be identifying the poet with the "singing bird" in the first line of "A Birthday." Critics from Rossetti's own day to modern times have speculated on the tension between her "imprisoned notes" and their need to "burst" out.

Author Ford Madox Ford, analyzing Rossetti's body of work nearly twenty years after her death, considered her range of subjects "limited very strictly within the bound of her personal emotions." However, he adds, "within those limits she expressed herself consummately." It is at least partly the conflict between what Rossetti felt and what she believed she should write about that gives her poems their energy. As Ford explained, her "infectious gaiety" shows through in the "metre of the verse" (the rhythm of her poems). Despite her suppression of subject matter that she feared was "too pagan or too sensual," Ford wrote, Rossetti's "faculty for pure delight and for esthetic enjoyment was expressed all the more strongly in her metre."

H. B. de Groot, writing in 1985, agreed with Ford, stating that Rossetti's "strong lyric gifts are often held in check by her moral and theological scruples, but at times it is that very tension which gives her best poems their distinctive quality." Her song seems determined to come out, whether in the content or the form of her poetry.

While Ford and de Groot found in Rossetti's poetic rhythm a vibrant expression of her feelings, not all her contemporaries concurred. Some, like Alice Meynell in her 1895 *New Review* article, objected to the poet's "lax metres which keep more or less musical time." And back in 1862 in an *Athenaeum* review of *Goblin Market and Other Poems,* in which "A Birthday" first appeared, an anonymous reviewer praised Rossetti's originality but regretted that she "should at times employ dis-

cords with a frequency which aims at variety but results in harshness." It may come to a surprise to modern readers, used to free verse (more loosely structured lines) and finding Rossetti's structure formal, that her experimentation with rhythm was considered daring by some of her fellow Victorians.

Despite the fact that not all critics approved of her techniques, Rossetti was popular in her lifetime, largely because of her ability to express moods and emotions. "A Birthday" stands out among many of her poems for its celebratory tone. As Edmund Gosse wrote in the 1890s, Rossetti's "habitual tone is one of melancholy reverie." However, whether she wrote of love or death, her work was charged by her intense aesthetic appreciation of beauty. "A Birthday" is full of detailed descriptions of beautiful things that occur in nature or were made by humans through art.

This is a love poem, specifically about loving and being loved in return. Rossetti reveals two sides to the experience. In the first stanza she describes the speaker's heart, showing the intense private joy of romantic love. This private view is symbolized by images from nature—a bird on its nest, an apple tree heavy with fruit, a shell in the sea. In the second stanza the speaker imagines a public pronouncement of that love. This takes place in the world of people, decorated with beautiful artistic objects. Here the birds and fruit are carved or formed in gold and silver. Although each stanza has the same meter and rhyme scheme, the tone changes dramatically. The beginning images are almost child-like in their view of the natural world. The description of the dais, on the other hand, is from the point of view of a woman directing a scene.

The overall effect of "A Birthday" is jubilation, but there is a tension between the two reactions to love. One way is a quiet, pure emotion, and the other is proud, a showing-off. In Victorian society a woman was expected to be modest and have humility, rather than exhibiting evidence of pride. As long as the love is self-effacing, the emotion is acceptable. However, the speaker first describes her heart as "gladder than all these" images from nature, then proclaims that love has brought about "the birthday of my life." There is a need, the poet seems to say, for both kinds of love.

Examining this tension is helpful in analyzing "A Birthday." Two Rossetti scholars, Lona Mosk Packer and Hoxie Neale Fairchild, explore specific connections to Rossetti's life to explain this conflict between private and public. They arrive at very different interpretations.

So convincing is the description of love that Packer, in a 1963 biography of Rossetti, explored the possibility that the poem was addressed to a specific person. It is well documented that Rossetti received two offers of marriage, one in 1848, when she was seventeen, and the other in 1866, when she was thirty-six. In both cases a difference in religious beliefs led her to refuse the proposals. However, "A Birthday" was written in 1857, at which time Rossetti was not known to be involved with anyone. While it is certainly possible that Rossetti could write love lyrics without being that moment in love, Packer suggests that the poet had a secret lover, a detail not noted in her earlier biographies.

According to Packer, the object of Rossetti's love was a Scottish painter and poet, William Bell Scott, who was married to another woman. Rossetti and Scott were friends and met at times in London; she visited him and his wife in Scotland, as well. Packer develops her idea by researching biographical information on both Scott and Rossetti. In addition, she studies the content of many of Rossetti's poems, especially the more melancholy ones, explaining the basis for the poetry about lost love and guilt for moral transgression. In Rossetti's world view, the thought of adultery was almost as serious an offence as committing it. Since Packer concludes that "A Birthday" was written at a happy time in Rossetti's and Scott's relationship, her thesis allows for the tension between the private and public views of love that are expressed in the poem. However, this hypothesis has not been proved indeed, it may be impossible to prove one way or the other and, thus, is not widely accepted.

Fairchild, in a 1957 essay, analyzes "A Birthday" as a religious poem. This view can be supported by biographical information. Rossetti was devout; she developed her own personal theology as well as being attached to the Anglo-Catholic church. She especially felt a closeness to Jesus, writing in *The Face of the Deep,* a work of religious prose, that she felt "towards the Divine Son as if he alone were our Friend." Fairchild, then, has a basis for suggesting that the love in "A Birthday" is holy, rather than human.

A review of the poem's images supports this view. The speaker first savors the sweetness by comparing her heart to natural things. It makes sense that a celebration of the natural world would follow a "mystical apprehension," or a belief arising from awareness, of Christ. The speaker's call

Her song seems determined to come out, whether in the content or the form of her poetry."

for the dais in the second stanza is also logical; she designs a beautiful place worthy for Jesus. Purple may symbolize the coming of Christ, and the dais could be construed as an altar. However, since Rossetti wrote many religious poems and did not actively acknowledge "A Birthday" among them, Fairchild's theory is no more widespread than is Packer's.

There may be yet another way to approach the poem in light of Rossetti's life. While "A Birthday" is obviously a love poem, whether to a particular subject or not, it may also refer to Rossetti's poetic art. That is, the poem may contain a subtext, or secondary meaning, in which the poet takes the opportunity to celebrate her joy of writing.

The images in the first stanza can be seen as connected to the creative process. Writing a poem is a private act, and one that gave Rossetti pleasure. The singing bird's nest and the tree laden with fruit may symbolize creation. The "rainbow shell" may represent the beauty of a poetic idea. In the last two lines of the stanza, the speaker says she is glad because her "love is come," which could be a reference to the muse (her source of inspiration). In the writing of a poem, the poet/speaker experiences a simple happiness.

The images in the second stanza refer to artistic creation, which relates to the creation of a poem. They describe works of art drawn from living things in nature a process not unlike Rossetti's own. Also, this stanza may be construed as a demand for public acknowledgement, with its directive to build a dais and decorate it so profusely. Rossetti was torn between her ambition for fame as a poet and her desire to be a modest, religious woman.

Here again is the tension found in her work as a whole, and it is revealed in the slight change in the structure of the last two lines. Line fifteen is the only line in the poem that is enjambed; that is, the reader must continue onto the next line to finish the sense of the phrase "Because the birthday of my life." All of the other lines in "A Birthday"

What Do I Read Next?

- *Sonnets from the Portuguese* (1850) is Elizabeth Barrett Browning's (1806–1861) most popular collection. She may have been a role model for, if not a direct influence on, Christina Rossetti's career as a poet. When Rossetti's first public book of verse was published around the time of Browning's death, the younger poet was hailed as the logical successor to Browning.

- *Alice's Adventures in Wonderland* (1881) and *Through the Looking Glass* (1872) by Lewis Carroll (1832–1898). Fanciful as they are, the Alice books may shed light on a young person's life in Victorian England. Carroll suggested in 1892 that Christina Rossetti should succeed Alfred, Lord Tennyson as Poet Laureate of England. Carroll, who was a photographer as well as a writer, photographed Rossetti and her brother Dante Gabriel in 1863. Like Carroll, Rossetti also wrote for children.

- Emily Dickinson (1830–1886) was an American contemporary of Christina Rossetti. Rossetti admired Dickinson's work, which she first read in 1890, citing its "startling recklessness of poetic ways and means." *Acts of Light* contains selected Dickinson poems as well as an essay on her life in Amherst, Massachusetts.

- A younger poet who was influenced by Christina Rossetti was Gerard Manley Hopkins (1844–1889). Like Rossetti, Hopkins celebrated the physical and spiritual world. And like Rossetti, Hopkins incorporated his religious beliefs in his mature poetry.

are self-enclosed, or end at the close of a phrase or sentence. Line sixteen is different from the other lines in meter. While it is still iambic tetrameter, there is a slight pause at the comma, so that the line sounds a little different in rhythm from the rest of the poem. The significance of this "glitch" in the meter no accident for a poet of Rossetti's skill comes as the speaker announces the arrival of her "birthday." Perhaps Rossetti is saying to the world

that she is a poet, she has found her calling, and means to stay with it for her life. And she does.

Source: Katrinka Moore, in an essay for *Poetry for Students,* Gale, 2001.

Elizabeth Judd

Elizabeth Judd is a freelance writer and book reviewer with an M.F.A. in English from the University of Michigan and a B.A. from Yale. In this essay, she discusses the ways in which Rossetti uses rhyme and rhythm to heighten and then complicate the speaker's emotions in "A Birthday."

One of Rossetti's best-known and most-often-quoted love poems, "A Birthday" is, in subject matter and tone, a departure from most of her other work. On the surface, "A Birthday" is a rhapsody on found love, an ecstatic outpouring of joy from a speaker who's finally come to be born through emotional fulfillment. Most of Rossetti's other poems are concerned with failed love, a morbid sense of impending death, and a lover who will not or cannot return the speaker's feelings. "A Birthday" is such an unexpected work from Rossetti—who was known for her reserved, serious demeanor and religious intensity—that its first line inspired a cartoon by the writer and artist Max Beerbohm. In that cartoon, Beerbohm depicts Christina Rossetti, dressed all in black and wearing a large dark hat that conceals most of her downturned face, being questioned by her more flamboyant brother Dante Gabriel Rossetti, who asks, " 'Well, Christina, your heart may be like a singing bird, but why do you dress like a pew-opener?' "

No matter how significant a departure the subject matter of "A Birthday" is, its meter and breathless, unforgettable rhythms *are* characteristic of Rossetti's poetry. "A Birthday" is a very carefully constructed poem. It consists of two octaves, or stanzas of eight lines each. The second and fourth lines of each stanza rhyme, as do the sixth and eighth lines. The poem is also written in iambs, or two-syllable pairs where the second syllable is the one on which the emphasis is placed. John Hollander demonstrated how an iamb works in this line from *Rhyme's Reason:* "Iambic meter runs along like this." Often, as in Hollander's example, iambs have such a strong rhythm that they can propel the poem forward in a rush of energy, a pattern that perfectly suits the excited speaker in Rossetti's poem.

In the first octave of "A Birthday," Rossetti uses repetition to give the impression of someone who's frenzied and anxiously trying to find a simile, or a comparison, that will aptly describe her happiness. The first three words of the first, third, fifth, and seventh lines are the same: "My heart is." In the speaker's first attempt to capture her own feelings, she compares her heart to "a singing bird / Whose nest is in a watered shoot." The "watered shoot" is a young branch that has grown out of a bud. Just as the shoot blossomed with water, the speaker has come alive with love. In the second comparison, the speaker likens her heart to "an apple-tree / Whose boughs are bent with thickset fruit." In a third try at finding a simile, the speaker compares her heart to "a rainbow shell." These three comparisons are similar in that they're derived from nature. In the seventh line, the speaker begins with the exact same pattern only to abruptly abandon it. Here she notes that the similes from nature are not sufficient because her emotions are more intense than these images can convey:

> My heart is gladder than all these
> Because my love is come to me.

The first octave ends in a hint that language can't fully capture the thrill of emotions that the speaker is experiencing. The second octave confirms that point by taking up a new strategy for expressing her emotions. Instead of searching for a simile, the speaker now suggests that a concrete action be taken—"Raise me a dais of silk and down"—so that she can convey her love in the creation of a work of art that employs elements of the natural world to her own ends. There is a suggestion that the carved representations will last, unlike the things of nature which are fleeting. Instead of comparing her love to a singing bird, the speaker now asks that the beautiful dais be carved with birds, specifically doves and "peacocks with a hundred eyes." In the second octave, the speaker is far less tentative and is now fully in command. It's as if the arrival of love has given the speaker a strength and confidence that she previously lacked.

Critics have noted that the shift in stanzas works very well. Theo Dombrowski said that in "A Birthday" "the comparatively subtle shift from the inward-looking first stanza … to the imperative stance of the second … is central to the success of the poem." And Katherine J. Mayberry noted, "Simile has collapsed into metaphor, experimentation has given way to command, and impermanence has been replaced by stability, but all these changes have been made possible by, and occurred within, the poem itself. In "A Birthday" we see the power of poetry to express strong feeling and to put it into more stable form."

> *No matter how significant a departure the subject matter of "A Birthday" is, its meter and breathless, unforgettable rhythms are characteristic of Rossetti's poetry.*

One mystery of "A Birthday" is the identity of the love that the speaker celebrates as having "come to me." Critics have speculated about whom this ecstatic love poem was written. Rossetti wrote this poem in November 1857, when she didn't seem to have close relationships with anyone outside her immediate family. Deepening the mystery is the fact that the two poems on either side of it in Rossetti's manuscript notebook were the exact opposite in mood: gloomy and regretful, instead of ecstatic. In one of the poems, "Memory," she writes, "My heart dies inch by inch; the time grows old / Grows old in which I grieve." And in the other, "An Apple Gathering," the speaker is mocked by her neighbors for being "empty-handed" when apple season comes because she's plucked the pink blossoms from her apple tree to wear in her own hair. These poems of thwarted fulfillment suggest that perhaps the love Rossetti describes in "A Birthday" was imagined rather than known through firsthand experience. Some critics have interpreted "A Birthday" as a religious poem, one about the speaker's rebirth through her love for Christ. Although this is a distinct possibility, neither Rossetti nor her brother William Michael Rossetti classified "A Birthday" among her other devotional poems.

No matter who, if anyone, the poem was written for, it is remarkable for its strong lyrical sense, its ability to capture in sound the heightened emotions of new love. "A Birthday" has an inescapable energy, and in that sense it's similar to some of Rossetti's children's poems, including:

> Who has seen the wind?
> > Neither I nor you:
> But when the leaves hang trembling
> The wind is passing through.
>
> Who has seen the wind?
> Neither you nor I:

But when the trees bough down their heads
The wind is passing by.

In both poems, Rossetti describes something unseen—in "A Birthday" love, and in the child's poem, the wind—by showing the dramatic effects that these forces can have on nature and on people. The wind makes the leaves tremble and the trees "bough down their heads," as if human. And in "A Birthday" love makes the speaker rush around to construct comparisons and then build a work of art in appreciation and gratitude. In both poems, the sounds of the words enhance their meaning. The rhythms carry the reader along with the speaker and with the wind itself.

Rossetti's greatest achievement in "A Birthday" rests in the music of her words. Virginia Woolf, a famous English novelist, praised Rossetti for the pureness of her tone and her wonderful ear: "Your instinct was so clear, so direct, so intense that it produced poems that sing like music in one's ears."

And yet what's ultimately most compelling about "A Birthday" is its strangeness. The identity of the speaker's beloved isn't the only mystery. The speaker's own state of mind, despite the fact that she speaks directly and emphatically, remains uncertain. There's an odd giddiness in the speaker's tone, something too frenzied in her habit of rushing from image to image, from singing bird to apple tree to rainbow shell. When she discards all of those images as inadequate, the speaker's emotions become suspect. Edmund Gosse, writing in 1896, said that "there is not a chord of a minor key in "A Birthday," and yet the impression which its cumulative ecstasy leaves upon the nerves is almost pathetic."

A reserved woman who never married, was often ill, and was deeply religious, Rossetti was considered almost unknowable by her family members and later by her biographers. There's a sense that Rossetti may have learned to write what's acceptable or expected, rather than what she truly felt. Elizabeth Bishop, a twentieth-century American poet, wrote,

> The art of losing isn't hard to master; So many things seem filled with the intent to be lost that their loss is no disaster.

Modern readers quickly realize that Bishop isn't saying what she means, but is in fact asserting the opposite. By putting on a brave front, Bishop shows us how unacceptable and deeply felt the pain of loss can be. Many decades earlier, Rossetti wrote words in a similar vein:

> Not to be first: how hard to learn
> That lifelong lesson of the past
> Line graven on line and stroke on stroke:
> But, thank God, learned at last.

Although Rossetti professes to be thankful for having learned to put her own desires second, this is a message that's hard to accept at face value. Equally, there's something in the manic ecstasy of "A Birthday" that doesn't sound like pure and natural joy so much as a conscious decision to act joyous, to announce the rebirth of love whether it's true or not. "A Birthday" may be a poem that apparently announces its intentions clearly, but behind the clarity lies doubt, and it's this doubt that makes the poem haunting and memorable.

Source: Elizabeth Judd, in an essay for *Poetry for Students,* Gale, 2001.

Kimberly Lutz

Lutz is an instructor at New York University and has written for a wide variety of educational publishers. In the following essay, she explores how the simplicity of "A Birthday" masks its deeper meanings.

The short poem "A Birthday" by Christina Rossetti diverges in tone from many of her other works. The feminist literary critics Sandra M. Gilbert and Susan Gubar describe Rossetti's style as an "aesthetic of renunciation." In other words, they see in Rossetti's poems a desire to renounce her own desire and to deny her feelings of passion and love. Again and again in her poetry do Gilbert and Gubar see Rossetti turning away from pleasure or fulfillment. In their assessment, "Rossetti, banqueting on bitterness, must bury herself alive in a coffin of renunciation." "A Birthday" stands in stark contrast to this aesthetic. This poem seems purely celebratory as the narrator relishes the coming consummation of her love, a love that on the surface appears to be both passionate and physical.

The first stanza begins with three similes that are separated by semicolons: "My heart is like a singing bird / Whose nest is in a watered shoot; / My heart is like an apple tree / Whose boughs are bent with thickset fruit; / My heart is like a rainbow shell / That paddles in a halcyon sea." The effect of these three clauses is to compare the narrator's heart with images found in nature. By connecting her emotions to the physical world, the narrator suggests that it is natural to express her love. She could no more suppress her feelings than the bird could stop singing or the apple not weigh down the bough. Such a love seems unbidden, not looked for by the narrator, but accepted as a gift of nature.

In the last couplet of the first stanza, however, the narrator stops using similes to describe her heart. As the long sentence of the first stanza ends, the narrator exclaims, "My heart is gladder than all these / Because my love is come to me." She holds herself superior to the natural images with which she began. The bird singing, the bough bending, the shell floating are all suspended in time. Their fates are precarious, and as literary critic Antony Harrison has argued, "the idealized images of nature that appear in the first stanza carry with them the inevitability of their own destruction." For the bird in its "watered shoot" is exposed to danger; the ripe apples threaten to fall to the ground or break the bough; and the shell that now floats in tranquil waters is, as Harrison shows, "vulnerable, as a delicate object, to the changing moods of the potentially destructive ocean." For these reasons, the narrator distances herself from these images. Her heart may be "like" the bird, the tree, and the shell, but it is not them. Her fate is not precarious because the suspense is over. She loves, and her lover has returned those feelings.

In the second stanza, then, as Harrison argues, the narrator signals her "need to retreat from mutability." She must move away from the natural world so as not to admit the possibility that her love or lover could change with time. In this second stanza, then, the narrator turns her gaze from the outside to the inside. Instead of looking at real manifestations of nature, the narrator wants the changeable physical world enshrined in art. Represented in art, the bird or the apple is frozen in time, impervious to change. The doves, pomegranates, peacocks, and grapes that are described in the second stanza, therefore, do not occur in nature, but only as images carved into a dais, or wooden platform. Is the narrator inferring, as Harrison suggests, "that the only true and permanent fulfillment of love is to be found in the art it gives birth to"?

Other readings could also explain the move from nature to art. Part of the narrator's desire to enshrine her love, to hold it unchangeable forever, is evident in the ceremony she demands in the second stanza. In the first stanza, the narrator describes the state of her heart, and it is unclear to whom she is speaking. In many ways it is as if she, like the bird she compares her heart to, is simply singing out loud the overwhelming emotions she feels. But in the second stanza, she is more concerned with audience. The first three couplets contain com-

> *The precariousness of the natural world, then, springs not from the transience of erotic love, but from the transience of human existence."*

mands to unknown servants: "Raise me a dais of silk and down; / Hang it with vair and purple dyes; / Carve it in doves and pomegranates, / And peacocks with a hundred eyes; / Work it in gold and silver grapes, / In leaves and silver fleur-de-lys." Causing a platform to be raised, the narrator infers that she wants a public celebration of her love. Natural love and passion, it seems, are unstable because they are potentially illicit. Marked by a ceremony, such as a wedding, this love becomes stable and legally binding. The delicate shell of a Victorian woman's desire can be potentially crushed by an ocean of social condemnation. Only when the love is publicly acknowledged, is she truly free to love.

The language of public ceremony, however, is overly exalted in the second stanza. The images used suggest a coronation, rather than a wedding. Purple is the color of royalty, and the fleur-de-lys is the symbol for the French royal family. A dais is commonly used as a platform for a throne. The narrator infers that love turns her into a queen. This image is both empowering and forbidding. Her passion "reigned" in, the narrator depends on outward symbols rather than the natural feelings of her heart to represent the strength of her love.

But, as the second stanza ends, the narrator returns to the simple declarative style she used in the first stanza, even repeating the same language, "my love is come to me." This repetition signals a return to the inward self. The outward show represented by the trappings of royalty and ceremony, after all, merely indicates the narrator's joy at fulfilled love. The last couplet, "Because the birthday of my life / Is come, my love is come to me," argues that life itself begins only in returned love. Reborn through love, the narrator has gained all the wealth in the world. The royal treasure, then, of "silk and downs," "peacocks," and "gold and silver" is a metaphor for what she has acquired through love.

A final question of the poem remains: of what type of love is the narrator singing? Harrison, for one, notes that "the poem is significantly ambiguous in defining the nature (erotic or spiritual) of the described love." Deeply religious, Rossetti refused two marriage proposals on the grounds that her suitors did not share her beliefs. Certainly, the idea of a rebirth, the "birthday of my life," can indicate a baptism, being spiritually born again. The precariousness of the natural world, then, springs not from the transience of erotic love, but from the transience of human existence. The permanence suggested in the artistic work that will enshrine her love is nothing to the permanence of Christian love. The narrator's command to the unseen servants to "Raise me" may, as Harrison suggests, refer to resurrection. In the promise of the next world, the narrator can confidently believe in the immutability of love. In the simple and sing-song-like "A Birthday," Rossetti raises profound questions about the nature of love.

Source: Kimberly Lutz, in an essay for *Poetry for Students,* Gale, 2001.

Sources

Arsenau, Marie, Antony H. Harrison, and Lorraine Janzen Kooistra, eds., *The Culture of Christina Rossetti,* Ohio University Press, 1999.

Deutsch, Babette, *Poetry Handbook, A Dictionary of Terms,* Harper Collins, 1974.

Dombrowski, Theo, "Dualism in the Poetry of Christina Rossetti," in *Victorian Poetry,* Vol. 14, No. 1, Spring, 1976, pp. 70-76.

Gilbert, Sandra M., and Susan Gubar, *The Madwoman in the Attic,* Yale University Press, 1979.

Gosse, Edmund, *Critical Kit-Kats,* Scholarly Press, 1971, pp. 135-62.

Harrison, Antony H., "Aestheticism and the Thematics of Renunciation," in his *Christina Rossetti in Context,* University of North Carolina Press, 1988, pp. 89-141.

Hinkson, Katherine, "The Poetry of Christina Rossetti," in *The Bookman,* Vol. 5, No. 27, December, 1893, pp. 78-79.

Hollander, John, *Rhyme's Reason: A Guide to English Verse,* Yale University Press, 1981, p. 8.

Mayberry, Katherine J., *Christina Rossetti and the Poetry of Discovery,* Louisiana State University Press, 1989, pp. 39-40.

Marsh, Jan, ed. *Christina Rossetti: Poems and Prose,* Everyman, 1996.

Smulders, Sharon, *Christina Rossetti Revisited,* Twayne Publishers, 1996.

Trilling, Lionel, and Harold Bloom, *Victorian Prose and Poetry,* Oxford University Press, 1973.

Woolf, Virginia, *Fortnightly Review,* Vol. LXXXI Old Series, p. 403.

For Further Study

Arsenau, Marie, Antony H. Harrison, and Lorraine Janzen Kooistra, eds., *The Culture of Christina Rossetti,* Ohio University Press, 1999.

> Subtitled "Female Poetics and Victorian Contexts," this book collects essays based on the most recent wave of Rossetti scholarship, beginning in the 1980s. This work is necessarily feminist, and is a revision of stereotypes of both the poet and her fellow Victorians. Most interesting to readers of "A Birthday" may be the final essay, "Dying to be a Poetess," by Margaret Linley, which describes some of Rossetti's conflicts as a woman and a poet in her time.

Marsh, Jan, ed., *Christina Rossetti: Poems and Prose,* Everyman, 1996.

> This volume contains a timeline and chronology of Rossetti and her era, biographical information, selected poetry, fiction, and excerpts from her nonfiction and letters. Its notes and background material provide a helpful overview for readers new to Christina Rossetti.

Smulders, Sharon, *Christina Rossetti Revisited,* Twayne Publishers, 1996.

> As part of the Twayne English Author series, *Christina Rossetti Revisited* is a critical study of the poet's life and works. Like *The Culture of Christina Rossetti,* it offers a modern viewpoint of Rossetti's career in the Victorian period. Compare Smulder's chapter interpreting Rossetti's famous *Goblin Market* with the essay "Tasting the Fruit Forbidden'" by Catherine Maxwell in *The Culture of Christina Rossetti.*

Black Zodiac

Charles Wright

1997

Many readers find Charles Wright's poetry difficult to understand or even inaccessible. Readers often assume that Wright's work is going to tell a story or be a neat, precise account that makes sense. This poet's work is, instead, like a loosely woven rug with threads of images, ideas, and descriptions winding in and out of one another, sometimes correlating, sometimes not. "Black Zodiac" is a typical meandering poem full of stark imagery and common themes that appear in the majority of Wright's poetry. A poem in the follow-up collection to *Black Zodiac, Appalachia,* illustrates what Wright's poems are usually about.

In "What Do You Write About, Where Do Your Ideas Come From?" the first two lines of the poem answer the questions: "Landscape, of course, the idea of God and language / itself, that pure grace." Indeed, these are the principles addressed in "Black Zodiac" "landscape, God (and death), and language" with each one standing alone as a theme, but also blending into one another, creating a mesh of nature, religious thought, and the ability to express ourselves. While it would be misleading, as well as futile, to analyze "Black Zodiac" in terms of what it tells us from beginning to end we can examine it in light of its pieces; the glimpses of lucid description and the obscure strings of images and broken thoughts. What this poem is *about,* then, is one man's attempt to express what he essentially feels is inexpressible and to describe that attempt through discourse on landscape, God, and language itself.

Author Biography

Charles Wright was born in Hardin County, Tennessee, in 1935. He spent most of his childhood in this Appalachian region, primarily in eastern Tennessee and western North Carolina. After graduating from Davidson College in 1957, he served in the army's Intelligence Service for four years, spending most of that time in Verona, Italy. Until this point in his life, Wright had not written poetry, but in Italy he discovered Ezra Pound's Italian *Cantos* and became engrossed in both reading and writing verse. The lush natural surroundings of Verona were a major impetus on his landscape descriptions. Upon returning to the United States, he attended the University of Iowa Writer's Workshop, graduating with an M.F.A. degree in 1963. Afterwards, he returned to Italy as a Fulbright Scholar to teach at the University of Rome. During his stay there, he also began translating the works of Italian poets whose style of poetry would find its way into Wright's own work as he crafted his poems.

The influence of growing up in the rural South is also evident in much of Wright's work, especially in the typical southern concern for the past and its power over present day life. The ideas of irrepressible memory, a sense of fatality, and personal salvation are concepts throughout many of his poems, including "Black Zodiac." While the collection *Black Zodiac* was written in the 1990s—three decades after his preliminary publications—much of the style and themes found in this recent book are only a continuation of those begun many years ago in his early material. Wright attributes his influences not only to Pound and various Italian poets, but also to his writing teachers, particularly fellow poet Donald Justice. While in the Writer's Workshop at Iowa, Wright learned not only the history of poetry and poetics, but also the importance of a poem's sound, or its "music" as Justice noted. Wright eventually began to connect his love of landscape with his love for language—like Pound, Justice, and others—and, after mixing in his own religious beliefs, doubts, and longings, he would arrive at the three themes most prevalent in his poetry.

Wright taught at the University of California, Irvine, from 1966 to 1983, then moved back to the South to take a position at the University of Virginia in Charlottesville. In 1992, Wright briefly returned to Italy, serving as a distinguished visiting professor in Florence.

Poem Text

Darkened by time, the masters, like our memories,
    mix
And mismatch,
       and settle about our lawn furniture, like air
Without a meaning, like air in its clear nothingness.
What can we say to either of them?
How can they be so dark and so clear at the same   5
    time?
They ruffle our hair,
      they ruffle the leaves of the August trees.
Then stop, abruptly as wind.
The flies come back, and the heat
      —what can we say to them?
Nothing is endless but the sky.
The flies come back, and the afternoon   10
Teeters a bit on its green edges,
      then settles like dead weight
Next to our memories, and the pale hems of the
    masters' gowns.

Those who look for the Lord will cry out in praise
    of him.
Perhaps. And perhaps not—
      dust and ashes though we are,
Some will go wordlessly, some   15
Will listen their way in with their mouths
Where pain puts them, an inch-and-a-half above
    the floor.
And some will revile him out of love
    and deep disdain.
The gates of mercy, like an eclipse, darken our
    undersides.
Rows of gravestones stay our steps,   20
    August humidity
Bright as auras around our bodies.
And some will utter the words,
    speaking in fear and tongues,
Hating their garments splotched by the flesh.
These are the lucky ones, the shelved ones, the
    twice-erased.

Dante and John Chrysostom   25
Might find this afternoon a sidereal roadmap,
A pilgrim's way …
    You might too
Under the prejaundiced outline of the quarter
    moon,
Clouds sculling downsky like a narrative for
    whatever comes,
What *hasn't happened to happen yet*   30
Still lurking behind the stars,
    31 August 1995 …
The afterlife of insects, space graffiti, white holes
In the landscape,
    such things, such avenues, lead to dust
And handle our hurt with ease.
Sky blue, blue of infinity, blue   35
    waters above the earth:
Why do the great stories always exist in the past?

The unexamined life's no different from
    the examined life—
Unanswerable questions, small talk,

Unprovable theorems, long-abandoned
      arguments—
You've got to write it all down.   40
Landscape or waterscape, light-length on
      evergreen, dark sidebar
Of evening,
      you've got to write it down.
Memory's handkerchief, death's dream and
      automobile,
God's sleep,
      you've still got to write it down,
Moon half-empty, moon half-full,   45
Night starless and egoless, night blood-black and
      prayer-black,
Spider at work between the hedges,
Last bird call,
      toad in a damp place, tree frog in a dry ...

We go to our graves with secondary affections,
Second-hand satisfaction, half-souled,   50
      star charts demagnetized.
We go in our best suits. The birds are flying.
      Clouds pass.
Sure we're cold and untouchable,
      but we harbor no ill will.
No tooth tuned to resentment's fork,
      we're out of here, and sweet meat.
Calligraphers of the disembodies, God's word-
      wards,
What letters will we illuminate?   55
Above us, the atmosphere,
The nothing that's nowhere, signs on, and waits for
      our beck and call.
Above us, the great constellations sidle and wince,
The letters undarken and come forth,
Your X and my X.   60
      The letters undarken and they come forth.

Eluders of memory, nocturnal sleep of the
      greenhouse,
Spirit of slides and silences,
      Invisible Hand,
Witness and walk on.
Lords of the discontinuous, lords of the little
      gestures,
Succor my shift and save me ...   65
All afternoon the rain has rained down in the mind,
And in the gardens and dwarf orchard.
      All afternoon
The lexicon of late summer has turned its pages
Under the rain,
      abstracting the necessary word.
Autumn's upon us.   70
The rain fills our narrow beds.
Description's an element, like air or water.
      That's the word.

Poem Summary

Lines 1-12:

The first stanza of "Black Zodiac" introduces us to the importance of memory. Memories, in fact,

Media Adaptations

- In 1991, fellow poet J.D. McClatchy interviewed Charles Wright for the Modern Poetry Association's "Poets in Person" series. Although Wright has done several published interviews, they were rarely recorded. Students may inquire about this tape by contacting the MPA in Chicago.

are compared to "the masters," but who the masters are is not certain. Given the title and the fact that they are "Darkened by time," perhaps there is a celestial reference, as in the figures that represent the 12 constellations in our solar system and which are best viewed at night. But whether these masters are considered in a religious sense or in the form of master poets or master philosophers, the connotation of the word itself is basically the same. Both memories and masters are at once elusive and yet very real. They "mix / and mismatch," the way our recollections often do and, on one hand, are "like air in its clear nothingness." Since Wright is known to compose many of his poems while sitting in his own back yard, the reference to lawn furniture is not uncommon. In fact, it brings the realness to memories and masters, giving them human characteristics as they "settle about our lawn furniture" and "ruffle our hair." Line 6 reveals the overall theme of this opening stanza, asking a rhetorical question about memories and masters for which there is no answer: "How can they be so dark and so clear at the same time?" Here, the word "clear" can be interpreted in two different ways. Set against the idea of entities that are "dark," the word "clear" may indicate that their reason or meaning is still very evident in spite of the fact that they are difficult to grasp and are so elusive. But "clear" may also imply transparency or invisibility, indicating no evident meaning or reason at all.

The second half of the first stanza brings nature and landscape into the poem in a more immediate sense. Wright details leaves, trees, wind, flies, heat, and sky, and the heat is apparently oppressive. The poet's description of the scene makes it easy to visualize, and the repetition of the line "The flies come back" helps paint the picture of a hot, stifling summer day. Wright uses the device of anthropomorphism (giving human characteristics to animals or inanimate objects) frequently in his work, and, here, the "afternoon" itself takes human form. As though it can't decide whether to expose its lush green summery side or wilt under the burn of its temperature, it "Teeters a bit on its green edges, / then settles like dead weight / Next to our memories, and the pale hems of the masters' gowns."

Lines 13-24:

The second stanza of the poem introduces fundamental religious beliefs in relation to death and the human reaction to it. Beginning with a biblical saying and including other religious imagery ("dust and ashes," "gates of mercy," "aura," and "speaking in tongues"), this stanza exposes the narrator as somewhat of a bystander in the events he describes, speaking mostly in third person and offering little personal judgment or concern. The first eight lines depict a variety of entrances into heaven from those who will "*cry out in praise*" to those who will "go wordlessly," to those who will "revile [curse or use abusive language] him out of love / and deep disdain." In line 19, Wright uses an astronomical allusion to describe the "gates of mercy," saying they are "like an eclipse" and serve to "darken our undersides." In other words, the sins which must be accounted for while standing at the entrance to heaven will appear even worse, or darker, at the moment of reckoning.

Lines 20-24 appear to take place in a cemetery where the dead are rising to enter into heaven, as recorded in various Christian doctrines. Wright reminds us again of the summer heat ("August humidity / Bright as auras around our bodies") and then continues to describe the reaction of the people facing a first-hand encounter with divinity: "And some will utter the words,/ speaking in fear and tongues." They hate their clothing that is "splotched by the flesh" because at this point the flesh is no longer necessary, nor even wanted, for it only serves to mask or hide the true beauty of the soul. The dead are "twice-erased" since they left the earth when they died, and are now leaving again with the second coming of Christ.

Lines 25-31:

In these eight lines, Wright shifts away from religious fundamentalism toward "sidereal" allusions, or, descriptions relating to stars and the con-

stellations. A "sidereal roadmap," for instance, is one based on the movement of the stars on a daily basis. Alighieri Dante, an Italian poet who wrote *The Divine Comedy,* and Saint John Chrysostom, born in what is now Turkey and noted for his eloquent speaking ability, are mentioned because of their associations with religious pilgrimages. Here, though, Wright suggests that they may find the afternoon *sky* a map for a pilgrimage, of sorts. In line 27, Wright addresses the reader directly, saying "You might too" find the "afternoon a sidereal roadmap."

Other references to the sky include the "prejaundiced [not yet yellow] outline of the quarter moon" and the "Clouds skulling [propelling] downsky." At this point, Wright brings the idea of *language* into the poem, the specifics of narrative and of words themselves. The clouds streaming across the sky are "like a narrative for *whatever comes,*" and "What *hasn't happened to happen yet*" is "Still lurking behind the stars." It's as though the speaker is analyzing astrological objects in literary terms, with the clouds and moon following a sequence as would a novel or short story.

Lines 32-36:

The last half of the third stanza presents a series of images connecting landscape, death, and memory. The mention of insects is a return to the flies pointed out in the first stanza, and the "space graffiti" implies the stars, moon, and sun splattered about the sky like words on a wall. Once again, the poet uses a reference to language itself (graffiti) to describe heavenly bodies. Wright calls the stars "white holes / In the landscape" and claims that they "lead to dust" in other words, to death and the biblical heaven in the sky. While we may feel pain or fear death, these "avenues" to our demise "handle our hurt with ease." Line 35 ("waters above the earth") is a striking metaphor for the sky, comparing its blue to the blue of the oceans. The stanza ends with another unanswerable rhetorical question, asserting that our memories are always better than present thought. In asking why the "great stories always exist in the past," Wright implies that we tend to recall events and experiences with undue intensity and romanticize or inflate those happenings through memory.

Lines 37-44:

The fourth stanza of "Black Zodiac" takes a philosophical turn, beginning with a reference to the Greek philosopher Socrates, who stated that, "The unexamined life is not worth living." Wright's sentiment flies in the face of Socrates by claiming that there is no difference in the unexamined life and the examined one. He lists some of the methods of philosophically examining a life's "Unanswerable questions, small talk,/ Unprovable theorems, long-abandoned arguments" and presenting them in a cynical, mocking tone. He then offers his own idea of how to study and attempt to understand life: "You've got to write it all down." Whether examining such tangibles or visuals as "Landscape or waterscape," the sunlight on evergreen trees, or the evening itself, it is best to express ourselves on paper. Just as students are told to take good notes and to write down questions and comments on a subject, the poet contends that written language is the key to self-examination. This is a point he will return to at the end of the poem.

Lines 45-48:

Wright ends the fourth stanza with strings of images that exemplify the poet's notion of examination through written expression. He lists natural, physical objects—the moon, spiders, hedges, birds, toads, and tree frogs—in an effort to describe as much of his surrounding as possible, thereby making it more comprehensible. He complements the attempt to understand, or examine, these aspects of living by embellishing the nouns with descriptive words. Depicting the moon as "half-full" or "half-empty" is an allusion to the philosophical adage regarding optimism and pessimism: if you're an optimist, your glass is half full; if you're a pessimist, your glass is half empty. Wright calls the night "starless and egoless," meaning that without its bright, shiny adornments, it has nothing to gloat about. He further emphasizes the darkness by describing it as "blood-black and prayer-black." Religious imagery is never far away in a Wright poem.

Lines 49-53:

The fifth stanza centers once again on death and employs celestial imagery, noting that when we die, we are like "star charts demagnetized." The first two lines imply a shortcoming or incompleteness in life. We take "secondary affections" and "second-hand satisfaction" to our graves, ending our lives only "half-souled." The speaker assures us, however, that though our bodies may be "cold and untouchable" we're well dressed and do not harbor any bad feelings or resentment over dying. Wright even jests about death in a playful tone, saying "we're out of here, and sweet meat."

Lines 54-60:

The last half of the fifth stanza continues the discussion of death, but also incorporates the metaphor of language down to its individual letters and words. Once we die, we become "calligraphers of the disembodied," protecting the sacredness of language as though we are "God's word-wards." Like constellations, our souls light up the night sky in the shape of letters. To emphasize the vast emptiness and expansion of the universe, Wright calls the atmosphere "The nothing that's nowhere" and implies that it simply waits there for us to "illuminate" against it. Eventually, our "letters undarken and come forth." The term "undarken"—while not found in a dictionary—is more appropriate than the term "lighten" would be, for it indicates a general progression from something that has been there all along, though too dark to see. In other words, we all have letters in the sky waiting for our deaths to illuminate.

Lines 61-66:

The first six lines of the final stanza return to religious imagery intertwined with the idea of memory and natural surroundings. Recall that in the first stanza the speaker questioned how memory could be "so dark and so clear at the same time," and here in the last verse, he begins with "Eluders of memory"—implying yet again the mysteries of recollection. The mention of the greenhouse simply interjects a concrete noun within the layers of wordplay and theological discourse, the "Spirit of slides and silences." Since the phrase "Invisible Hand" is capitalized, we may assume it refers to God whom the speaker is asking to "Witness and walk on." The "lords" in line 64 may refer back to the "masters" in the first stanza, and the speaker is asking that his own shifting and discontinuity be succored (relieved) and that he be saved by the lords of such.

Lines 67-73:

The blending of the tangible and the intangible continues through to the end of "Black Zodiac." Not only is it raining "in the gardens and dwarf orchard," but also "in the mind," implying sadness or a gloomy outlook. Lines 68-70 reemphasize the need to find the right language for adequate expression and that the speaker has spent all afternoon trying to describe his environment by thinking of it as a dictionary—the "lexicon of late summer" which is also "Under the rain." Finally, the speaker acknowledges that "Autumn's upon us" and that the "rain fills our narrow beds," meaning garden plots, literally, but, figuratively, our homes and our beds may be cheerless and gray, as though they are being rained on. Finally, the speaker reaches a conclusion, finding what he has been looking for throughout the entire afternoon (and the entire poem). What he has found is *"the word"*— the language that captures the vitality of expression. Wright italicized line 72 to stress its significance. He tells us that *"Description's an element,"* meaning that the act of expressing ourselves and the use of language is as important to human life as are *"air or water."* The three words that end the poem (line 73) are like an exclamation point on the entire work. And the poet has reached "that pure grace," which is language itself as he refers to it in the later collection, *Appalachia.*

Themes

Religion and Death

Charles Wright's personal religious views play a significant role in much of his work, and they are obviously flavored with the fundamentalism of southern denominations. But admitting a basic belief in a supreme being does not tell the entire story of one of this poet's common themes. In "Black Zodiac," as in all his work, there is a tension kindled by his faith in God, almost a love-hate relationship that often occurs when strong and fervent feelings come into play. From the outset of the poem, the religious references, the "master's," in the first stanza, are described as elusive and difficult to understand. They "mix / And mismatch" and are "like air / Without a meaning." The second stanza brings religion and death together and contains biblical citations as well as language associated with fire-and-brimstone doctrines: "dust and ashes," "revile him," and "speaking in fear and tongues." Wright seldom mentions religion without incorporating some relation to death and, therefore, a direct meeting with God. He acknowledges that some people will be happy with that encounter, some will be angry, and some will be fearful. Regardless of the emotion, however, eventually "we're out of here." In this poem, Wright appears ambivalent in his own feelings. On one hand, he expresses old-fashioned sentiments of a religiously fundamental nature, and on the other hand he intellectualizes the idea of God, thinking in more abstract terms. He blends heaven and the constellations, eternity and astrological signs, the afterlife and a zodiac of letters. Our souls become calligraphers and "word-wards" for God, all of which

Topics for Further Study

- This assignment has two parts. First, write a brief essay describing a natural setting that you see on a regular basis, perhaps your own backyard. Write the essay from memory. Next, go to the place you have described and write a second brief essay about the landscape as you are observing it. Notice how the two writings differ and how they are alike.

- Read a collection of poetry by a southern poet (other than Charles Wright) and write an essay discussing any southern influences that are evident in the work.

- The connection and disconnection between God and the physical universe has been debated for centuries. Write an essay describing your own feelings on the subject.

- Pretend you live in a time and place in which written language has not yet developed. Describe what your typical day may be like, what your activities may be and how you "communicate" with other people in the community.

- If you wrote a poem leading up to the final line, "That's the word," what would your "word" be and why would it be worth writing a poem about?

sharply contrasts to—and yet mixes with—the biblical notion of crying out in praise and of speaking in tongues. "Black Zodiac" leaves room for both evangelical and philosophical thought on religion, but death goes hand in hand with whichever side we fall.

Landscape

Poets do not often get so much inspirational mileage out of their own back yards, but Wright's entire *Black Zodiac* collection is full of imagery, allusion, and description based upon Sunday observations from a lawn chair. In the poem "Black Zodiac," he includes several landscape reflections, but is even more extensive in describing "skyscape." He moves through the afternoon into evening, from oppressive heat to a late summer rain shower, philosophizing on religion, death, and memory, but always including a layer of nature—what color the sky is, what the wildlife is doing, how hot it is, etc. This is because human beings are inseparable from the natural environment. We depend on it, and it depends on us. Rather than ignore that fact, Wright is a poet who incorporates, blends, and layers landscape, waterscape, and skyscape into nearly everything he writes. He compares abstractions such as "masters" and "memories" to a summer breeze: "They ruffle our hair, / they ruffle the leaves of the August trees. / Then stop, abruptly as wind." In this poem, insects have an afterlife and stars are "space graffiti, white holes / In the landscape." The poet insists that we write down our observations or else we'll forget them or memory will distort them. Given this, he sometimes simply records what he sees and hears: "Spider at work between the hedges, / Last bird call, / toad in a damp place, tree frog in a dry." As evening comes on and daylight fades, the stars begin to appear, some of them perhaps the souls of the "disembodied": "Above us, the great constellations sidle and wince, / The letters undarken and come forth." "Black Zodiac" ends with yet another blend of the abstract and the concrete. The notion of "description" is likened to the very real and very natural elements of air and water. Regardless of the theological or philosophical twists and turns that a Wright poem takes, one sure foundation is the presence of nature.

Language and Expression

Perhaps the most dominant theme in "Black Zodiac" is that of language itself. While it may be obvious that any writer, regardless of genre, is concerned about creative, interesting, or accurate expression, Wright goes an extra step in turning that concern into a quest. He is constantly in pursuit of the "right" phrase or the "right" word. Sometimes he finds it and does not hesitate to point it out. In "Black Zodiac" the word is "element," and the last line says so. Ironically, in this poem the search for the right description involves looking for a way to describe description itself. But long before the end of the poem, Wright displays his language crusade with remarkable, unlikely imagery. The hot summer afternoon "Teeters a bit on its green edges" and the "gates of mercy, like an eclipse, darken our undersides." Instead of portraying the outline of an early evening moon as pale or vague, he calls it "prejaundiced," not yet bright and yellow in the sky. The clouds are not simply moving across the heavens, nor racing, nor drifting—they are "sculling downsky." A scull is a long oar used to propel a boat through water, so, here Wright employs a nautical term and a play on the word "downstream." Considering the poem ends with rain moving in, this line is a forecast for what is to come. Another example of the poet not settling for common verbiage is his description of the emerging constellation as the stars and planets become visible. The heavenly bodies do not merely twinkle—they "sidle and wince." Clearly, Wright's search for unique expression is often rewarded, and he proves over and over the essential connection between language and all that we do, all that we think, and all that exists.

Style

At first glance, Wright's poetry may appear highly unstructured, composed of long meandering lines that are sometimes complete sentences and sometimes just strings of phrases. While long lines and phrase groups are certainly present in his poems, a close look also reveals a very carefully constructed work, even mathematical in some instances. Wright's typical "divisor" is three. "Black Zodiac" is made up of 73 lines—six stanzas with 12 lines each. Even entire collections are grouped into what Wright calls "triptychs," a term more often used in the art world to describe three painted or carved panels that are hinged together. In literature, three books in a series is considered a "trilogy." To date, Wright has composed three triptychs, the most recent consisting of *Chickamauga, Black Zodiac,* and *Appalachia.* The style of poetry in these three books is very similar, as are the themes, most notably God, landscape, and language.

Language, of course, has already been heavily discussed in this article, but its use and its results are at the very core of the poem's style as well as its themes. In Wright's collection of "improvisations and interviews" called *Halflife,* he has this to say about expressing himself on paper: "Mostly I like the sound of words. The sound, the feel, the paint, the color of them. I like to hear what they can do with each other. I like layers of paint on the canvas." In regard to the structure of entire lines, Wright mentions that, "a well-known poet once said to me, 'I don't worry about the ends of my lines. I feel if the beginnings are good, the ends will take care of themselves.' Wrong. They will not. Things have ends as well as beginnings. The

Compare & Contrast

- **1993:** In Waco, Texas, the United States Bureau of Alcohol, Tobacco, and Fire Arms raided the compound of the Branch Davidians religious cult under charges of child abuse and other law violations. Eighty cult members died when the compound went up in flames.

  1996: An Israeli Internet access company began delivering e-mailed messages to God to Jerusalem's Western Wall for people who cannot get there in person. The messages are printed out and stuffed into cracks in the wall.

  1996: The Oakland, California, school system voted unanimously to recognize "Ebonics" as the primary language of its African American students. The decision brought fierce protests from both black and white communities and the government denied federal funding for teaching the new "language."

  1998: NASA's Hubble Space Telescope revealed a glimpse of previously unseen galaxies 12 billion light years away. The "Deep Field South" image is a long-exposure view of the constellation Tucana, visible only from the Southern Hemisphere.

  1999: President Bill Clinton made a stop in Hazard, Kentucky, on a four-day tour aimed at bringing business to the poorer regions of Appalachia.

line must be strong all the way through and not finish in a dying fall." Wright resorts to art terms often in his discourse on poetry, from calling his collections "triptychs" to talking about the "paint" and the "color" of words. Keeping the poet's philosophy about language and lines in mind, we can see how "Black Zodiac" came to be filled with such colorful imagery and word-paint, and with lines that remain "active" to their very ends.

Historical Context

Since 1983, Charles Wright has lived and taught in Charlottesville, Virginia. While he spent several years in both Europe and California, his roots are in the American South, and that is where he has returned. Some of his earlier poetry was obviously influenced by his visits to Italy (and Ezra Pound), but even while there on military assignment, most of his writing focused on the lush Verona landscape and on the poet's own contemplation about life, death, and God, not war, the human condition, poverty, and other topical issues. "Black Zodiac" could have been written in any time period and in any back yard. Because Wright does not generally call attention to social or political events, human

rights issues, or "causes" throughout the world, it is difficult to pin down an exact historical or cultural perspective on his work. Even though he writes exhaustingly about nature, we cannot call him an "environmental" poet because social responsibility, economics, and politics do not come into play. What we can say is that this poet puts more creative effort into the metaphysical than the cultural and deals with history more in the personal sense than the universal, concentrating on the inevitability of memory and our distortions of it. The influence of growing up in the South is evident in his allusions to the past and its powers, but he avoids direct references to specific historical occurrences. Rather, he abstractly asks, "Why do the great stories always exist in the past?" This line, however, is more a comment on the tricks that memory plays instead of an observation on any particular "great" story.

In his article "Between Soil and Stars," teacher and critic James Longenbach states that, "by his own admission, Wright has focused on three subjects for the last thirty years: language, landscape, and the idea of God. *Black Zodiac* is the synthesis of Wright's contrary drives toward waywardness and compression, the soil and the stars." This tendency toward "waywardness and compression"—

or freedom and restriction—may be the strongest evidence of cultural influence on Wright and his work, from the beginnings of his life through the writing of the poem and ever since. Brought up in the "Bible belt" and remaining there until after college graduation, Wright must have felt the common tug between strict, religious conservatism and the temptations of secular curiosity and desire. The poem "Black Zodiac" demonstrates both the longing to be wayward, or free, with thoughts and actions, as well as the compressing, or restricted, tendencies that seem inescapable. The speaker offers a religiously charged quote: *"Those who look for the Lord will cry out in praise of him"*—and then immediately interjects his own opinion: "Perhaps. And perhaps not." He flirts with the idea of an astrological afterlife in which our souls light up as letters in the constellation, and yet God is not out of the picture—as star-letters, we become his "word-wards." Beyond the southern influence any further attempt to date and place "Black Zodiac" would be superfluous and far-reaching. Considering the intellectual and creative intricacies of the bulk of Wright's work, we cannot find fault with an indeterminate setting.

Critical Overview

Wright's poetry has been highly praised from early publications on. His second book *Hard Freight* was nominated for a National Book Award and received a National Endowment for the Arts grant and a Guggenheim Fellowship, among other awards. Most critics have given a thumbs up for Wright's style, pointing to the layering of fragmented images and the shifting/blending of dominant themes as very interesting to "watch" as well as just read. *Black Zodiac,* in particular, has drawn favorable attention, as much for its intriguing subject matter as for its striking language. In a review of the collection in *America,* critic Robert Ellis Hosmer Jr. addresses the speaker who presents a consistent voice throughout the book: "[t]he voice we become accustomed to hearing often expresses hesitation, ambivalence, contradiction and doubt. At the same time, the narrator acknowledges that there is "great radiance." Every single notated element in these poems has no importance greater than pointing beyond." Many other critics picked up on the "looking beyond" aspect of *Black Zodiac,* comparing it to the tendency to "look backward" in the previous collection *Chickamauga.*

Wright's technique of piling up images, however, is not praised by all critics. Some have complained that the poet tries so hard to find the "right" language that he ends up sacrificing quality for quantity. Because many of his poems contain themes that wind in and out of one another, some readers find him confusing at best, boring at worst. In spite of these charges, however, Wright is one of the nation's most prolific poets, and his positive critics far outnumber the negative.

Criticism

Greg Barnhisel

Barnhisel holds a Ph.D in American literature. In this essay, he examines how Charles Wright responds, in "Black Zodiac," to the question of what relationship a poet should have to the material world, especially the world of nature. He also discusses how Wright, in answering that question, enters into a conversation with such predecessor poets as Wordsworth, Keats, and Wallace Stevens about these topics.

In her 1988 book *The Music of What Happens,* the eminent critic Helen Vendler writes of Charles Wright that "Wright's poetry reproduces the circling and deepening concentration that aims at either obliteration or transcendence, blankness or mysticism. But Wright stops short of either polarity because he remains bound to the materiality and temporal rhythm of language, whereas both Eastern nothingness and Western transcendence, at their utmost point, renounce as meaningless both materiality and time." For Vendler, Wright's poetry attempts to come to a resting-place between the desire for nothingness, for obliteration, and the desire to transcend or go beyond the material world. Wright ends up accepting and even embracing the material world, but without the uncritical admiration characteristic of such poets as Wordsworth. "Black Zodiac," the title poem of his 1997 collection, illustrates and describes the answers that Wright comes up with to the poetic dilemma of obliteration or transcendence.

Probably at no point have poets' attitudes toward nature and toward artistic representation of nature changed so much as during the Romantic period of approximately 1760-1830. A long tradition of nature poetry existed, of course, before the Romantics; the Greek pastoral elegy, for instance, survived the Greeks to become popular among the

> *In this poem, the motions of the stars provide him with the raw material for his meditations on "the masters," both poetic and religious."*

Romans and to endure to the Renaissance, Milton, and Tennyson. Virgil, Rome's most important poet, wrote so-called "bucolic" poetry in praise of the country life. But in the Romantic period, and especially in the poetry of William Wordsworth, Nature became all. Wordsworth saw the poet as the servant of Nature, and for both Wordsworth and his close friend and collaborator Samuel Taylor Coleridge, the experience of the "sublime" was the most powerful sensation a human could have. The sublime, a popular philosophical concept of the eighteenth century, was the sense of the overwhelming, a feeling of being dwarfed. Experience of the sublime was an experience of awe. For Wordsworth, only nature could provide an experience of the sublime, for nothing human-created (such as art) could convey the sense of infinity, power, and divinity that nature (being a direct creation of God) has.

John Keats, another important poet of the Romantic era, used these ideas of Wordsworth's but changed them slightly. Keats was in awe of nature, but unlike Wordsworth, Keats counted his experiences of art as the most important and powerful in his life. Where Wordsworth wrote of rambling in England's Lake Country and of climbing Mount Snowdon, many of Keats' most famous poems recount his experiences with artworks such as a translation of Homer or a Greek amphora. In "Ode on a Grecian Urn," perhaps Keats' best-known poem, he describes a scene on a Greek amphora. He is transfixed not just by the nature portrayed on the urn, but by the question of *representation*. In art, Keats feels, natural beauty cannot fade. Time and its ravages have no effect on art, and in this sense Keats feels the sublime gazing upon the urn. Keats' reaction is to aestheticize: "'Beauty is truth, truth beauty,'" the urn tells him, and he responds: "that is all / Ye know on earth, and all ye need to know."

The Romantics, therefore, questioned the relative power of art and of nature, and these conflicting ideas have influenced every poet who has written on nature since. A third poet, though, Wallace Stevens, took his questioning even further. Stevens was concerned, for his entire poetic career, about whether the outside world really has an objective existence or whether it is simply a projection of the mind. He wavered between the two principles; in poems like "Tea at the Palaz of Hoon" or "The Snow Man" he seems to feel that the world is only a projection of the mind, whereas in others—"Debris of Life and Mind," for instance—he sides strongly with the idea that the world does have an objective existence. And in "Thirteen Ways of Looking at a Blackbird," Stevens adopts a Picasso-like approach and examines this question from thirteen different angles, coming up with thirteen different ideas about the outside world.

Charles Wright has always been a poet deeply concerned with the outside world and especially with nature, but at the same time he (like almost every other American poet of his generation) carries with him the deep influence of Stevens. In "Black Zodiac," he addresses questions of the existence of nature and of how poets can or should represent nature. In Wright's early poetry (much of which is collected in the volume *Country Music*), Wright concentrated on the description of nature and seemed to be taking the middle ground between Wordsworth and Keats. But as with Keats, the poet does not call attention to his own place in the perception of nature—he seems to assume that all people would perceive and understand nature in the same way. Vendler, in an earlier essay on Wright, complains that he claims, "like all poets, a return to original nature: the refusal to particularize his individual existence implies his utterance of universal experience, predicable of everyone."

In "Black Zodiac," though, as in much of his later verse, Wright has gotten beyond his youthful tendency to generalize his impressions of nature. In this poem, the motions of the stars provide him with the raw material for his meditations on "the masters," both poetic and religious. The poem begins, as do so many of his, in his yard. The August heat and humidity hang about him in their palpable "clear nothingness," and this invisible omnipresence reminds Wright of these "masters," who in this first stanza remain unnamed.

But the next stanza begins with a hint of who these "masters" are: "Those who look for the Lord will cry out in praise of him." The stanza begins, and we understand that these masters are the masters of theology as well as the masters of poetry. This stanza muses on humans' relationship with God: is it painful and agonizing? Is the cry one of joy, or is it from "where pain puts them, an inch-and-a-half above the floor"? What is unclear in this stanza is how nature fits in—it was introduced in such strong and permeating terms in the first stanza, but it almost disappears in the second, replaced by a discussion of holy men.

The third stanza begins to bring the two terms together in its use of the figures of Dante and St. John Chrysostom. Dante, of course, was the 14th century Italian poet whose *Divine Comedy* attempted to construct an architectural model of the temporal and spiritual worlds, linking the two partially astronomically, while St. John Chrysostom is one of the Doctors of the Roman Catholic Church. "Chrysostom" means "golden-mouthed," and St. John Chrysostom was famed as one of the great orators of the early church, a man who became the Patriarch of the city of Constantinople and attacked the material excesses of the Empress Eudoxia. In this stanza Wright starts drawing together his themes—nature, astronomy, God, and poetry—in a carefully-constructed web. In the first line, he links Dante, a poet who encompassed religion, the stars, and art, with St. John Chrysostom, whose fame was also due to his use of language. Both of these men might / find this afternoon a sidereal roadmap, / A pilgrim's way ... /

Wright's use of the term "sidereal," or having to do with the stars, again brings us back to the notion of astronomy, as well as the humid air, representing nature. "The afterlife of insects, space graffiti, white holes / In the landscape, / such things, such avenues, lead to dust / And handle our hurt with ease." Wright compares the dust and ashes that are the inevitable final states of any living creature with the dust that forms planets and stars as well as filling the void of space.

Much of the rest of the poem develops this theme, in quite abstract and cosmic terms, but in the final stanza we return to homely, quite terrestrial nature. We have returned from space and are back in Wright's yard, by the greenhouse, and he is still questioning the process by which the mind understands and represents nature. The "lexicon of late summer," both the poetry that Wright is responding to and the lexicon of nature (heat, insects, humidity), is "abstracting the necessary word," causing the poet to think in these broad, abstract, cosmic terms. But it is to the particular that Wright

must return. "Autumn's upon us," he notes, "the rain fills our narrow beds." These "beds" recall the graves that Wright has discussed earlier, in the previous stanza when he talks about human death, and death, to Wright, is not a particularly important event: "we're out of here, and sweet meat."

So what is the enduring part of human existence, if we turn to nothing but dust and "sweet meat"? The answer comes in the final lines: "*Description's an element, like air and water. /* That's the word." Wright's stance on the relative places of the poet, of poetry, and of nature, then, comes somewhere between Wordsworth's and Keats'. Art is immortal: it is "an element, like air and water." In this, the poem seems an affirmation of Keats' "Grecian Urn" ode. However, this poem, and human existence, are buffeted by and in a sense determined by nature. If art does end up being as enduring as (or even more so than) nature, as Keats would have it, the artist is not entirely in control, as in Keats. Rather, nature must determine the subject matter of poetry, which achieves immortality in that it depicts of nature. Artists, destined to be dust or "sweet meat" in the grave, simply record the atmosphere of the thirty-first of August, 1995, or the zodiac, the motions of the stars themselves.

Source: Greg Barnhisel, in an essay for *Poetry for Students*, Gale, 2001.

David Caplan

David Caplan is a doctoral candidate at the University of Virginia, writing a dissertation on contemporary poetry. In this essay, he places "Black Zodiac" in the context of Charles Wright's poetic career.

An air of almost pure meditation distinguishes Charles Wright's poetry. Characters rarely inhabit its landscapes. Extremely few actions occur; the poems never tell stories. More often than not, they direct their gazes inward, meditating upon the nature of poetry. Again and again Wright's verse returns to the basic questions one might ask of this art. How is it written? What inspires it? What does it accomplish? What, if any, consolations does poetry bring?

The answers Wright provides might strike some as intolerably bleak. During the Vietnam War, many poets and readers wanted politically committed writing. Art, the argument went, could help stimulate opposition to an unjust war. It could raise consciousness and protect a nation from its worse impulses. Wright viewed these claims with

> *... a writer claims originality not by composing a wholly unprecedented poem but by bringing together a unique combination of influences."*

characteristic skepticism. His widely noticed poem, "The New Poem," categorically rebuts these hopes:

It will not attend our sorrow.
It will not console our children.
It will not be able to help us.

As this stanza suggests, "The New Poem" presents a series of negative propositions, an austerity that extends to its nearly monotonous cadences. Though extremely bracing, such poetry does not remain "new" for very long.

Wright published *Black Zodiac* in 1997, a time when Americans enjoyed peace, not endured a divisive war. *Black Zodiac* expresses a less severe pessimism. The difference can be heard in the poem's lush rhythms. While "The New Poem" presents a dirge-like monody, "Black Zodiac" avails itself of a much wider variety of cadences. The writer of "The New Poem" is a young man, laying down prohibitions. In "Black Zodiac," Wright asks a series of questions directed toward himself and his art. The questions include:

What can we say to either of them?
How can they be so dark and so clear at the same
    time?
. . . .
The flies come back, and the heat—what can we
    say to them?
. . . .
Why do the great stories always exist in the past?

Appropriately for such a self-questioning poem, "Black Zodiac" opens with a tone of humility. Meditating upon the poet's relationship to his precursors, the great poets who preceded him, the speaker pays homage to "the masters," a term suggestive of a great humbleness, an almost religious deference to these artists' authority. Like a supplicant, the speaker stands at the level of "the pale hems" of their gowns. Yet these "masters" also form the poet's inspiration and his audience. The poem starts:

Darkened by time, the masters, like our memories,
    mix
And mismatch, And settle about our lawn furniture,
    like air
Without a meaning, like air in its clear nothingness.

In the terms of contemporary literary criticism, this passage considers the nature of poetic influence: that is, the nature of a poet's relation with earlier writers. Some scholars characterize this relationship as essentially competitive, as poets fight each other for a chance at poetic immortality. Wright, though, describes a different dynamic. The "masters" gather as the poet writes. The act of creation summons them because poet starts to "mix / And mismatch" his great influences as he writes. In other words, a writer claims originality not by composing a wholly unprecedented poem but by bringing together a unique combination of influences.

Wright's notes for this poem confirm this strategy of eclectic influence. The mere presence of these notes in the back of *Black Zodiac* suggests a certain meticulousness; Wright does not try to hide the fact that previous works inspired his poem. Instead, his notes acknowledge that his poem borrows phrases and ideas from sources as diverse as the posthumously published work of the twentieth-century American poet Wallace Stevens, a translation of the German poet Paul Celan, and the journals of St. Augustine, a leading figure in early Christianity.

Mixing and re-mixing these god-like influences, the poet faces the challenge of drawing sustenance from "the masters" without being mastered by them. He twice distills this problem to its crux, asking, "What can we say to them?" In the presence of these "masters," the poet experiences a tongue-tied sense of awe. They reduce him to acting like a child, letting them tussle his hair.

Of course the poet is not actually tongue-tied; he remains articulate about his inability to craft a response worthy of the visiting spirits:

They ruffle our hair, they ruffle the leaves of the
    August tree.
They stop, abruptly as wind.
The flies come back, and the heat—what can we
    say to them?

Several characteristics mark these lines as Wright's. As in much of his work, this passage uses a split line as a means to control the tempo and cadence. For example, the first line features a caesura, a comma that forces the reader to pause, after the word, "hair." Wright then splits the line, leaving it unbalanced, as the first part remains shorter than the second. The next line features a caesura after its second word, "stop," and the fifth word, "wind." All of these lines move toward an iambic meter, an arrangement of the syllables into a pattern where an unstressed syllable precedes a stressed one. Yet the lines do not quite adhere to this pattern. For example, in the following line I have italicized each syllable that I read as stressed:

The *flies come* back, and the *heat*—
What can we *say* to *them?*

Mixing the lines' cadences and arrangements of stessed and unstressed syllable, Wright produces this distinctive rhythm.

"Black Zodiac" comes closest to articulating a solution to the question, "What can we say to them?" in its third section. "You've got to write it down," the poet tells himself three times:

Memory's handkerchief, death's dream and
    automobile,
God's sleep, you've still got to write it down,
Moon half-empty, night half-full,
Night starless and egoless, night blood-black and
    prayer black,
Spider at work between the hedges,
Last bird call, toad in a damp place, tree frog in a
    dry ...

This passage's details remain mysterious; they more evoke a state of mind than describe an experience. Memory takes a sorrowful form, a handkerchief to wipe away tears. While the poet enters death's "dream," God moves into a deeper distance. God sleeps while death fills the poet's consciousness. A darkness surrounds him. In the poem's opening section, "the masters" humble the poet in their presence. In this section, he achieves a state of grace, entering the "starless and egoless" landscape. "The unexamined life's no different from / the examined life," he declares. Humbled as in his encounter with "the masters," the poet realizes that, though poetry brings no consolation, he must continue to pursue its examinations.

Source: David Caplan, in an essay for *Poetry for Students*, Gale, 2001.

Dean Rader

Dean Rader has published widely in the field of twentieth-century poetry. Here, he offers a comparative reading of Charles Wright's "Black Zodiac" and Wallace Stevens's poetry.

"Description is an element, like air or water" writes Wallace Stevens in his "Adagia," a collection of adages and aphorisms that appear in *Opus Posthumous* (1957), a collection of ideas, poems

> *You've got to write it all down. Landscape or waterscape, light—length on evergreen, dark sidebar Of evening, you've got to write it down."*

and plays published a few years after Stevens' death. This passage also appears in the second-to-the-last line in Charles Wright's enigmatic poem "Black Zodiac": *Description's an element, like air or water. / That's the word.* And that's the poem. It ends right there. One wonders what, precisely, Wright refers to with the word "it." Possibly air, possibly water, but most likely he is suggesting that description is the word in question. In fact, the entire poem is a description, not so much of the external landscape but of the landscape within. For Wright, as for Stevens, there is a fuzzy (if even detectable) border between the self and nature, or better put between interior and exterior spaces. At times, both spaces are imbued and altered by the perspective of the poet. Thus, the poem "Black Zodiac" and the book of the same title see the poetic process as descriptions of the ways in which the individual positions himself and his ideas against the backdrop of this utterly complex and inhibiting world.

Wright's final line, "That's the word," recalls the first line of the Gospel of John, "In the beginning was the word, and the word was God." However, in Wright's universe, the word is not God but description. Such a configuration means a decidedly different role for the poet. It's not so much God that speaks the world into being or even defines the world but the individual capable of description. That leaves the poet in a pretty good place. Indeed, in Stevens' wonderful poem "Description without Place," he begins section four with an aphorism worthy of Wright, one that brings home the idea that description carries an element of apotheosis: "Description is revelation." Like most of Stevens' assertions, this one proffers multiple meanings. On one hand, Stevens suggests that description is not a fixed endeavor, that it reveals itself over time. On the other hand, Stevens endows

What Do I Read Next?

- Editors Robert Bain and Joseph M. Flora explore both the changing and the traditional values of the American South in *Contemporary Poets, Dramatists, Essayists, and Novelists of the South* (1994). The book includes critical comments and personal glimpses of 50 southern writers and provides an excellent overview of the nuances of "southern" writing.

- Diane Jarvenpa's 1996 publication entitled *Divining the Landscape: Poems* is a splendid collection of poems reflecting this Finnish-American's love for the Minnesota landscape. She brings a remarkable sensibility to everyday subjects and also deals heavily with mother-daughter ties.

- Australian theologian Peter Jensen provides a unique Christian perspective in understanding man's place and purpose in the universe in *At the Heart of the Universe: The Eternal Plan of God* (1997). The book is written in an easy-to-understand literary style without a great deal of heavy-handed theological doctrine.

- Under the fun and provocative title *On Kissing, Tickling, and Being Bored: Psychoanalytic Essays on the Unexamined Life* (1993) author Adam Phillips presents a collection of essays focusing on issues rearely discussed in the field of psychoanalysis: kissing, worrying, risk, etc. He debunks the Socratic notion that the unexamined life is not worth living, asserting that good mental health depends on maintaining aspects of life that resist interpretation.

- *Christianity in Appalachia: Profiles in Regional Pluralism* (edited by Bill Leonard, 1999) brings together articles on the many religions represented by the "hill-folk" of the Appalachians. While many publications portray people from this region as simple and unsophisticated, this collection presents them as genuine, sincere believers in God who do not always fit the mold that the rest of society has created for them.

the act of description with a palpable holiness by linking it with God himself—a revealed deity. Thus, for both Stevens and Wright, the poetic act is a sacred act, one that turns the mundane into the divine.

For Wright and Stevens, the divine may not exist in heaven but on earth, which is to say that some may seek the divine not for purposes of praise but simply to engage it. It would seem, then, that for both poets, the first step toward this engagement is to desire it. Wright begins section two of "Black Zodiac" with a passage from St. Augustine:

Those who look for the Lord will cry out in praise
of him.
Perhaps. And perhaps not—dust and ashes though
we are,
Some will go wordlessly …

Wright suggests that we each look for divine out of different motivations. For him, looking does not equal praise. But, that's not a problem, for both Stevens and Wright, finding is not as important as looking. Indeed, both poets locate the divine in the act of desire itself. In "Description without Place," Stevens claims that description "is an expectation, a desire" and in "Primitive Like an Orb," he says that "The Lover, the believer and the poet. / Their words are chosen out of their desire." In the final moment, we may never actually find God, we may never experience the grand revelation. Thus, when we cannot count on the celestial, we can count on the terrestrial. We can count on language. Language, the ability to articulate, the description of the processes of life remains our most reliable avenue toward making sense of a senseless world. As Wright writes in "Black Zodiac."

The unexamined life's no different from the
examined life—
Unanswerable questions, small talk,
Unprovable theorems, long abandoned arguments—
You've got to write it all down.
Landscape or waterscape, light—length on
evergreen, dark sidebar
Of evening, you've got to write it down.

Simply thinking about the world is not enough. Our memories, our moments of insight and understanding, slip away from us like minutes and hours, like sunlight. Writing down the world, describing the internal landscape fixes your perception of the world in a medium we all share—language. Stevens would agree. It's all about articulation:

That's it. The lover writes, the believer hears,
The poet mumbles and the painter sees …
As a part, but part, but tenacious particle,
Of the skeleton of the ether, the total
Of letters, prophecies, perceptions, clods

Of color, the giant of nothingness, each one
And the giant ever changing, living in change.

This idea of change haunts Wright as well. Elsewhere in "Black Zodiac," he writes, "Mine is a brief voice, a still, brief voice / Unsubject to change or the will to change." According to James Longenbach, one of the best readers of twentieth-century American poetry, Wright's poetic style, his means of expression, put him in touch with both tangible and intangible experiences: "The possibility of change depends on what Wright calls 'celestial similes' or 'the slow dream of metaphor': Wright's style is the arc of his own salvation." Longenbach adroitly notes that Wright creates his mode of salvation through the poetic process; he understands that Wright changes the landscape from one of emptiness to one of possibility. To combat the "giant of nothingness," as Stevens would say, one must construct somethingness; one must call attention to the somethingness that is there as opposed to the nothingness that is not there. In section five of "Black Zodiac," Wright invokes Stevens' famous poem "The Snow Man" to underscore his system of belief-description: "Calligraphers of the disembodied, God's word-wards, / What letters will we illuminate? / Above us the atmosphere, / The nothing that's nowhere, signs on, and waits for our beck and call." For Stevens and Wright, there is little evidence that God resides in the atmosphere above us. For the modern and postmodern writer, God is an absence, but language, words, poems are a presence. They sustain us. Wright's question is a provocative one. In a world in which there are no monks creating illuminated manuscripts of sacred texts, we must make our own sacred text out of the world around us, the world mediated through language.

That we make not only the sacredness of the world but the world itself is the ultimate theme of both "Black Zodiac" and "Description without Place." How do we make these things? Out of words:

It is the theory of the word for those

For whom the word is the making of the world,
The buzzing world and lisping firmament.

It is a world of words to the end of it
In which nothing solid is its solid self
As, men make themselves their speech: the hard
     hidalgo
Lives in the mountains character of his speech;

According to Stevens, the word is the only solid thing in the world. What's more, the world issues forth from the word. We are nothing more than our speech. What we say of the world is part of what the world becomes. For Wright, the words desire us as much as we desire the words: "The letters undarken and come forth, / Your X and my X. / The letters undarken and come forth." The revelation that Stevens speaks of translates into letters for Wright. Instead of God revealing himself in a burning bush or in a flame in a cave, the divine comes to us in symbols, in letters, that we translate, through our own language, into the world itself.

Stevens and Wright are both difficult poets. There is no easy interpretation for "Black Zodiac," or, for that matter, for "Description without Place." In his poem, Stevens, more overtly than Wright, argues that the poet has the ability to do anything through description; he can even bring about "the invention of a nation in a phrase." To speak is to reveal. It is to utter the holy. For Wright, to speak is to make sense of the world. Without language, the world, our heads, the past, the future are a junkpile of words, a dark map with no markings. So connected to the external world is the poetic process, that both Wright and Stevens accord it elemental status: "Description is an element, like air or water." For the reader, the philosopher, the poet, the lover, and the believer, words are part and parcel of our world. They connect us not only with each other but with the divine and the idea of the divine. In fact, without them, the divine would not be the divine, merely the "nothing that's nowhere," waiting "for our beck and call" to reveal the divine and our world to each other.

Source: Dean Rader, in an essay for *Poetry for Students,* Gale, 2001.

Sources

Amazon, www.amazon.com (March 28, 2000).

CNN News, www.cnn.com (March 28, 2000).

The History Channel, www.historychannel.com (March 28, 2000).

Hosmer, Robert Ellis, Jr., Review of *Black Zodiac,* in *America,* Vol. 177, No. 20, December 20-27, 1997, p. 24.

Longenbach, James, "Between Soil and Stars," in *Nation,* April 14, 1997, pp. 27-30.

————, Review of *Black Zodiac,* in *The Nation,* April 14, 1997, pp. 27-31.

Stevens, Wallace, *Opus Posthumous,* Alfred A. Knopf, 1957.

———, *Wallace Stevens: The Collected Poems,* Random House, 1982.

Vendler, Helen, *The Music of What Happens: Poems, Poets, Critics,* Harvard University Press, 1988.

———, *Part of Nature, Part of Us: Modern American Poets,* Harvard University Press, 1980.

Wright, Charles, *Appalachia,* Farrar, Straus, and Giroux, 1998.

———, *Black Zodiac,* Farrar, Straus, and Giroux, 1997.

———, *Halflife: Improvisations and Interviews, 1977–87,* University of Michigan Press, 1988.

For Further Study

Stitt, Peter, *Uncertainty and Plenitude: Five Contemporary Poets,* University of Iowa Press, 1997.

Stitt is a noted critic and editor of the *Gettysburg Review.* In this book, he presents a very poignant study of five contemporary American poets: John Ashbery, Stephen Dobyns, Charles Simic, Gerald Stern, and Charles Wright. He concentrates on the poets' writing strategies, subject matter, cultural issues, and artistic strengths and weaknesses.

Wright, Charles, *Chickamauga,* Farrar, Straus, and Giroux, 1995.

This is the first book in the "triptych" which contains *Black Zodiac.* In it, Wright sets the stage for the issues he ponders in the subsequent two collections, concluding that what he has learned in the 30 years since he began writing is "not communicable."

———, *The Grave of the Right Hand,* Wesleyan University Press, 1970.

The is Wright's first full-length collection of poetry, and it demonstrates an early attention to the "architecture" of a book. The poems are shorter and more precise than those in his later work, but there is still an emphasis placed on overall structure and connections between the poems included.

The Bustle in a House

"The Bustle in a House," first published as "Aftermath" in Dickinson's posthumous first collection, *Poems by Emily Dickinson,* in 1890, was probably written in 1866. In this poem, Dickinson writes about the brief, busy, suspended period of time between the death of a loved one and the private grief that follows. It is during this time that the bereaved must busy themselves with mundane, or ordinary, tasks in order to get through the experience without emotional collapse. Though it may seem absurd to clean and straighten a house where a loved one has passed away the night before, Dickinson describes this behavior almost as if it were a ceremonial rite. On a practical level, these activities are necessary because friends and neighbors will come calling to the house to pay their last respects to the deceased and they will be comforted by cleanliness and order. On a spiritual level, these activities are cathartic, or emotionally cleansing, because they allow the bereaved some time to prepare themselves for the real work: living the rest of their lives without the loved one.

Emily Dickinson

1890

Author Biography

Dickinson was born in Amherst, Massachusetts, in 1830 and lived there all her life. Her grandfather was the founder of Amherst College, and her father Edward Dickinson was a lawyer who served as the treasurer of the college. He also held vari-

Emily Dickinson

zine. Over the years Dickinson sent nearly one hundred of her poems for his criticism, and he became a sympathetic adviser and confidant, but he never published any of her poems. Dickinson's isolation further increased when her father died unexpectedly in 1874 and her mother suffered a stroke that left her an invalid. Dickinson and her sister provided her constant care until her death in 1882. Dickinson was diagnosed in 1886 as having Bright's disease, a kidney dysfunction that resulted in her death in May of that year.

Poem Text

The Bustle in a House
The Morning after Death
Is solemnest of industries
Enacted upon Earth—

The Sweeping up the Heart   5
And putting Love away
We shall not want to use again
Until Eternity.

ous political offices. Her mother Emily Norcross Dickinson was a quiet and frail woman. Dickinson went to primary school for four years and then attended Amherst Academy from 1840 to 1847 before spending a year at Mount Holyoke Female Seminary. Her education was strongly influenced by Puritan religious beliefs, but Dickinson did not accept the teachings of the Unitarian church attended by her family and remained agnostic throughout her life. Following the completion of her education, Dickinson lived in the family home with her parents and younger sister Lavinia, while her elder brother Austin and his wife Susan lived next door. She began writing verse at an early age, practicing her craft by rewriting poems she found in books, magazines, and newspapers. During a trip to Philadelphia in the early 1850s, Dickinson fell in love with a married minister, the Reverend Charles Wadsworth; her disappointment in love may have brought about her subsequent withdrawal from society. Dickinson experienced an emotional crisis of an undetermined nature in the early 1860s. Her traumatized state of mind is believed to have inspired her to write prolifically: in 1862 alone she is thought to have composed over three hundred poems. In that same year, Dickinson initiated a correspondence with Thomas Wentworth Higginson, the literary editor of the *Atlantic Monthly* maga-

Poem Summary

Lines 1-2:

On the morning after a loved one has died, the house of the deceased is full of so much activity that it forms a surprising contrast to the lifeless corpse that would have been laid out in the parlor or elsewhere in the home in Dickinson's day. The word "bustle" is used brilliantly here, for it can mean an excited activity or a violent commotion. Indeed, the aftermath, or consequences, of death are almost always harsh and violent. In line 2, it is no accident that Dickinson used a homonym for "mourning." Mourning is the outward, customary expression of grief which Dickinson will elaborate upon in the poem.

Lines 3-4:

This "bustle" mentioned in the first line of the poem is "solemn." "Solemn," too, has several meanings. It can mean serious, or it can mean sacred and ceremonial. There is reason to believe that Dickinson intended both meanings, for she uses it to describe "industries," a word with the archaic meaning of "diligence." "Diligence," in turn, can also mean "assiduity," or pious devotion. In these lines, the spiritual and the practical are intertwined

Media Adaptations

- *Poems and Letters of Emily Dickinson: Unabridged,* Caedmon Audio, 1992.

because the sacred rituals and ceremonies performed for the dead are the closest that most people "upon Earth" will ever get to the mystery of immortality before passing away themselves.

Lines 5-6:

In these lovely lines, Dickinson uses housekeeping as a metaphor for the process of letting go of the dead. The heart, broken to pieces by grief, must be swept up and hidden from sight. Love, like memory, must be stored in a safe place. Order must be created to counteract the chaos of death. On a more literal level, it is true that many people, when they are in crisis, turn to thoughtless tasks like housework in order to maintain control of the situation. In fact, Dickinson plays with language by using the "heart," a word similar to "hearth," or fireplace, which would have needed to be swept out before the mourners arrived. The house must be straightened up in order for the family of the deceased to receive visitors, but every home is full of evidence left behind by the person who has died.

Lines 7-8:

These final lines escape being melodramatic because of Dickinson's use of the verb phrase, "shall not want to use." After great loss, many grief-stricken human beings react by vowing that they will not love again if love is inevitably lost, and loss brings such great suffering. Others hide their love away out of a profound sense of loyalty to the deceased, swearing that they live only with the memory of their lost love until the grave. Both of these reactions, though somewhat irrational, are an important part of the process of grief for many people. Finally, the idea that we will all be reunited with our deceased loved ones in the afterlife ("Eternity") has been a comfort to the bereaved since the beginning of time.

Themes

Death

Readers with just a passing familiarity with the Dickinson's work, including "The Bustle in a House" often come to the conclusion that the poet was "obsessed with death." Certainly death and dying are frequent subjects in Dickinson's more than 1,750 poems, but to accuse her of such a fixation is to underestimate her contributions to American literature. Many of her male poetic contemporaries are equally concerned with death, but have not been thought to be so eccentric on account of it.

There are reasons why nearly 600 of Dickinson's poems to have to do with death and dying. First, as the descendent of Calvinists Dickinson grew up in a culture that viewed mortal life as a temporary interlude before the moment of death and judgement, and, one hopes, ascension to heaven. Though she rejected her family's strict religious views, Dickinson would have certainly absorbed the attitudes. Second, death was common in Dickinson's life. People died of common illnesses and in childbirth with a frequency that is hard for modern readers to imagine. She lost three young friends growing up and was greatly affected by their deaths. Finally, Dickinson's great strength as a poet is her interest in probing and describing moments in the human psyche, and the moment of death is without a doubt the most dramatic of all possibilities.

In "The Bustle in a House," Dickinson depicts the state of a household after someone has died. The pairing of death and domesticity is a common theme in Dickinson's poems. In the poem she describes the noticeable escalation of activity, the bustle, that follows death. In the nineteenth century these activities would include preparing the corpse for burial, packing up belongings, and preparing for guests. Such domestic activities are important to her exploration of the dimensions of death, "solemnest of industries."

Domestic Sphere

That many of Dickinson's poems employ imagery of domestic activity is not surprising: she lived virtually her entire life inside her house in Amherst, Massachusetts. She had some household help with the chores, but she still devoted more time than contemporary readers can imagine to her domestic duties. Her letters often reveal an impatience with and a distaste for the routines of housework, but her poems show how she came to see this kind

Topics for Further Study

- Write a long poem describing exactly what the "bustle" consists of, what actions are taken the morning after death. Use specific, clear details.

- Compare the emotion in this poem to Walt Whitman's "O Captain! My Captain!" Whitman's poem was written at almost the same time as Dickinson's. What do the two poems have in common?

- What do you think the author means by "putting love away"? Is this idea realistic or hopeful?

of work more abstractly, more metaphorically, as a defense against the death and decay that always threatens to overwhelm human beings. Critic Cynthia Griffin Wolf argues that "a reader must understand the routines of housework to appreciate" the poem. This is "no daily chore of dusting off and throwing out," Wolf continued. Instead it is *seasonal* work with *cyclical* implications, the careful folding up and putting aside of summer or winter clothes that will not be used again until a new year has begun. In other words, sweeping up and putting away provides an emotional outlet for the speaker and gives her the chance to contemplate the possibility of an afterlife. She would know from years of experience that what is stored away is usually brought back out in another season.

Style

"The Bustle in a House," is written in two quatrains, or stanzas of four lines each. As in the majority of Dickinson's works, the rhythm of the poem is rooted in iambs, regularly recurring two-syllable segments in which the first syllable is unstressed and the second is stressed. In the first, second and fourth lines of each quatrain, Dickinson uses a three-foot metric line called an iambic trimeter ("tri" meaning three). In the third lines, she changes to a four-foot line, called iambic tetrame-

ter ("tetra" meaning four). This pattern—two lines of six syllables, followed by one of eight, then one of six—is called the short meter. It is one of the English hymn meters familiar to her from childhood.

In the 17th and 18th centuries, common English nouns and other words were often capitalized. Dickinson adopted this out-of-fashion form of capitalization to her own purposes and in this poem applies it in "Bustle," "House," "Morning," "Death," "Earth," "Sweeping," "Heart," "Love," and "Eternity." She does this, perhaps, because her poetry is a celebration of the exact, perfect word, and capitalization can be used to highlight the intensity of meaning.

She punctuates the poem by separating the two quatrains with a dash, her signature mark. Here, the dashes seem to divide the poem between a general, universal topic and specific, personal examples.

Historical Context

Women's Lives

The truth about Dickinson's life in Amherst has been both intentionally and unintentionally distorted in literary and popular accounts. The basic facts are indisputable: she lived almost her entire life in one house, she never married nor seriously entertained any proposals; and she left behind more than 1,700 poems hand-bound and sewn. The myth of the lonely spinster whose delicate nature poems emerged from her broken heart is a modern-day fiction, however. In order to separate Dickinson the artist from Dickinson the myth, it is important to understand why she would have chosen the life she did, given what was available to her at the time.

As the female child in an old and very prominent family with a great many connections, Dickinson was groomed and educated to assume the roles of wife and mother, and would have had certain civic responsibilities as well. At the very least, she would have raised and educated her children, run the household and supervise the staff, and support her husband in his professional life. In the nineteenth century, however, these roles were much more onerous than they seem to readers now. She would have had almost no control over when and how many children to bear and would risk death every time she delivered. She would have spent part of every day dressing to go out and then calling on the old and sick, visiting with members of the

Compare & Contrast

- **Late Nineteenth Century:** The Civil War, as well as bacterial infection and widespread diseases such as consumption, makes death a familiar part of daily life in the United States.

  Today: Through live news reports from both network and cable television, Americans viewers are presented with images of death and tragedy from around the world with an immediacy previously inconceivable.

- **Late Nineteenth Century:** New Englander death rituals take place in the home, with the dying being surrounded by friends and family in household rooms temporarily made into death chambers. There, the company awaited signs of the dying's heavenly salvation, received last requests and wills, and witnessed the repentance of sins during the last rites sacrament. The faithful dying sometimes gave witness to the approach, then presence of heavenly salvation. For the onlookers, contact with the dead and dying is considered an important part of living, in that it reminds them of the temporality of the body and the potential passage of the spirit into heavenly eternity.

  Today: In most cases, the dying are removed from their homes and cared for in specialized facilities such as hospitals, nursing homes, and hospices. In all cases—and by law—corpses are removed from houses and prepared for burial by mortuary specialists. Even in instances in which the dead are viewed postmortem, their bodies are carefully prepared and doctored. In the eyes of the general public, contact with the dead and dying is seen—both rationally and irrationally—as dangerous, harmful, and disturbing.

- **1830-1855:** Transcendentalism, an American philosophical and literary movement born in New England, is at its height. An outgrowth of Romanticism, the transcendentalist attitude opposed middle-class commercialism and looked for evidence of the divine in the world while conceiving very liberally of godliness. It gave priority to personal intuition, organized mysticism, and a broad optimism about human nature.

  Today: While many people espouse views of divinity and have faith in a transcendent mover of the world we see, the domain of the mysterious—concerning aspects of everything from causes of death to weather patterns to human behavior—in increasingly collapsed by advances in human sciences.

---

church, and generally fulfilling civic and social responsibilities. Even if she could have found the time and the solitude to read, contemplate, and write, her work would likely have been seen as completely unseemly, even downright dangerous, for a woman.

Under the circumstances it makes sense that a young woman with towering artistic ambitions, like Dickinson, would chose solitude. She was fortunate that she had some money of her own and did not have to marry for support or protection, which would have been true for a woman without her social status. Dickinson gave up the chance to marry and have a family; in exchange, she had the independence, time, and solitude to devote herself to her writing. She was not an isolated and heartbroken eccentric, having enjoyed many correspondents and a dear relationship with her sister-in-law.

Poetic Tradition

Dickinson's unconventional way of life and her poetry still strikes readers today as daring and original. Earlier critics have suggested that she published so few of her poems while she was alive because she had no intention of ever releasing them. More recent scholarship suggests that Dickinson regarded herself as a serious poet and imagined an audience for her work beyond her primary reader, who was her sister-in-law.

Dickinson was an avid reader and was well aware of the kinds of poetry popular in her day. She also knew, therefore, how little hers resembled it. Popular poetry of the time was sentimental and genteel. Not even the radical transcendentalists (Ralph Waldo Emerson, Henry David Thoreau, and others) produced much poetry that looked or sounded new. Women's poetry at the time was even more sentimental, describing emotional states or re-iterating conventional behavior. Dickinson's radical new lines and use of dashes would have been jarring enough, but her unsentimental questioning, and her often erotic imagery, would have offended some editors and readers alike, if she could even have reached them. It's likely that Dickinson knew she would be wasting her time in battling the literary establishment, especially as a woman poet; even if she succeeded in getting her work into print, it would bring unwanted attention that would distract her from the more important task of writing more poems.

Critical Overview

Harold Monro, a British poet and editor whose criticism of Dickinson is included in *The Recognition of Emily Dickinson: Selected Criticism Since 1890,* argues that Dickinson has been "overrated," claiming that she was "partially deaf [and] mostly dumb, to the art of poetry." He goes on to point out how her poems are riddled with mistakes that a better editor would have noticed and corrected. In spite of this negative opinion, he does offer a relatively positive reaction to "The Bustle in a House," writing that the poem is "clumsy enough, but redeemed entirely by a magic of pathos and loveliness."

In contrast, W. D. Howells, writing in his *W. D. Howells as Critic,* offers more sympathetic critique of Dickinson's poetic talent. Howells writes of her poetry 's "rarity" and "singular worth" in his 1891 review of her first collection of poems, posthumously. Howells' enthusiastic opinion garnered respect for Dickinson's writing by contrasting the negative opinions held by many of his contemporaries. Howells describes "The Bustle in a House" and poems like it as "terribly unsparing … but true to the grave and certain as mortality."

Criticism

Sarah Madsen Hardy

Madsen Hardy has a doctorate in English literature and is a freelance writer and editor. In the following essay, she discusses the metaphors in

"The Bustle in a House" in the context of Dickinson's life and culture.

Emily Dickinson's poem "The Bustle in a House" is a poem of mourning. Unlike typical poems of mourning, called elegies, however, readers do not learn from Dickinson's poem specifically who died and who is mourning. Dickinson instead refers to the activities in a household where a death has taken place and to the feelings of the deceased's loved ones. At first glance, the poem may seem quite simple—a description of how, on the morning after a death, the living begin to confront the love they still feel for the departed. However, it uses the unconventional metaphor of housework to describe the process of mourning. In this essay I will explore the cultural and personal contexts of this metaphor in order to shed light on Dickinson's original concept of the relationship between life and death.

Dickinson was singularly fascinated with death, both the experience of dying itself, and how loss is experienced among the living. Death is one of the most prominent themes in her large body of work. This can be attributed to the fact that the mystery of death raises questions of what it is to live, to be, to have a soul or consciousness—questions at the very center of Dickinson's poetic inquiry. But it also reflects the fact that death was far more closely woven into the texture of everyday life in the mid-nineteenth-century when Dickinson wrote than it is today. Because antibiotics had not yet been discovered, people frequently died from sicknesses that we now consider mild. Death in childbirth and early childhood were common. Furthermore, less medical intervention was available at each stage of physical decline. The majority of all deaths took place at home, instead of in hospitals, hospices, and nursing homes; thus, people in Dickinson's time were much more likely to witness the death of their family members. Death was an experience that was closer at hand for Dickinson and her contemporaries than it is for most Americans today—an experience associated with, rather than divorced from, the intimate setting of home.

Dickinson witnessed a number of deaths in her lifetime, describing them from the point of view of an attendant in poems such as "The Last Night that She Lived." The closing stanzas of this poem describe the dying woman's moment of passing and the actions and feelings of her intimates immediately afterward as they handle and then contemplate her body. It reads, "She mentioned, and forgot— / Then lightly as a Reed / Bent to the Water, struggled scarce— / Consented, and was dead— / And We—We placed the Hair— / And drew the head erect— / And then an awful leisure was / Belief to regulate—." In other poems like "The Sun Kept Setting—Setting—Still" and "I Heard a Fly Buzz When I Died" Dickinson describes death even more daringly and intimately from the point of view of the dying person, both during and after the moment of death. The latter, one of her most famous poems, is striking because it interposes a buzzing fly upon the dying speaker's grand spiritual passage to the afterlife. At the moment of "that last Onset—when the King / Be witnessed—in the Room—" it is this common household pest whose presence the dying person feels, rather than that of God. Dickinson juxtaposes the great theological concepts of mortality and eternity with a mundane detail from daily life. "While what is expected [at the moment of death] is the storm of dissolution, the sublime moment of passage," wrote Judith Farr in *The Passion of Emily Dickinson,* instead is an awareness of a fly, "its stupid aimlessness a suggestion of the puzzlement that is life as well as its homely sweetness."

The scene of dying at home is important to Dickinson's representations of death throughout her body of work. Indeed, it can be argued that Dickinson's "image of house or home, touching the tangible and imaginative worlds at once, is perhaps the most penetrating and comprehensive figure she employs," as Jean McClure does in *Emily Dickinson and the Image Home.* McClure elaborates that Dickinson uses images of the house and home to "treat all of her most pressing concerns, concerns which relate to her place in the universe. *Home* thus reflects her inner landscape … a sensitivity to space dependent on both personal and social factors." McClure refers to women's role in nineteenth American culture as inextricably tied to domesticity, as well as to Dickinson's personal history—she lived as a recluse, seldom venturing from her family home, from her early twenties until her death at age fifty-five.

Death poses difficult philosophical questions for all who contemplate it. Most people rely on some culturally prevalent form of explanation, such as science or religion, for death's mysteries. However, Dickinson was in critical dialogue with the dominant ideas of death circulating in her day. Her poetry is steeped in Protestant theology and the rhythm of Protestant hymns. But Dickinson sets her poetic vision of death against the religious doctrine representing God in authoritative, impersonal, and patriarchal (male authority) terms that she would

> *For Dickinson … home is, foremost, a metaphor for the self."*

have heard preached at church on Sundays. Another culturally dominant understanding of death to which Dickinson responded in her poetry was derived from sentimental literature—a form of fiction and poetry that was wildly popular in the nineteenth century. Popular sentimental literature was predominantly written by women from whom Dickinson was eager to distinguish herself. As Maria Magdalena Farland described it in her article, "That Tritest/Brightest Truth," sentimental literature renders death less threatening by using "human emotions to symbolize divine love [and] using homey scenes of life on earth to represent the less-familiar prospect of life-after-death." Just as Dickinson's poetry uses ideas and aesthetics from the strict Protestant religious culture in which she was steeped, it also uses ideas and aesthetics from the dominant popular culture of sentimental literature. But, "while sentimental fiction and poetry overwhelmingly tended to affirm the value of such comparisons" between home and the afterlife, Farland argues, "Dickinson's poems contest and often negate them."

"The Bustle in a House," as in "I Heard a Fly Buzz," poses large spiritual questions pertaining to mortality using modest, homely imagery—a deliberate and provocative juxtaposition. The first verb in the poem, "bustle," has none of the grand solemnity associated with death and formal, ritualized mourning. Bustle is the somewhat trivial action that is associated with the many small necessities of everyday life, necessities that do not cease for the living even when a death has just taken place. While men—notably, religious leaders—were traditionally in charge of the spiritual preparations for the soul's passing, it was women's work to deal with the practical and logistical preparations. Thus, Dickinson refers to the morning-after bustle as the "solemnest of industries," characterizing it as part of women's realm of home industry or housework. As in "I Heard a Fly Buzz," this poem situates death in the home, dramatizing a confrontation between the seemingly meaningless activities of life and the specter of a final Meaning endowed by death. The

What Do I Read Next?

- *A Room of One's Own* by Virginia Wolf makes the argument that women cannot be great writers until they create domestic space in order to read and write and think.

- *Diary of Emily Dickinson* (1993) by Jamie Fuller and illustrated by Marlene McLoughlin is a fictional account of the poet's inner life and includes several poems written in Dickinson's style by Fuller, herself a poet.

bustle that opens the poem is a counterpoint to the weighty word, "Eternity," with which it ends. The poem is filled with similar contrasts. It is set on "the Morning after Death," setting up a contrast between the night, with its associated darkness and surrender of consciousness, and the day that inevitably follows—and with it, life's mundane but unstoppable flow.

In the second stanza, Dickinson extends her central metaphor. After a death in the house, life goes on with "the sweeping up the Heart / And putting Love Away." Thus, it becomes clear that she is not just talking about the general cleaning and straightening up of house that continues to be necessary even after the occurrence of a death within its walls, or even the more intimate and dramatic preparations of the body. Rather, she uses such activity to symbolize the internal, emotional activity of mourning. In "The Bustle in a House" she describes a housekeeping of the heart that must go on even after it has experienced a great loss. For Dickinson—who lived an adventuresome life of the mind between the same four walls of the house where she was born—home is, foremost, a metaphor for the self. Homes and houses in her poetry represent different dimensions of selfhood-consciousness, the mind, imagination, and spirit. To die is, then, to surrender the only known home of the self, rather than to "come home" to God, as the prevalent theological metaphor would have it. Witnessing a death is a partial loss of self for Dickinson; it requires a setting aside of a piece of the

self—one's love for the deceased—until "Eternity," a concept impossibly abstract for the homebound, grieving heart to comprehend.

"The Bustle in a House" does not offer the reassurances of either Home in an all-powerful God or those of a homey afterlife that is not so different from the world we know. In the poem death is simultaneously an intimately familiar event and one of awesome mystery. What is familiar and homelike is the love of the deceased that the living carry with them. Eternity is, by definition, not-home, a radically other and unknown place. The living are stuck in the metaphorical houses of themselves, in a place or state radically disconnected from Eternity—disconnected except for the ties of love for the dead that the living must struggle to "put away."

Source: Sarah Madsen Hardy, in an essay for *Poetry for Students,* Gale, 2001.

Elisabeth Piedmont-Marton

Elisabeth Piedmont-Marton teaches American literature and directs the writing center at a college in Texas. In this essay she discusses Dickinson's use of domestic imagery in her poems about death and dying.

Readers who encounter only a handful of Dickinson's poems remark how frequently she writes about death and dying. Her interest in the moment of death is not surprising to critics who recognize, like Adrienne Rich noted, that "she is *the* American poet whose work consisted in exploring states of psychic extremity." Less critical attention has been paid to domestic life and work, another persistent theme in her poetry.

These activities, which include sweeping, dusting and other household labors, have been overlooked for a couple of reasons. First, early critics belonging to the male literary establishment would have read her use of domestic imagery as an indicator of her femininity and reclusiveness. Then, the first feminist critics of the 1970s devoted little attention to her domestic imagery because its identification with "women's work" made their project of reconstructing her as a feminist more difficult. More recent critics, primarily feminists, however, understand her use of domestic imagery in more subtle ways. Cynthia Griffin Wolff, for example, notes that "many of the poems that give voice to despair most forcefully and poignantly are strung together with this stabilizing imagery from the domestic world." "The Bustle in the House," together with another poem, "How many times these low feet staggered" reveal Dickinson's deft and layered use of domestic imagery in poems that also concern death.

That the moment of death seems often less momentous than ordinary is one of the most disturbing and powerful characteristics of Dickinson's poems. Where one expects the sublime, she offers the mundane. Instead of grand passion, she delivers quiet rumination. In both of these poems, for example, the finality of death is set against the insistent cycle of housework. Dickinson uses the image of housework to suggest ways that humans can stem the tide of decay that death signifies. The routine labors of tending to the house and family, Dickinson suggests, anchors women and keeps them from despair.

In "How many times have these low feet staggered," Dickinson describes a housewife after her death. The first stanza wonders how many times has this humble woman failed or stumbled under the burden of all the work she has to do. There can be no answer, however, because only the "soldered mouth can tell," and it will never open again. No one else knows because no one else paid attention. The housework, like the woman, was invisible. In the second stanza the poem insists that the woman be seen and touched. It reminds observers that her now cold forehead was frequently hot with exertion or fever, and it dares those present to touch her hair and handle her fingers. The last line of the stanza can be read as a rebuke to those who still see her only as the embodiment of work, reminding them that in death her fingers "never a thimble-more-shall wear." As is often the case with a Dickinson poem, the final stanza destabilizes the meaning of the poem that had developed to that point.

In contrast to the rather oblivious and callous human viewers of the "low" woman's body, the household "spirits" in the second stanza are quite animated and attentive. On the occasion of the housewife's death, they stage a kind of celebration. Flies buzz, the sun shows off the proudly speckled window, and cobwebs fear no retribution. The woman can take a day off and be "indolent," or lazy, pampering, self-indulgent, only in death. Dickinson uses housework to signify two things. First, the housewife's work represents the human instinct to fight against death and decay, however futile the battle. As soon as she "staggers" for the last time, death defeats her and her efforts. At the same time, however, it's hard to miss the celebratory note in the last stanza, as if the poet secretly wants to endorse the victory of dust and finger-

> *That the moment of death seems often less momentous than ordinary is one of the most disturbing and powerful characteristics of Dickinson's poems."*

prints over drudgery. What if, she seems to say, the forces of entropy—represented by cobwebs and fingerprints—have always been in sympathy with the housewife? What if they're not mocking her, but are instead rejoicing because she is finally liberated from the burden under which she has staggered for too long?

The Bustle in a House also takes housework and death as its subject. In this poem, Dickinson describes the escalation of activity in a household where someone has just died. In this poem, however, the housewife is absent. In the first of the two stanzas, the "bustle" is the subject of the sentence. The impersonal effect is intensified by the Dickinson's word choices. She describes the deeply personal and intimate acts of cleaning up after death as "industries." Even more striking, however, is her location of this solemnest of industries not in a particular house, not even indoors, really, but "on Earth." This is an unusual gesture for Dickinson: in most poems she consistently chooses the particular over the general, the concrete over the abstract, and her poems tend to take place in enclosed spaces.

The second stanza continues to focus on the act and not the person doing it. The subject of its single sentence is two gerunds (verbs that represent uncompleted action), "sweeping" and "putting away." In a marvelous visual pun, Dickinson allows a glimpse of the material reality of this kind of "industry" in the line "The Sweeping up the Heart." She knows that reader's eyes will mistake Heart for Hearth, because that's the thing housewives ordinarily sweep. The moment of confusion this causes allows both meanings to hang in the air and asserts the deep connection between both kinds of women's work, the care of both hearths and hearts. In the poem's last two lines, Dickinson finally introduces a pronoun. But in the choice of "We," she nevertheless keeps the housewife hidden from view while insisting beneath the surface that the reader make the housewife present. The poem's concluding lines suggest that the one doing the sweeping and putting away does so for the benefit of others, the "we" who will not want to use them "until Eternity."

Dickinson scholar Griffin notes that "the speaker's deep insight is that this is no daily chore of dusting off and throwing out. Instead it is *seasonal* work with *cyclical* implications, the careful folding and putting aside of summer or winter clothes we shall not 'want to use again' until a new year has begun." By suggesting that the rituals of grief are like the rituals of domestic duty, Dickinson offers a measure of consolation: death is a stage in a cycle, not an end; love will return in time. But the poem strains against its own imagery and invites readers to reconsider housework as much as it illuminates the cyclical nature of death and grief. The result is a poem that uses housework as a metaphor, but which also distances itself from the work itself and she who would do it.

This attitude toward housework reflects what we know about Dickinson herself, who often expressed resentment at the feminization and futility of domestic duty. According to Ellen Louise Hart and Martha Nell Smith, scholars who edited Dickinson's intimate letters to her sister-in-law, the two women shared a resentment toward housework because it impinged on their intellectual, artistic, and private lives. Hart and Smith assert that Susan Huntington Dickinson spoke for both women when she wrote to Emily about the burden of "the Spring siege of sewing" that had put her "quite in despair." In the letter she complains, "I find no time to read or think, and but little to walk—but just go revolving round a spool of 'Coat's cotton' [thread] as if it were the grand centre of mental and moral life."

Dickinson and her sister-in-law share the daring view that housework—traditional and compulsory women's work—is an enemy of "mental and moral life" of the independent and creative lives they would choose. Because she never married, Dickinson was able to give to her art much of the time and energy she would have been compelled to devote to sweeping and putting away if she had had a family. When housework appears in Dickinson's poems, therefore, it must be understood as more than a handy metaphor. As Wolff argues, domestic imagery does act as a stabilizing and grounding force in Dickinson's despairing poems about death. But metaphors work both ways, illuminating and complicating both terms in the pair. "The Bustle in a House," and others like it, can also be read as poems about housework in which death is a metaphor. For Dickinson, who used domestic imagery in so many poems, housework was no minor annoyance. It represented the entire complex of social and economic constraints under which women labored and which both literally and figuratively deprived them of intellectual and artistic opportunity.

Source: Elisabeth Piedmont-Marton, in an essay for *Poetry for Students,* Gale, 2001.

Michael Lake

Lake holds an MA in English and is a poet residing in California. In the following essay, Lake examines Dickinson's use of the "exact" word and how her style infuses her poetry with its "subtle power."

Among people who really know little of Emily Dickinson's work, there are two predominant prejudices: her poetry is morbidly preoccupied with death, and her style is grammatically and syntactically confusing. As with some prejudice, there is at least some basis for making these complaints. Dickinson was at once fascinated with and appalled by death. Out of her own misgivings about the meaning of life and death, she thought often and deeply about the mysteries of death's seeming extinction of the self. As much as she longed for the comfort of traditional Christian belief or Romantic pantheist mysticism, she found she lacked the ability to believe with simple faith in either. She was, in other words, the consummate nineteenth century agnostic. But she still struggled ceaselessly with the ultimate contradiction death seemed to pose to life. And she was also a keen student of human behavior, having observed death and dying and their effects on all concerned many times first-hand. And as far as Dickinson's linguistic peculiarities go, her style was unique and arose from her self-developed style of poetic meditation. Early exposed to Webster's dictionary and his unusual linguistic theories about the relationship between verbs and nouns, Dickinson spent her life searching for the "exact word" to express her insights into the human condition.

In fact, the magic of Dickinson's poetry lies in its ability to say so much with so few words. She can conjure up an entire scene with a single noun and tell a whole story in a mere phrase. In fact, her work is highly prized for its crystalline compactness in Japan, where haiku reigns supreme. Even in translation, her poetry comes across as almost native to the Japanese. Understanding Dickinson's technique of using select words and phrases to elicit a scene or to penetrate to the core of human experience helps us to appreciate such a tidy gem as "The Bustle in a House" with a sense of profound wonder. There are absolutely no wasted words in this short poem! Each reveals the depths of an emotional experience that we who live in the twenty-first century seldom encounter. Much in the tradition of the meditation poetry that Dickinson so admired in George Herbert, a seventeenth-century Metaphysical poet, "The Bustle in a House" meditates on the figures of a "grief delayed" in compressed language, syntactical "elision," and choice imagery. It is a poetic achievement that in many ways anticipates Imagism and other modern poetic movements because of its use of single words and phrases to tell its story through pictures that reveal so much about the human condition with an economy of language.

Today dying is often hidden from us, obscured behind the facade of high-tech "life-support" systems in alien clinical environments. And death is disguised, cosmetically "sanitized," and made unreal in corporate "funeral parlors." But in Dickinson's day, death was "up close and personal," an entirely domestic affair. The dying often remained in their own beds at home during their illness and later "lay in state" in the family's front room or parlor. Given the tightness of living quarters at the time and the socially required Puritan ethic of self-control, grieving survivors in Dickinson's social circle often had nowhere to "hide" emotionally from their inward torment. But according to thanatologists, the psychologists who study the phenomena of death and dying, denial is usually the first of many stages in the grieving process in most cultures anyway. It is logical, then, that retreat into the everyday details of domestic life would be, especially for women of that era, the safest place to hide from the pain of losing a loved one.

Indeed, Dickinson creates an image of quick and efficient domesticity in the poem's very fist line, "The Bustle in a House." The repeated sibilants in "Bustle" and "House," occurring in the first and third stressed syllables of the trimeter line, onomatopoeically produce the swishing sounds of skirts and petticoats moving swiftly about the house. And the second line immediately discloses the reason for all this activity by locating its time and circumstance, "The morning after Death." No-

> *She can conjure up an entire scene with a single noun and tell a whole story in a mere phrase."*

tice, however, that the circumstance under which the "Bustle" occurs ("after Death") and the time at which it occurs ("The morning") are really the same because "morning" homophonically echoes "mourning," the real circumstance under which the housekeeping takes place. The "Bustle," therefore, is part of the "mourning" due to the "Death" of the beloved.

But the third and fourth lines of the poem actually exalt the housework beyond the pale of merely mundane labor and simple psychological denial, asserting that it "Is solemnest of industries / Enacted upon Earth." With characteristic irony, Dickinson plays with the multiple meanings of words in the dictionary. Consulting Random House's *Unabridged Dictionary* (Second Edition), we discover that cleaning house is aptly named an "industry" in this line, for it is indeed an ancient "systematic work or labor," traditionally performed by women. But "industry" also means "energetic, devoted activity … ; diligence." As such, it implies "application, effort, assiduity, [and] industriousness." Dickinson, of course, had all these meanings in mind. But as an industrious effort performed in dedication to the dead, this particular housework reveals an assiduity that approaches spiritual devotion. By calling it the "solemnest of industries," Dickinson also invokes an older meaning of "solemn" to portray this house cleaning as a "sacred," even a "ceremonial," activity. In fact, the choice of the word "Enacted" completes the valorization of housework from "just woman's work" to a sacramental office of religious devotion.

But note that at the end of the first stanza, we find one of Dickinson's characteristic dashes. Usually used to slow the reading of her poetry's hymn meter for verbal emphasis, it acts syntactically here to list the contents of the "solemnest of industries" enumerated in the last stanza. Part of the "Bustle in a House / The morning after Death" lies in "The Sweeping up the Heart." In this, Dickinson plays with the similarity in spelling between "hearth" and "heart," for sweeping up the hearth was an onerous chore too often performed by women during the nineteenth century. In sweeping up the ashes of the fireplace, the grieving one is actually sweeping up the pieces of her burnt out and broken heart. Of course, along with sweeping comes the folding up of linens for storage in cedar chests, but here the mourner is also folding up "And putting Love away / We shall not want to use again / Until Eternity." Shutting away one's love for the deceased with such utter finality is a sign of the state of psychological denial mentioned earlier. But Dickinson's poem is a verbal snapshot of that precarious time after the personal disaster of a loved one's death before those suffering from it can integrate its trauma into their lives and get beyond their pain. There is no reason to believe, however, that the grieving will stop at this stage and not proceed further towards healing. Beyond the scope of this poem's dramatic vignette, there is still a chance this love will be opened up again when the mourner is able to stand love's ultimate loss in death.

The fact is that Dickinson's economy of language and syntactical compression empower her poetry to expose so much about the nature of human suffering. Many readers, as mentioned above, find her syntactical deletions and obtuse style confusing. We must understand, however, that Dickinson delighted in telling "all the Truth but tell[ing] it slant—" because in her opinion "Success in Circuit lies" (poem 1129, lines 1 and 2, in *The Complete Poems*). Telling all the truth "slant" entails an indirect approach that reveals rather than prosaically states the inner dimensions of life. It is a revelation that replicates for the reader Dickinson's own "evanescent" or fleeting insight into the "Truth" of the human condition. Dickinson's unusual syntax and her dependence upon isolated words and phrases to tell her story actually reveals the intensity of her thoughts and feelings, as well as the situation she is meditating upon. In fact, her

fusion of intellect and emotion accounts for her poetry's power to involve the reader in an act of consciousness, a direct apprehension of her vision. It is for this quality her poetry is admired in Japan, and it is this subtle power that makes "The Bustle in a House," for all its brevity, a true masterpiece among Dickinson's many exquisite poems.

Source: Michael Lake in an essay for *Poetry for Students,* Gale, 2001.

Sources

Griffin Wolff, Cynthia, "Emily Dickinson," in *The Columbia History of American Poetry,* Edited by Jay Parini, Columbia University Press, 1993.

Hart, Ellen Louise, and Martha Nell Smith, eds., *Open Me Carefully: Emily Dickinson's Intimate Letters to Susan Huntington Dickinson,* Paris Press, 1998.

Howells, W. D., "Emily Dickinson Announced," in *W. D. Howells as Critic,* Edited by Edwin H. Cady, Routledge & Kegan Paul, 1973, pp. 189-195.

Monro, Harold, "Emily Dickinson—Overrated," in *Recognition of Emily Dickinson: Selected Criticism Since 1890,* Edited by Caesar R. Blake and Carlton F. Wells, University of Michigan Press, 1966, pp. 121-122.

Rich, Adrienne, "Vesuvius at Home: The Power of Emily Dickinson," in *Critical Essays on Emily Dickinson,* G.K. Hall Press, 1984.

For Further Study

Ferlazzo, Paul, *Emily Dickinson,* G.K. Hall, 1976.
    Though a little old, this book provides an excellent introdcution to the life and work of Dickinson.

Griffin Wolff, Cynthia, *Emily Dickinson,* Knopf, 1986.
    This excellent and engaging biography looks at Dickinson's life from a femininst point of view and goes a long way toward ending the myth of the poet as a frustrated old maid.

The Cremation of Sam McGee

Robert W. Service
1907

Service wrote "The Cremation of Sam McGee" while working as a bank teller in the Yukon Territory several years after the gold rush of 1898. In addition to his writing, Service entertained by reciting the works of Rudyard Kipling, Ernest Lawrence Thayer ("Casey at the Bat"), as well as his own rhymes and ballads. He refused to call his writing "poetry" for fear people would think his pieces were too intellectual and they would not buy his books.

Along with "The Shooting of Dan McGrew" and other poems for the book *Songs of a Sourdough,* "The Cremation of Sam McGee" exhibits the elements that mark Service's style: internal rhymes, stressed rhythms, a dash of stereotypical Yukon *machismo* ("manliness"), ironic and slightly macabre humor, and a smattering of Klondike slang and jargon.

The poem tells a story of Cap (the speaker of the poem) and his mushing companion, Sam McGee. On a bitter cold Christmas Day, Sam exacts a promise from Cap: to cremate his remains when he dies. Cap finds Sam dead by nightfall the next day. Wanting to honor his friend's final request, Cap hauls the frozen body of Sam McGee across the frozen land. When they arrive at the shores of Lake LaBarge, Cap spies an abandoned ship jammed in the ice. After making his way to the ship, Cap uses planks and coal remnants to build a fire in the ship's boiler. Into this blaze Cap stuffs the body of Sam McGee. When Cap returns later to the ship, he opens the furnace door to find Sam

Robert W. Service

McGee sitting up and smiling. Sam tells Cap to
shut the door so as not to let in the cold.

Author Biography

Robert William Service was born on January 16,
1874, in Preston, Lancashire, England, to Robert
and Emily (Parker) Service. When Emily's father
died and left a bequest of ten thousand pounds, the
family moved to Glasgow, Scotland. The oldest of
ten children (Service had six brothers and three sisters), Service was sent to live with three maiden
aunts and his paternal grandfather. He returned
home at age eleven and was enrolled in the Hill-
head School. Expelled three years later for defying
the drillmaster, Service was apprenticed at age fifteen to a branch of the Commercial Bank of Scotland, where he stayed until 1896.

Service resigned from the bank at the end of
March, 1896, to emigrate to North America. He
crossed the Atlantic as a steerage passenger to
Montreal, took a "colonist" train to Canada's west
coast, and ended up as a farm laborer on Vancouver Island. A little more than eighteen months later,
he headed for California. In his autobiography, Service claims to have worked as a tunnel builder in

Oakland, a handyman in a San Diego brothel, and
a guitar-playing singer in Colorado. Whatever the
actual truth to those claims might be, by 1899 Service was again working on a Vancouver Island
ranch. In October of 1903, Service returned to the
banking industry with the Canadian Bank of Commerce in Victoria, British Columbia. In 1904 he
was transferred to Whitehorse in the Yukon Territory, and, at the end of the summer of 1906 he became the branch's teller.

Service was never a miner. Rather, he learned
of the 1898 Gold Rush through conversations with
old-timers and the research of old records. His volume of poetry about life in the northern wilderness,
Songs of a Sourdough (1907), quickly went through
fifteen printings, and Service was earning royalties
of several thousand dollars a year while still working as a bank teller in Dawson, even farther north
in the Yukon Territory.

In 1910, Service made his way to Toronto and
New York to arrange for the publication of his
novel, *The Trail of '98*. On his return trip Service
visited his family, who had settled in northern Al-
berta, then set out alone on a perilous journey of
more than two thousand miles to Dawson by canoe
through wilderness waterways. His experiences,
real or imagined, provided material for the best
chapters of his autobiography and inspired the
Mackenzie River ballads of *Rhymes of a Rolling
Stone* (1912). Service planned to follow in the foot-
steps of Robert Louis Stevenson and travel to Tahiti
in 1912, but the editor of the *Toronto Star* hired
him as a foreign correspondent, and Service left the
Yukon, never to return.

In 1913, Service arrived in Paris. He married
Germaine Bourgoin on June 12, 1913. Denied admission to the armed forces because of varicose
veins, Service assumed the role of war correspondent for the *Toronto Star*. Service joined an Amer-
ican-organized ambulance corps in Paris, and from
these experiences came *Rhymes of a Red Cross
Man* (1916). For nine months the book topped the
best-seller lists in the United States.

From 1919 to 1929, Service and his wife lived
in Paris, where their only child, a daughter named
Iris, was born. During this time Service became interested in film. Cinematic adaptations of some of
his poems received mixed reviews. By 1931, the
family had moved to Nice, France. The American
edition of *The Complete Poems* in 1933 recon-
firmed Service's reputation, although many people
in North America assumed Service was already
dead. In 1940, Service and his family returned to

Canada, but they soon moved to Hollywood to be close to the film industry. Service and his family returned to Europe in 1946 and took up residence in Monte Carlo. Service continued to publish and remain active until his death from a heart attack on September 11, 1958. He is buried in the Brittany region of France.

Poem Text

There are strange things done in the midnight sun
*   By the men who moil for gold;*
The Arctic trails have their secret tales
*   That would make your blood run cold;*
The Northern Lights have seen queer sights,   5
*   But the queerest they ever did see*
Was that night on the marge of Lake Lebarge
*   I cremated Sam McGee.*

Now Sam McGee was from Tennessee, where
    the cotton blooms and blows.
Why he left his home in the South to roam   10
    'round the Pole, God only knows.
He was always cold, but the land of gold seemed
    to hold him like a spell;
Though he'd often say in his homely way that
    he'd "sooner live in hell."

On a Christmas Day we were mushing our way
    over the Dawson trail.
Talk of your cold! through the parka's fold it
    stabbed like a driven nail.
If our eyes we'd close, then the lashes froze till   15
    sometimes we couldn't see;
It wasn't much fun, but the only one to whimper
    was Sam McGee.

And that very night, as we lay packed tight in
    our robes beneath the snow,
And the dogs were fed, and the stars o'erhead
    were dancing heel and toe,
He turned to me, and "Cap," says he, "I'll cash
    in this trip, I guess;
And if I do, I'm asking that you won't refuse my   20
    last request."

Well, he seemed so low that I couldn't say no;
    then he says with a sort of moan:
"It's the cursèd cold, and it's got right hold till
    I'm chilled clean through to the bone.
Yet 'tain't being dead — it's my awful dread of
    the icy grave that pains;
So I want you to swear that, foul or fair, you'll
    cremate my last remains."

A pal's last need is a thing to heed, so I swore   25
    I would not fail;
And we started on at the streak of dawn; but
    God! he looked ghastly pale.
He crouched on the sleigh, and he raved all day
    of his home in Tennessee;

And before nightfall a corpse was all that was
    left of Sam McGee.

There wasn't a breath in that land of death, and
    I hurried, horror-driven,
With a corpse half hid that I couldn't get rid,   30
    because of a promise given;
It was lashed to the sleigh, and it seemed to say:
    "You may tax your brawn and brains,
But you promised true, and it's up to you to
    cremate those last remains."

Now a promise made is a debt unpaid, and the
    trail has its own stern code.
In the days to come, though my lips were dumb,
    in my heart how I cursed that load.
In the long, long night, by the lone firelight,   35
    while the huskies, round in a ring,
Howled out their woes to the homeless snows
    —O God! how I loathed the thing.

And every day that quiet clay seemed to heavy
    and heavier grow;
And on I went, though the dogs were spent and
    the grub was getting low;
The trail was bad, and I felt half mad, but I
    swore I would not give in;
And I'd often sing to the hateful thing, and it   40
    hearkened with a grin.

Till I came to the marge of Lake Lebarge, and
    a derelict there lay;
It was jammed in the ice, but I saw in a trice it
    was called the "Alice May."
And I looked at it, and I thought a bit, and
    I looked at my frozen chum;
Then "Here," said I, with a sudden cry, "is
    my cre-ma-tor-eum."

Some planks I tore from the cabin floor, and I   45
    lit the boiler fire;
Some coal I found that was lying around, and I
    heaped the fuel higher;
The flames just soared, and the furnace roared
    —such a blaze you seldom see;
And I burrowed a hole in the glowing coal, and
    I stuffed in Sam McGee.

Then I made a hike, for I didn't like to hear him
    sizzle so;
And the heavens scowled, and the huskies   50
    howled,and the wind began to blow.
It was icy cold, but the hot sweat rolled down my
    cheeks, and I don't know why;
And the greasy smoke in an inky cloak went
    streaking down the sky.

I do not know how long in the snow I wrestled
    with grisly fear;
But the stars came out and they danced about
    ere again I ventured near;
I was sick with dread, but I bravely said: "I'll   55
    just take a peep inside.

I guess he's cooked, and it's time I looked"; ...
   then the door I opened wide.

And there sat Sam, looking cool and calm, in the
   heart of the furnace roar;
And he wore a smile you could see a mile, and
   he said: "Please close that door.
It's fine in here, but I greatly fear you'll let in
   the cold and storm —
Since I left Plumtree, down in Tennessee, it's   60
   the first time I've been warm."

There are strange things done in the midnight sun
   By the men who moil for gold;
The Arctic trails have their secret tales
   That would make your blood run cold;
The Northern Lights have seen queer sights,   65
   But the queerest they ever did see
Was that night on the marge of Lake Lebarge
   I cremated Sam McGee.

Poem Summary

Stanza 1:

In this opening stanza, Service sets a mood of
mystery and suspense. By using words like strange,
midnight, and secret, and phrases like "make your
blood run cold," "queer sights," and "the queerest
I ever did see," the reader anticipates that something unnerving will occur. The final line of the
stanza ("I cremated Sam McGee.") suggests a violent end to Sam McGee and the involvement of the
speaker in that death. Even before Service uses the
word "cold," he chills the reader by introducing the
"midnight sun," "the Arctic trails," and "the Northern Lights." The inclusion of icy Lake LaBarge reinforces the feeling of coldness.

Stanzas 2-3:

Service introduces Sam McGee. Hailing from
the warm South, Sam is always cold in the Yukon.
There appears to be some confusion as to why Sam
left his warm Southern home. He says "he'd
'sooner live in hell'," but this land of gold holds
him "like a spell." Interestingly, it is "the land of
gold," not the gold itself, that has this strange hold
on Sam McGee. The Christmas Day trip over the
Dawson trail begins the action of the poem in a bitter, menacing cold. The speaker describes the cold
in stark, uncompromising terms—it "stabbed like
a driven nail" and froze eyelashes shut. "It wasn't
much fun," adds the speaker, and the other mush-
ers recognize the hazards of this way of life. They
don't complain, but Sam not only complains, he
"whimpers."

Media Adaptations

- A 12-minute short film, directed by Bob Jacobs,
  was released in 1982 by The Film Farm and distributed by EBE.

- A website featuring the work of Tom Byrne, an
  actor who has performed the works of Robert
  W. Service for more than 20 years, can be found
  at http://www.interchange.ubc.ca/service/index.
  htm. The site features CDs, audiocassettes,
  videos, and show bookings.

- At www.rwservice.com, Les McLaughlin, Tracey
  Brown and Randall Prescott have produced a
  CD of Service's work set to music. Sound clips
  are available at the website.

- Blue Frog Records, which can be found at www.
  bluefrogmusic.com, presents an album of songs
  inspired by the poetry of Robert W. Service, titled *Out of Service.* Two additional poems from
  Robert Service complement "The Cremation of
  Sam McGee." "The Shooting of Dan McGrew"
  tells of the "spell of the Yukon" and the "gnaw-
  ing hunger of lonely men for a home and all that
  it means." By the end of the poem, ironic comedy comes into play: there is shooting; someone
  steals a cache of gold, and Lou turns out to be
  no lady at all. "The Ballad of Blasphemous Bill"
  is a good comparison poem to "The Cremation
  of Sam McGee." A similar plot line results in a
  more comical approach and an equally comical
  ending. "The Ballad of Blasphemous Bill"
  makes no pretense of being serious.

Stanzas 4-6:

In these stanzas, Sam tells the speaker ("Cap")
about his fear of being buried in an icy grave and
makes Cap promise to cremate his corpse when he
dies. Service prepares the reader for Sam's demise.
First, Sam states that he will "cash in this trip,"
adding, "I guess," which suggests more finality
than uncertainty. Sam seems depressed, moans,
looks "ghastly pale," and becomes incoherent

("rave[s] all day"). By nightfall, Sam is a frozen corpse.

The stunning visual beauty of the night sky ("the stars o'erhead were dancing heel and toe") might be overlooked in these stanzas is. The word "dancing" should stand out as providing an undercurrent of joy and happiness to contrast with the bitter cold and the strangeness of Sam's last request. It might offer an explanation of the spell of the land that holds men like Sam. Also, the dancing stars echo the Northern Lights of the opening stanza and foreshadow the flames of Sam's "crematorium."

Stanzas 7-9:

These stanzas detail the speaker's trials and tribulations with the frozen body of Sam McGee. Cap has lashed the frozen corpse to the sled as he continues on his journey across the frozen land. There is little description of the landscape, the weather, or anything else in this section unless it refers to the frozen body of Sam McGee. It appears that Cap makes the travels alone, with no other companions than the dogs. The speaker appears to be driven to the brink of madness. He is described as "horror-driven" in stanza 7; he curses "that load" in stanza 8; he talks of the "quiet clay" growing "heavy and heavier," and that he "felt half mad." He even refers to the corpse as a "hateful thing" at the end of stanza 9.

The mood of these stanzas is bleak. Long nights, lone firelight, and dogs howling indicate the gloom. The frozen corpse of Sam McGee "talks" to Cap and listens ("harkens") when he sings to it. Additional elements, no breath in the land of death, tired dogs howling their woes, a low food supply, a bad trail, and the near-madness of Cap coupled with the grin of the frozen corpse all contribute to a dark picture of despair and misery.

Stanzas 10-11:

Cap's arrival at the shores of Lake Lebarge signals a shift in mood and action. This section begins by suggesting the oppressive bleakness of the previous nine stanzas will continue. But, the use of the verb "stuffed" in the last line of stanza 11 and the frenetic action of tearing out planks and lighting a fire begin the transition from the somber to the comic. The overplayed sudden cry of "Here … is my cre-ma-tor-eum" lightens the mood. When Cap stuffs Sam into the fire, the questioning of whether the poet's motives are comic or tragic begins.

Stanzas 12-13:

Before the poem's climax, Service takes a brief pause, a two-stanza caesura. The activities of stanza 12 echo the despair of stanzas 6,7 and 8, with scowling heavens, howling winds, and icy cold. The dancing stars, however, replace the death images with one of delight and amusement, cleverly anticipating the poem's unforgettable ending.

Stanza 14:

The unexpected sight of Sam McGee sitting in the middle of the fire presents a far more comic image than the scriptural portrayal of Shadrach, Meshach, and Abednego who come out of the furnance unscathed in the Book of Daniel. The smile that Sam wears is far warmer (pun intended) than the grin his frozen corpse displayed back in stanza 9. The admonition to close the door or the cold will get in contrasts with Sam's earlier situation where he whimpered and slept beneath the snow. Sam's earlier insistence for cremation is also transformed from a morbid request to a signal that nothing untoward will happen. The twist of the final line of stanza 14 elicits a nod of admiration to Service for evoking humor from a man "freezing to death."

Stanzas 15:

The cold and frightening images of the opening stanza have been completely transformed even though the words are repeated in the conclusion. The unnerving images of Lake Lebarge, and the secret tales of the Arctic have lost their power to chill. The bleak descriptions of death are replaced by the image of Sam McGee sitting in the middle of the fire, telling Cap to shut the door so as not to let in the cold.

Themes

Nature, and Survival in the Wilderness

The first nine stanzas of "The Cremation of Sam McGee" discuss at length the problem of survival in the Arctic wilderness. The deathly cold is but one element. Long distances between pockets of civilization and extreme loneliness also factor into how one survives in this environment. The mood of the first half of the poem points to failure, rather than success, in this particular endeavor. Sam is frozen solid, and Cap, the speaker, appears to be fighting a descent into madness. The arrival at the shores of Lake Lebarge, the building of the fire, and the poem's final twist do not detract from the

Topics for Further Study

- Compile a list of what a modern day prospector might need for a six-month journey into the Yukon wilderness. Use a camping supplies catalog (such as L.L.Bean's or Cabela's) to determine weight as well as cost. Decide if the results would be worth the time and expense.

- Compose a poem that mimics the rhythm and rhyme of "The Cremation of Sam McGee." You might use a title such as "The Citation of Tommy B" or "The Vacation of Peggy Lee." Remember to start by creating two lines of 17 syllables each. The fifth syllable, the tenth syllable, and the final syllable in each line should rhyme.

- To get pure gold, the ore must be mined, treated, and refined. Research the environmental impact of each of these processes.

seriousness of the fight for survival in the unforgiving Yukon.

Death

"The Cremation of Sam McGee" is filled with images of death. The frozen corpse of Sam McGee is the most obvious. But, from the opening lines, Service talks of "tales / That would make your blood run cold" and includes at least one reference to death in succeeding stanzas. Sam says he'd "sooner live in hell" in stanza 2, and the speaker talks of the cold that stabs "like a driven nail" in stanza 3. In stanzas 4 and 5, Sam refers to "cash[ing] in" and makes his "last request." The fear of the "icy grave" prompts him to exact the promise that Cap will "cremate [his] last remains."

Cap finds Sam's frozen corpse on the sled at the end of stanza 6. "There wasn't a breath in that land of death" is the most chilling and direct reference, not only to the death of Sam, but the deaths of the many "sourdoughs" claimed by the Yukon cold. Sam's body changes into a "load" and a "thing" that is "loathed" in stanza 8 and is "quiet clay" and a grinning, "hateful thing" by stanza 9.

The final act of "letting go" takes place over stanzas 11, 12, and 13. Cap prepares the "cre-ma-tor-eum," unceremoniously "stuff[s] in Sam McGee," and removes himself from the place because he does not "like to hear him sizzle so." Having "wrestled with fear" and "sick with dread," Cap checks to see what has happened to the body of Sam. Although not directly stated, it appears Cap is preparing to retrieve Sam's ashes as his final act of mourning. Instead, Service turns the tables with the image of Sam sitting in the middle of the fire, telling Cap to shut the door so as not to let in the cold. This element of redemption and salvation negates the power of death even in the hostile and unforgiving cold of the Arctic.

Loyalty

Sam cannot defeat death by himself. Without Cap's help, Sam will die. Sam has to depend on Cap's loyalty to follow through on his last request. It is clear from Cap's thoughts that loyalty is what compels him to honor Sam's wish to be cremated. Such beliefs as "A pal's last need is a thing to heed" and "a promise made is a debt unpaid" drive Cap to comply with Sam's dying request.

Style

"The Cremation of Sam McGee" is written in the form of a ballad. Ignoring the eight-line opening, the poem follows a regular pattern of four-line stanzas composed of two rhyming couplets. The regular, metronome-like rhythms make this poem (and others from by Robert Service) easy to memorize and recite, reminiscent of Edgar Allan Poe's, "The Raven." The reliance on internal rhyme drives the action of the ballad and enhances the performance aspect. The opening and closing lines follow the same metrical and rhyming patterns of the narrative stanzas, but Service reconfigures them into eight-line stanzas and puts them in italics to create a mood of mystery and suspense at the beginning, and comic irony at the end.

Historical Context

In 1896, gold was discovered in the Klondike River. Because the location was so remote and getting to the strike was a difficult journey, it wasn't until 1898 that the "gold rush" actually began in

Compare & Contrast

- **Late 1890s:** Prospectors flock to the Yukon looking for gold. Boom towns spring up all over the Klondike region. More than 20,000 people swarm into the town of Dawson alone.

  Today: Just over 1300 people brave the wintry weather in Dawson.

- **Late 1890s:** Gripped by "gold fever," people sell everything they have for a chance to strike it rich in the Yukon. A few are lucky. Many lose everything.

  Late 1990s: Fascinated by the strongest economy in history and mesmerized by a rising stock market, many people go into debt to ride the stock market boom. Some cash out their retirement funds to become involved in "day-trading." Many of these investors lose everything.

  1896: The Olympic Games are revived through the efforts of Baron Pierre de Coupertin.

  1998: The Olympic movement survives a major scandal involving bribes to the International Olympic Committee to influence the site selection for future Olympic Games. Salt Lake City, site of the 2002 Winter Games, comes under particular scrutiny.

---

earnest. Even with hardships brought on by some of the world's most unforgiving weather, prospectors managed to extract small and large fortunes in gold from the region. The annual output of gold reached a peak of 22 million dollars in 1900. Production steadily declined after that, until it fell to 5.6 million dollars in 1906. By 1910 most of the population had left for Alaska and other regions.

The Klondike was the fourth and last major "gold rush" of the nineteenth century. Earlier strikes in California (1849), Australia (1851), and South Africa (1886) proved profitable for some who braved the weather and distances to lay claim to riches. Many more, however, left with dreams of gold, but returned with a broken spirit and empty pockets. Some never came home at all. The great gold rushes of the 1800s were an aspect of frontier movements on three continents. With the end of the gold rush period, mining was largely taken over by corporations and governments. The flow and uses of gold became much more controlled than in those frenzied "Wild West" days that glamorized the settling of once open territory.

By the time Service publishes "The Cremation of Sam McGee" and embarks on his new career as a writer of verse, Klondike fever has evaporated and the attention of the world has turned to other matters. The US and Spain have completed their war, but a Mexican Revolution is brewing, there is unrest in the Balkans, and Korea is annexed by Japan. Peary and Amundsen race toward the respective Poles. Henry Ford has started his assembly line system of manufacturing automobiles. But, the sun never sets on the British Empire and Edward VII reigns as King of England. Neither the *Lusitania* nor the *Titantic* has sunk yet, and the World has not yet begun "the war to end all wars." Things will become more complicated in a few short years, but Service can entertain his fascination for the Yukon, including his famous two thousand mile solo canoe trip before relocating to France and becoming a war correspondent for the *Toronto Star* during World War I.

Critical Overview

Praised in 1921 for their spontaneity and liveliness, Service's rhymes have most often been lauded for their energy but criticized for their lack of "true" emotion. For many years serious criticism simply ignored Service's work, or found it of limited interest. While Arthur Phelps recoiled from the "grotesque gruesomeness" of "The Cremation of Sam McGee," he also claimed that the poem was

"

*At the word "sizzle,"
in stanza 12, the thaw of
the poem begins."*

"a folk tale of unquestioned natural vitality." Phelps further distinguished between readers with literary pretensions (who dismissed Service's sentimentality, metronomic rhythms, simplicity, and limited range) and those who used these same criteria to praise his verse for being memorable, recitable, and sympathetic to ordinary people. More recent critics have attempted to isolate the folk-poetry features of his work and to analyze his structural patterns. Edward Hirsch, for example, reads the Yukon ballads as a closed structure opposing Dionysian and Apollonian (body and mind) elements in human behavior. Service represented tensions between nature and culture, and he claimed to espouse nature before all. The continuing appeal of the poems about Sam McGee and Dan McGrew, however, rests not in any intellectual paradigm they employ but in the sly humor and metrical regularity that initially made them so readily adaptable to parlor performance.

Criticism

Bill Wiles

Wiles teaches and writes in the shadow of Vermont's Green Mountains. In this essay, he explores the idea of cold and the meaning of keeping promises.

"The Cremation of Sam McGee" presents an interesting look into the life of prospectors. Extracting gold from the Klondike and Yukon Rivers in less than favorable weather conditions offered challenges to the "sourdoughs" who came to seek their fortunes, and provided material for writers like Robert W. Service and Jack London.

The term "moil" in the opening lines carries with it the meaning of digging under wet, dirty conditions. That is an unpleasant task in any climate, but set that action in the Yukon and the significance becomes more apparent. The very fact that days and nights are much different than they are in the

lower 48 creates an atmosphere of disorientation. Couple that with a landscape covered in snow where many landmarks can be obliterated with a mere shift of the wind, not to mention a full-blown blizzard, and the search for gold becomes more a tale of survival than adventure.

There is no mention in this poem of Cap and Sam's particular search for treasure. Instead, the poem focuses its attention on surviving the cold. For Cap, that means to keep moving. Throughout the poem, Cap is active, moving across the ice and snow. He appears to have no particular destination, but no particular place he can use for shelter or refuge either. When Cap does stop for the night, he wraps himself tight in his robes and buries himself in the snow. There is no specific mention, but the reader could assume at least one of the dogs would share the snow cave with Cap, their bodies providing the heat.

Whether Sam uses this method of keeping warm is not clear. He does "whimper," though, and says that he'd "sooner live in hell" than in the Yukon. His chief complaint is that he is "chilled clean through to the bone." It is interesting that Sam does not appear to be afraid of dying; he is fearful, however, of being cold for eternity. Thus, he requests to be cremated.

From the finding of Sam's corpse in stanza 6 to Cap's wandering just after stuffing Sam into the fire, the poem does not mention the cold. The previous six stanzas presented such a palpable presence of the cold that it remains with the reader even though there are no further references to it until stanza 12. There, the cold is brought in as a contrast to the hot sweat Cap is experiencing, an emotional and physical reaction to having built the "cre-ma-tor-uem" and putting the body of his friend in it.

At the word "sizzle," in stanza 12, the thaw of the poem begins. The defrosting continues and increases when Cap mutters, "I'll just take a peep inside / I guess he's cooked, and it's time I looked." By the time Cap opens the door to reveal Sam sitting in the middle of the furnace, it should be no surprise to the reader. The path to warmth has been clearly marked. Sam's remark that it's the first time he has been warm should resonate with the reader as well. All the Arctic cold of the beginning of the poem has given way to humor and the warmth of Sam's personality.

Some might say this poem is about salvation, but that argument would be difficult to make. Instead, it appears this poem deals more with the power of friendship and loyalty, and the meaning of making a promise. The promise on its face first seems distasteful, maybe even gruesome. But, As Cap says, "A promise made is a debt unpaid." It is that notion of following through, of honoring the commitment, that comes to the forefront. The poem shows in a humorous way the effect of keeping a promise.

Source: Bill Wiles, in an essay for *Poetry for Students*, Gale, 2001.

Carl Mowery

Mowery holds a Ph.D. from Southern Illinois University in Rhetoric and Composition and American Literature. He has written numerous essays for the Gale Group. In the following, Mowery examines the poetic style and imagery found in the ballad as well as the poetic techniques used by Robert W. Service.

"The Cremation of Sam McGee" reflects Robert W. Service's knowledge of the Yukon territory, where he lived much of his early adult life. It was there that he was exposed to the rough and tumble world of the gold miners and other outdoorsmen of the Canadian northwest. "The only society I like," he once said, "is that which is rough and tough—and the tougher the better. That's where you get down to bedrock and meet human people." Those kinds of images, experiences and people fill much of his poetic output. His ballads vibrate with the sounds and smells of the frontier saloons, with the piano playing in the background, the men and women talking and arguing, and the occasional gun fight erupting. His verses reflect his personal search for balance between the social life of the mining camps and the solitude of the north woods.

His most famous ballad, "The Shooting of Dan McGrew," is a serious tale of intrigue and treachery ending with the deaths of McGrew and the stranger who did the shooting. This ballad, first published in 1907 in a collection called *Songs of a Sourdough* and later reissued with the title *The Spell of the Yukon,* was inspired by an actual event. Service had gone into a bank where he worked during the day looking for a quiet place to write. He did not tell the night watchman he was coming, and the startled watchman shot at Service, missing his head by inches.

Included in the *Songs of a Sourdough* collection was "The Cremation of Sam McGee," a lighthearted ballad with an unexpected twist at the end. A ballad is a poetic form that tells a tale, usually in a very rhythmic fashion. These kinds of poems

> *'They understood him, and knew that [his] verse ... would be a lilting thing, clear, clean and power-packed, beating out a story with a dramatic intensity that made the nerves tingle.'"*

are not filled with deep symbolism; rather, they are straightforward explications of a story, serious or comedic.

"The Cremation of Sam McGee" opens with a stanza that establishes the tone of the work, giving it a mysterious air that the following tale will then unravel. The stanza is repeated at the close of the ballad, and thereby frames it. When it was published, Service instructed that this stanza be printed in italics for added emphasis, in much the same way that Rudyard Kipling used italics to set apart and add emphasis to stanzas in many of his poetic pieces. Service used this same publication practice in other verses, including "The Ballad of One-eyed Mike." Such stanzas function like the choruses of ancient Greek dramas. While they are important to the telling of the story, they are not directly connected to it. Instead, they offer background or other information that helps the reader understand the literary work more completely. For Service, these mini-choruses set the tone and establish the mood of the verse they bracket.

The stories in Service's ballads are very easy to follow. He was deliberately anti-intellectual and did not include in his verse obscure imagery and hidden meanings. But this fact does not make his poetry any the less important in the history of poetry, nor does it make other poetry any more important. It just makes their styles different. Service's obituary in the Pittsburgh *Sun-Telegraph* of September 16, 1958, stated: "He was a people's poet. To the people he was great. They understood him, and knew that any verse carrying the by-line of Robert W. Service would be a lilting thing, clear, clean and power-packed, beating out a story with a dramatic intensity that made the nerves tingle."

What Do I Read Next?

- Jack London's short story "To Build a Fire" documents the darker side of what can happen to someone who doesn't follow the advice of the more experienced "sourdough." Also, London's *Call of the Wild* offers another view on life mushing in the Yukon

- The story of a youth shipwrecked on an iceberg in the Arctic in 1757 with only a polar bear cub for a companion comes to life when Arthur Roth details seventeen-year-old Allan's seemingly hopeless struggle for survival in *The Iceberg Hermit*.

An important aspect of Service's style is the generous use of dialogue. In "The Cremation of Sam McGee," many of the important parts of the story are carried along by the spoken words of its two characters, the unnamed narrator and Sam McGee. And at one important moment even McGee's corpse seems to speak. In other verses, like "The Shooting of Dan McGrew," several speakers are active in telling the tale. The use of speakers in this way descends from the practice of Edgar Allan Poe, especially in his poem, *The Raven*. Poe uses both spoken word and the thoughts of his narrator to tell the story. The other speaker is, of course, the Raven. Service has also been strongly compared to Rudyard Kipling and is sometimes called "The Canadian Kipling." Service adopted similar rhythmic and rhyming approaches as well as the occasional use of the italicized stanzas that are found in the poetry of Kipling. Both poets were very conscious of the language they used, often incorporating slang and jargon in their poetry.

Service's verse (he did not call his ballads "poems") is in the style and tradition of oral folk lore. In this tradition the poet tells the story using simple language in catchy meter and rhyme scheme. Despite the use of plain language, his characters and their stories mythologize the adventure and masculine vigor of life during the Klondike gold rush. The narrator has given his word to Sam and then endures severe hardships in order to keep his word. The characters achieve, in the hands of Service, a stature that belies their humble origins and surroundings. They become icons of the north woodsman who lived by a special code of honor and duty to keep one's word.

Service's verses are marked by their playful rhythms and unusual rhyme schemes. The rhyme pattern of the present verse is *abcb defe* and the meter is a lilting iambic pattern, with four and three beats in alternating lines. An iamb is a two-syllable foot, with an accent on the second syllable; a foot is a metrical unit consisting of two or three syllables. The interesting aspect here is the occasional inclusion of an anapest foot or two where the story line needed the extra syllables. An anapest foot is a three syllable foot with two unaccented and one accented syllables. The first line is a good example of this. "There are strange" (the anapest foot) "things done" (the iambic foot) "in the midnight sun" (a second set of an anapest foot followed by an iambic foot).

An obvious reflection of Service's youth in the Yukon is much reliance on images of the north county, including the northern lights (the Aurora Borealis), sparkling stars, scowling heavens, and the sky seen through the smoke of a fire. But most of the feel of the north is revealed through the constant references to the cold—the cold that "stabbed like a driven nail," the cold that froze their lashes shut, and the cold that froze the grinning, departed Sam McGee on the way to the Lake.

But in contrast to this biting cold, the poem also reflects on Sam's home state, Tennessee, and the warmth that Sam remembers there. Also there is reference to that hottest of all places, Hell, where Sam said he would "sooner live" than in the cold northern parts of Canada. The last scenes, as the narrator builds a huge fire into which he puts Sam McGee's frozen corpse, combine cold and hot: "It was icy cold, but the hot sweat rolled / down my cheeks."

A tale of travel in the north woods would not be complete without mention of the dogs that pull the sleds. In this verse Service makes several references to the huskies, who lie in circles to keep themselves warm during the long, cold and windy nights. The dogs howling is reminiscent of wolves at night. Despite their fatigue, they are pushed onward to help the narrator fulfill the promise made to Sam to cremate his remains.

Service makes use of a pun on the word "grisly" (calling to mind the grizzly bear) as he describes the narrator's wait in the snow while the fire burns up Sam's remains. In the first and last stanzas, Service uses two words that now seem odd, "marge" and "moil," that these words were commonly used at the beginning of the century but have since fallen out of use. They mean margin and toil, respectively.

When they arrive at "the marge of Lake Lebarge" the narrator finds an old, derelict steam boat, an image of death and ruin. He is pleased to see it and determines to use its furnace as the crematorium. Out on the derelict (dead) boat he builds a fire into which he puts Sam. When he can no longer refrain from avoiding the fire and is curious about how the cremation is progressing, he opens the door and sees Sam sitting up. Sam says, "Please close that door ... it's the first time I've been warm." Out of cold and death now rise warmth and life!

On August 17, 1975, the Canadian Postal Service paid tribute to Robert Service with an eight cent stamp. The stamp depicts Sam McGee grinning out from an open fire on Lake Lebarge in the Yukon.

Source: Carl Mowery, in an essay for *Poetry for Students,* Gale, 2001.

Sources

Kellner, Bruce, "Robert Service; Overview" in *Reference Guide to English Literature, 2nd ed.,* edited by D. L. Kirkpatrick, St. James Press, 1991.

Klinck, Carl F. and New, W. H., "Robert W(illiam) Service," in *Dictionary of Literary Biography, Volume 92: Canadian Writers, 1890-1920.* A Bruccoli Clark Layman Book. Edited by W. H. New, University of British Columbia. The Gale Group, 1990, pp. 342-348.

The Original Homepage of Robert W. Service, www.ude. net/service/service.html (March 20, 2000).

For Further Study

Mossman, Tam, *The Best of Robert Service,* ed., Running Press, 1990.

An interesting collection of Robert Service poems, including "The Cremation of Sam McGee," "The Shooting of Dan McGrew," and others. Vintage photographs from the Klondike days add a sense of realism. There is also a helpful glossary of the more exotic words and phrases Service uses in his poems.

Kellner, Bruce, "Robert Service; Overview" in *Reference Guide to English Literature,* edited by D.L. Kirkpatrick, St. James Press, 1991.

Provides an overview of Service's work and leads to other critical sources.

Review of *The Spell of the Yukon and other Verses, The Sewanee Review* 1. Vol. XVII, No. 3, July, 1909, pp. 381-82.

An unnamed critic discusses Service's style, stating that, although it shows considerable skill and vitality, the poetry deals "too rawly" with the harsh realities of life in the Yukon.

Dear Reader

James Tate

1970

As readers of James Tate's poems, *we* are the subject of this one, aptly titled "Dear Reader." Upon finishing it, we may not think there is much "dear" involved, but, to the contrary, Tate is skilled at underlining the seemingly offensive with a hint of loving concern and drawing on the absurd to make almost-sense. "Dear Reader" is a typical Tate poem in its surreal setting, placing both speaker and subject in a bizarre place performing bizarre actions, but the poet presents the scene as though it is natural and, therefore, not too obscure to understand. Often, when a poet or fiction writer indulges in unreal and unusual circumstances, readers are left out in the cold—becoming bystanders to actions that take place only in the writer's mind. "Dear Reader" may leave us perplexed at first, but the poem's intention manages to work its way into our own heads by the time it is over. We may be in the cold for a while, but we are not left there.

Writing a poem that directly addresses the person(s) reading it is by no means unique to James Tate, nor to the genre of poetry. Most often, however, the sentiment is one of "gentleness" and appreciation. A common practice in nineteenth-century writing—especially fiction—was to break up a sentence with the direct address "gentle reader," serving to draw us more closely into the events taking place or the thoughts of the persona. Tate's poem certainly draws us in, from the title on, but not with such softness or kindness. Still, a close read reveals less of the speaker's curtness, or rudeness, and more of his feelings of inadequacy and

despair. In the end, we may indeed be a little more "dear" to him than it would first appear.

Author Biography

James Tate was born in Kansas City, Missouri, in 1943 and was educated at the University of Missouri, Kansas State College, and the University of Iowa Writer's Workshop. He received his M.F.A. from Iowa in 1967. Tate claims not to have begun writing poetry until his freshman year in college but over the years he has become one of the most prolific poets in America, publishing more than thirty books, many of which are small-press publications and reprints from earlier volumes. His first full-length collection, *Lost Pilot,* won the Yale Series of Younger Poets Award in 1966, making Tate, at twenty-three, the youngest poet ever to receive this distinguished honor. He began teaching immediately after graduation, with positions at the University of Iowa, the University of California at Berkeley, and Columbia University. Since 1971, he has been on the English faculty at the University of Massachusetts, Amherst.

In 1976, Tate wrote an autobiographical article for *North American Review,* called "The Route as Briefed." He recently used the title again for a collection of essays, stories, and interviews, published in 1999. If we may take this account of his first eighteen years as an accurate, unembellished autobiography, we may understand where much of the erratic, despairing, dark humor of many of his poems derives. Tate tells a story of violent stepfathers, contemplation of murder, humiliating experiences at camp, an affinity for tarantulas, a mentally impaired stepbrother, poor grades, drunkenness, and crazy friends of the family. One recollection involves fleeing in a car from Kansas City to Detroit with his mother at the wheel, his stepfather hiding under a rug in the back seat, and the six-year-old Tate wondering why he had been pulled from school to suddenly move out of state. A month or so later, upon returning to Kansas City with just his mother, he learned that his stepfather was wanted for murder and was seeking protection from his own parents in Detroit. He was eventually captured and sentenced to the electric chair for killing his first wife. Tate's real father was a fighter pilot killed during World War II before ever seeing his infant son, born five months earlier. The fact that Tate never met his natural father played heavily into his work and was the impetus behind the *Lost Pilot* collection. While there may be no direct connection between specific

childhood events and the "Dear Reader" poem, its general macabre setting and tortuous language could understandably evolve from early encounters with violent behavior and an insecure home life.

Poem Text

I am trying to pry open your casket
with this burning snowflake.

I'll give up my sleep for you.
This freezing sleet keeps coming down
and I can barely see.   5

If this trick works we can rub our hands
together, maybe

start a little fire
with our identification papers
I don't know but I keep working, working   10

half hating you,
half eaten by the moon.

Poem Summary

Line 1:

Tate draws us into a strange scene at the very beginning of this poem. The first thing we find out about the "dear reader"—about *ourselves,* in other words—is that we are dead. Or, at least, we are thought to be dead because the reader addressed here has been placed in a casket, the lid sealed. If we pulled this line out of the poem and read it as a separate, freestanding sentence, it would connote a sense of desperation on the part of the speaker. If we saw the line scrawled alone on a piece of paper, or across a wall, it would likely conjure up chilling images about the person who wrote it— horror, despair, a mad attempt to bring a loved one back to life, the frantic refusal to let go. But all these macabre pictures derive from taking the line in its literal sense. We can also consider a figurative option. Perhaps we are "dead" to the speaker— the poet—because we no longer respond to his work. And perhaps the poet is so desperate to have our attention that he is willing to "pry open" our closed minds. These metaphorical references are more in line, of course, with where the poem takes us and will become more evident in the end.

Line 2:

The second line of the poem swings the reader 180 degrees in relation to the first one. Suddenly the allusion to death and the dark, horrific imagery

Media Adaptations

- If you have audio access on your computer, you can hear James Tate read his poem "Restless Leg Syndrome" by clicking on the "Hear James Tate Read" icon at http://www.poets.org/LIT/poet/jtatefst.htm.

- A 1996 cassette recording by James Tate includes his witty, comedic reading of several poems, including "How the Pope Is Chosen" and "An Eland, In Retirement" from *Worshipful Company of Fletchers*. Tate is introduced by fellow poet Jon Ashbery. The tape runs 60 minutes and is available from The Academy of American Poets Tapes Program in New York.

are counteracted by an absurd, impossible, comedic admission. The speaker is using a "burning snowflake" to pry open the coffin. Now an act we thought of as desperate and determined is nothing more than foolish and half-hearted, if that. The sarcasm toward readers of his poetry in this line comes quickly and unexpectedly. But the about-face is not that unusual in Tate's poetry, and the use of incongruous images is one of his specialties. In a 1982 interview for *The Poetry Miscellany* (reprinted in *The Route as Briefed*) with critic Richard Jackson, Tate stated that he attempts to "set expressions in motion against whole new meanings so that you can't classify them as simple statements. The reader thinks that the poem is making a statement and then all of a sudden the poem insists that the reader think about words, not about content." The second line in "Dear Reader" does force us to think about the *words,* especially in conjunction with the first line—"burning," "snowflake," and "casket" are all unlikely companions.

Line 3:

Line 3 is a declaration of the self-sacrifice that the poet is willing to endure to connect with us, but now we are leery of his sincerity. "I'll give up my sleep for you" tells us that he will work all night

to write a poem if that is what it takes to satisfy us, to create something that we appreciate. This line is "softer" than the one preceding it and several of those that follow, and it *seems* like an honest gesture of eagerness to please. Given the previous tongue-in-cheek remark, however, we need to see where the rest of the poem goes before deciding on the poet's intent.

Lines 4-5:

These lines return to the exaggeration of the entire surreal scene. At this point, we picture a desperate man standing over a casket late at night during a blizzard, trying to use a snowflake as though it is a crowbar. With the sleet pouring down, he can barely see what he is doing or whether he is progressing in prying the coffin open. All of this, of course, is a metaphor for how difficult it is to create a good poem for a fickle audience. The scenario is full of self-pity, opposing the struggling writer against the unimpressed "dear reader" who is still waiting to be entertained.

Lines 6-7:

Lines 6 and 7 indicate that the poet is indeed sincere in his effort to stay in touch with his readers, and he admits that it will be a "trick"—or a real feat—to make that connection. He will go so far as to "rub our hands" to bring some life back into the relationship between poet and reader, but the "maybe" that ends line 7 once again throws a little doubt into the mix. The word is ambiguous here, for it can be seen as the bridge to the next line so that we read it as "maybe / start a little fire," or it can leave in limbo the idea of reviving a lost reader: " we can rub our hands / together, maybe."

Lines 8-9:

Line 8 may be an extension of the thought begun in the previous two lines, but it also implies starting a fire with something other than hands—in this case, "identification papers." Perhaps Tate means here that our hands *are* a form of our identities, but the term also reflects an estrangement or a lack of familiarity between the poet and the reader, or the desperate would-be savior and the dead, so to speak. If we must show someone ID papers, we must not already be acquaintances, much less friends.

Line 10:

Line 10 presents the speaker as both doubtful and determined. Exactly what he does not "know" is not spelled out, but it seems that he is not sure whether we will be able to rekindle ("start a little fire") the connection between him as poet and us as readers. There may also be a less apparent reference here, one hidden within the statement, "I don't know." Perhaps the speaker does not know why he is even trying to please us, why he struggles so to appease an audience that will likely remain aloof and unappreciative. Regardless of the implication, the speaker continues to "keep working, working," determined not to stop writing—or, to carry the metaphor through, not to give up trying to pry open the casket with a burning snowflake.

Lines 11-12:

The last two lines of "Dear Reader"—"half hating you, / half eaten by the moon"—are, essentially, half understandable and half vague. The poet/speaker has already established the notion of a love-hate relationship with his readers, fluctuating between frantically trying to reach us and mockingly putting forth the effort of a snowflake on fire. Line 11, therefore, is clear: the poet hates his readers, but not completely. His feelings of animosity stem from the pressure to "produce" for us, to create poetry that we will read and, hopefully, appreciate. The possibility of achieving that keeps him from walking away from the work altogether. Line 12 is Tate insisting the reader "think about words, not about content," as mentioned above. The moon plays no real part in this poem because there is no reference to it throughout and, more importantly, it is unlikely that the moon would "appear" during a blizzard—in the sky *or* in the poem. Nonetheless, it is there, but why the poet is "half eaten" by it is unclear, and intentionally so. Perhaps he feels so inadequate in his efforts that even this heavenly body is a foe, eating away at his confidence. Perhaps *moon* is just an overused cliche in so much poetry that Tate drops it in here as another tongue-in-cheek move. And perhaps it is just a phrase that sounds "poetic" and defies analysis altogether. Whatever the impetus behind its inclusion, is typifies this poet's typical "play" with language.

Themes

Surrealism

Surrealism refers to artistic or literary works that attempt to express subconscious thoughts through the use of fantastic imagery and incongruous juxtaposition of subject matter. Many of James Tate's poems are grounded in surrealistic and bizarre settings, including "Dear Reader." The most obvious juxtaposition of subjects in this poem is the notion of prying open a casket with a burning snowflake. Certainly, the idea of a "burning snowflake" itself is not only unrealistic, but physically impossible. We could dismiss this conflict as simply a touch of sarcasm to express how much the speaker is *not* attempting to pry the casket open, but just the presence of a coffin—and, therefore, death—introduces a macabre, surreal element into it. Tate's speaker is not perplexed by his situation and his dilemma. Rather, he too expresses strange desires and exhibits freakish behavior. In the reader-as-corpse metaphor, he contemplates rubbing the hands of the dead person in order to bring back life in the same manner we may rub two sticks or stones together to spark a fire. He describes himself as working feverishly in a surreal scene, perhaps in a cemetery where a sealed coffin stands in the open, and snow, sleet, and the moon complement the eerie setting.

Surrealism and fantastic imagery in this poem are effective devices that make the poet's point. If he were to forsake metaphor in favor of "plain talk," he would, ironically, end up with a poem that drives readers even further away, making our caskets even more difficult to pry open, so to speak. Take away the figures of speech from this poem and it would read something like, "Dear Reader, you do not seem to like or read my work anymore, no matter how I slave over it, but I will keep trying to write something that pleases you because I crave your attention." Obviously, the poem needs strong imagery to keep it from lapsing into mere pathos.

Loneliness and Despair

Loneliness and despair are common themes in James Tate's work, and he is capable of packing quite a few melancholy, depressing thoughts into a short poem such as "Dear Reader." In spite of the gloomy tendencies, however, he is not a poet who gives in to despair. Instead, he usually finds a way to introduce a comedic effect or to incorporate such odd language pairings that we are distracted from the hopelessness by curiosity and amusement. In "Dear Reader," the very first line sets a despondent tone. But the about-face comes quickly here, as the poet resorts to a snide, yet whimsical, remark about a snowflake on fire. The rest of the poem is not so easily rescued from despair, but settles into a nagging sense of loneliness and disheartenment that is overcome only by the speaker's decision to "keep working, working." Even *that* notion is something

*Topics for
Further
Study*

- Pretend you are a composer of classical music and are writing a poem entitled, "Dear Listener." What would you say to your audience and how would your thoughts and sentiments compare or contrast to James Tate's in "Dear Reader"?

- Write an essay exploring the basic differences between realistic and surrealistic writing. Beyond the obvious, what sets the two apart and which style do you find more appealing to read. Incorporate your opinion into the essay.

- Research the topic of starting fires by rubbing sticks or stones together and write an article explaining how this phenomenon occurs. Be scientific, but accessible to informed readers, in your essay.

- James Tate's father was shot down over Germany in WWII, and his remains were not found until many years after the war. Do some research into soldiers missing-in-action (for any war) and write an article discussing the main issues on why these men and women were never found.

less than positive, for it implies a pathetic perseverance to attain the unattainable.

Tate's persona has chosen the lonely profession of writing poetry, made even lonelier by being rejected or ignored by readers. In the metaphor that he sustains throughout the poem, the speaker/poet operates in a self-inflicted vacuum. Alone and sleepless, he works in the freezing weather, and his attempt to accomplish the job is hardly more than futile. He appears to acknowledge that futility, but then relieves his despair by opening the door—only slightly—to possibility: "*If* this trick works" and "*maybe* start a little fire." The fact that he and the person inside the casket would have to show "identification papers" to one another further indicates a lack of relationship or closeness. While darkness and "freezing sleet" are obviously gloomy images, we may expect that the introduction of the "moon" at the end of the poem provides

a touch of optimism or accomplishment. Instead, however, the moon slips easily into the themes of loneliness and despair, for the speaker feels "half eaten" by it. Once again, though, Tate does not relinquish the entire poem to hopelessness. In the end, the word "half"—used twice—tells us that his hatred for readers and the viciousness of the moon do not make a complete picture; there is still room for the *better* half.

Style

"Dear Reader" is a 12-line, free-verse poem, divided into five stanzas that alternate between two and three lines each. There is no obvious rhyme and very little alliteration, with the exception of the long "i" sound in "I am trying to pry" and the long "e" sound in "freezing sleet keeps." The poem is made up of simple, declarative sentences that depend on surreal language for effect rather than any stylized approach to its appearance on the page. Tate's earlier work tended to be more formally structured with attention to the number of syllables and an intentional rhythm. With the publication of *The Oblivion Ha-Ha* in 1970, which contains "Dear Reader," the poet presented a looser style, showing much less poetic restraint than in his previous work. Commenting on the poems in this collection, critic Stephen Gardner stated that "the strengths and weaknesses of his style become evident. For Tate is a skilled poet, a turner of metaphors and a shaper of images. When he is terrifying, the fear is universal. And when his stories are captivating, there are few poets who can be more successful." "Dear Reader" is an example of Tate's resorting to metaphors and images to tell a "captivating" story—a brief and limited story, yes, but one that piques our curiosity and holds our attention.

Historical Context

In "Dear Reader," there is no specific time or place in which the events occur. To the contrary, any work of surrealism tends to defy certain markers that would set it in a particular year or decade, or in any particular area of the world. By definition, metaphysical poetry is boundless and more in tune with the intellect than actual surroundings. This, of course, is not to say that concrete images and natural objects do not play a role in this type of work. "Dear Reader" is full of images that, by themselves, are very "normal" or easily recognizable. We can

Compare & Contrast

- **1960:** Alfred Hitchcock's now-classic film *Psycho* appeared in theaters across the country.

  1999: At Columbine High School in Colorado, two students went on a killing spree that left more than a dozen dead and many others injured.

- **1969:** The Woodstock Music Festival lasted for four days in the Catskill Mountains. Illegal drugs and sexual freedom were widespread.

  1992: Euro Disney opened in France, causing many French citizens to complain about the unwelcome spread of American culture.

- **1973:** Direct American involvement in Vietnam ended, but the bombing of Cambodia continued in efforts to retrieve P.O.W.s.

  1993: In Cambodia, the monarchy was reestablished, and Sihanouk became king.

all picture and understand caskets, snowflakes, sleet, hands rubbing together, fire, and the moon. It is what Tate does with these images—how he uses them together—that turns the real into the surreal.

What we can say about the historical and cultural perspective of this poem, or about Tate's work in general, must come from the poet himself. During an interview conducted over a three-year period, from 1975 to 1978, Tate answered questions from fellow poets and critics Helena Minton, Lou Papineau, and Cliff Saunders for an article which eventually appeared in various journals and in Tate's own collection, *The Route as Briefed.* The discussion centered on all of the poet's collections up to that point, including *The Oblivion Ha-Ha.* When asked whether he saw himself and other poets as social historians, Tate responded, "I wouldn't mind that particularly, but I think it happens to you unwittingly. If one succeeds in being spoken through by one's times, then you're bound to reflect it." Given that Tate's early work was written and published during the Vietnam War era, it would have been easy for him to use that conflict and the resulting social turmoil as a backdrop for his work as so many other poets and writers were doing in the 1960s and 1970s. But when asked the question, "Did you ever write any blatant antiwar poems?" Tate said, "I find that all too obvious; you can get all that matters on the news, and I'm not a bit interested in some poet's righteous opining. In fact I find it offensive to be slapping yourself on the back because you don't believe in killing babies, as so many poets were doing at the

time. I mean, did you ever meet anybody who said, 'Yeah, I *like* to kill babies'?"

The most revealing point in Tate's comments is the fact that he finds antiwar poems—and, presumably, other blatantly opinionated pieces—as "all too obvious." This would account for his preference for a more obscure use of language and metaphors that are sustained throughout poems. He may in fact write a poem that speaks out against war on one level, but that level may be buried beneath layers of surreal imagery and bizarre occurrences, leaving the actual meaning lost to the reader. Tate would make no apology for this and appears content to have his poems enjoyed, if not completely understood. He reemphasized his feelings when asked whether he had written what he would call political poems: "What is obvious is seldom worthy of poetry. I do think poets must be committed to being certain kinds of 'outlaws.' They can't 'fit in,' as it were. I definitely mean for most of my poems to ridicule our performance in life: it is shoddy and not what it should be. I am political in that I speak for failure, for anger and frustration." In "Dear Reader," this sentiment is at work. The speaker/poet expresses both anger and frustration in not being able to please his readers, and that in turn gives him a sense of failure.

Critical Overview

As critic Stephen Gardner noted about James Tate's poetry in his article for the *Dictionary of Literary*

Biography, "Critic after critic has pointed out the obvious: his imagery is dreamlike, although clear; his stance is often ironical, ranging from involvement to objectivity; his major themes confront (although some would say avoid) the confusion, terror, emptiness, or boredom that defines the times." In general, Tate's work has been well received, most readers referring to his ability to convey the inner human psyche and all our dark thoughts without pitching the entire poem into despair and hopelessness. He has also been applauded for his humor in the face of anguish and whimsy in the midst of melancholy.

Not all critics have been so accepting, however. Those who find fault with Tate's poetry most often site the lack of *real* substance it contains. They point out that the "cleverness"—the unusual imagery, odd juxtapositions, bizarre occurrences, and so forth—sometimes present only confusing fluff that *sounds* interesting but means nothing. Despite the harshness of these criticisms, Tate's overall acceptance is recognizable in the numerous accolades he has won over the years, including the Yale Series of Younger Poets Award in 1966, a National Institute of Arts and Letters Award in 1974, and a Pulitzer Prize in 1992.

Criticism

Jeannine Johnson

In the following essay, Johnson examines the conflicted sentiments the poet has toward his reader, revealing that Tate ultimately concedes it is better for a poem to be read than to remain unread.

In "Dear Reader," James Tate explores the nature of poetry by examining the relationships that coexist with it. The poem first appeared in the 1970 collection *The Oblivion Ha-Ha* and is reprinted in *Selected Poems.* In "Dear Reader," though he is interested in the creation of meaning and other theoretical issues involving verse, Tate is more concerned with the ways that we use poetry and with its role in a unique kind of interaction between people. Tate has said that "The poem is man's noblest effort because it is utterly useless" (*Contemporary Poets of the English Language*). However, it is clear in "Dear Reader" that, even if it is true that poetry is useless, Tate continues to act as if it were not. He wants to believe that poetry can serve some constructive purpose and that it can contribute to our efforts to know ourselves and each other.

The tension between Tate's knowledge that poetry is useless and his desire for poetry to be useful is reflected in the conflicted feelings the poet directs toward his reader. On the one hand, the poet resents the reader, as he is forced to "keep working, working / half hating you." On the other hand, there is no doubt that the poet needs a reader, that he cannot work without imagining that someone hears him, and that he is willing to make extraordinary sacrifices for that person: "I'll give up my sleep for you. / This freezing sleet keeps coming down / and I can barely see." The poet is willing to risk fatigue, illness, and even compromised vision for the sake of a reader, demonstrating just how important it is for his voice to be received by another person.

In his introduction to *The Best American Poetry 1997,* Tate claims that poets "write their poems with various degrees of obsessiveness mostly for themselves." A good poet, he contends in that essay, does not write with his audience in mind, nor for the primary purpose of being read, recognized, or understood. Instead, a poet writes poetry to serve his own needs and to fulfill his own intentions. And yet, somewhat paradoxically, it is this method of composing exclusively for himself that makes it worthwhile for others to read his poetry. Tate continues, "It is precisely because the poet has written his poems in solitude for himself to satisfy unanalyzable hungers and to please his highest standards with negligible prospects of any other rewards that the poem is incorruptible and may address issues unaddressed by many people in their daily lives." In other words, a poet writes best when he refuses to consider the demands of others or the possible acclaim he might receive for his work. When he does so, he can concentrate on grooming the poem for its own sake and can ensure that everything in it contributes to its success. Thus, in writing for himself, the poet makes it more likely that his poems will be effective and, therefore, that they will be valued by his readers.

Tate may have felt more secure about his ability to attract readers in 1997—by which time he was sufficiently well-known to have been named to the prestigious position of editor in the *Best American Poetry* series—than he was in 1970 when he published "Dear Reader." Thirty years before his assignment at *Best American Poetry 1997,* he was not as eager to ignore his reader, and this dependence created considerable conflict in the poem. Here and elsewhere in Tate's work, the intimate relationships that are engendered by poetry are almost familial. Poem, poet, and reader interact with each other as naturally and as contentiously as do the members of any family. The familial relationship is arbitrary and inescapable, and it is one that both produces resentment and generates exceptional devotion. In "Poem to Some of my Recent Poems," published in 1983, Tate calls his works of art "My beloved little billiard balls, / my polite mongrels, edible patriotic plums _" (*Selected Poems*). Tate's poems are contradictions unto themselves, as they are meant to be played with, trained, and consumed, all at once. More than this, his poems are his children, and their mother is a beautiful firelog who, as he tells his offspring, "scorched you with her radiance."

In "Poem to Some of my Recent Poems," as in "Dear Reader," fire is central to the experience of poetry, indicating both poetry's power and its potential danger. Tate pays tribute to the mother of his "recent poems," announcing that "I shall never forget / her sputtering embers, and then the little mound." The poet wistfully recalls the past and the flame that, in giving his poem life, also guaranteed its own demise. He assures his children, "you are beautiful, and I, a slave to a heap of cinders." Fire is a symbol of the creation and appreciation of beauty, and, as such, both phenomena are necessarily fleeting.

The image of death with which "Poem to Some of my Recent Poems" ends supplies the starting point for "Dear Reader": "I am trying to pry open your casket / with this burning snowflake." The poet's first words reveal the paradoxes involved in this art. They intimate that poetry can revivify the reader with its flames; in other words, the opening lines suggest that fire, instead of destroying something, can renew it. These first words also signal the hazards—and perhaps even the impossibility—of successful poetry: after all, poetry is an endeavor that is similar to that of burning a snowflake. The fact that the reader is dead further complicates the poet's project, and confirms the difficulty of his task. Tate says that "What we want from poetry is to be moved, to be moved from where we now stand. We don't just want to have our ideas or emotions confirmed" (*The Best American Poetry 1997*). In "Dear Reader" this task of moving the reader is literalized: for only when the reader is removed from his casket and returns to life can the real work of poetry begin.

In this poem, the creative moment seems to be in the future rather than in the past, and therefore the poet expresses a measured hope for his encounter with the reader: "we can rub our hands /

> *And yet … it is this method of composing exclusively for himself that makes it worthwhile for others to read his poetry."*

together, maybe / start a little fire / with our identification papers." Yet, even if the poem reveals expectation for an event that is still to come, it also testifies that the present is marred by discord. The reference to "identification papers" seems to locate the poet and reader in wartime and link their meeting with each other to destruction as much as to creation. Furthermore, the poem ends with an image of incompletion, as the poet goes about his task "half hating you, / half eaten by the moon."

The poet remarks that he is "half eaten by the moon," which may be the same "black moon" of "Shadowboxing," another poem included in *The Oblivion Ha-Ha*. The latter poem ends with a confrontation between a universal "you" (who is a proxy for the poet) and an unnamed figure who perhaps represents life or God or conscience or even art. This figure asks, "How come you always want to be / something else, how come you never take your life seriously?" The poet, speaking for "you," responds, "Shut up! Isn't it enough / I say I love you, I give you everything!" In the final stanza, the poet recounts a scene in which "you" confronts a higher power: "He comes closer. Come close, you say. / He comes closer. Then. *Whack!* And / you start again, moving around and around / the room, the room which grows larger / and larger, darker and darker. The black moon." Here Tate illustrates that it is both futile and inevitable to fight against that for which we are destined. The person identified as "you" expresses love for someone (or something) while at the same time throwing punches at that person or thing. Likewise, in "Dear Reader," Tate dramatizes the way in which the poet contradicts himself as he both entreats and resists his reader.

"Dear Reader" is one of the last poems to appear in *The Oblivion Ha-Ha*. Tate might have placed this poem first in the book, in which case it would have served as an invitation to participate

What Do I Read Next?

- In 1997, *The Best American Poetry* series celebrated its tenth anniversary, and James Tate was the guest editor who selected the 75 poems included in the volume. It is interesting to read the works that Tate considered the "best" that year and to read his introduction, in which he states that, "The daily routine of our lives can be good and even wonderful, but there is still a hunger in us for the mystery of the deep waters, and poetry can fulfill that hunger."

- Editor Joe David Bellamy put together a collection of poets discussing their own work in the 1984 collection, *American Poetry Observed: Poets on Their Work.* This book is very accessible to readers and provides interesting insight on poetic perspectives from the poets themselves, including James Tate.

- Known as a "science fiction poet," Keith Allen Daniels published his collection *Satan Is a Mathematician: Poems of the Weird, Surreal and Fantastic* in 1998. These poems have been called exotic, horrific, bizarre, and uncanny—all characterized by inventive uses of language and imagery.

- Maurice Nadeau's *The History of Surrealism* (translated by Richard Howard) was first printed in 1965, but has been reprinted in several later editions. This book has been called the "bible" of surrealism and covers the art movement's history through the artists who employed it, the culture in which it thrived, and its progression into the various arts. It is lengthy, but worth the read.

---

actively in the sequence of verses to come. Instead, "Dear Reader" stands near the end of the volume, intoning a final plea and forecasting the uncertain effect of the collection's poems: "If this trick works we can rub our hands together…." The poem is no more reliable or sincere than a "trick," and, even if it works, its effects are unpredictable: the poet concedes that only "maybe" will a fire start. "I don't

know," he confesses, declining to name the nature of his ignorance, and burdening the last lines with a conspicuous silence. Nevertheless, he assures us that he will "keep working, working," repeating that word to emphasize the unceasing nature of the poetic process. Even if the poet writes in solitude, he will return to his work in part because well-crafted poems are the only ones worth writing, or worth reading. Tate cheers on the poems in *Best American Poetry* by concluding his introduction with the line, "Go, little book, make some friends if you can." Tate reconstitutes a few words from the end of *Troilus and Criseyde,* written by the English poet Geoffrey Chaucer, and in so doing he echoes several other writers, from Ovid and Horace to John Bunyan and Lord Byron. Like many poets before him, Tate understands that, although the measure of good poetry is not whether or how well it is received, there is nothing wrong with a successful poem that makes a few friends along its journey.

Source: Jeannine Johnson, in an essay for *Poetry for Students,* Gale, 2001.

Sean Robisch

Sean Robisch is an assistant professor of ecological and American literature at Purdue University. In the following essay, Robisch discusses Tate's "Dear Reader," examining how Tate's surrealist influences structure this poem and form its images.

Regardless of what labels are given to them according to their styles or eras, poets have always been shockers. Many of them love the odd juxtaposition, the surprising turn, the line break that makes a word seem to fall on us from a little higher up. The temptation for readers who encounter a poem filled with strangeness is to run for the comfort of those labels; and so James Tate has been called an absurdist, a free-associator, and most often, a surrealist. The odd imagery in his poems may seem on the surface to be mere cleverness or gamesmanship, but the poetry in *The Oblivion Ha-Ha,* in which "Dear Reader" appears, holds together with an order and clarity that seep up through the poems, come to us slowly, and therefore may affect us deeply.

The surrealist movement with which Tate is often associated includes Rene Magritte, Salvador Dali, and Andre Breton, who wrote, "I madly love everything that adventurously breaks the thread of discursive thought and suddenly ignites a flare illuminating a life of relations fecund in another way." They loved to poke fun at death, to chat about revolution, to make grandiose claims about their own works and the way those works awakened readers from their slumber. How readers make sense of something surprising to them is the matter at hand for the surrealists. In "Dear Reader," we see an opening image that gives some support to James Tate's being known in that tradition—the narrator trying "to pry open your casket / with this burning snowflake."

Surrealist images at their best are written by poets who aspire to clarity, not just cleverness. When the reader comes to a poem in an effort to make sense of it, the poet that only frustrates that effort is writing questionable poetry, material in which the gamesmanship may have taken over. On the other hand, readers are in the constant position of training themselves to understand more and more writing, to keep at it, to work with the poet and the text to expand their consciousness and hammer out their definitions of art.

This is, of course, hard work, and "Dear Reader," is very much about frustration and effort. Although Tate uses many strange images and wild juxtapositions in *The Oblivion Ha-Ha,* he does so in order to bring the reader close to his poems, to let the reader sit and think through the possibilities, to give us material that keeps our minds alive and awake. There is an old joke in which a party clown hires a person to write cue cards for him, in case the clown forgets what he wanted to say. The clown goes to a party with a crowd that does not like him much. So he turns to his writer, who holds up a cue card reading, "Tell a funny joke." In "Dear Reader," Tate seems to understand both the clown's position and the cue card writer's.

The poem is addressed as a letter, resembling a letter that comes from a magazine or journal to one of its readership. The obvious implication here is that the poet is writing to one person, but this poem goes out to many readers. Given that one of the criticisms of Tate's poetry is that it is too clever, too aware of its own jumps and surreal junctions, we might consider that the poem is written so that critics, who are also readers, may better understand their relationship to poets.

The narrator of the poem establishes a strained relationship with its reader. The reader is being sent a letter, but is, as is assumed from the first line, dead. It might also be possible that the narrator is trying to pry open a casket the reader has not yet entered. In the latter case, the impossible (a burning snowflake, a snowflake as a pry-bar) might indicate what is to come; the poet is looking ahead

> *Surrealist images at their best are written by poets who aspire to clarity, not just cleverness.*

to the reader's inevitable demise, to only the poem being left behind.

In the second stanza, the narrator makes a trade. It is hard to tell the emotion or motivation behind the line because it is a flat statement. The narrator could be reluctant or enthusiastic to give up sleep for the reader. But one clue might be that throughout the second stanza, Tate uses the double-e sound, a kind of keening in "sleep," "freezing sleet," "and see." The narrator shares the reader's confusion as to what is happening at this point in the poem. The white-out, the inability to see, is a winter image that adds weight to the sense of sleep and death, indicating that the narrator is as "blind" to how to pry open the casket as the reader is.

The third stanza indicates that a poem is a trick, a sentiment in keeping with the surrealists. But it takes a turn into a cooperative image, a little bit of hope in that the trick might work. There is a possibility here that ends in a line break at "maybe" and, in stanza four, becomes a fire to warm the reader in the winter sleet. Tate's use of "identification papers" may imply several things: one is that readers give up their official selves and connections to the establishments that identify them when they unite with the writers of poems. Another image is that of a wartime poverty, a place in which the poet and reader stand over a fire because the infrastructure has collapsed. This reading may be a tie to Tate's use of surrealist influences, because surrealism did not follow the standard infrastructures of traditional poets. In this image then, the narrator and the reader burn their papers—which further implies that they are in this together, and that the papers to be burned could well be poems.

The narrator moves out of stanza four with a kind of plea, a throwing up of the hands and getting back to work despite the confusion, the honesty of how he or she feels as the poem comes together. Readers frustrate the narrator. They require something. They are to be satisfied somehow, and while at work, the narrator is upset by that fact.

Many writers would write without fanfare or expectation; perhaps many of readers consider writing as something one does for one's self. But the narrator of "Dear Reader" understands that putting words on a page in some way makes the act public because the poems can now be found and read, if not published. This narrator is trying to be present with the reader, so that perhaps the crafting of a poem makes a little more sense. In some ways, this is a paradoxical position, given that surrealist images, such as a burning snowflake, are designed to bend perceptions of reality, not straighten them out.

"Dear Reader" ends with mention of the moon, the cliched muse of poets throughout the centuries. The narrator says that he or she is "half eaten" by it. The muse has taken its toll; writing is a chore. This is the answer to the critic who assumes that poetry must be a precious, sentimental, formal, and easily accessible thing. As surrealism goes, Tate's is strong because it actually confronts the very people upon whom poems depend most: the readers. Tate ends the poem, leaving the narrator in the position of diligently writing despite the frustrations of trying to reach someone else with the work. Rather than feeling detached from poetry by the clever turns and odd images that appear, the reader is challenged in "Dear Reader" to sympathize with the poet, to work a little harder and entertain the possibilities of what could happen when one is willing to participate in the exchange.

Source: Sean Robisch, in an essay for *Poetry for Students*, Gale, 2001.

Cliff Saunders

Cliff Saunders teaches writing and literature in the Myrtle Beach, South Carolina, area and has published six chapbooks of poetry. In the following essay, Saunders asserts that "Dear Reader" is a surrealistic poem that probes two key concerns of author James Tate at the time of its writing: his ambivalent feelings toward his readership and Americans' complacency and obsession with superficial materialism.

Perhaps more than any other poem in *The Oblivion Ha-Ha* (1970), "Dear Reader" lays bare the conflicting feelings that James Tate had toward his readership at a crucial time in his career. Actually, Tate had found himself grappling with this dilemma ever since his first book, *The Lost Pilot,* won the Yale Younger Series of Poets award in 1966 and thrust him into the national poetry limelight at the tender age of 23. In an interview conducted by Lou Papineau and myself in the early

1970's and included as part of a larger interview published in *American Poetry Observed* (University of Illinois Press, 1984), Tate went into considerable depth about this issue. Asked whether any pressures had been placed on him by the Yale award, Tate responded that for the first time as a writer of poetry, he had to consider the possibility of an audience, and although he mused that this was probably a "phony" (i.e., foolhardy) consideration, he admitted undergoing a struggle with the concept of reader expectation in the wake of his impressive early success.

Other poems in *The Oblivion Ha-Ha,* such as "Shadowboxing," deal on some level with Tate's love-hate feelings toward the reader, but none does so more overtly than "Dear Reader." It is right there in the title, of course, for without it, the "you" addressed in the poem could be interpreted in any number of ways, such as a lover or even the poet's own "second self." So Tate wastes no time in defining the battleground, so to speak. Of course, the unassuming reader encountering the poem for the first time is likely to be surprised, if not outright shocked, that a poet would have the gall to come right out and say *I kind of hate you,* and those readers unaware of Tate's proclivity for biting irony might just toss the book aside. Until the publication of "Dear Reader," no poet had come nearly as close to facing in print the dilemma of readership as directly as Tate had. Such bold, risk-taking moves are sure to alienate a number of readers, and truth be told, Tate got raked over the coals a bit by critics for *The Oblivion Ha-Ha,* which is surely a more bitingly ironic and caustically intoned collection than *The Lost Pilot.* As noted by Chris Stroffolino in his entry on Tate for the *Dictionary of Literary Biography, Oblivion* "was almost universally panned for lacking the restraint" of *The Lost Pilot.* Looking back, however, Tate's second collection seems a seminal one, and in poems like "Dear Reader," one can see Tate taking off the "kid gloves" and adopting a "take-no-prisoners" stance that encompasses not only his struggle with society's penchant for the conventional and superficial but also his mixed feelings about poetry's readership. The rules of engagement that had guided him so well in *The Lost Pilot* were no longer adequate for a time when "everything" (not just the social status quo and America's involvement in the Vietnam War) had to be questioned, including one's modus operandi for writing poetry in the first place.

And so, in fearless fashion, Tate forged ahead in *The Oblivion Ha-Ha,* viewing no ground too sacred for investigation, least of all the implied covenant between poet and reader based on certain assumptions of how "the game" should be played. At a time when a new generation was attempting to tear down the status quo, Tate was trying to strip away any veneer that might stand in the way of his quest to shock the reader into a fuller, deeper awareness of life's possibilities. For Tate, a primary concern was that people were so locked into an entrenched system of conventional thought and superficial values that anything less than a direct frontal assault would be insufficient. Paul Christensen addresses this central concern quite cogently in his article on Tate for *Critical Survey of Poetry,* in which he points out that "[t]he central theme running throughout Tate's canon is the desire to shatter superficial experience, to break through the sterility of suburban life ..." Indeed, in "Dear Reader," the implication in the poem's first line, "I am trying to pry open your casket," is that the reader is dead—if not literally, then at least figuratively. Tate sees the reader as someone "boxed in," and though this reader may feel safe within the confines of a secure haven, Tate suggests that this attitude represents a kind of death for the reader. Moreover, he implies that it is the poet's mission to revitalize and even resurrect the reader from a death of the spirit brought on by bourgeois materialism. This task, though, may be an impossible one, for W. H. Auden may have been right when he said in his profound elegy "In Memory of W. B. Yeats" that "poetry makes nothing happen"? Is the task of prying open the reader's "casket" an impossible one if you are using a "burning snowflake" to perform the operation?

The burning snowflake initially strikes one as maddeningly paradoxical and irrational. How can a snowflake burn, let alone be held in order to pry open a casket? It cannot, of course, in any rational sense, but its powerfully symbolic suggestiveness cannot be dismissed. Aside from implying that the job of awakening the reader from a deathlike state may be doomed from the start, Tate may be using the burning snowflake as an indication of his mixed feelings toward the reader. The snowflake could mean that the prospect of having to awaken the reader from a figurative death leaves him "cold," yet a passionate need to at least attempt such a daunting task "burns" within him, so much so that it enables him to overcome the "chilly" prospect of any such foray into the private world of the reader.

It is this insular world with which Tate ultimately is concerned, the personal worlds that people protect and will seemingly do anything to maintain a safe, orderly existence. Yet it is this private

> *The rules of engagement that had guided him so well ... were no longer adequate for a time when "everything" ... had to be questioned, ..."*

place within everybody, this storehouse of subconscious energy, that manifests in dreams and in the irrational that Tate wants to penetrate. It is there, as many poets believe, where the real living is taking place, not in the mundane world of job sites, supermarkets, gas stations, and the like. This quest constitutes a kind of prime directive for the surrealist writer. Like many of the European and Latin surrealists who had preceded him, Tate was very much involved with the odd juxtapositions and incongruous combinations of words and dreamlike images that mark surrealism around the time when *The Oblivion Ha-Ha* was published. In Line 3 of "Dear Reader," Tate boldly proposes making what can only be seen as the surrealist's ultimate sacrifice: "I'll give up my sleep for you." This line emphasizes Tate's need and determination to make a connection with the reader. The bridge to the reader is a slippery one because Tate's journey toward the reader is being compromised by "[t]his freezing rain [that] keeps falling down," blinding him ("I can barely see") and thus compromising his attempt to reach the reader. The "freezing rain," which can be seen as a type of static gumming up the lines of communication between Tate and his readership, reinforces the references to cold and numbness (that is, "casket" and "snowflake") in the first stanza.

Is Tate implying that there is a "big chill" in the public imagination that he is having a hard time negotiating? The poem would seem to support such an interpretation, especially in Lines 6-9, where Tate suggests that if contact between poet and reader can be made, then a spark can ignite and spread like wildfire through the public imagination. He muses that perhaps this spark can be stoked if his readers would just contribute their "identification papers" to a community fire. Here is another image packed with possible associations. On the one hand, the image draws parallels to a very real situation occurring in America around the time when "Dear Reader," was composed: the burning of draft cards as a protest against the Vietnam War. With his choice of "identification papers," however, Tate proposes something even more fundamentally revolutionary. Whereas the burning of draft cards attempts to negate one aspect of what is perceived to be an unjust system, the burning of identification papers would be a protest directed at the entirety of such a system. This move would require great sacrifice on the part of all involved, including the loss of creature comforts and material possessions that keep most everyone safe and happy within a sense of false security. In keeping with the revolutionary tenor of the times, Tate seems to be implying that such a sacrifice may be the only means of breaking through to the heart of what really matters, of scraping off the "freezing sleet" that coats society in a numb, impenetrable gloss of superficiality. He is saying, in a sense, *Let's fire up the public imagination and get our priorities straight.*

In the poem's final stanza, however, this burning desire dissipates under the weight of doubt and the realization that his goal of communal passion will likely never come to fruition. "I don't know," Tate remarks with a tinge of helplessness, "but I keep working, working ..." In other words, he is determined to keep striving for this ideal conception of shared passion, to keep plugging away in his poetry despite the possibility that his words will make "nothing happen," will fail to spark the communal intensity he so desires. This struggle is not uncommon among serious writers, who are often caught in the dilemma of trying to push their creative powers to new heights and worrying about whether an at-large readership will jump ship for something "safe" and less demanding. This dilemma is clearly at play in the poem's last stanza, where Tate implies that his quest for artistic growth is being fueled by two contradictory forces: hatred for the reader (or, perhaps more precisely, for the kind of reader expectation that might force him to stop taking risks and thus compromise his artistic growth) and the all-consuming needs of the muse, as represented by the moon eating away at him.

In the poem's context, however, the hungry moon of the last stanza is as loaded an image as the "burning snowflake" of the first stanza. Both are images of "cold fire" being used in an irrational way, for just as a snowflake cannot burn, the moon cannot eat. Yet the moon is surely an object of "cold fire" in that it "burns" or glows but is known to be largely a frozen stone in the sky. In one sense, Tate may be saying by way of this surreal image that the muse will always burn within him, regardless of his concerns about his readership. In another sense, given that the moon has traditionally functioned as a literary symbol of longing and desire, Tate may be saying that no matter how strongly he convinces himself that the reader is an enemy of sorts, he will always long for a stronger connection between the reader and himself. Though this connection may have its high points and low points (much as the moon waxes and wanes), it will serve as a source of sustenance for poets and poetry readers alike for as long as there is a moon in the sky.

Source: Cliff Saunders, in an essay for *Poetry for Students,* Gale, 2001.

Sources

Amazon, www.amazon.com (April 18, 2000).

The History Channel, www.historychannel.com (April 18, 2000).

Tate, James, *The Oblivion Ha-Ha,* Little, Brown & Company, 1970.

———, *The Route as Briefed,* University of Michigan Press, 1999.

For Further Study

Tate, James, *The Lost Pilot,* Yale University Press, 1967.
This is Tate's first and most highly acclaimed collection. Taking its title from the actual event of his father's plane being shot down during World War II, the poet blends childhood memories, personal encounters, and his own imagination to create this award-winning book

———, *Worshipful Company of Fletchers,* Ecco Press, 1994.
This recent collection was the winner of a National Book Award. In these poems, Tate continues his surprising twists of metaphors and comedy/horror effects by placing in bizarre situations such ordinary things as toy poodles, gum wrappers, crayons, and Camp fire Girls.

Upton, Lee, *The Muse of Abandonment: Origin, Identity, Mastery, in Five American Poets,* Bucknell University Press, 1998.
As the title suggests, this book is a close and comprehensive look at how and why five poets produce the work they do. Poets include: Russell Edson, Louise Gluck, James Tate, Jean Valentine, and Charles Wright.

Drifters

Bruce Dawe
1999

"Drifters" is from the book *No Fixed Address,* Bruce Dawe's first book of poetry. Over the years, Dawe has become one of Australia's most popular poets. He is credited with bringing about a cultural shift in Australian poetry. Australians had previously considered their language to be a slight alteration of the English spoken in Britain, much as Americans did in the mid-1800s, but Dawe, like Mark Twain, showed with his writing that a particularly Australian idiom had developed, separate from Britain, spoken in a way that only people in his country spoke. Dawe combined his mastery of Australian English with his deep understanding of people on the outskirts of society and a sense of rhythm that owed more to common discourse than traditional poetic forms, and the result was a surprisingly direct style that captured the public imagination.

Author Biography

Donald Bruce Dawe was born in 1930 in Geelong, Victoria, which is just outside of one of Australia's largest cities, Melbourne. He did not care much for school and was poor at his studies, leaving school at the age of sixteen and working as a gardener and a postman. In his twenties, he finished school through a series of equivalency courses, and in 1954 he entered the University of Melbourne. Although his career at the University was brief—just less than a year—Dawe made a lasting impression on Australian poetry through his association with other writers who went on to be counted as the greatest names in Australian literature, including Vincent Buckley, Chris Wallace-Crabbe, R.A. Simpson and Andrew Taylor. This was an educated group, well-versed in their command of English, and Dawe stood out in his use of the vernacular and his command of dialect as it was used in his particular area of the country at that particular time in history.

Dawe left the University of Melbourne, worked for a few years in a factory, and then joined the Royal Australian Air Force, where he served from 1959-1968, rising to the rank of Captain. During that time he began his literary career, publishing poetry collections (including *No Fixed Address,* which this poem is from), continued his college studies, and married Gloria Desley. He received a Bachelor of Arts from University of Queensland in 1969; a Master's in 1975; and a Ph.D. in 1980. He taught until the early 1990's at University of Southern Queensland, and upon retiring from there was awarded an honorary professorship. Dawe continues to write, is published frequently, and is recognized as one of the leading literary voices in Australia. He has received numerous awards for his writing, including the Myer Award for Poetry in 1965; the Patrick White Literary Award in 1980; and the Order of Australia, for his contribution to Australian literature, in 1982.

Poem Text

One day soon he'll tell her it's time to start
 packing,
And the kids will yell "Truly?" and get wildly
 excited for no reason,
And the brown kelpie pup will start dashing about,
 tripping everyone up,
And she'll go out to the vegetable-patch and pick
 all the green tomatoes from the vines,
And notice how the oldest girl is close to tears 5
 because she was happy here,
And how the youngest girl is beaming because she
 wasn't.
And the first thing she'll put on the trailer will be
 the bottling set she never unpacked from
 Grovedale,
And when the loaded ute bumps down the drive
 past the blackberry-canes with their last
 shrivelled fruit,
She won't even ask why they're leaving this time,
 or where they're heading for
—she'll only remember how, when they came 10
 here,

she held out her hands bright with berries,
the first of the season, and said:
'Make a wish, Tom, make a wish.'

Poem Summary

Line 1:

This poem begins in the middle of some lives that are already in progress, without indicating who these people are or what has happened to them in the past. The references to "he" and "her" in the first line are left unexplained, so that readers only come to know these characters through what happens in the poem. Similarly, there is no further information given about why "it's time to start packing," about where they are or why they have to leave. To some degree, they are leaving because, as the brief title of the poem states, they are "drifters," and as such it is in their nature to not stay in one place. As the details of the poem are going to explain, though, the entire family does not agree with the idea of leaving just for the sake of leaving. The mother, for example—the "her" of the first line—has hopes of establishing some permanence here. She is willing to leave in order to be supportive of the father, which is an aspect of their relationship that is clear in the poem's first line, when a major decision for the family is made by him alone, without discussion, and told to her.

Lines 2-4:

All of the activity in these lines serves to show how unexpected the decision to move is. The narrative voice makes a judgment on this activity by commenting that the children's excitement is "for no reason," but the poem has not yet established its point of view. It would seem to be the man's perspective given by the narrator. To the children, there is quite a good reason to be excited, and to people who lead stable lives it makes sense that moving would cause some turbulence, but the man is the one who is calm about the decision he announces, and so the excitement would seem to him to be "for no good reason." It is not until later that the poem attaches itself to the woman's point of view, and that gives this phrase new meaning: instead of meaning that the children shouldn't be excited, it means that she wished they wouldn't.

The scene around the house is chaotic, a sense that Dawe adds to by having the dog run around barking. A "kelpie" is an Australian sheepdog, descended from the breed of collies, but in Scottish the word also refers to an evil water spirit that takes the form of a horse and drowns travelers. This cross-meaning gives the poem a sense of danger, implying that the family is not only traveling with a puppy for the children but also an omen of bad luck. The unexpectedness of the move is conveyed by the fact that the tomatoes are still green on the vine; the mother's reluctance about leaving is clear in the fact that she picks the tomatoes even though they aren't ripe, having become too attached to them to drive away and leave them.

These lines are the first three of eight in a row that begin with "and." This is a technique that helps the poem's style imitate the chaos in the family's life. By starting with "and" over and over, the thoughts presented in each line seem to be added with no large scheme in mind, as if the speaker of the poem is just realizing important details while going along, feeling finished at the end of each line but then finding that something else needs to be mentioned.

Lines 5-6:

The attitudes of the two daughters represent the attitudes of the parents: the older one has been happy living there and is upset to be leaving, while the other is glad to go. Although these are the only two mentioned, the implication is that there are more children, enough to create a hectic situation while running around. Lines 5 and 6 are not only about how the daughters react, but about the mother noticing their varied reactions, even though the poem does not tell readers what this information means to her.

Line 7:

Australians use the word "bottling" the same way that Americans use "canning." The woman in this poem has a kit to make preserves out of the vegetables that she has grown in her garden, but is forced to leave before they become mature enough to be useful. In Australian slang, a "bottler" is also something that is excellent. The extent to which she thinks her vegetables will be excellent is a reflection of the hope that her garden raises in her. This family is poor enough to count on the crop of their small vegetable garden, and they probably would be much more comfortable with those canned vegetables than without them, but, to her disappointment, they have not been in that place long enough for one crop cycle.

Lines 8-9:

"Ute" is Australian slang for a utility vehicle. The shriveled fruit on the blackberry vines that is

Media Adaptations

- Dawe can be heard discussing his work on a cassette recording made in 1989 for ABC Radio, in Sydney, Australia. The title of the tape is *Bruce Dawe in Conversation.*

- Another audiocassette, titled *Bruce Dawe Reads His Poems,* was released in 1983 by Longman Cheshire of Melbourne, Australia.

- Dawe is featured on a 1973 recording from University of Queensland Press at St. Lucia, titled *Australian Writers on Tape.*

- *Some Poems of Bruce Dawe* is a 1973 audiocassette released by A.B.C. of Sydney as part of their "Poet's Tongue" radio series.

- The most comprehensive website about Australian literature is *OzLit,* which can be found at www.vicnet.net.au/. This site has reviews, biographies of authors, and updates on recent articles in Australian literary publications.

mentioned in line 8 is a foreshadowing of the memory to come at the end of the poem, which takes the woman back to the time when the fruit was new. There is a sense of weariness and despair in the way that the woman decides, in line 9, to not ask why they are leaving or where they are going; these would be natural questions, but she apparently knows from experience that asking will not change the man's mind or make any difference whatsoever. The hope that she may have once had, symbolized by the garden and the bottling set, is so far gone that she lacks any strength of will to make her own wishes known.

Lines 10-12:

This flashback presents the hope that the woman once had, which has been hinted at throughout the poem. The woman's hands are mentioned, showing readers her physical connection to the place in a more tangible and personal way than if the poem only mentioned that she "held" the berries. In addition, her hands are "bright," while brightness usually indicates hope and optimism, a goal that one can see beyond the dismal present. In line 12 the berries that are dying at the time of the poem are fresh and new, "the first of the season— all looks encouraging for her plans to reap the bounty of the land and to capture the sweetness that is just beginning in jars or cans, so that they can not only see it, or experience it, but keep it too.

Line 13:

This is only the second time that anyone in this poem speaks—the first is in line 2, when they children ask "Truly?" with just as much optimism about leaving as the mother had about arriving. It is only in this line, when the woman is most enthusiastic about life, that anyone in the poem is given an identity. When she looked forward to what life would bring them at the new location, he was "Tom," but when they are leaving after a few months without having improved their lives at all she knows better than to think that their lives will be any better in the new place. Her mind is so deadened that in the present she does not even think of him by name anymore, as if "Tom" were someone from a different time, with whom she wanted to share life, and not the man that she blindly, reluctantly follows.

Themes

Permanence

"Drifters" is about a family that regularly packs all of their worldly belongings into their car, driving off to a new home. In the scene presented here, the mother, anticipating the pattern, imagines that they will not stay at their latest location for the tomato harvest to ripen in the garden. She knows that the odds are great that the father can come home and announce at any time that "it's time to start packing." There is no evidence to show why they have to leave, whether it is because of his job, or legal complications, or just because he is the type of person who likes to change addresses often. There is also no evidence that anyone in the family expects any more stability to life than theirs offers. The oldest girl is displeases because she has been happy where they are, and the mother appears to be vaguely dissatisfied about leaving her garden crop unfinished, but the basic idea of having a permanent address does not seem to enter into their thoughts. These are people who do not know what permanence is and cannot imagine what it would

be like, who only have a general feeling that it would be better to linger at any place a little longer than they do.

Cycle of Life

'For the woman in this poem, time is measured by the blackberries that grow at the end of the road. She remembers that the first berries of the season had just ripened when the family arrived, filling her with hope, prompting her to tell the man to "Make a wish" in anticipation of a better life to come. She expects him to want to leave before the end of blackberry season, her withered hopes symbolized by the unripe fruit that is left to ripen on the vine and rot. There is another method used to measure both the length of time that the family has been in one place and the hope that they had and then lost; the vegetable patch, where, unlike the blackberries, fruit was cultivated by the family when they arrived. The tomatoes there are green, not having been given a full cycle to mature, but the woman is willing to pick them prematurely, to cut them down like her hopes, before they reach their fullest potential. Without the plant-growing cycle to measure how long they have been in one place, the woman's disappointment about having to leave so soon would be nothing but a vague sense of discontent; when held up against the cycle of life, her feelings become much more real for readers.

Loyalty

This poem raises the question of why, if she is so dissatisfied with the life that the man forces her family to leave, this woman does not just leave and pursue a life that would make her happy. One answer might be that she is bound by social convention, that whether they are married or not society would still judge her harshly if she left. This social pressure would not, however, be as strongly felt in a family of drifters as it would be felt in a stable situation. An even stronger motive for her loyalty is presented at the very end of the poem, where the woman is shown sharing her hope for the future with the man. When she says, "Make a wish, Tom," it is clear that the future looks bright to her, and that she wants him to experience that same feeling. The poem does not record his response, whether he felt the same way she felt upon arriving, but the important thing is that she thought, if only for a short time, that she could stir in him the believe that life was going to be better. When she anticipates his plans, the poem explains, "she won't even ask why they're leaving this time or where they're headed for." In spite of her disappointment, she is

Topics for Further Study

- Study an occupation that would have migratory workers and report on the lives they lead.

- Find out what services are available in your community to help people who have just arrived there. Interview someone from one of these organizations to find out what they have to offer transients.

Instead of holding this poem together by using repeated sounds at the ends of the lines, as a traditional rhyming pattern would do, Dawe uses repetition at the beginnings of the lines. Of the thirteen lines, seven begin with the word "and," and another three begin with "she." The effect of this is to give emphasis to those particular words—repeating "and" makes the poem seem spontaneous, as if the speaker is tacking on new thoughts while going along, while saying "she" often makes readers more aware of the woman's consciousness. It also serves to hold the poem together, to give the whole piece a sense of unity and order. A clear-cut rhyme scheme makes readers aware of the controlling hand of the author, while this sort of repetition achieves the same purpose to some degree, while appearing to occur within the natural boundaries of speech.

committed to staying with him and possibly making him happy.

Fear

The thing that the woman in this poem fears—that her life will be uprooted once again, that the stability she had hoped for will dissolve without warning one day—does not happen here. This detailed account of how the family's next move will come about is not her reality, it is only what she fears is going to happen. "One day ..." the poem starts—she has no way of knowing for certain that this will actually happen, but her sense of inevitability reflects how much she fears that it will come about. She thinks of these future events as being a foregone conclusion so that she can come to grips with what she fears and start learning to accept it even before it comes to pass.

Style

"Drifters" is written in blank verse, which means that the ends of the lines are not rhyming words. Often, blank verse will be written with a regular rhythm, such as alternating stressed and unstressed syllables, with the same number of syllables on each line. In this case, though, there is no distinct style given to the meter (which is the term poets use for the rhythmic pattern) or to the lengths of the lines. Dawe has not organized this poem around any poetic style, but has given it the natural structure that occurs in speech.

Historical Context

The history of Australia is often associated with the history of the United States, because both were British colonies that developed their national characters by ignoring the rights of their indigenous people and prevailing over rugged geographical conditions. The comparisons between the two countries are valid, but they are also limited. Australia became known to Europeans on 1770, just as tensions in America were leading toward the War of Independence. It was in that year that English captain James Cook found a port near what is now Sidney that was useful for docking his ship, claiming the southern coast of Australia for England. Following the American Revolution, England needed a place to send convicted felons, and so in the 1780s prison camps were established in Australia. Governors were sent from England to manage the new land, and former convicts who had earned their freedom formed a middle class, while the convicts were used as slave labor to build roads and buildings in the rugged terrain. Unlike America, which has vast tracts of fertile land available for farming, Australia is mostly made up of barren, rocky ground that is unfit for growing. There was no tradition of hopeful expansion, as there was in America; the prison camps along the periphery of the continent were the end, not the start, of growth. Also, this heritage as a prison colony has left a lasting impression on the country's cultural identity. Before the penal colony there was closed in 1887, the number of people sent there to serve out prison

Compare & Contrast

- **1962:** The United States sealed the island nation of Cuba after its spy satellites revealed that Cuban dictator Fidel Castro was being supplied with Soviet nucelar weapons. After tense negotiations, the Soviets removed their weapons from Cuba. Historians recognize the Cuban Missile Crisis as being the closest that the world has come to nuclear war.

  Today: The Soviet Union, which was the only superpower that could match the United States in the 1960s, collapsed in 1990. Cuba is still a Communist state and still ruled by Fidel Castro.

- **1962:** The first K-Mart stores and the first Wal-Mart stores were opened that year. K-Mart grew rapidly throughout the 1960s and 1970s, but Wal-Mart caught up in the 1980s and eventually became the highest grossing department store.

  Today: Increasing numbers of people are staying away from large stores and shopping online.

- **1962:** Philip Morris Company started a new advertising campaign aimed at making people associate its top-selling brand with the rugged, outdoor masculinity of cowboys. The "Marlboro Man" campaign eventually was to make Marlboro cigarettes the top-selling brand in the world.

  Today: In an effort to reduce teenagers' infatuation with cigarettes, the government has restricted the use of advertising images such as the Marlboro Man.

- **1962:** The United States was still largely segregated, particularly in the south. James Meredith, an Air Force veteran, was faced by thousands of angry protestors when he tried to attend class at the University of Mississippi. Federal guards stayed at Meredith's side for ten months, and his life was in danger every moment.

  Today: Laws against discrimination due to race, disability, or gender give victims of discrimination a chance to sue for their rights.

---

sentences topped 160,000, and it was mostly their descendants who make up the modern population. Some parts of the island, such as Dawe's native Victoria, were settled by Europeans who were not involved in the penal system, and these areas carried a sense of pride over the western colonies, which developed an identity of half-civilized toughness. In Australian literature of the late-1800s and early-1900s, the struggle against nature became a dominant theme, just as it had been for American writers when the country was being settled. Among the stereotypes that became popular in Australian literature were the drovers (whose job it was to drive herds of sheep across great distances) and swagmen, who were transient workers who went from job to job with their belongings in blanket rolls ("swags") on their backs.

Unlike the United States, Australia did not fight to get out from under the rule of Britain, but instead was generally content with being a British colony. Australian culture reflected English culture, so that the emerging national identity was overshadowed for many years whenever it contrasted with the European way of seeing things. It was not until 1901 that Australia became an independent federation, and even after that the country still maintained close ties with London, technically but not spiritually separated. A wedge was driven between the two during World War I, when Australian interests became more clearly defined as something distinct from European interests. One famous turning point in the growth of Australia's self-identity was the famous battle of Gallipoli, in Turkey, during which British strategists sent Australian troops into a senseless attack to their certain death; this incident highlighted the courage of Australian soldiers and the foolishness of following British rule. In World War II, England concentrated its defenses against Germany, which was just across the English Channel in France. Australia, on the other hand, was much more concerned with possible attacks from Japan, which was not far away in the Pacific Ocean. This war, in the 1940s, pushed Australia into the global community as a completely separate political entity.

In the United States, the late 1950s and early 1960s are seen as a peaceful time curing which the country enjoyed economic prosperity and stability, in part because it had become the world's leading economy after the nations of Europe and Asia had suffered the destructive effects of World War II. As the trauma of the war receded into the past and the economy grew, Americans became uneasy with comfort and complacency; the social conformity of the 50s led to social revolutions in the 60s. Australians picked up American social values, mostly through the visual media, such as television and movies. The country did not have a film industry, and these media mostly showed products that were made in the United States. Thus, a poem like "Drifters" shows influences of the Australian swagman tradition, of John Steinbeck's *The Grapes of Wrath,* of the independent spirit of American "beat" poetry of the late 50s and of the independent spirit that defines both countries.

Critical Overview

Bruce Dawe is associated with a small, intellectual group of poets who worked at or around University of Melbourne in the late 1950s. Writing in 1967, Clement Semmler categorized these writers for their sense of irony, identifying Dawe in particular as a "sardonic urban poet," depending upon "the native ironic shrug to counter a tendency toward sentimentality" in his work. History has shown that this post-modern irony was not unique to Australian writers, and that Dawe was not very unique in his urban toughness, when looked at from a global perspective. Still, Semmler's focus on Dawe as a leader in his field has withstood the test of time.

Dawe is one of the most popular poets to come out of the Australian movement of the 1960s. One of the reasons for his popularity was that he made his mark in the public's conscious early, with his first collection, *No Fixed Address,* which included the poem "Drifters." While the other young Melbourne poets of the day were intellectual and showed at least some debt to English and American literary tradition, Dawe wrote in a new style, practically rewriting the rules of poetry by himself. Thomas Shapcott, an Australian writer who assembled the volume *Contemporary American & Australian Poetry,* credited Dawe with bringing about "a very real re-thinking": "at once vernacular and expressive of the new, post-war, outer-suburban hinterland," was the way that Shapcott characterized Dawe's work. "It was the language of a culture previously untapped in our writing, and Dawe gave expression to it with humor and very considerable skill." No one had captured the way Australians talk so exactly, nor recognized the beauty of everyday Australian life. Dawe was the first writer to face the new reality of Australia's poor as they shifted from a country to an urban background.

"Drifters" is one of the most influential poems from Dawe's early period, standing out not just for its theme but for its humanity. "'Drifters' is a poem to compare with Hardy and Larkin," Vivian Smith wrote in *The Oxford History of Australian Literature,* putting Dawe in league with two of the twentieth century's greatest poets, both known for their understanding of ordinary people. She further praises "Drifters" not only for the empathy it shows toward the underclass, who Smith refers to as the "down-and-outers," but for presenting its empathy with a calm and controlled tone. "The remarkable achievement of this poem is in its dynamic movement," Smith explains: "it moves forward and upward rather than drifting down, to show how in a life of drifting, the elation of hope and happiness and surprise are sustaining elements. This capturing of a sense of unquenchable hope in an otherwise hopeless situation adds to the poignancy of the poem."

Since the 1960s, Bruce Dawe's reputation as a major Australian poet has been solidified. Having made an early reputation for writing in an innovative style, he has remained fairly consistent throughout the decades, growing in compassion, not inventiveness. His early, immense popularity led some critics to initially make light of his artistry, but over the decades those writers have come to respect his work. He is still considered one of his country's greatest poets, and is considered an innovator who opened Australian poetry up to a new awareness of the lives and verbal style of the ordinary people.

Criticism

David Kelly

David Kelly is an instructor of creative writing and composition at two colleges in Illinois. In the following essay, he examines aspects that make "Drifters" a distinctly Australian poem.

> "*Drifters*" offers a picture of hopelessness and ineffectuality that taps one strain of the Australian personality without capturing the nation's good humor."

Because of the similarities of experience, Americans can generally pick up Australian writings without much background, aside from the definitions of a few words that are exclusively theirs. Much Australian poetry, if it is not concerned with specific natural conditions, reflects life and sensibilities that could be our own. This has been especially true since World War II, when the bonds between Australia and the United States became closer as we fought a common enemy.

Bruce Dawe's poem "Drifters," which comes from his 1962 collection *No Fixed Address,* is accessible to American readers. On the other hand, this is a particularly Australian poem, and if we look at where it came from we can see that, though it fits our circumstances, it fits its own land even better.

Geography tells the tale most eloquently. Australia is a huge island that, like America, is thousands of miles away from Europe. Much has been written about the country's roots as a prison colony, a dumping ground for England's criminals for nearly a hundred years. Such a history is undeniably important, and will show a residual trace in nearly all things Australian, such as the deep-seated, almost maniacal struggle for freedom hinted at in "Drifters." Even more important, though, is the topography of the continent.

In America the wilderness is lush and fertile, and going into the wilderness in our literature may be dangerous, but more often than not it means beginning a new and better life. American expansion moved in one direction, from east to west, with some of the most fertile soil in the world found in the Great Plains of the center. Australia's center, on the other hand, is a desert, barely inhabitable and certainly not a garden of prosperity. The penal

colonies were so successful because they offered nowhere to escape. Prisoners left on the western edge of the continent stayed there. Over the generations, the descendants of former convicts and their jailers developed a civilization, but they certainly did not plunge into it with the optimism that drove America's settlers.

It is not pessimism, exactly, that hangs over the lives of the people in "Drifters," but they do see life as a cycle of hope followed by hope's abandonment. America has its share of idealists, always pulling up stakes to look for something better, and its share of desperados who are always on the run, but "Drifters" comes from a more subtle frame of mind than that. The people it shows are not going anywhere; the reader knows that as well as the wife in the poem does. The phrase "make a wish" at the end of the poem means different things to Australians than to Americans. An American speaker could, even in the circumstances given, imbue this phrase with a greater belief that prosperity actually is just over the next ridge, but Australia, settled around the edges of a harsh island, offers the drifters only three possibilities: somewhere like where they are, or the ocean or the desert. Of course this is a generalization that ignores all of the beauty of the land, but it applies to the poem in a general sense.

"Drifters" offers a picture of hopelessness and ineffectuality that taps one strain of the Australian personality without capturing the nation's good humor. Dawe captures a feeling of what life is like for his characters by using the language that he uses. This poem is specifically, pointedly, as "unpoetic" as the unhappy lives it presents, relying on the strength of its well-placed images to keep readers' attention. Dawe does not let his technical skill draw attention to itself, but it is all over the piece, such as the alliteration of "how," "happy," and "home" and assonance of "tears," "she," and "here" in line 5. He makes it read like the kind of poem that might have been written by the kind of people that it talks about.

Dawe was considered a master of rendering common lives in their own terms, of seeing poetry in the ordinary. In the early 1960's, when his work first started to appear, Dawe was considered a pioneer who ignored Australia's cultural ties to England and America and developed an Australian voice to present Australian people and their concerns. His direct relation to the people of his land was ground-breaking, but it was also long overdue.

A reader does not need to know anything about the society or circumstances a poem like "Drifters" was written in to understand or appreciate it. The kinship between American and Australian poetry is a close one, maybe even closer than our relationship to other Western civilizations, owing to our nations' similar histories, but there is also much that makes Australia different. The sort of people in a poem like this are in fact universal types, but there will always be assumptions in the culture they came from that require a slightly deeper examination.

Source: David Kelly, in an essay for *Poetry for Students*, Gale, 2001.

Erica Smith

Erica Smith is a writer and editor. In this essay she explores Dawe's "Drifters" as an illustration of the poet's social concerns.

Bruce Dawe's "Drifters" begins with a simple declaration—"One day soon he'll tell her it's time to start packing"—given without an explanation. That simple statement brings a surge of theoretical consequences, tumbling out in a rapid-fire series of images that comprise the poem. Over the course of the poem the reader comes to a full realization of the tensions inherent in a family of migrants.

In the beginning of the poem the reader feels the electricity of the anticipated announcement travel through the house: "the kids will yell 'Truly?' and get wildly excited for no reason, / and the brown kelpie pup will start dashing about, tripping everyone up." It is significant that the reactions of the children and the dog are mentioned first, for the reader can most closely identify with them. A reader, like a child or an animal, can sense commotion, and react to it, without yet knowing the full spectrum of what exactly is going on. For now, the poet chooses to withhold the reason for the announcement.

The following lines depict the more contemplative reactions of the wife and two daughters. First the wife goes into the garden and picks the green tomatoes, presumably saving them because she needs to conserve her resources. Then the poet asks, "notice how the oldest girl is close to tears because she was happy here, / and how the youngest girl is beaming because she wasn't." This double-snapshot of the two sisters is both a nostalgic look at childhood's ups and downs, and a serious portrait of two children who are thrown into upheaval. The lines carefully bring out the daughters' inner thoughts, and a phrase such as "she was happy here" further implies that "here" is but one in a chain of places in which the daughter has lived.

> *... We seem either too smug or too shy to have a good hard look at the world we live in ... the suffering, poignant and necessary world."*

That recognition, when made by the reader, can be deeply saddening.

Along those lines, it is interesting to note that the poet positions the "announcement" as a foregone conclusion, setting it sometime in the future. Thus, as with the girls' reactions, the reader senses that the family has been through this upheaval numerous times already. The poet can imagine, down to the last emotional nuance, what will happen when the inevitable comes to pass.

The action of the poem then turns back to the wife: "And the first thing she'll put on the trailer will be the bottling-set she never unpacked from Grovedale." This detail indicates another crucial element of the family's life. Not only does the family move on a regular basis, but they move so frequently that they do not have time to unpack their belongings. The last thing to be removed from the trailer is the first to be put back on.

Suddenly the action of the poem jumps ahead. The family is already packed and leaving, the trailer bumping down the drive, "past the blackberry canes with their last shriveled fruit." The image of the shriveled fruit mirrors the family's circumstances: the family's time of thriving in this home, and town, has passed.

As the family is leaving, the focus of the poem turns again to the wife's thoughts: "she won't even ask why they're leaving this time, or where they're heading for." This is a harrowing reality. Still, the reader does not know exactly why the family must go. The reader may surmise that the father is a tenant farmer (suggested by the image of dying fruit), or perhaps he is another kind of laborer who is hired only long enough to complete a specific job. Like the wife, the reader remains unable to ask why.

Despite the terror of having to leave, and quite possibly of having nowhere to go, the wife's

What Do I Read Next?

- One of the most recent studies of Dawe's poetry is Peter Kuch's *Bruce Dawe,* published in 1996 by Oxford University Press. Kuch examines Dawe's poetry using post-Structural and post-colonial theory.

- Ken L. Goodwin's 1988 biography *Adjacent Worlds: A Literary Life of Bruce Dawe* is considered one of the most influential works about the poet, although it is difficult to find in America.

- One of the most famous and influential books about migrant farm workers in the United States in John Steinbeck's 1939 novel *The Grapes of Wrath.* This influential book, describing life during the Great Depression, fills in ideas about the transient life that are hinted at in "Drifters."

- "Drifters" is included, with many other significant contemporary Australian poems, in one of the best anthologies available, *The Bloodaxe Book of Modern Australian Poetry,* edited by John Tranter and Philip Mead. Published in 1991 by Bloodaxe Books, England.

- Judith Wright is the most respected Australian poet of the generation before Dawe's (she was born in 1915). Her poetry is sharp and amusing. One of her best collections is *The Double Tree: Selected Poems, 1942-1976,* published in the United States by Houghton Mifflin.

---

thoughts are presented with a tone of resignation rather than fear. It is likely that the wife feels this resignation after having moved so many times already. But rather than communicating with her husband, she yields to her own inner thoughts. It is indeed alarming that she does not even know where they are going, and reader is left to wonder if the husband knows, either. The wife's train of thought then trails back into the past:

> —she'll only remember how, when they came here,

she held out her hands bright with berries,
the first of the season, and said:
'Make a wish, Tom, make a wish.'

Here, the wife's introspection turns bittersweet. She remembers that, upon arriving at this home, the future seemed promising. The same berries that are now shrivelled were once full and ripe, and she was full of hope. The woman holding out her hands, full of berries, to her husband was both giving a gift and issuing a plea. She entreated him to "make a wish," and she may have made a wish herself. Most likely both of them wished to stay, prosper, and be happy. The wish is now unfulfilled with their leaving. As the poem concludes on this poignant note, the reader is left hoping that the family will find the prosperity they desire.

This poem embodies many of the concerns that have prevailed in Bruce Dawe's work. An Australian poet, cited by Thomas W. Shapcott in *Contemporary Poets* as "the most central and pivotal poet in Australia during the decade of the 1960s," Dawe is known for portraying the ordinary lives of those in his country. Within Dawe's body of work the migrant family of "Drifters" coexists with residents of the suburbs, soldiers in Vietnam, and a raped girl, and many others. By shining their lives in the light, Dawe demonstrates a deep empathy for these people. In fact, the title of his 1999 volume *A Poet's People* is both an acknowledgment of, and an ironic spin on, his distinction. He remains one of Australia's most popular, and most widely taught, poets.

Despite the presence of Dawe's poetry in the schools, the poems themselves are not literary or academic. Instead, they are precise and compassionate pictures of outsiders—"battlers," Dawe has called them—communicated in plain language. Dawe merges these pictures with his overarching conscience. This conscience is comprised of a deep commitment to political, social, and religious concerns. In 1964, early in the course of his work, Dawe spoke at a Commonwealth Literary Fund lecture, elaborating his views on this aspect of poetry:

> [There is a] a painful lack of social awareness in our poetry ... So few genuine poems reflect directly or indirectly an awareness of the social problems of our country ... those which concern people everywhere one way or another ... I mean such issues as graft and corruption in government, business and industry, spiritual wickedness in high places. I mean the never-ending tussle of State versus the individual ... There are the lost people in our midst for whom no one speaks and who cannot speak for themselves ... We seem either too smug or too shy to have a good hard

look at the world we live in … the suffering, poignant and necessary world.

"Drifters" indeed, is a portrait of what goes on in that "necessary world." It is the empathy of the poet that keeps his ideologies, when depicted in a poem, from becoming overzealous. One of the beautiful aspects of "Drifters" is that the reader is left feeling as if he or she has witnessed a stark and melancholy moment. Others of Dawe's poems have a similar effect. Consider these lines from "Phantasms of Evening," concerning the Vietnam War:

Light fails. From here
it's hard to see
whether those young men ghost-dancing into there
        graves
are Viet Cong or Sioux …
Say, are those plumed shadows

Flying Horsemen of the First Air Cavalry
        Division,
or Hittites bringing the gospel of iron
to confound the Egyptians?
Whose war are we up to now?
Whose mourning is it?

These lines passionately and concisely covey the poet's moral stance, and the result is aching. Likewise, of the poem "Home-coming" the critic Geoffrey Lehmann of the *Bulletin* wrote: "There is a tolerance point where excruciating pain becomes angelic singing, and this poem exists at that point." To strike such a note of purity is a major accomplishment.

One of the wellsprings for Dawe's conscience is his Christian belief, although few of his poems are overtly religious. Interestingly, though, selections from Dawe's 1999 volume, such as "Some Old Testament Characters with Big Problems Get the Latest Treatment" (presumably by negotiating with one of the new gods: psychiatry), do use religious themes to expose perceived hypocrisies in society.

If one were to search for a salient criticism of Dawe, it would be that his effort to make his poems sound like everyday speech (through use of the vernacular) at times comes across as affected. However, one might argue that that is a far less grievous fault than the transgressions of academic poetry.

Dawe takes on personal and cultural issues full throttle, and remains a force to be reckoned with.

Source: Erica Smith, in an essay for *Poetry for Students,* Gale, 2001.

Sources

Lehmann, Geoffrey, "Beyond the Subdivisions," review, in *Bulletin,* May 2, 1970, p. 56.

Martin, Philip, "Public yet Personal: Bruce Dawe's Poetry," in *Meanjin Quarterly,* Vol. 25, No. 3, 1966, p. 21.

McLaren, Greg, "I Think I Must Write This Down," review, in *Southerly,* Spring-Summer, 1999, p. 403.

Semmler, Clement, *Twentieth-Century Australian Literary Criticism,* Oxford University Press, 1967, pp. 350-51.

Shapcott, Thomas, "Introduction," in *Contemporary American & Australian Poetry,* University of Queens Press, 1976, pp. xxiii-xxxiii.

Smith, Vivian, "Poetry," in *The Oxford History of Australian Literature,* edited by Leonie Kramer, Oxford University Press, 1981, pp. 269-426.

For Further Study

Australian Literature: An Anthology of Writing from the Land Down Under, edited by Phyllis Fahrie Edelson, Ballentine Books, 1993.

> This overview has examples from the greatest writers in all periods throughout Australian history. Edelson's introduction gives an especially concise and helpful chronology of the country's civic and literary growth.

Buckley, Vincent, *Essays in Poetry, Mainly Australian,* Books for Libraries Press, 1969.

> This collection is out of print and a little dated, but it still provides a good analysis of the Australian literary scene at about the time "Drifters" was written.

Clark, Manning, *A Short History of Modern Australia,* Mentor Books, 1963.

> Published at about the same time as this poem, Clark's book concentrates on the country's history as a prison, with plenty of interesting tales that illuminate how the Australians came to be who they are.

Tranter, John, "Australian Poetry 1940–1980: A Personal View," in *Poetry,* October-November, 1996, pp. 86-93.

> This essay, published in *Poetry* magazine's special Australian issue, is written by one of the most influential writers on the Australian poetry scene.

Dulce et Decorum Est

Wilfred Owen

1920

Many of Wilfred Owen's poems, including "Dulce et Decorum Est," paint in stark images the brutality of war. Having fought in some of the bloodiest action of World War I, Owen wished to warn his English countrymen that the horrors of combat far outweigh its glory. He believed that those writers and politicians at home who championed the necessity of war did so only because they had not experienced its suffering—the suffering of the poem's dying soldier poisoned by mustard gas, his "white eyes writhing in his face," the blood "gargling" from his lungs. Such images were intended to make civilians experience the troops' fear and pain. Owen hoped that by displaying in such vivid terms the reality of war he might encourage others to let pity inform their patriotism.

"Dulce et Decorum Est," like much of Owen's work, relies on irony—a figure of speech in which the actual intent is expressed in words which carry the opposite meaning—to help convey its message about war. An example of this is title itself, from the Latin poet Horace: *"Dulce et decorum est pro patria mori"* ("Sweet and fitting it is to die for one's country"). Although patriotic and romantic depiction's of war run through British poetry of the Victorian period (see, for instance, Tennyson's "The Charge of the Light Brigade"), Owen hoped to direct poetry in a new direction. He shows us nothing "sweet" in a gas attack, nothing "fitting" or heroic about bootless, "blood-shod" soldiers marching "like old beggars" and "coughing like hags." Compared with war's absurd violence,

Owen suggests, patriotism becomes an absurd matter: the poem never tells us what country the poisoned soldier is dying for.

Owen himself was killed in 1918, a week before the armistice that ended World War I. He had just returned to the front after recuperating from illness in a Scottish hospital. While in the hospital, he met and was encouraged by the English poet Siegfried Sassoon, who published much of Owen's work in a volume titled *Poems* in 1920. Today Owen is regarded as one of the finest war poets of the century.

Author Biography

Owen was born in 1893 in Oswestry, Shropshire, the eldest son of Susan Shaw Owen and Thomas Owen, a railroad station master. After attending schools in Birkenhead and Shrewsbury, and failing in an attempt to win a scholarship to enter London University, Owen became an unpaid lay assistant to the Vicar of Dunsden in Oxfordshire. After trying unsuccessfully for a scholarship again in 1913, he spent time in France, teaching for a year at the Berlitz School of Languages in Bordeaux, and then privately tutoring for an additional year. Shortly after his return to England, Owen enlisted in the Artist's Rifles. He was later commissioned as a lieutenant in the Manchester Regiment, and in late 1916, with World War I raging, was posted to the Western Front, where he participated in the Battle of the Somme. Suffering shell-shock after several months of service at the front, Owen was declared unfit to command and was taken out of action in May, 1917. In June he was admitted to Craiglockhart War Hospital in Edinburgh, where he met Siegfried Sassoon, an outspoken critic of the war who encouraged him to use his battle experiences as subjects for poetry. Owen returned to the front in early September 1918, shortly afterwards being awarded the Military Cross for gallantry. He was killed in action at the Sambre Canal in northeast France on November 4, 1918—one week before the Armistice. He is buried at Ors, France.

Sassoon's respect and encouragement confirmed for Owen his ability as a poet. Under Sassoon's guidance he first adapted his poetic techniques to nontraditional war subjects, writing most of his critically acclaimed poems in the fifteen months prior to his death. Having had only five poems published during his lifetime, Owen's reputation as a poet was only established in 1920, with

Wilfred Owen with young boy, possibly his son.

the publication of *Poems*, a volume edited by Sassoon. A second collection edited by Edmund Blunden caught the attention of W. H. Auden and the poets in his circle who admired Owen's artistry and technique. Owen is widely considered among the finest English poets of World War I, gaining further recognition through an additional collection edited by C. Day Lewis and the inclusion of his works in numerous anthologies.

Poem Text

Bent double, like old beggars under sacks,
Knock-kneed, coughing like hags, we cursed
    through sludge,
Till on the haunting flares we turned our backs
And towards our distant rest began to trudge.
Men marched asleep. Many had lost their boots   5
But limped on, blood-shod. All went lame; all
    blind;
Drunk with fatigue; deaf even to the hoots
Of tired, outstripped Five-Nines that dropped
    behind.

Gas! GAS! Quick, boys!—An ecstasy of fumbling,
Fitting the clumsy helmets just in time;   10
But someone still was yelling out and stumbling,
And flound'ring like a man in fire or lime ...
Dim, through the misty panes and thick green light,
As under a green sea, I saw him drowning.

In all my dreams, before my helpless sight,   15
He plunges at me, guttering, choking, drowning.

If in some smothering dreams you too could pace
Behind the wagon that we flung him in,
And watch the white eyes writhing in his face,
His hanging face, like a devil's sick of sin;   20
If you could hear, at every jolt, the blood
Come gargling from the froth-corrupted lungs,
Obscene as cancer, bitter as the cud
Of vile, incurable sores on innocent tongues,—
My friend, you would not tell with such high zest   25
To children ardent for some desperate glory,
The old Lie: Dulce et decorum est
Pro patria mori.

Poem Summary

Lines 1-4:

In contrast with the title, which suggests that war, patriotic duty, and even death for one's country are "sweet and fitting," the poet shows us nothing noble about the wretched condition of the soldiers on their march. These troops appear far different than the ones the British people might have been used to reading about. They are "bent double" under the weight of their packs, but bent also, perhaps, under the weight of duty itself. Using simile—a figure of speech expressing the similarity between two seemingly unlike things—the speaker compares the troops to "old beggars" and "hags." The effect of the comparisons is to create a frightful, almost medieval atmosphere. Moreover, the comparison of the soldiers with "hags," or witches, creates the sense of the unnatural and introduces the possibility of some kind of evil at hand. The "haunting fires" reinforce this sense. Also notice, beginning the second line, the sequence of participles—"knock-kneed, coughing," etc.—that suggest the sounds and persistence of battle.

Line 2:

In the second line, the speaker defines his relationship to the situation: "we cursed through sludge." By identifying himself as one of the soldiers, he establishes the authority necessary to comment on the hardships he describes. In addition, he reminds us that war is not a far-away spectacle, not the heroic scene described by Tennyson in "The Charge of the Light Brigade," but as real and as close to us as the speaker himself.

Lines 5-8:

The speaker lists the soldiers' tribulations in short, direct phrases, varying at times from the dominant iambic meter to highlight certain details. A number of figurative uses are introduced here as well to demonstrate the suffering of the troops. They are "blood-shod"—a use of metaphor since it is an implied, rather than directly stated, comparison between the blood on the troops' feet and the boots they have "lost." Also note a similar use of hyperbole—a figure of speech based on exaggeration—when the speaker says the men are "deaf" to the cries of their comrades and that "all went lame; all blind." The troops are "drunk with fatigue"— an ironic echo of the "sweetness" in the title. Even the falling artillery shells, or "Five-Nines," are "tired" and "outstripped" by the grave nature of the men's fatigue. The images presented thus far create a somber, static, and miserable world, one in which the indignities the soldiers suffer seem as if they will go on indefinitely. This stasis, however, provides a grim contrast with the explosive violence of the second stanza.

Lines 9-11:

A shift in voice brings on the sudden gas attack. In two sharp syllables someone—we cannot tell who—warns the men of a gas attack. We watch the men scramble for their gas masks in "an ecstasy of fumbling." Owen might intend irony in the use of the word "ecstasy," which can mean "a frenzy of exalted delight." Certainly the men should not be delighted about the attack. In an older sense of the word, however, Owen might simply mean that the soldiers have entered a state of emotion so intense that rational thought is obliterated. A third possibility is that Owen is suggesting a kind of mystical experience. As the men fight for their lives, they may feel the kind of religious ecstasy associated with near-death experiences. At any rate, one soldier fails to put his mask on in time and is poisoned by the gas.

Lines 12-14:

In World War I both the allies and the Germans used mustard gas as a way of both attacking and striking fear into the enemy. If breathed without the protection of a mask, the gas quickly burns away the lining of the respiratory system. Thus the speaker compares the soldier with a man consumed in "fire or lime." Such a fate is not often compared with "drowning," yet the speaker knows that victims of mustard gas effectively drown in the blood from their own lung tissues.

In addition, mustard gas has a particular hue—"as under a green sea." The speaker views the "floun-d'ring" man as if through an underwater mask, adding to the nightmarish and surreal atmosphere of the poem thus far.

Lines 15-16:

In these two lines the incident is transformed to one that seems like a dream to an actual dream—a recurring vision or nightmare that the speaker cannot escape. In this dream the "guttering, chok-ing" soldier "plunges" at the "helpless" speaker, seeking assistance. Although the speaker can do nothing for the man, there is still a feeling of re-sponsibility and guilt. Perhaps many survivors of such attacks felt the same sense of guilt, wonder-ing why they lived while their friends died.

Lines 17-24:

In this last stanza the speaker directly ad-dresses the reader—one who, presumably, is read-ing in the safety of England and who has not per-sonally witnessed the type of horror just described. The speaker suggests that if the reader too were subject to such memories, they would "smother" the reader's conscience in the same way the mus-tard gas has suffocated the soldier. The images that follow depict the aftermath of the attack: the sol-dier's slow death, the "eyes writhing" in his face, the "blood come gargling from his lungs." Note among these descriptions the powerful use of allit-eration, or the repetition of initial consonant sounds in closely related words. A good example of this can be found in lines 18 and 19: "wagon," watch," white," "writhing." The speaker combines this sound device with the most discomforting words he can conjure. The soldier's face is like "a devil's sick of sin"; his lungs are "corrupted" and "obscene as cancer, bitter as the cud / of vile incurable sores on innocent tongues" that suggest unseemly diseases.

Lines 25-28:

If the reader—"my friend"—could see such horrors, the speaker insists, then his or her attitude toward war would change. The reader would not encourage war-like fervor, would not repeat patri-otic slogans such as *Dulce et decorum est / pro pa-tria mori,* a saying which would have been famil-iar to Owen's contemporaries. In this part of the poem, the Latin phrase is used without irony: it is simply called a "Lie." Owen suggests that if the reader continue to spread that lie to young men prone to believing romantic sentiment, then those

Media Adaptations

- The audiobook *English Verse: Early 20th Cen-tury from Hardy to Owen* covers the great Eng-lish poetry written from 1880-1918, including the "poignant realism of the War Poets Rupert Brooke, Wilfred Owen, and Siegfried Sassoon." The audio anthology is published by Penguin Audiobooks.

- Created in 1999, the on-line Wilfred Owen As-sociation at http://www.wilfred.owen.associa-tion.mcmail.com/ offers visitors a virtual tour of Owen's life and poetry. There is also a member-ship offer, including a twice-a-year newsletter.

- Another website—http://www.hcu.ox.uk/jtap/—with information on Wilfred Owen is the Wil-fred Owen Multimedia Digital Archive (WOMDA). Created by the Humanities Com-puting Unit at Oxford University, this site in-cludes not only Owen's manuscripts, but also has a selection of World War I publications and an archive of period documents.

- Artist Robert Andrew Parker has created an ex-hibition based on the poems of Wilfred Owen. Published in catalog format by the Saint Paul Art Center in Saint Paul, Minnesota, the title of the portfolio is *Watercolors by Robert Andrew Parker: My Subject is War and the Pity of War.*

young men will likely receive a fate like that of the fallen soldier. Thus the final line is the shortest of the poem, bringing on the full effect of the three crucial words, *Pro patria mori:* to die for one's country.

Themes

Death and Human Suffering

Owen's poem, describing the death of a sol-dier caught in a gas attack, is at once a realistic por-trait of the brutality of war and a lesson in moral-ity to those who would romanticize patriotic duty.

Topics for Further Study

- Contrast a poem of Owen's to Richard Lovelace's "To Lucasta," a poem that expresses the honor of being called to military duty. How does tone (the speaker's attitude) help create the vastly different themes in each poem?

- Trace the developments of modern warfare from World War I to today. What major technologies have helped define warfare along the way?

- Research the effects mustard gas has on the human body. Include various systems (e.g. nervous, respiratory, etc.).

- Think of an abstract concept (like Love, Hate, Death, Confusion, etc.). Now, without naming the abstract concept, write a poem describing it, using only concrete sensory details (sight, sound, smell, taste, and touch). When finished, share your poem with a classmate and see if they can tell you what you've written your poem about.

- As a class, create your own War Memorial. Include family members and friends of families who have served during wartime. You may also add artists like Wilfred Owen, Yusef Komunyakaa, Tim O'Brien, John Singer Sargent, and others. Be creative! Include photos, poems, letters, artwork, etc.

Owen's representation of death and human suffering within the poem is significant in terms of its depth; on the surface the poem chronicles the physical destruction of men at war. "Dulce et Decorum Est" achieves its power, however, through the equally compelling discussion of both the emotional and spiritual destruction with which war threatens the individual.

Death and human suffering, on a purely physical plane, are abundant throughout the poem. The first stanza depicts the horrors of the war on the human body-even for those lucky enough to survive their tour of duty. It takes young, healthy, empowered men and turns them, metaphorically, into aged transients and pathetic invalids. War has exacted such a physical price on those asked to wage it that they are literally transformed with exhaustion, unable to appreciate the deadly reality surrounding them. They are, in Owen's words, " … Drunk with fatigue; deaf even to the hoots / Of gas-shells dropping softly behind." The remaining lines of the poem focus on the horrific death of one young man caught in the devastating fumes of mustard gas. Owen's use of water imagery makes this scene all the more uncomfortable to witness, as the soldier's death is compared to a drowning. He is described as "flound'ring," "guttering," and "choking." Owen twice uses the very word—"drowning."

While the physical pain is noteworthy, the death of the soldier is rivaled by the emotional suffering present in the poem. The men themselves face the most primal of emotions, fear. First, Owen repeats the word "gas" at the beginning of the second stanza; the capitalization of all three letters in its second usage clearly indicates a heightened sense of panic. Interestingly, while the impact of the poem in no small measure comes from the candid nature of its witness, the narrator does not need to embellish the account with exaggerated punctuation. The images speak for themselves. It is only here, as the reader hears the dialogue of the soldiers, that we see the use of exclamation points. This combined with the aforementioned use of capitalization serves to convey a strong emotional investment. The true emotional impact, though, is on the solitary soldier. It is not, however, to be focused on the dying man, whose terrified confusion can easily be imagined in "the white eyes writhing in his face." It is on the man condemned to replay this grisly scene again and again in his tortured sleep. The speaker in "Dulce et Decorum Est," so clearly identifiable as Owen himself, is forever plagued with visions of his comrade's demise, evidenced by lines 15-16: "In all my dreams before my helpless sight/He plunges at me, guttering, choking, drowning" Just as there was nothing either man could do to prevent the gas from killing the soldier once he has inhaled the noxious fumes, the guilt-stricken speaker seems equally incapable of forgetting what he has seen in surviving the attack. The soldier's literal death—suffocation by "froth-corrupted lungs"—is symbolically preserved in the speaker's "smothering dreams."

Finally, the poem revolves around spiritual suffering and death. Owen once described himself as "a conscientious objector with a very seared conscience," further stating that "pure Christianity will not fit with pure patriotism." There is a distinct irony that should be acknowledged here. Owen's reputation as a poet is a direct result of the impact the war had on his poetry. While his earlier work evidences a commitment to the Romantic precepts of Love and Beauty and the trappings of fantasy, it is his role as a soldier in one of the most costly wars in the history of mankind that reveals his true growth as an artist. War confronted Owen with reality, with Truth; however, these same horrible realities that signal a maturation for the poet, also coincide with the destructive force the war had on all who fought it. For Owen, the war became a symbol for the ugliness of human nature. The last stanza, then, represents for the speaker a sacrifice, with the doomed soldier's face "hanging … like a devil's sick of sin." The death is "Obscene," compared to "vile, incurable sores on innocent tongues." These comparisons are not those of the man who is dying, but instead of the man left to remember the death. In the end, it is the poet's innocence—his tongue—which has been violated. It is his responsibility to at once reveal the ugly truth of war to the world, and warn others of the danger of romanticizing this truth. In one stanza Owen connects the guilt a surviving soldier feels when his brother-in-arms falls with the guilt others should feel who either ignore or willfully dismiss the truth of war.

Style

"Dulce et Decorum Est" is divided into four stanzas, each addressing situation or idea. The first stanza describes a group of marching soldiers in a shell-shocked, wretched condition. The second stanza shows a gas attack in which one of the soldiers is stricken. The third stanza describes the event's nightmarish effect on the speaker, while the fourth suggests that the reader should be similarly impacted.

The dominant meter of the poem is iambic. This means the poem's lines are constructed in two-syllable segments, called iambs, in which the first syllable is unstressed and the second stressed. As an example of iambic meter, consider the following line from the poem:

> Till on the haunting flares we turned our backs.

If we divide the iambs from one another and mark the unstressed and stressed syllables, the line appears like this:

> Tillon / the haun / ting flares / we turned / our
> backs.

Reading the line normally, you will notice the emphasis on the stressed syllables. Iambic meter is natural to the English language and is the most common measure in English verse. Shakespeare employed iambic meter throughout much of his work. In fact, to remember what iambic meter is, you can always sound out the syllables of these famous words: "To be, or not to be."

While "Dulce et Decorum Est" is written primarily in iambic meter, Owen deviates from the pattern at times to heighten the sense of certain words. Consider, for example, this line:

> But limped on, blood-shod. All went lame; all
> blind;

If you read the line naturally, you will find only one weak, or unstressed, syllable: the first. All others are strong, or stressed, in order point out the crippling reality of the soldiers' physical condition. The poet varies his iambic meter in lines like this to achieve a specific effect. Yet to do so, he has had to set up a dominant pattern from which to deviate.

Finally, note that the poem's stanzas include quatrains, or groups of four lines each, in which the last syllables of first and third lines as well as the second and fourth lines rhyme with one another. This form of rhyme scheme is often used in ballads and in heroic verse. Owen might have chosen the form to make readers think about the contrast between his poem and more traditional war poems.

Historical Context

"Dulce et Decorum Est" is historically useful because it so poignantly shows both the changes in the way war was to be fought as well as the necessary metamorphosis war poetry would have to undergo in the face of such change. To understand this, it is vital to consider the two major differences the twentieth century brought on to the battle field—namely, technology and trenches.

It has been estimated by war historian Leon Woolf that somewhere in the neighborhood of 10,000,000 men died fighting in World War I. This does not include the 21,000,000 soldiers wounded, and only accounts for a million of the 7,750,919 captured or missing in action. While such numbers are certainly staggering, none include the loss of civilian life during the war. It is under this dark

Compare & Contrast

- **November 11, 1918:** The Armistice agreement is signed at 5:50 a.m.; at 11:00 a.m. all fighting ceases. World War I is over.

September 1939: The German attack on Poland precipitates World War II. Over 6,000,000 Jews and millions of others will be persecuted and murdered under Nazi tyranny.

May 8, 1945: Germany surrenders to Allied forces.

August 6, 1945: The first atomic bomb to be dropped on Japan is dropped on Hiroshima.

August 9, 1945: The second atomic bomb to be dropped on Japan is dropped on Nagasaki. The Japanese surrender September 2, 1945, bringing an end to World War II.

June 1950: The North Korean army launches a surprise attack on the thirty-eighth parallel, marking the beginning of the Korean War.

July 27, 1953: The Armistice signed in Panmunjon brings an end to the Korean War.

March 8, 1965: The first American combat troops land in Da Nang, Vietnam, marking the "Americanization" of the war in Vietnam.

1968: The number of American forces in Vietnam reaches over 500,000. Over 14,000 U.S. soldiers will be killed in 1968.

March 28, 1973: The Last of the American troops and prisoners leave South Vietnam. The United States has lost over 45,000 men killed in action and a further 300,000 have been wounded.

1982: The Vietnam Veteran's Memorial—"The Wall"—is dedicated in Washington, D.C.

1990-2000: Wars continue to be waged, throughout the world and for a myriad of different reasons. From the Persian Gulf War to the warfare in Bosnia-Herzegovina, peoples of the world continue to fight each other.

---

umbrella that Wilfred Owen both fought, wrote, and died. The numbers alone would seem to support Owen's caustic message in "Dulce et Decorum Est"; anyone witnessing such a tremendous loss of life would be hard put to continue feeding young children the romantic rhetoric of patriotism and heroism associated with warfare going into the twentieth century. But what caused such loss? Simply put, mankind became more efficient. The Great War was the first war in which technology was implemented in order to achieve military objectives. Men were equipped with machine guns, capable of spraying the enemy with bullets; the battlefields were bombarded with explosives and gas shells. And with this efficiency, this speed of death, came the demise of the romantic notion of the war hero. As Arthur E. Lane writes in his book *An Adequate Response:*

> The war was a lesson in humility, not an exercise in cultural style: death came unseen and from a distance, and the inoffensive ex-clerk in an ill-fitting uniform who dutifully placed shell after shell in the breechlock of a gun which pointed only at the sky never knew if heroes or cowards or corpses awaited dismemberment in the distance. Men died asleep or playing cards, eating breakfast, writing letters, quarreling, picking lice from their clothes and hair. They died praying or cursing, weeping or dumb with horror, comforting each other or fighting for shelter.

Owen captures this in his poem, too. There are no heroes, only dog-tired men struggling for survival. None knew where the "tired, outstripped Five-Nines" were fired from, and most only have time to retreat beneath the relative safety of their gas masks before it is too late. Owen does not depict the men valiantly overcoming the effects of the gas to help their dying comrade. This is dirt-level survival. This is life on the battlefield. The cost is great and Owen reflects the sheer volume of death wrought by the war when he describes the way the men treated the dying soldier. There is no time for tears; last rites are muffled beneath panes of glass and clouds of gas. The soldiers merely fling him in

An American soldier is wounded as troops advance across a field in France, WWI, 1918.

a wagon. In the end, no one can claim heroism—not the unknown man shelling them, not the unfortunate soldier left to die, and certainly not the guilt-ridden witness whose only response is to follow behind the wagon as the rest of the troops retreat from danger.

Just as the *way* in which war was fought forced a change in poetic perception, so too did *where* it was fought. The use of trenches is yet another hallmark of World War I. Wet, cold, and muddy, there was no retreat for the men forced to endure these conditions. In *The Truth of War,* author Desmond Graham writes of this harsh reality: "Physically, despite the inaction, the soldier is still assaulted, by cold; and physically, just as mentally, he is not left alone but reminded of his defencelessness by the snow which reaches his face. In this state, dreams do remain, and the soldier succumbs to them." While Graham is specifically relating to Owen's poem "Exposure"—a detailed account of life in the trenches—the same realities are reflected in "Dulce et Decorum Est" The reader can clearly see the effects living and fighting in the trenches has had on the men in the first stanza. They are not under direct military attack, and yet are "bent double" and "coughing like hags." Owen makes mention of "the sludge" in which they march, some without boots. Here, too, we see the devastating toll the exposure

to the harsh climate has taken on the men before the gas attack even commences. Again, this is not a poem of heroism; it is a poem of fact.

Critical Overview

Many writers, including the prominent British poet C. Day Lewis, have commented that Owen's war poems are among the best written in our century. Though Owen lived to see only four of his poems published, he wrote nearly all of his best work, including "Dulce et Decorum Est," in a span of only one year, the twenty-sixth and last year of his life. Lewis notes the maturity of these poems: "It was as if, during the weeks of his first tour of duty in the trenches, he came of age emotionally and spiritually." Lewis cites "the originality and force of [the poems'] language" as well as their passion and "harsh realism." "Dulce et Decorum Est" marks the period which, according to Lewis, made Owen a major poet capable of changing people's minds about war. The sudden maturation of Owen's work, writes Lewis, represents "a forced growth, a revolution in his mind which, blasting through all the poetic *brick-a-brack,* enabled him to see his subject clear—'War, and the pity of War.'"

Not all have agreed that "the pity of war"—Owen's own phrase—is a basis for sound poetry. William Butler Yeats, for one, determined the "passive suffering" in Owen's work an unfit theme. Critic Samuel Hazo has challenged the notion that many of the poems spring from pity at all. Instead, Hazo suggests, the bulk of Owen's work arises from uncontrolled indignation. "Many of them," he writes in *Renascence,* "are revelations of acrimony, protest, pessimism, outrage and hatred." While Hazo admits Owen manages to achieve a degree of objectivity in some poems, he finds "Dulce et Decorum Est" to be merely didactic. "Whatever is poetic in it," Hazo writes, "is subordinated to a rhetorical end."

Criticism

Daniel Moran

Daniel Moran is a secondary-school teacher of English and American Literature. He has contributed several entries and essays to the Gale series Drama for Students. *In the following essay, Moran examines the ways in which Owen's poem can be read as a reaction to pro-war sentimentality.*

Shakespeare's *Henry V* contains one of the Bard's most popular and rousing speeches: When King Henry learns that the morale of his soldiers has sank, he realizes that he must rouse them to action for their upcoming battle against the French at Harfleur. The English are outnumbered five to one by the well-rested French—a fact that has caused Henry's men to lose heart about their cause and fear their seemingly inevitable deaths. Henry turns all of his rhetorical skills to the effort of boosting his soldiers' confidence and convincing them that, whatever happens, they will be remembered for their dedication and courage:

> If we are marked to die, we are enow
> To do our country loss; and if to live,
> The fewer men, the greater share of honor.
> God's will! I pray thee wish not one man more …
> Rather proclaim it, Westmoreland, through my
>   host,
> That he which hath no stomach to this fight,
> Let him depart; his passport shall be made,
> And crowns for convoy put into his purse;
> We would not die in that man's company
> That fears his fellowship to die with us.

Already Henry is playing the "masculinity card" and inviting his soldiers to side with him—for who among them will take the King's offer of "crowns for convoy" after hearing these words? Henry then reminds them of the holiday on which they are about to fight and offers them a vision of a future which, according to his propaganda, is the only one that a *real* true-born Englishman would want:

> This day is called the Feast of Crispian:
> He that outlives this day, and comes safe home,
> Will stand a-tiptoe when this day is named,
> And rouse him at the name of Crispian.
> He that shall see this day, and live old age,
> Will yearly on the vigil feast his neighbors
> And say, "Tomorrow is Saint Crispian."
> Then he will strip his sleeve and show his scars,
> And say, "These wounds I had on Crispian's day."
> Old men forget; yet all shall be forgot,
> But he'll remember, with advantages
> What feats he did that day …
> And gentlemen in England, now abed,
> Shall think themselves accursed they were not
>   here;
> And hold their manhoods cheap whiles any speaks
> That fought with us upon Saint Crispian's day.

Henry's men—now roused by the words of their King—proceed to slaughter the French, who lose ten thousand men while the British only part with twenty-five. "O God, thy arm was here!" the King proclaims, and the viewer, stirred by Henry's charisma, is apt to agree with him.

That is, unless the viewer is Wilfred Owen, or any sensitive reader of "Dulce Et Decorum Est," a poem that is as savage and merciless to the rhetoric spouted by Henry as the King's armies are to the French. Owen's poem, which describes a gas-attack upon a British company during World War I, attacks the kind of sentimental notions about war that Henry espouses so skillfully. Owen's title, when read before the actual poem, leads a reader to think that the poem will be in a vein similar to Henry's speech at Harfleur, but by the end of the poem, the title becomes (like many other moments in the poem) ironic and bitter. Saint Crispan's Day never arrives, and the speaker's scars are mental ones that never heal—and that are definitely never shown to his neighbors as examples of his manhood.

The poem begins with the speaker's description of his company:

> Bent double, like old beggars under sacks,
> Knock-kneed, coughing like hags, we cursed
>   through sludge,
> Till on the haunting flares we turned our backs,
> And toward our distant rest began to trudge.

Owen's depiction of the soldiers is the first of the poem's ironies: They are not completing the "feats" of which King Henry speaks, but are instead scrambling, with all the stature and courage of "old beggars under sacks," for cover. The sound of these opening lines echoes their sense: "Bent double" jars the ear just as the men's backs are "jarred" under the weight of their packs, and the fourth line—

And *toward* our *dis*tant *rest* be*gan* to *trudge*

—"trudges" along in the reader's ear as the men "trudge" toward their unattainable relief. (Also note the rhyming of "trudge" with "sludge," which connects the action of trudging with the terrain.) This trudging continues:

Men marched asleep. Many had lost their boots
But limped on, blood-shod. All went lame, all
        blind;
Drunk with fatigue; deaf even to the hoots
Of tired, outstripped Five-Nines that dropped
        behind.

Bereft of all their senses (they are "blind" and "deaf"), these men are exhausted to the point where their fatigue intoxicates them; They cannot hear the jeering "hoots" of the gas shells that mock their efforts to escape.

This description of solders in battle is far removed from those urged on by King Henry in another part of his play, where he advises them to

Imitate the action of the tiger:
Stiffen the sinews, conjure up the blood,
Disguise fair nature with hard-favored rage …
Now set the teeth, and stretch the nostril wide,
Hold hard the breath, and bend up every spirit
To his full height!

As Owen points out in the opening words of his poem, these men are incapable of "bending up the spirit," for the war has made them "Bent double," not like tigers, but "like old beggars under sacks."

Once the men realize that they have been gassed, the poem again imitates, through its meter, the sense of what is happening:

Gas! GAS! Quick, boys!—An ecstasy of fumbling,
Fitting the clumsy helmets just in time,
But someone still was yelling out and stumbling
And flound'ring like a man in fire or lime …
Dim through the misty panes and thick green light,
As under a green sea, I saw him drowning.

There is an "ecstasy of fumbling" to the ear here as well, when the verse sounds as clumsy as the soldiers trying to get their masks on before the gas grasps their lungs. The line depicting the solders' realization of the gas attack—with its first four words stressed and monosyllabic—heightens the reader's sense of the soldiers' urgency; Likewise,

> *Owen's poem, which describes a gas-attack upon a British company during World War I, attacks the kind of sentimental notions about war that Henry espouses so skillfully."*

the verbs "fumbling," "stumbling," "flound'ring," and "drowning" are connected by the sounds of their endings as well as their depictions of the men made graceless and spasmodic. The image of the "green sea" of gas—and the soldier in it, appearing to the speaker as a drowning man, struggling for air but eventually collapsing under the pressure of the poison—conveys the speaker's helplessness and provokes the reader into considering another irony of war, where men drown on land. Everything in Owen's poem is thus reversed, both literally (the soldiers seek rest but are instead attacked) and metaphorically (the title is held up as a "lie" that perpetuates the horrors depicted in the poem.

While Henry told his men that their futures would reward them for their bravery, the future of Owen's speaker is one haunted by (rather than enhanced by) the memory of battle. The next two lines—

In all my dreams, before my helpless sight,
He plunges at me, guttering, choking, drowning.

—personalize the action of the poem and connect it to the memory of the speaker. The Germans are never mentioned by name in the poem, because, in a sense, they are not the real enemy here. Rather, the memory of the dying man, that "plunges at" the "helpless" speaker as if in attack, turns out to be more powerful than the Germans because it can never be vanquished. Long after the armistice, this formidable foe continues to threaten the speaker.

As the poem begins with a description of a company and then narrows its focus to a single victim, the final stanza becomes more focused still, with the speaker making a direct address to a nameless individual. He states,

If in some smothering dreams, you too could pace
Behind the wagon that we flung him in,

What Do I Read Next?

- Randall Jarrell is a writer who, like Owen, uses powerful imagery to convey the horror of war. His poem "Death of the Ball Turret Gunner," in particular, has themes and incidents similar to those in "Dulce et Decorum Est." Specifically, the reader is shown the fear and nightmarish reality surrounding a gunner's last living moments. The poem is included in Jarrell's 1945 collection, *The Complete Poems.*

- In the September 18, 1997 issue of *English in Australia* authors Peter McFarlane and Trevor Temple discuss an innovative plan for teaching Owen's poetry by having students develop meaning with a dramatic reading of the poem, interpretive music or dance, or artwork. McFarlane and Temple note that the method seems to have fostered for their students a better understanding and student "ownership" of Owen's poetry. The title of their article is "Making Meaning: A Teaching Approach to the Poetry of Wilfred Owen Using the Visual and Performing Arts."

- Vietnam veteran and poet Yusef Komunyakaa offers another excellent example of a soldier who recaptures "in country" experiences in his poetry. Like Owen, Komunyakaa saw fellow soldiers fall in action. His poem "Facing It" depicts the physical and emotional reflection a veteran has when visiting the Vietnam Veterans Memorial. This poem can be found in Komunyakaa's 1988 *Dien Kai Dau.*

- A true sense of the talent of an artist can not possibly be gained through the analysis of a single piece of that artist's craft. Students interested in Owen's poetry should read his other works, including "Anthem for Doomed Youth," "Strange Meeting," "Arms and the Boy," "Spring Offensive," and "A Terre." These poems and many others can be found in Owen's *Collected Poems,* published in 1964.

- R. L. Barth's 1983 *Forced Marching to the Styx: Vietnam War Poems* is yet another example of the impact war has on humanity. An excellent place to begin is with Barth's poem "The Insert."

- Students interested in the fiction arising from wartime experience should read the works of Tim O'Brien. An excellent place to start is O'Brien's 1979 National Book Award-winning novel *Going after Cacciato.*

And watch the white eyes writhing in his face,
His hanging face, like a devil's sick of sin …

The speaker not only wants to convey the horror of his experience—he positively *wants* the nameless "you" to see what he has seen. ("You, too, should have these dreams," he suggests, for reasons that become apparent later in the poem.) The image of a man not gingerly lowered into the ground in a casket but instead "flung" into a wagon stresses the indignity of the soldier's impending death, while the simile "like a devil's sick of sin" creates the impression that the soldier has become other than human—a revolting, almost supernatural creature.

Even this imagery (and such powerful imagery it is, with the "white eyes writhing in his face") is not enough for the speaker. He also wants "you" to hear the soldier die as well, in full cinematic sound:

If you could hear, at every jolt, the blood
Come gargling from the froth-corrupted lungs
Obscene as cancer, bitter as the cud
Of vile, incurable sores on innocent tongues,—

Recalling the notion of the soldier "drowning" in gas, these lines offer the *sounds* of drowning— except that the "gargling" is not water, but blood. The soldier is, in effect, drowning in himself—in his own blood—which compounds the initial irony of a man drowning on land. The speaker also appeals to the sense of taste here as well, comparing the soldier's taste of his own blood to "the cud / Of vile, incurable sores"; the rhyming of "blood" and "cud" emphasizes their relationship in terms of taste, while the overall impression of the taste is one as revolting as the "white eyes writhing in his face." The once innocent soldier has been corrupted ("froth-corrupted," to be exact) by the war, and his body is the brutal proof of that fact.

But who *is* the "you" upon whom the speaker is forcing these images, sounds, and tastes? The answer lies in the poem's final lines, after the speaker finishes cataloguing the horrors of the dream he wants this "you" to have: If you could have dreams as vivid as these, he implies, then

> My friend, you would not tell with such high zest
> To children ardent for some desperate glory,
> The old lie: *Dulce et decorum est*
> *Pro patria mori.*

The "you" is not specifically King Henry V, but all those *like* him, who clothe the horrors of war in beautiful words and appeal to those "children" (automatic symbols of innocence) who yearn for a glory made "desperate" by the fact that it is only attainable through wounds or death. Nor is this "you" actually the speaker's "friend," since that address in this context is a sarcastic one. Horace's adage—like Henry's bombast—is an "old lie," and the poem attacks those who propound it. The final, awful irony is that Owen himself died fighting in World War I, a week before the armistice was declared. Like millions of others, there was no Saint Crispin's Day for him.

Source: Daniel Moran, in an essay for Poetry for Students, Gale, 2001.

Tyrus Miller

In the following essay, Tyrus Miller examines the vivid images of Owen's poem.

Wilfred Owen's "Dulce et Decorum Est" is justly one of his most celebrated poems and a landmark amidst the poetry written by combat soldiers during World War I. Owen combines vivid sensory immediacy, conveyed through his careful composition of sound, imagery, and syntax, with a powerful psychological and ideological denunciation of war. Juxtaposing an implied schoolboy past when he still believed in the "Old Lie" of glory in war, the horrifying recent past of the gas attack, and the present of dreams and writing in which the Old Lie of glorious death appears in all its falseness, Owen weaves a complex pattern of time and changing consciousness throughout his poem. In a few terse lines, he manages to contrast the classical age of the Latin poet Horace to his own modern age, the idealizing words of the schoolbook to the reality of

> *Juxtaposing an implied schoolboy past when he still believed in the "Old Lie" of glory in war, the horrifying recent past of the gas attack, and the present of dreams and writing in which the Old Lie of glorious death appears in all its falseness, Owen weaves a complex pattern of time and changing consciousness throughout his poem."*

warfare, the blind patriotism of the homefront to the cynical demystified attitude of the frontline soldier, and the naïvety of the child to the dismaying recognitions of the adult.

The Latin phrase "Dulce et decorum est pro patria mori," which lends the poem its title and concluding lines, comes from a poem of Horace, writing under the emperor Augustus Caesar. It means, "It is sweet and fitting to die for one's country." For Owen, a junior officer in the British army who died in combat in 1918, the line has a number of resonances that make it an appropriate target of his anger and criticism in his poem. First, the sentiment the line expresses is obviously an incentive to patriotic self-sacrifice, to be willing to die in war for one's country so as to experience the glory of one's deeds. Yet equally importantly, such lines were the mainstay of British classical education, which stressed learning classical languages and experiencing the morally uplifting quality of the literary culture of the ancients. While the less savory or sexually racy parts of the classical canon were edited out, the textbooks and anthologies were full of such edifying phrases as the one that gives Owen his theme. Owen, thus, is primarily interested in the latter-day uses of the classics rather than in their historical reality. He not really concerned whether

Horace himself was being sincere or hypocritical when he penned his lines. Rather, he is pointing to the hypocrisy or blindness of those who continue to feed children on classical ideals in a modern world in which these values no longer correspond to any reality: the terrifying new world in which the trench soldier found himself, an infernal landscape of mud, flares, devastated houses, machine guns, gas grenades, barbed wire, and long-range artillery. If the schoolmaster and the war recruiter could really experience what modern warfare was like, Owen believes, they would not be so eager to trot out the well-rehearsed lines written hundreds of years in the past: "My friend, you would not tell with such high zest / To children ardent for some desperate glory, / The Old Lie."

Owen begins his poem in confusion and apparent violence, strongly implying that the reader has entered in the middle of some action already well underway. With the first two words, "Bent double," the reader gets the impression of a blow that has been struck or a dangerous near-miss that has compelled a tense, rapid, violent contraction of a body. Owen reinforces this sense of contortion and displacement by withholding the person who has been bent until the second line ("we") and adding several other images further contributing to this impression of a body knocked out of kilter: "Bent double, like old beggars under sacks, / Knock-kneed, coughing like hags, we cursed through sludge." Up to this point, these figures have no definite location or features. Soon, the reader will learn that they are drawn from the trenches of World War I; but in the opening lines, they might just as well be damned souls trudging all eternity through the hell of the medieval Christian poet Dante. Only with the flares of line 3 and the "trudge" to a distant rest does the reader finally begin to intimate who and where "we" are: a group of trench soldiers withdrawing from combat at night.

The next four lines draw a veil of extreme weariness over the scene. The men are marching in a half-sleep. They are insensate to pain. Many have lost their boots in the sludge and mud of the rain-filled trenches and shell holes, and they trudge on wearing their own blood as a kind of boot ("blood-shod"). In their fatigue, they are stunned and senseless, as if lame, blind, drunk, and deaf. So tired are they that the artillery shells that fall short of their lines seem to miss them because the shells themselves are fatigued. Clearly, the men are projecting their own tiredness onto everything around them.

In the midst of this dull, thudding atmosphere, Owen portrays a sudden, violent event that shatters the deadened mood of the previous stanza. As if the reader were present on the scene, the gas attack is announced only by the desperate warning of the officer in charge: "Gas! GAS! Quick, boys!" They have only a few seconds to get their gas masks on to save themselves from the acrid, searing, toxic gas that has been released from a shell. Again, Owen captures the confusion and fear of a panicky mass of men scurrying to save themselves from threatening death: "An ecstasy of fumbling, / Fitting the clumsy helmets just in time." Yet if the gas masks render the soldiers literally faceless, one man, a soldier who has failed to get his mask fitted in time, stands out from the rest: "But someone still was yelling out and stumbling, / And flound'ring like a man in fire or lime … / Dim, through the misty panes and thick green light, / As under a green sea, I saw him drowning."

In one of the most surprising turns of the poem, Owen suddenly pulls the reader out of the narrated war scene and into his own dreams: "In all my dreams, before my helpless sight, / He plunges at me, guttering, choking, drowning." The shift is, in its own way, as violent as the gas attack that broke into the dozing fatigue of the first stanza. Once again, as at the beginning, the reader is unsettled and dislocated: was the vivid narration of the night march and gas attack a real event or a traumatic dream? Owen implies that in the end it does not really matter which it is, dream or reality. To have experienced this scene in real life is to be doomed to repeat it in dreams, and to dream it so vividly is to suffer its real agony all over again. Owen reinforces this sense of identity of dream and reality in his only departure from the otherwise strict alternating rhyme scheme (ABABCDCDEFEF etc.). In the two line stanza that mentions Owen's dreams, rather than rhyming with the word "drowning" in line 14 from the previous stanza, Owen exactly *repeats* the word "drowning," thus implying that this scene must recur over and over without change.

In the final stanza, the poem once again shifts, now from the poet's dream to his address to a reader, presumed to be a person on the homefront who has experienced nothing of the horror of war and who still believes that war is glorious and ennobling. Owen angrily wishes that his reader could be haunted by dreams like his own, to feel drowned and smothered with guilt and horror as he does over the gassed soldier that had been under his command. Although he cannot literally bring this haunting about, through his poem and its grotesque details, he can force his reader to confront the ugly reality of war that masks behind fine phrases and edifying sentiments. Thus, Owen lingers over the sounds and sight of the dying body, destroyed by the poisonous gas. In six horrifying lines, he drags his reader slowly up to the brink of death. He displays the eyes moving convulsively about in the paralyzed face, expressing in this contradictory figure the soldier's unspeakable suffering. He exhibits the blood and fluid that bubble up from the burned and blistered lungs, describing the gargling and croaking noises that the man makes as his wracked body is jolted along the road in the wagon in which it has been "flung." And finally, the poet even takes us into the mouth of the man himself, forcing us to feel with him the sensation of his chewing and biting to relieve the pain of his burnt, ulcerated, swollen tongue.

Owen insists on the innocence of this tongue, so as to contrast it with the lack of innocence of those whose tongues continue to speak and teach "the Old Lie." It is as if Owen were wishing that the innocent tongues of his men would be left unharmed, while those who continue to participate in the lie of the war, feeling no risk themselves, would have their tongues burned and blistered as soon as they tried to speak. Thus, Owen's final lines are addressed to the teachers and parents who have helped prepare these young men to go to war, but left them unprepared for anything they would actually face. Many of these soldiers, he implies, were little more than children who thought they were going off to some high adventure, having been taught that war was a glorious thing, that death ennobles youth, and that they would prove their courage and virtue in combat. But the war being fought in the trenches, with gas and machine guns, Owen makes clear, is nothing like the idealized scenes of the one-on-one strife of valorous heroes fighting in classical poetry. Its violence strikes anonymously, destroys young bodies in the ugliest and most disgusting ways, makes men scurry to survive like rats, and give rise to a necessary cynicism and indifference towards the dying and dead. This, Owen implies, is the real face of "dying for one's country," and we should cease to fool ourselves and others about it. His final rhyme and closing line let the full irony of this phrase ring past the ending: glory rhymes with "mori" (die) as if glory is swallowed up in death. In the poem, as in real life, Owen has seen too clearly, it is death that has the last word, not glory.

Source: Tyrus Miller, in an essay for *Poetry for Students*, Gale, 2001.

Even more hauntingly, Owen writes of the fear of those who survive. The images of battle, ever imprinted on their minds, will haunt their sleep. The nightmare of the trenches can never be erased."

Kimberly Lutz

Kimberly Lutz is an instructor at New York University and has written for a wide variety of educational publishers. In the following essay, she examines how Wilfred Owen broke from literary tradition in "Dulce et Decorum Est."

Generally regarded as the *the* poet of World War I, Wilfred Owen broke with many of the literary conventions of war literature in his poetry. Most strikingly, Owen does not present his soldiers as necessarily heroic. Instead he shows frightened men in pain, dying gruesomely. Their last thoughts are not of joy at having, in the words of American revolutionary patriot Nathan Hale, "but one life to give for their country." Instead, they fight aimlessly for life. As they gasp their final breaths, Owen suggests that they have no comprehension of a righteous cause or a meaning behind their sacrifice. Even more hauntingly, Owen writes of the fear of those who survive. The images of battle, ever imprinted on their minds, will haunt their sleep. The nightmare of the trenches can never be erased. Indeed, Owen biographer and critic Dominic Hibberd records that Owen himself "deliberately stayed up late in order to shorten his sleeping hours" during his wartime hospitalization in Scotland, trying hopelessly to escape the memories that invaded his dreams. Hibberd believes that in "Dulce et Decorum Est" Owen was describing his own recurrent nightmares, "directly facing the central experience of his war dreams, the sight of a horrifying face which ... renders him a 'helpless,' paralyzed spectator."

This sensibility of the cost of war to both the dead and surviving soldier stands in stark contrast to the types of poetry with which Owen's readers would have been familiar. Take for instance, "The Charge of the Light Brigade," a famous poem by the Victorian era's most famous poet (and poet laureate) Alfred, Lord Tennyson. Written in 1854 in response to a newspaper account of a military mistake that sent hundreds of men to die battling the Russians in the Crimean War, the poem acknowledges the awful cost of war. However, the reader learns only that "horse and hero fell." The bloodshed, the smells, the confusion that go along with battle are not depicted. Further, Tennyson describes how these soldiers, even while knowing that they are being sent to die because "Someone had blundered," accept their fate ungrudgingly: "Theirs not to make reply, / Theirs not to reason why, / Theirs but to do and die." Abandoning the ethos of self-sacrifice, the narrator of Owen's poem does question why he and his fellow soldiers must miserably die in what seems to be a fruitless campaign. Directly addressing the reader, Owen argues that "If you could hear, at every jolt, the blood / Come gargling from the froth-corrupted lungs, / Obscene as cancer, bitter as the cud / Of vile, incurable sores on innocent tongues,— / My friend, you would not tell with such high zest / To children ardent for some desperate glory, / The old Lie: Dulce et decorum est / Pro patria mori." The Latin line, taken from the ancient poet Horace, means "It is sweet and meet to die for one's country." Calling this "The old Lie," Owen shows how dying is anything but sweet and questions the pursuit of "glory" that leads boys to the trenches. Breaking from the not too distant past—Tennyson died the year before Owen was born—Owen sets out to both question authority and to show realistically what World War I was like from the perspective of the trenches.

In trying to capture the feeling of modern warfare, however, Owen not only violated the literary conventions of poets like Horace and Tennyson, but of the popular poetry of his own time. In the newspapers, poets were writing of the glory of war, enjoining young men to rally to the cause and fight in the trenches. More than his other poems, "Dulce et Decorum Est" was written in direct response to such patriotic and sentimental dribble, and particularly in response to one prolific pro-war poet, Jessie Pope. In an earlier version of the poem, Owen actually named this woman, indicating that she was the "friend" who tells "children" the "old Lie." One of her poems, "A Cossack Charge" describes soldiers in action: "The wine of war they're quaffing,/ The glorious draught of swift, resistless death." Death in her vision is heroic and almost de-

sirable.

Owen's argument with such patriotic writers was not well received by the early critics of his work. Critic D. S. R. Welland (who in 1960 called "Dulce et Decorum Est" "moralising") cites a 1921 review in the *Times Literary Supplement:* "The suggestion is that a nation is divided into two parts, one of which talks of war and ordains it, while the other acts and suffers. We can understand how such a thought might arise, but not how it can persist and find sustenance." In other words, this reviewer believed that Owen's strong feelings of betrayal are overstated. In a 1924 letter, Sir Henry Newbolt, another patriotic poet who as critic Gertrude M. White records "had called death in battle sweet," heartily disagreed with Owen's conclusions: "Owen and the rest of the broken men rail at the Old Men who sent the young to die: they have suffered cruelly, but in the nerves and not the heart—they haven't the experience or the imagination to know the extreme human agony .... what Englishman of fifty wouldn't far rather stop the shot himself than see the boys do it for him?" Newbolt thought Owen blind to the sorrow of those who stay at home awaiting news of further casualties. A more recent critic, Adrian Caesar, while believing that Owen's anti-war message was important in 1917, argues that there is a "tendency in a poem like this to substitute different types of glorification and heroism for those being satirised." Particularly, Caesar finds that "Dulce et Decorum Est" wants the reader to admire the "sufferings ... not only those of the gassed soldiers, but also Owen the poet's." In over seventy years of criticism, many see Owen as a little too satisfied in his own righteousness.

But if "Dulce et Decorum Est" is didactic—tending towards preachiness—it is a highly effective sermon. And it is effective for two reasons. First, Owen successfully captures the ugliness of war, and particularly his war—World War I. Second, Owen is able to create new and powerful metaphors to describe war, metaphors that can replace the truisms of heroism and glory that poets had for so long depended on.

In the first stanza, Owen places his reader immediately in the experience of war. "Bent double, like old beggars under sacks,/ Knock-kneed, coughing like hags, we cursed through sludge." Nothing is pretty about this world, and the soldiers, far from seeming manly, have been reduced to "beggars" and "hags." Old women, rather than young men, they cannot stand upright. Instead of victoriously marching they "trudge," not to battle, but away from it: "on the haunting flares we turned our backs / And towards our distant rest began to trudge." Having already deflated the sentimental picture of soldiers, Owen in the second stanza turns his eye to what battle and death actually look like: "Gas! GAS! Quick, boys!—An ecstasy of fumbling, / Fitting the clumsy helmets just in time; But someone still was yelling out and stumbling." In this war, the men desperately try to defend themselves, not from an attacking enemy, but from the almost unseen poison gas deployed by the enemy. They defend themselves not by reaching for their guns to fight but by ineffectively "fumbling" for protective gas masks. The man who fails to reach his mask in time is doomed to die, "guttering, choking, drowning" with "the white of his eyes writhing in his face," and "the blood / ... gargling from the froth-corrupted lungs." This vividly described death is far from "sweet." Some critics suggest that Owen tried for an even less palatable realism in his line about "incurable sores on innocent tongues." Merryn Williams, for one, believes that in this description, Owen "seems to have been thinking of venereal disease." This interpretation furthers the idea that Owen's soldiers are not heroic. Far from being youthful boys, they are corrupted and diseased men. The corruption and the disease, however, spring directly from the experience of war. Soldiers on short leave infamously frequent prostitutes, the implied source of the "incurable sores."

What is most effective about this poem, however, is that Owen does not merely turn to realism to combat the literary images of the past. Rather he creates new metaphors and images. The narrator of the poem who watches the man being gassed describes, "As under a green sea, I saw him drowning." Here Owen leaves the realistic description of guns and mud behind, and instead through figurative language seeks for images to convey the world of war. The green gas becomes the green sea. The man choking on the gas is pictured as drowning in that sea. Next, Owen moves from the battlefield to his nightmares: "In all my dreams, before my helpless sight,/ He plunges at me, guttering, choking, drowning." The war is at once real and unreal, happening in life, but repeated in dreams. It is the unnaturalness of war, its nightmarish qualities that Owen wants his readers to see. He does not ask the reader to join him on the battlefield, but to join him in his dreams: "If in some smothering dreams you too could pace / Behind the wagon that we flung him in." Dream my dream, says Owen. Bringing his reader with him under the sea, Owen demands that his audience recognizes what it really means to die for one's country. D. S. R. Welland notes that "Dulce et Decorum Est" is a bit "unpolished." For of course, as he points out, Owen was unable to make his final corrections before his slender book of poetry went to press. Owen died on the battlefield in 1918, one week before World War I ended.

Source: Kimberly Lutz, in an essay for *Poetry for Students,* Gale, 2001.

Sources

Blunden, Edmund, ed., *The Poems of Wilfred Owen,* New Directions Books, 1949.

Caesar, Adrian, "Wilfred Owen," in his *Taking It Like a Man: Suffering, Sexuality, and the War Poets,* Manchester University Press, 1993, pp. 115-171.

'Dulce et Decorum Est'—A Literary Writer's Point of View, www.writerswrite.com/journal/sept97/mika.html (September 1997)

Ellis, John, *Eye-Deep in Hell: Trench Warfare in World War I,* Pantheon Books, 1976.

Graham, Desmond, *The Truth of War,* Carcanet Press, 1984.

Hazo, Samuel J., "The Passion of Wilfred Owen," in *Renascence,* Vol. XI, Summer, 1959.

Hibberd, Dominic, *Owen the Poet,* The University of Georgia Press, 1986.

Kennedy, X. J., and Dana Gioia, eds., *Literature: An Introduction to Fiction, Poetry, and Drama,* Harper Collins, 1995.

Lane, Arthur E., *An Adequate Response: The War Poetry of Wilfred Owen & Siefried Sassoon,* Wayne State University Press, 1972.

Lewis, C. Day, introduction, in *The Collected Poems of Wilfred Owen,* edited by C. Day Lewis, Chatto & Windus, 1963.

Lewis, C. Day, ed., *The Collected Poems of Wilfred Owen,* New Directions Books, 1964.

McPhail, Helen, and Philip Guest, *On the Trail of the Poets of the Great War,* LEO Cooper, 1998.

Newbolt, Henry, *The Later Life and Letters of Sir Henry Newbolt,* edited by Margaret Newbolt, Faber and Faber, 1942, p. 314.

Pope, Jessie, "A Cossack Charge," in her *Jessie Pope's War Poems,* Grant Richards, Ltd., 1915, p. 24.

Silkin, Jon, *Out of Battle: The Poetry of the Great War,* St. Martin's Press, Inc., 1998.

Tennyson, Alfred, "The Charge of the Light Brigade," in *The Norton Anthology of English Literature,* Edited by M. H. Abrams, Norton, 1993, pp. 1132-1133.

Welland, D. S. R., *Wilfred Owen: A Critical Study,* Chatto and Windus, 1960.

White, Gertrude M., ed., *Wilfred Owen,* Twayne Publishers, Inc., 1969.

Williams, Merryn, "Poetry," in her *Wilfred Owen,* Seren Books, 1993, pp. 46-114.

The Works of Wilfred Owen with an Introduction and Bibliography, The Wordsworth Poetry Library, 1994.

For Further Study

McPhail, Helen, and Philip Guest, *On the Trail of the Poets of the Great War,* LEO Cooper, 1998.

> This book is a part of the Battleground Europe series, and provides not only a look at Owen's development as a poet, but offers a detailed timeline of his military career. Complete with photographs and correspondences, the text serves the historian or traveler as a guide to the battles and events that would be reflected so powerfully in Owen's poetry.

Welland, D. S. R., *Wilfred Owen: A Critical Study,* Chatto & Windus, 1960.

> This book remains a definitive look at the critical importance of Wilfred Owen's poetry. Welland offers insight into Owen's earlier, pre-war poetry; analyzes the effect his service in World War I had on his craft; and discusses Owen's place and reputation in the 20th century.

White, Gertrude M., ed., *Wilfred Owen,* Twayne Publishers, Inc., 1969.

> Much like Welland, White traces Owen's growth as a poet, discussing his early work and the forces that brought about his poetic maturity. After a detailed study of Owen's work-including commentary on his early adherence to the Romantic tradition and the qualities, themes, techniques of his mature poetry-White too chronicles the growth of Owen's reputation following his death.

A Farewell to English

Michael Hartnett

1975

"A Farewell to English" is a political poem, presenting to readers a moment in the poet's life when his consciousness awakened to the problem of being an Irish writer who wrote in the English language. The scene depicted shows the poet in a pub, listening to the bartender talk to other patrons in the smooth flow of the Gaelic language. Although the poet does not understand all of the words, the music of the language stirs some sort of genetic memory in him, connecting his life to the ancient history of the Irish people. He goes on to muse about the complex thought processes that he regularly undertakes while writing in English, but becomes convinced that obeying the laws of the English language is not the best approach.

At the time, Ireland's struggle for independence England had reached a violent stage, reminiscent of past conflicts. In Northern Ireland, citizens were being killed in the streets, caught between rebel actions and retaliations from the British government. The more mundane incident in the bar in this poem was powerful enough to change Hartnett's life. Up to 1975, Hartnett had spent most of his career writing in English. Two years later he published *Poems in English 1958-1974,* concluding his poetry composition in English. He continued to write essays and translations in English, then returned to writing verse in the English language in 1985.

Author Biography

Michael Hartnett was born in Newcastle West in County Limerick, Ireland, in 1943. He attended National University of Dublin, graduating in 1962, and later graduated from Trinity College in Dublin in 1972. In between, he worked a variety of jobs, including dishwasher, postman, house painter and security guard. Already a recognized poet in the 1960s, his *Collected Poems* was published in 1970. With his popularity as a writer, he could have easily secured a job teaching, but preferred working for the Irish telephone company. He turned to teaching, in 1976, the year after *A Farewell to English and other Poems* was published.

Along with his numerous collections of poetry, Hartnett is a respected translator, ranging from a translation from Old Irish of the ancient tale *Hag of Beare* to an edition of the *Romancero Gitano* by Frederico Garcia-Lorca, a Spanish poet who was executed by the government after the start of Spain's civil war in 1936. Lorca's poetry and his political commitment served as powerful influences on Hartnett. Through the 1960s and early 70s, Hartnett wrote in English, increasingly using Irish words. The poem "A Farewell to English" marked, as its title implies, a break away from his use of the English language in his poetry. After that, he wrote almost exclusively in Gaelic, often publishing under his Gaelic name, Micheál Ó hAirtnéide, until he eased back into using English in 1985. He served as co-editor of the literary magazines *Arena* and *Choice,* and was the poetry editor of the *Irish Times* newspaper for a short time. He died in Dublin, where he had lived most of his life, on October 13, 1999.

Poem Text

for Brendan Kennelly

Her eyes were coins of porter and her West
Limerick voice talked velvet in the house:
her hair was black as the glossy fireplace
wearing with grace her Sunday night-dance best.
She cut the froth from glasses with a knife   5
and hammered golden whiskies on the bar
and her mountainy body tripped the gentle
mechanism of verse: the minute interlock
of word and word began, the rhythm formed.
I sunk my hands into tradition   10
sifting the centuries for words. This quiet
excitement was not new: emotion challenged me
to make it sayable. The clichés came

at first, like matchsticks snapping from the world
of work: mánla, séimh, dubhfholtach, álainn, caoin: 15
they came like grey slabs of slate breaking from
an ancient quarry, mánla, séimh, dubhfholtach,
álainn, caoin, slowly vaulting down the dark
unused escarpments, mánla, séimh, dubhfholtach,
álainn, caoin, crashing on the cogs, splinters   20
like axeheads damaging the wheels, clogging
the intricate machine, mánla, séimh,
dubhfholtach, álainn, caoin. Then Pegasus
pulled up, the girth broke and I was flung back
on the gravel of Anglo-Saxon.   25
What was I doing with these foreign words?
I, the polisher of the complex cause,
wizard of grasses and warlock of birds
midnight-oiled in the metric laws?   29

Poem Summary

Lines 1-4:

This poem is set in a pub where the speaker is watching a serving woman as she prepares drinks for the customers and talks to them in Gaelic, the traditional language of Ireland. Her eyes are "coins of porter": porter is a very dark, strong beer served in Irish pubs, so this image makes the woman desirable while blending a reference to beer and money. Limerick, the city mentioned in the second line, is a working-class town in the middle of Ireland, a port on the river Shannon. Limerick is surrounded by some of Ireland's most fertile land, and it is a natural center for local farmers and for sailors around the world. The fireplace in this pub is glossy, indicating that it is probably made of inexpensive painted steel that has been scrubbed, not black with caked-on soot. In this humble setting, the serving woman is wearing her best clothes, the clothes that she would wear to a dance. The effect of these first few lines is to present a scene of a pub and a woman who looks comfortable and neat in humble circumstances.

Lines 5-9:

Having introduced the bartender and implied the speaker's attraction to her, the second part of the poem puts her into motion. Because beer is carbonated and tends to foam when it is poured, she scrapes the top of glasses, removing excess foam. In addition, she slams a glass of whiskey on the bar to knock any sediment in the drink to the bottom, where it will be left when the glass is drained. These two mechanical gestures, common to the bartender's trade, create a swish-and-bang rhythm that draws the attention of the poem's speaker to the rhythm of the speaker's language. The adjective "mountainy" in line 7 should not be taken to mean that the server is huge in stature, in which case she would be called "mountainous": mountainous" implies one large thing, "mountainy" gives the idea of having many curves, in addition to giving the idea of being a part of a larger landscape, as the woman and her language is part of the larger Irish culture. Watching the woman, the speaker follows the rhythm of her work. Then, the vague musical pattern of the language she is speaking becomes more and more understandable, even though the words themselves are not clear.

Lines 10-13:

In lines 10 and 11, tradition is represented as a substance like dirt or sand that can be sifted through to find buried objects. That symbolism relates the traditions of culture to region. The poem's speaker, having had his interest in his own culture awaked by the bartender and her flowing use of Gaelic, becomes involved with the language, giving himself over to it by burying his hands in it, a metaphor that connects dirt and sand and also alludes to the act of writing. The break between lines 11 and 12 draws attention to the fact that the poem is forcing two contrasting ideas together, "quiet" and "excitement." The feeling the speaker has about hearing this language is one he experienced before, but he does not know how to express it. It is significant that at the same time he is excited about recognizing the sound of Gaelic, he is discovering that speaking English is insufficient to capture the excitement he feels. He is driven to form his ideas in Gaelic in response to a "challenge" from his emotions.

Lines 14-15:

Gaelic words that keep going through the speaker's mind head are identified by him as "cliches," as words that have lost their significance by being used over and over, possibly in such situations as he is experiencing—the poetic moment of describing an attractive woman in melodious language. The very point of the poem is that the Gaelic words do not have English equivalents; any translation has to be recognized as very loose, not even nearly able to capture the true sense of what the Gaelic words mean to the poet. For example, the meaning of "álainn" has to do with "beauty" and "beautiful"; "dubhfholtach" refers to a person with black hair; and "mánla" "séimh" and "caoin" are all close to the meaning that the English language gives to "graceful" and "gentle." These

rough translations let readers know that he is thinking about the bartender, but it is almost impossible for someone not familiar with the language to relate to the feeling the poem is trying to capture. In this case, the words are not just tools to capture the meaning of what he wants to express, they affect what he is feeling. They are part of the emotional experience.

Lines 16-19:

The experience of hearing the Gaelic language spoken so beautifully is one of liberation and of inevitability. The words liberate the mind of the speaker of the poem, allowing it to fall free, like a large slab of slate that breaks free of a quarry wall. It is no coincidence that the stone mentioned is slate, material used to make chalkboards that are used in schools of formal teaching. The reference contrasts the social acceptability of English with the poem's point, that Gaelic is innate to the Irish. The "unused escarpments" in line 19 are the recesses of the speaker's natural mind, his instinctive nature, which he has not had use while thinking in English. These lines repeat the Gaelic words— "mánla, séimh, dubhfholtach, álainn, caoin"—like a mystical incantation, as if they can free his mind if he keeps chanting them to himself.

Lines 20-22:

Slate cracks into splinters when it breaks, and Hartnett mixes the image of slate shattering with an idea of a machine. Machine cogs are often referred to by poets when they want to point out something that is a small part of a large man-made scheme. In this case, the implication is that the speaker, by speaking and writing in English, has been part of an "intricate system," a tool. Using the Irish language, then, not only liberates him, but it helps damage the machine that had used him.

Lines 23-25:

In Greek mythology, Pegasus was a winged horse. Bellerophon, the prince of Corinth, captured Pegasus and tried to ride him to the top of Mount Olympus, which was the home of the gods, but Pegasus threw him off and he fell back to the ground. The speaker of this poem feels that he is just about to ascend to heaven via his experience of hearing the Celtic language spoken so beautifully. Abruptly, however, the spell is broken—the "girth" that he refers to is the strap that goes around a horse's waist to hold its saddle on. He ends up using plain, worldly English again, "the gravel of Anglo-Saxon."

Lines 26-29:

The speaker of the poem is pulled back from the magical spell that the Gaelic language had drawn him into, back into the ordinary reality that he knew before. The same words that he described in line 10 as "tradition" he describes here as "foreign words." The poem uses the sound of the English language more conspicuously in the last lines, especially the device of alliteration, the repetition of consonant sounds, such as the hard "c" in "complex" and "cause," the "w" sound formed with the lips ("wizard" and "warlock"), and the "m" of "midnight" and "metric." This sort of wordplay is referred to as "metric laws" at the end of the poem, implying that English-language poetry is more a matter of trickery than of actual meaning. The last three lines of the poem are graceful, for English, but they still prove weak when compared with the ennobling experience of the speaker in hearing Gaelic.

Themes

Language and Meaning

"A Farewell to English" addresses an old, long-running philosophical question of whether language describes meaning or creates it. The poem's speaker is inspired by the sound of the Irish words he hears, particularly their rhythm, and not by their meaning. As a poet, he is of course aware of both the sounds and meanings of words, but the few Gaelic words are not significant to him for what they say. They express the sorts of ideas that might be expected to drift through one's mind in a social setting—beautiful, black-haired, graceful, gentle—but they do not combine in meaning to make a life-altering experience.

The speaker's life is definitely altered, though. The metaphor he uses for his new awareness, slabs of slate falling, break the forms of meaning he used to know. In this poem, it is language that destroys old meanings and creates new ones, but, ironically, it is the sounds of the words, not their definitions, that changes this person's sense of meaning.

Identity

The setting of this poem, a pub, is a typical Irish gathering place. The bartender, with her black hair and deep, dark eyes, is a typical symbol of Irish beauty. The speaker of this poem is a poet, though, and it is the Gaelic language that awakens him to

Topics for Further Study

- Because of the use of English in international business, several countries have passed resolutions declaring their original language to be the "official" one. Choose a country and research its official language and report on what measures are taken to assure its use.

- Study the history of England's involvement with Ireland. Explain why you think the Irish language has become so rare.

- Old Irish is used more often in music than in poetry. Find some recordings of people singing in Old Irish, and explain what is musical about the rhythm and sounds of the words used.

- Do you think people of one culture could have a "cultural memory" that would allow them to recognize a language they have never heard before? Explain why or why not.

- Some people see the Irish Republican Army as a group of freedom-fighters who have made it possible for Ireland to stand up against the tyranny of Britain, while others consider them murderers for their terrorist acts that have taken many lives. Research the history of this organization and support your own judgement about them.

- Read about County Limerick, and explain why you think Hartnett makes a point of mentioning that this event happened there.

his true Irish identity. Through the middle of the poem, the excitement that he experiences, that sends him "sifting the centuries for words," is all expressed in the fine Irish words that he keeps repeating: "mánla, séimh, dubhfholtach, álainn, caoin." Even after the music of the words has stopped exerting its effect on him, though, he realizes that he will never be able to look on his Irish identity in the same way as before. The Anglo-Saxon words he once used now look foreign to him: in fact, his former business as a poet of English strikes him as questionable at best. The poem's title tells readers that the cultural awakening described here led Hartnett to turn away from using English to express himself, and to embrace his Irish identity.

Culture Clash

Writing in English, as it is presented in this poem, is polishing "the complex cause," which implies both the sense of urgency that a cause would have and the dedication to minute details that comes with complexity. The English-language poet is considered a "polisher," a "wizard" and a "warlock": all of these imply someone who makes things out of reality, instead of just appreciating it as it is found. Irish language, in the other hand, controls the poet, rather than being in his control: the "minute interlock of word and word" pulls him in. He is not able to manipulate reality because the words are "sunk." The culture clash presented here is between one group that understands the past and another that has no use for the past because it is busy controlling the present. It is natural that an intellectual poet would work in English. It is also natural that the poet, aware of his feelings, would be drawn to a deep understanding of the Irish culture, as Hartnett is here. As it is presented, English is about thought and Irish is about experience.

Consciousness

The speaker of this poem is evidently an intelligent, self-aware person, a "polisher of the complex cause," who knows how to control his perception of reality by manipulating words in English. Still, his experience with the true force of Gaelic awakens in him a new kind of consciousness about his cultural identity. It starts with a fairly common situation; sitting in a pub, admiring a pretty bartender, listening intently to her. But in lines 8-11 he becomes more aware of how the musical sound of the Gaelic language connects him with the tradition of his people, and he becomes conscious of how his life is intertwined with the traditions of centuries gone by. It is a vague awareness that he has felt before: "This feeling was not new," he explains. Still, having the feeling and opening his consciousness up to what it means are two different things. He is not able to achieve full awareness of his link to the past because he has never had the right words to describe the way he feels. The few Gaelic words that he knows take him in the direction of consciousness, but, as he points out, they are cliches. Even though they come close, they are never able to capture the feeling exactly. In the end, he is able to fully open his conscious-

ness up to his Irish heritage, and he becomes more conscious of the shortcomings of the Anglo-Saxon language, which had previously been his chosen method of expression.

Style

It is interesting to note that this poem, which praises the Irish language for its "gentle mechanism of verse" and faults English for its "metric laws," is written in the most common meter that there is in English, iambic pentameter. "Iambic" means that means that the basic unit of rhythm in the poem is the "iamb," which consists of one unstressed syllable followed by one stressed syllable. For example, in the first line of the poem, the even-numbered syllables receive greater emphasis when read aloud: "her *eyes* were *coins* of *por*-ter." Pentameter" means that there are five of these units, five iambs, per line, adding up to a total of ten syllables in each line. In some cases, the rhythm might not seem to be strictly iambic. For instance, the seventh line, taken by itself without the context of the poem, would begin with the first three and the seventh syllables stressed: *and her moun*-tainy *bo*-dy." Overall, though, iambic pentameter is the dominant rhythm, which sometimes forces readers to adjust their pronunciations of words to fit the pattern.

The iamb is the most naturally-occurring rhythm in English speech. Iambic pentameter is the most common meter used in English poetry. It is possible that Hartnett used this form to capture the simplistic sound of English, while working against this language's simplicity with the multi-syllabic complexity of the Irish words he includes. This shows off their free-floating grace in contrast to the English language's more rigid formality.

Historical Context

The Division of Ireland

Many Irish people had been opposed to the country's domination by Great Britain ever since it had been annexed in 1801. Most of the history of Ireland during the twentieth century is marked by the violent struggle for independence. A turning point came in 1916 with the Easter Rebellion, during which several Irish nationalists took over key government buildings, to protest the British taking away Irish political power a few years earlier. The

Compare & Contrast

- **1975:** After nearly twenty years' involvement in the war between South Vietnam and North Vietnam, the United States withdraws the last of its troops.

  Today: Hostile relations between Vietnam and the United States have ended. The two governments share economic programs.

- **1975:** Nineteen-year-old computer wizard William Henry Gates III drops out of Harvard to form software manufacturer Microsoft.

  Today: Bill Gates is the world's wealthiest individual.

- **1975:** Belfast, Northern Ireland, is widely considered one of the most dangerous places on earth. The Irish Republican Army, fighting for Northern Ireland's freedom from Great Britain, and British forces often engage in open warfare.

  Today: Peace treaties have been signed between Great Britain and the Irish separatists, but a lasting accord has not yet been reached.

Easter Rebellion was quickly put down by British troops, and its leaders were executed, but in memory they became martyrs to the cause of freedom. More rebellious organizations formed, including the Irish Republican Army. In 1920, Britain tried to solve the trouble between Irish who wanted independence and those who wanted to remain a part of the British United Kingdom by passing the Government of Ireland Act. This act divided the country into separate parts: the six northernmost counties became Northern Ireland, and the rest became the Irish Free State, or Eire (which changed its name to the Republic of Ireland in 1949).

Beside political divisions, religion also played a part in the tensions; the majority of the people in the north were Protestant and they identified themselves with Protestant Britain, while the Catholic minority in Northern Ireland supported reunion with the rest of the island, which was predominantly Catholic.

The Troubles

As the decades went by, the animosity deepened between the Protestant majority, which supported staying tied to Britain, and the Catholic minority. who thought of Britain as a foreign invader. In 1955, the Irish Republic Army, which had been formed in the 1920s as a reaction against the country's separation, became more active in terrorist violence to push toward reunification. During the 1960s, a period of civil strife that came to be known around the world as the Troubles began in Northern Ireland. A cycle began: Catholics protested, the government made new rules to punish the protestors, and this repression led to more protest. Housing allocation and voting rights were the areas of greatest discrimination against Northern Ireland's Catholics. Protests in Northern Ireland became larger and more vocal, so British troops were sent to keep the peace. Incidents followed: a protestor died of wounds after being beaten by police following an incident at a parade, then a soldier died fighting a violent mob.

Bloody Sunday

One of the definitive moments in Northern Ireland's struggle against British rule came shortly before this poem was written, on January 30, 1972. At a Catholic protest in Derry, British paratroopers opened fire on the crowd, killing fourteen people. The troops claimed that they acted in self-defense, that the protestors were turning violent, but observers say that the attack was unprovoked. A British inquiry, led by the country's Lord Chief justice, found that the soldiers did nothing wrong, which only infuriated the Catholics more and led many angry Catholic youths to join the IRA. This date has come to be referred to as Bloody Sunday. Historically, it marks the end of the period of hostility between the Unionists (for a united Ireland) and the Nationalists (supporters of Great Britain), and the beginning of all-out warfare between the two sides.

The Language

The very first examples of a language that resembles the modern Irish language appear on stones dated to around 300–400 BC; this language is called Ogham. Though the language was adapted through the years, it has basically stayed the same. In the 1100s, when the Anglo-Normans from the European mainland came to Ireland, the Irish language remained the dominant one spoken. By the 1500s, Irish was almost exclusively spoken.

In the 1600s, wealthy English lords settled large estates in Ireland, and they promoted laws that would curtail the Irish language and make English the official language spoken. A series of Penal laws enacted in 1695 did much to suppress the Irish language, as well as much of Irish culture, in Ireland. By the mid-1800s, when the Irish Potato Famine wiped out half of the farming population, the vast majority of Irish people spoke English. Some areas in the west and northwest of Ireland, such as West Limerick mentioned in the poem, still maintain a strong cultural personality and have many Irish speakers, but they are the minority.

Critical Overview

Hartnett was already a moderately well-known writer in Ireland by the time "A Farewell to English" was published in 1975: James Simmons, discussing his work in the 1974 anthology *Ten Irish Poets,* made a point of mentioning that Hartnett's work was "well thought of in Dublin, and in the North he is the most widely admired Southern poet." Since "A Farewell to English," however, it has been difficult for critics to discuss Hartnett's poetry without giving their opinions of his decision to write in a dead language. As Denis Donoghue explained in the *Sewanee Review* in 1976, "Irish writers find it particularly difficult to know what they are doing; they live on a fractured rather than an integral tradition; they do not know what voice is to be trusted. Most of them speak English, but they have a sense, just barely acknowledged, that the true voice of feeling speaks Irish, not a dead language like Latin but a banished language, a voice in exile." Soon after publishing this poem, Hartnett received several awards from Irish patriotic associations, serving more as recognition of his nationalism than of his poetic ability.

Even looking beyond nationalistic sentiments, though, Hartnett has not gained a very broad reputation outside of his native country. In his review of Hartnett's 1996 *Selected and New Poems,* Ben Howard recounts the period of time when Hartnett only wrote in Irish, but he is also able to consider the post-Gaelic period. Howard praised Hartnett, but found that "his characteristic tone is one of grievance, historical and personal"; still, he noted, "the black clouds of Irish history sometimes lift, revealing the freshness of the physical world." Eamon Grennan, whose relationship with Hartnett went back to college days in the early 1960s, was less reserved in his review for the *Southern Review,* calling *Selected and New Poems* "a gift to Hartnett's admirers, as well as to those readers approaching his work for the first time." Grennan's, like most reviews, gives readers a background of the poet's career of over thirty years: during that time, Grennan recognizes that Hartnett's reputation has not spread beyond a small audience of poetry enthusiasts and Irish patriots.

Criticism

David Kelly

Kelly is an instructor of Creative Writing and Composition at two colleges in Illinois. In the following essay he examines the causes and problems that can arise from the sort of separation that Hartnett proposes in "A Farewell to English."

Most of us will never know what it must be like to be a colonized people, to have to contend with two different histories—the official one, which is the history of the colonizers, and also the suppressed history of your own people. Even worse would be the terrible responsibility of having to decide how much of the pre-colonial past should be held on to. Making it even more difficult is the fact that much of the past in question is not even a personal matter, not the past of people living now but of their ancestors, people who left the earth long ago. When is the right time to stand up against the ugly idea that history is written by the victors? When is it time to give in and focus on the here-and-now?

The Irish poet Hartnett took his stand with a 1975 poem entitled "A Farewell to English," in which he described a common incident—hearing Old Irish, or Gaelic, spoken in a bar—that led him to the resolution to quit writing in English and to

> *His statement was artistic, it was political, and of course it was personal; it was one of those choices by which one defines one's own identity"*

work from then on in Irish, even though his mother-tongue has for several centuries been a near-dead language. His statement was artistic, it was political, and of course it was personal; it was one of those choices by which one defines one's own identity. It only lasted ten years, and then Hartnett was back to writing in English again. In some respects, it hardly seems that Hartnett's good intention was worth the embarrassment of seeming shallow in the long run. On the other hand, Hartnett's declaration drew attention to an issue he felt strongly about then, and it eventually led him to a voice of his own, a way of poetic expression more important than either English or Irish.

The poem is an expression of pride in his culture and tradition, and readers, naturally, support the poet in his stand against the oppressive forces from England that had leached Ireland of its heritage. If cultural identity were clearly, undeniably right, then we might be able to say that the idea behind "A Farewell to English" is a good thing, or that it is a bad thing. Strong cultural identity has as many evils as virtues, however. For every heart surging with patriotic pride, there is someone dead on a battlefield somewhere, killed when the balance shifted from "love of us" to "hatred of them."

Colonized people are supposed to forget their old ways, to take on the ways of those who are their new rulers. In America, our clearest example of this is the treatment of the indigenous people who were here before Europeans arrived. When the land was taken from the Indians, those who were not killed were moved onto reservation lands, where they were allowed to follow their own traditions and customs and speak in their native tongues. About the 1930s, though, there arose a new way of thought that said that Indians were being held prisoners within their small societies; maintaining their culture was seen as a racist trick to keep them out of

the wider American culture. New programs and policies from the thirties to the seventies were aimed at encouraging Indian youths to leave the reservations and assimilate. This theory was reversed in the 1970s, at about the time that Hartnett wrote "A Farewell to English." The government came to realize that it was destroying hundreds of years of Indian heritage in order to offer young people a chance to make money, and opponents argued that a better job could be done to promote both prosperity and culture. The primacy of retaining tribal ways was established once again on the reservations.

Around the same time—in the late 1960s and early 1970s—black Americans began to assert their own cultural identities. The situation of blacks was in some ways worse than the cases of either the Irish of the Indians because they were so far removed from their original situations. Their ancestors had been from different tribes across the African continent, taken from the physical setting which had formed their cultural identities, without any relics to remind descendants of why practices developed as they did. The culture of former slaves should be considered the pure American experience if anything is, since they were so detached from their former lives and had to create an almost entirely new cultural identity here. Instead, they were rejected by the dominant American culture as well. In the 1960s and the 1970s the Black Pride movement raised public awareness about the rich cultural history of African-Americans. The Civil Rights movement of the 1950s and 1960s had struggled to establish that there was nothing wrong with being black, and the Black Pride movement pushed beyond that with the assertion that there was in fact everything right about it.

As with life on the reservation, though, establishing a cultural identity had the unwanted effect of separating African Americans from mainstream society, which meant that those who made their culture an obvious part of their identity could not rise to America's highest political or economic levels. Today there is a debate about the language used by America's blacks that has parallels to the issues Hartnett was addressing with "A Farewell to English." At different times in the country's history, educational groups have recommended that the public school system should accept the pattern of speech that has developed among black Americans, calling it Black English, or, more recently, Ebonics (a phrase coined from "ebony" and "phonics"). Recognition of this way of speaking could be taken as a political gesture, as an affirmation of a black culture's separation from the mainstream. It could also be used as a tool to convert speakers from Ebonics to standard English more effectively. As is the case with Irish opponents of Gaelic, a considerable number of African Americans are cautious of Ebonics because they can see that giving the minority their own language without teaching competence in standard English would exclude them from the overall economic competition—the word we use for political separation like this is that it "ghettoizes" them.

In Hartnett's poem, the Irish language is liberating, a chance for the speaker to return to his true nature. The Irish words that he recalls hearing in a bar stir an excitement that "was not new," but that he felt compelled by emotion to express in words, finding English inadequate to the task. The language he needed was definitely not language of business, and in fact the few Gaelic words that he recognized broke down the smooth functioning of commercial discourse, "clogging the intricate machine." English had been the language of Ireland since the 1690s, when British landowners passed laws requiring its use. Gaelic remained common in the country, where it was not necessary to conduct formal business transactions. The famous potato famine of 1847 though, severely depleted the rural population of Ireland. The population went from 10 million people in 1841 to 6.5 million just a decade later, and dwindled yet another million in the following twenty years. The number of Irish people speaking Gaelic cut in half during the famine, from four million to two million. Millions died, and a million others emigrated to other countries, specifically Australia and the United States, which were both English-speaking countries. Those who remained in Ireland, no longer able to feed themselves with what they grew in their fields, shifted further and further into the English-speaking economy. Today, English is the language of international business, required for transactions throughout Europe, Africa and Asia.

It is understandable that victims of the potato famine, struggling to make ends meet, would abandon Gaelic and take up English if it would give them an economic advantage. It is also understandable that Hartnett would, in the 1970s, take up Gaelic. First, there are aesthetic reasons, which are clearly identified in "A Farewell to English." Some emotions that Hartnett felt just could not be captured by the logic of English, and needed the sweet flow of music that Old Irish offered. The poem hints at some sort of genetic code that is tickled by the sound-combinations of the mother

What Do I Read Next?

- Hartnett's last volume of poetry, *The Killing of Dreams,* was published after his death, in 2000, by The Gallery Press.

- *The Selected Poems of Federico Garcia-Lorca,* available from New Dimensions, provides a good sampling of the work of the Spanish poet who was a major influence on Hartnett.

- The Irish poet best known in America today is Seamus Heaney, the 1995 winner of the Nobel Prize in Literature. His works are available in many anthologies, and his career is on display in *Opened Ground: Selected Poems, 1966-1996.*

- Thomas Kinsella, one of Ireland's most respected poets and a contemporary of Hartnett, edited *The New Oxford Book of Irish Verse,* which includes poems from the sixth century to today. From Oxford University Press, 1986.

tongue, an assumption that seems less and less plausible the more you think about it, but then, the point of getting away from English is precisely to leave over-analysis behind.

Another reason his decision is a sound one is that it reminds us that economic dominance is no reason to forget one's own culture. As already mentioned above, someone has to fight against the concept that the winners of any fight are the ones who get to leave their mark on history. The 1970s were a time of struggle for dependence in Northern Ireland (where, by the way, Hartnett did not live nor work: most of his life was spent in County Limerick and Dublin, in the south). The fight for freedom from Great Britain reached was at the height of its violence, and Hartnett sought the preservation of the Irish culture by pumping life back into a language that was nearly dead.

At least he was doing what he could to counter the forces that would have caused his tradition to disappear. Throughout the twentieth century, the world became aware of the systematic removal of any sign of a defeated culture. The example of the

> " *I propose that the language of the poet, the poet's ability to elicit intense feeling with a minimum of words and a wealth of image and sound, is a language unto itself.* "

American Indians has already been mentioned, with the late-found respect for their ways, which were nearly obliterated by a few well-meaning people and many racist enemies. It took Hartnett's generation, raised in the shadow of World War II and its subsequent revelations about the Nazis' plan to erase all signs of the gypsies, Jews, and homosexuals from the land they conquered, to realize that an entire culture could in fact be erased as if it had never existed. Since then, there have been plenty of examples, from Pol Pot's Cambodia to the massacre of the Hutus by the Tutsis of Rwanda to the tragedy of the former Yugoslavia to illustrate the need for people like Hartnett to defend dying cultures against genocide.

A third benefit is that his shift to Gaelic, though it did not last, made Michael Hartnett a better writer, a more introspective poet, in tune with the world around him. In a little collection called *Ten Irish Poets* published just before "A Farewell to English," James Simmons acknowledged Hartnett's popularity, but was himself unimpressed. "He seems to me to have considerable talent and dedication, perhaps a little turned in on himself and obscure," Simmons wrote. "There is certainly a strong ambition to be a poet which is well on the way to being fulfilled." Hartnett became an important writer during his ten years away from English. This might have been a result of working with a language that was more attuned to what he had to say, as he anticipated in his "Farewell." It might have been the natural maturation process, taking him to that point he was "well on the way to" anyway. Most likely, though, the very act of making a choice about language and identity, of looking deeply at who he was and what he wanted to say, had more to do with his development than his connection with the faded language of centuries gone by.

Source: David Kelly, in an essay for *Poetry for Students*, Gale, 2001.

Karen D. Thompson

In this essay Thompson discusses the ambiguities that cast doubt upon Hartnett's intention to bid farewell to English language, politics, and poetry and embrace his Irish heritage.

Geometry students learn early that any point on a line can be divided into an infinite number of points. Some students may further understand that since every point can be infinitely divided, a line actually has no finite beginning, middle, or end. Those students may go on then to make connections and end up pondering a similar quality of infinity in, for example, history class. When does a war actually begin? Did World War II (1939-1945) really start with ill feeling over the Treaty of Versailles (1919)? If that's so, then isn't the real first cause of World War II the end of World War I because without it there would have been no Versailles Treaty? And on and on and on. Ultimately the conclusion may be drawn that every beginning, middle, and end is likewise ambiguous and cannot be discussed in finite terms, but only in terms of defining moments.

This theory transposes nicely upon the work of Hartnett. At some time in his life, a civil war began to rage within the writer between poetry and politics, Irish and English, heart and head. He chronicled this war in "A Farewell to English," and as is the case with most wars, the battle rages back and forth; and even when it reaches its supposed end, there is an uncertain peace and a great many unanswered questions.

Astute readers, those who pay attention to the nuances of language, first question Hartnett's true intentions after considering the title "A Farewell to English." If the reader knows anything of Ireland's tempestuous relationship with England or of Hartnett's poetic background, the reader rather quickly deduces that Hartnett intends to take leave of English influence, including English poetry, language, and politics. Yet the word "farewell" is gentle and conveys connotations of amicable partings and kind wishes. "Farewell" is an unusual word to use in regard to a conflict as passionately violent as that between things English and things Irish.

Readers become more uncertain of Hartnett's intentions by the end of the first stanza. Visually, readers are prepared for a ballad, definitely Irish, by the poem's appearance on the page and its division into short stanzas. The beautiful woman at the bar in stanza one inspires in Hartnett the need for poetry, and by line 15, he has slipped into Gaelic with these descriptions: "mánla, séimh, dubhfholtach, álainn, caoin." These Gaelic phrases are repeated over and over until the reader is caught up in the intoxicating beauty of the barmaid and of the poetry. Hartnett's preference for Gaelic seems unquestionable when he uses the image of being "flung back on the gravel of Anglo-Saxon."

But no sooner does the reader become satisfied that Hartnett is condemning English in favor of Gaelic, than the reader is confronted by contradictory images in lines 20-22. These lines could have been overlooked among the overwhelming evidence of nationalistic love for Irish form and language. In lines 7 and 8, Hartnett shares that the beautiful woman pouring ale has "tripped the gentle mechanism of verse" within him, and he begins "sifting the centuries for words." Immediately, lilting adjectives rise to his consciousness. And then? His romance with the language of his ancestors explodes in his image of Gaelic words like slabs of stone "crashing on the cogs, splinters / like axeheads damaging the wheels, clogging / the intricate machine" which is poetry. These words ("mánla," "séimh") are foreign to him and awkward, not sensual like the barmaid, not intimate like a lover.

The poem continues then with distinct Irishness. In the second stanza, Hartnett's words are pastoral, glorifying nature with evocative images of "a gentle bench of grass" and strawberries that "looked out with ferrets' eyes." He brings forth the old men who shuffle toward Croom and Cahirmoyle. These black-coated men are the bards of early Ireland who, we are told in *The New Princeton Encyclopedia of Poetry and Poetics,* descended from the mystical *filidh* and held an esteemed position in Irish society. However, Hartnett introduces another paradox. These traveling bards, dressed in mourning black and carrying ashplants along with a "thousand years of history in their pockets" are also "snotnosed" and "half-drunk." Regardless of his justification, Hartnett has conveyed an ambiguous message about the rank of his ancestral poets.

A look backward at poets would not be complete without a consideration of, perhaps without a tribute to, William Butler Yeats. According to Hartnett's analogy, "Chef Yeats, that master of the use of herbs / could raise mere stew to a glorious height" by stirring in a "soupçon of philosophy." In other words, Yeats could combine philosophy and poetry and produce excellent results. Hartnett

then seems to honor contemporary Irish poets by calling them chefs also, but he calls his own sincerity into question by calling them "commis-chefs." By tying the newer poets to the "commissary" chefs, Hartnett has thrown them under the questionable light of politics; "commissary," according to *Webster's Unabridged Dictionary,* is closely related to "commissar," a decidedly political word that carries the connotation of an autocrat or dictator. The culinary efforts of these commis-chefs result in an "Anglo-Irish stew" flavored with allusions to Ireland's great mythology and poetic tradition. In this description the emphasis is not on the "glorious heights" as it was in the description of Yeats's poetry. Instead the emphasis is on the stew, a many-ingredient meal in which every ingredient loses its distinct flavor.

The poem moves through stanza after stanza offering contrasting political points of view as it moves through different battles within Hartnett's internal war. While the first three stanzas specifically consider the value of the Irish and English language and Irish and English poetry, the fourth shifts to a perspective on politics which is continued through the fifth and sixth stanzas. Still, ambiguity permeates these sections. In the fourth stanza, Ireland becomes the brood sow raped by the English boar, but the description is not as simple as perpetrator and victim. Instead, Ireland is depicted as a wanton whore who would "allow / any syphilitic boar / to make her hind-end sore ..." Towards the end of the fourth stanza, Hartnett criticizes Ireland for the failure, in 1922, to make a clear stand on self-determination. Ireland's failure to make her own fate certain is the exact type of ambiguity, or ambivalence, that this poem examines and mirrors.

The fifth stanza begins as a requiem for the murdered Spanish poet Garcia-Lorca and the banished Russian writer Boris Pasternak. Though Garcia-Lorca died as the result of a heinous act of violence, Hartnett offered a memorial to him that was celestial in its imagery and symbolism: "my Lorca holding out his arms / to love the beauty of his bullets." Then, at the end of the stanza, Hartnett changes his tone as he lauds his contemporaries, including those who "write / with bitterness in their hearts," and proclaims that the very "act of poetry / is a rebel act."

In the sixth stanza Hartnett overtly criticizes politicians and condemns them for not "wanting freedom— / only power." He blasts them for lacking a conscience and thus forgetting the political dominance of Ireland by England, even though he previously established that the Irish sow was not unwilling. The final line of this stanza casts doubt once again over Hartnett's intention. The miasmatic spectacle of dwarf-riding dwarves racing toward an obscene prize ends in a "dead heat." Figuratively, this means that nothing was decided, no resolution reached. But even the two words considered separately present a paradox. "Dead" means the absence of life. The absence of life in a human would leave the body cold, with no heat. Additionally, "heat" connotes the same sexual images that Hartnett supplied in the first stanza with the sensual bartender. It also reminds us of the sow "in heat." A "dead heat," then, is an oxymoron and further representation of the paradox presented throughout this poem.

At last Mr. Hartnett leaves his political discourse for a more personal one. In his final lines, he seems to consider—more than art or country or politics—his own heart and mind. Is he clear here? No more than in the preceding stanzas. He says that he has "made my choice / and leave with little weeping: / I have come with meager voice / to court the language of my people." Even in the final line, Hartnett's meaning is enigmatic. Consider the use of the word "court" in the final line. Is Hartnett simply rounding out the poem, finishing it nicely by alluding back to the intimate encounter between the poet and the beautiful woman he is possibly "courting"? Perhaps. Or, perhaps his diction is intentionally conflicting. "Court" has numerous meanings. One would be the pursuit of a romantic interest, but another would be a place of law, a political place. Hartnett may be saying that he still has not made a decision; he has not quite committed himself to the language of his heart, Irish, or the language of his "well-oiled" previous poetry, English. And what does he think of his English poetry: is it simply "smooth," or is it mechanical?

If Hartnett's honest intention was to cast off English and use only his Irish poetic heritage, why did he not make a final transition back to the Gaelic he had used in the first stanza of the poem? Is it because some of his readers might not understand Gaelic or because he could not say precisely what he wanted to say without using the English?

This last question will remain unanswered, but the question of whether Hartnett would compose in English or Irish was answered finally in later works. He chose the language of his people, Gaelic, almost exclusively after 1975. This decision could not, as evidenced by the raging conflict within this poem, have been one made lightly.

One cannot deny the power of this poem, "A Farewell to English." No scathing governmental report, no angry editorial could lay claim to the effectiveness of Hartnett's assertion that "We woke one morning / in a Dublin digs / and found we were descended / from two pigs." Furthermore, only rare prose could capture the image Hartnett put forth when he described the governments of Ireland and England as "horribly deformed dwarfs" racing "towards the prize, a glass and concrete anus." These descriptions are written in English; would they lose or gain impact if written in Gaelic?

Certainly not. They may lose the slightest bit in translation, but no more so than a melody transposed to a different key—especially if the translator is one as gifted as Hartnett. Language is a tool only, employed by a poet as Bach employed notes. Does Bach's genius disappear if a piece is performed on a piano as opposed to an organ or a harpsichord? I do not believe so. I do not believe Hartnett's poetry achieves its heights because of the language in which he wrote. In fact, I propose that the language of the poet, the poet's ability to elicit intense feeling with a minimum of words and a wealth of image and sound, is a language unto itself.

Hartnett is an artist. His work rises above the scrutiny of government censors, breaks the bonds of language, and transcends the page. Consider once again the beautiful maid in stanza one. At the same time that "her West / Limerick voice talked velvet" and she wore "with grace her Sunday-night-dance best," her "mountainy body" "cut the froth from glasses with a knife / and hammered golden whiskies on the bar." Her paradoxical description brings to mind Haphaestus, huge and disfigured, using hammer and anvil and brute strength to turn out spectacular metal ornaments for the gods of Olympus.

That is what Hartnett accomplished in "A Farewell to English." Shackled by a language which he feels inferior, which cripples him, he still delivers a thing of beauty.

Source: Karen D. Thompson, in an essay for *Poetry for Students,* Gale, 2001.

Sources

Bradley, Anthony, "Irish Poetry," in *The New Princeton Encyclopedia of Poetry and Poetics,* Princeton University Press, 1993.

Donoghue, Denis, "Being Irish Together," in *Sewanee Review,* Vol. 84, No. 1, Winter 1976, pp. 129-33.

Grennan, Eamon, "Wrestling with Hartnett," in *Southern Review,* Vol. 31, No. 3, Summer, 1995, p. 655.

Howard, Ben, "Review of *Selected and New Poems,*" in *Poetry,* May 1996, pp. 109-11.

Simmons, James, *Ten Irish Poets,* Carcanet Press, 1974.

For Further Study

Hoagland, Kathleen, ed., *1000 Years of Irish Poetry: The Gaelic and Irish Poets from Pagan Times to the Present,* William S. Konecky, 1999.

This anthology shows how the Irish tongue evolved over the centuries, to the Anglicized form that Hartnett turned his back on with this poem.

O'Brien, Conor Cruise, *Ancestral Voices: Religion and Nationalism in Ireland,* The University of Chicago Press, 1996.

O'Brien is one of the most respected contemporary observers of Irish politics. His analysis of the violence in Northern Ireland is very helpful to understand the sentiments Hartnett expresses in this poem.

Taylor, Peter, *Behind the Mask: The IRA and Sinn Fein,* TV Books, Inc., 1999.

Based on Taylor's award-winning documentary that was telecast in England and America, this book gives a contemporary view of the terrorist acts and the negotiations for peace that divide Northern Ireland.

Funeral Blues

W. H. Auden

1936

The Auden poem called "Funeral Blues" first appeared in *The Ascent of F6,* Auden's 1936 play written with his longtime collaborator Christopher Isherwood. This version of the poem was known by its first line: "Stop all the clocks, cut off the telephone." Later, Auden discarded the last three stanzas of the poem and added three new ones and the title, "Funeral Blues." The rewritten stanzas converted a musical comedy piece to a melancholy lament. Auden offered this revised version as a cabaret song, which was set to music by Benjamin Britten and sung by soprano Hedli Anderson for the stage. In 1940 Auden included "Funeral Blues" in *Another Time,* a collection of his poetry.

The 1994 cinema hit *Four Weddings and a Funeral* helped bring the poem to the attention of the general public, when a character played by actor John Hannah reads an excerpt at the film's emotional climax. As a result of overwhelming public demand for copies of the poem, *Tell Me the Truth About Love: Ten Poems by W. H. Auden,* a collection of Auden's verse and cabaret songs from the 1930s including "Funeral Blues", was rushed to press soon after the film's release. Reviewer David Gritten noted in the *Los Angeles Times* that the film created "a sudden demand all over England" for Auden's works. Americans have also shown an increased interest in the author. Filmgoers and readers responded to "Funeral Blues'" heartfelt expression of grief over the death of a loved one. The poem expresses a rhythmical, intimate portrait of the totality of love and the devastating consequences of its absence.

Author Biography

W. H. Auden was born on February 21, 1907, in York, England, to George (a physician) and Rosalie (a nurse) Auden. His father's love of the mythology of his Icelandic ancestors and his mother's strong religious beliefs would have a great influence on Auden's poetry. After being admitted to Oxford University to study engineering, Auden switched to the literature. His interest in science would later be evident in his poetry. At Oxford Auden became an important member of a group of writers that became known collectively as the "Oxford Group," and later as the "Auden Generation." This group, which included Stephen Spender, C. Day Lewis, and Louis MacNeice, often expressed their decidedly leftist political views in their work. Stephen Spender arranged in 1928 for the publication of Auden's first work, *Poems.* That work, commercially published in 1930, coupled with Auden's next collection, *The Orators* published in 1932, earned him, at age twenty-five, a reputation as an important new poet.

After his graduation from Oxford, Auden taught in England until 1939, when he relocated to the United States and became a U.S. citizen. The critical success that followed the publication of his *The Collected Poetry* helped set his literary reputation as a versatile and inventive writer. He continued to write poetry, plays, and essays while teaching at various colleges and universities, including Bryn Mawr, Bennington, and Oxford. After his death in 1973, he was buried in Poet's Corner in Westminster Abbey. Auden won several awards during his lifetime, including the Pulitzer Prize in Poetry for *The Age of Anxiety* (1948); the National Book Award for *The Shield of Achilles* (1956); the Feltrinelli Prize (Rome), 1957; Honorary Student (Fellow), Christ College, Oxford University, 1962-73; and the Gold Medal of the National Institute of Arts and Letters, 1968.

Poem Text

Stop all the clocks, cut off the telephone,
Prevent the dog from barking with a juicy bone,
Silence the pianos and with muffled drum
Bring out the coffin, let the mourners come.

Let aeroplanes circle moaning overhead   5
Scribbling on the sky the message He Is Dead,
Tie crépe bows round the white necks of the public
        doves,
Let the traffic policemen wear black cotton gloves.

W. H. Auden

He was my North, my South, my East and West,
My working week and my Sunday rest,   10
My noon, my midnight, my talk, my song;
I thought that love would last forever: I was wrong.

The stars are not wanted now: put out every one,
Pack up the moon and dismantle the sun,
Pour away the ocean and sweep up the wood;   15
For nothing now can ever come to any good.

Poem Summary

Lines 1-4:

The title "Funeral Blues" sets the somber tone that Auden reinforces in the first stanza, where the speaker prepares for a funeral. The speaker uses an imperative voice throughout the poem. John G. Blair in *The Poetic Art of W. H. Auden* noted that "Auden frequently chooses the imperative to attract attention." This technique, according to Blair, brings the poem "closer to the dramatic immediacy of dialogue, for the speaking voice is usually directed not to the reader but to an audience or another character whose presence is implied by the framing of the poem." The technique also helps the speaker try to gain a sense of control that was lost when their loved one died. Using this imperative voice, the speaker tries to encourage others to al-

Media Adaptations

- Actor John Hannah in the 1994 film *Four Weddings and a Funeral* read an excerpt from "Funeral Blues." The 1994 film starred Hugh Grant and Andie MacDowell and became a huge box-office success. It was directed by Mike Newell and produced in the United Kingdom by Working Title Films.

- The poem was also released as a Random House Audio Book, read by John Hannah.

ter the landscape to more closely reflect the speaker's emotional state.

In the first two stanzas, the speaker demands that certain rituals be performed during the funeral ceremony. In the first stanza, the speaker, expressing an overtly sensitive response to everyday sounds, calls for a silence that is both respectful and representative of his internal state of mind. Clocks, telephones, dogs, and pianos must not make a sound in honor of the one who has died. Clocks must stop, since time, in essence, has stopped for the speaker after the loss of love. Telephones must be cut off since no further communication is desired. Dogs, who often bark during play, must be quieted since the speaker does not feel playful. Not even the music from a piano can be appreciated. The only sound the speaker wants to hear is the somber beat of a "muffled" drum as the funeral procession begins. Only after these careful preparations have been completed can the coffin be brought out and the mourners allowed to arrive.

Lines 5-8:

In these lines, the speaker insists that the surroundings reflect the somber occasion and the speaker's mood. The only sound called for besides the muffled drum is the "moaning" of airplanes overhead that write "He Is Dead" in the sky for onlookers. These two sounds more closely reflect and perpetuate the speaker's mood. The processional path must be appropriately decorated with "crepe

bows round the white necks of the public doves" and black gloves must be worn by policemen.

Lines 9-12:

The focus shifts in these lines from the funeral procession to a description of the speaker's relationship with the deceased. All the images in this stanza illustrate the prodigious effect the loved one had on the speaker. The first three lines describe the completeness of their relationship in images of distance and time. The ninth line, "He was my North, my South, my East and West," suggests that he gave the speaker direction and a sense of constancy. The next line and a half, "my working week and my Sunday rest, / My noon, my midnight" describes him as an integral part of every moment of the speaker's daily life. He influenced the speaker's communication ("my talk") and mood ("my song"). These lines suggest that he was, in fact, the speaker's life. The final line of this stanza expresses the genuine sorrow the speaker experiences over his/her loss and points to a growing sense of disillusionment. The speaker had previously believed "that love would last for ever" but now admits, "I was wrong." Auden reinforces this sense of disillusionment with a caesura (a break in rhythm) in the middle of this line, separating the speaker's previous romantic illusions from the harsh reality of the present.

Lines 13-16:

The sense of disillusionment continues in the poem's final stanza and becomes coupled with feelings of bitterness. The ceremony so carefully constructed by the speaker in the first two stanzas does not seem to be enough to express or reflect his/her intense grief. As a result, the speaker expresses a desire to alter the universe. Auden employs a caesura in the middle of the thirteenth line to show the effects of the speaker's sorrow and his/her desire to recreate the universe in order to objectify that sorrow. The beauty of nature cannot be appreciated anymore. Since the stars "are not wanted now," the landscape must change. The speaker's "star" has been effectively "put out," and so the moon, the sun, the ocean, and the woods must be packed up, dismantled, poured away and swept up since they can no longer offer comfort. As in stanza two, the speaker here calls for all to recognize and echo his suffering. The world has changed after the death of his love, and as a result "nothing now can ever come to any good." There is no romantic sense in the finality of that statement of the transcendence of love or the possibility of regaining that love after death.

Themes

Death

Death is the subject and main theme of "Funeral Blues." Through the poem Auden makes a compelling statement about the devastating effects that the death of a loved one has on those left behind. The speaker has just lost someone for whom he/she had a deep love. During the course of the poem, the speaker will plan a funeral procession, reveal details about their relationship, and consider the future.

Love

The speaker describes the love he/she felt for the deceased in the third stanza. The lines "He was my North, my South, my East and West, / My working week and my Sunday rest, / My noon, my midnight, my talk, my song;" express the impact the loved one had on the speaker's life. The naming of directional points suggests that the deceased provided direction and meaning for the speaker. The time elements that encompass an entire week and a twelve hour day point to a sense of constancy in their relationship. Even as the speaker expressed him/herself through "talk" and "song," the deceased's influence was felt. Auden's modern view in this poem contradicts the romantic notion of love lasting through eternity. The loss of love is final here, as expressed in the twelfth line: "I thought that love would last forever: I was wrong."

Order and Disorder

When we lose a loved one who provided a sense of meaning and order, chaos can result. The speaker feels a sense of disorder as a result of losing a relationship that was such an integral part of his/her life. Their love provided the speaker with a sense of time and space and so helped delineate the boundaries of his/her life. The loss of that order prompts the speaker to try to regain some semblance of it through the planning of the funeral procession. First everyday objects are attended to as a somber mood is set. The speaker's use of the imperative voice helps regain a sense of control. The death has caused a sensitivity to noise, and so the speaker instructs the listener to silence telephones, dogs, and pianos. Telephones are silenced since communication is no longer possible in this chaotic state and playful, barking dogs become an annoyance. Even art, in the form of music from a piano, cannot be appreciated. Clocks must be stopped because time stands still now for the speaker who cannot see any sense of meaning in the future. This at-

Topics for Further Study

- Write a poem about a loss you have experienced. How did that loss alter your view of the world?

- Consider the stages of grief, focusing on the psychological effects of death on the griever. How does your research relate to the speaker in "Funeral Blues"?

- Compare and contrast the statements on suffering in Auden's "Funeral Blues" and "Musee des Beaux Arts." How does the style in each reflect the theme?

tempt to control and order existence continues as the funeral procession begins. The speaker informs listeners that the only sounds heard shall be the mournful beating of a "muffled drum" and the engines of the "moaning" airplanes as they write the message "He is Dead" in the sky. Further efforts at control include instructions to appropriately decorate the processional path with "crepe bows round the white necks of the public doves" and policemen wearing "black cotton gloves."

After ruminating on the meaning of the relationship with the loved one, the speaker admits to the disorder that results from death when noting that he/she wrongly assumed "love would last for ever." In a final attempt to restore order, the speaker turns to the cosmic, instructing listeners to put out stars, pack up the moon, dismantle the sun, pour away the ocean, and sweep up the woods. Since the speaker's world has been inexorably altered, nature must be as well, for its beauty can not longer offer comfort.

Meaning of Life

Ultimately though, the speaker's efforts to restore order fail. The absurd situation that results from the complete disruption of the universe after the death of a loved one cannot be explained or resolved. Where the speaker had previously felt a sense of meaning in life through the relationship with the loved one, after his death, that meaning has vanished. In this overwhelming and nonsensi-

Compare
&
Contrast

- **1936:** Edward VIII abdicates the English throne to marry Wallis Simpson, an American divorcee.

  1998: The House of Representatives approves two articles of impeachment against American President William Clinton as a result of his relationship with Monica Lewinsky, a young White House intern.

  1999: The Senate acquits the President on both impeachment charges. The scandal however, has severely damaged his reputation.

- **1936:** Adolph Hitler reoccupies the Rhineland on March 7.

1939: Great Britain enters World War II.

2000: Economically and politically, the United States has become the most powerful nation in the world.

- **1936:** The British Broadcasting Corporation (BBC), a publicly owned institution, sets up the world's first electronic television system.

  2000: The BBC is watched more than any other single broadcaster in the United Kingdom. Shows produced by the BBC, especially historical series and comedies retain their popularity with American viewers.

---

cal universe, the speaker expects little, since "nothing now can ever come to any good."

Style

Auden presents "Funeral Blues" as an elegy to a loved one who is deceased. The poem presents a mixture of traditional and nontraditional elements, reflecting one of its dominant themes: order and disorder. Its somber tone is reflected in its four quatrains (four-line stanzas), each containing two couplets (end rhyme pattern *aabb*), and a regular meter of four feet per line. Yet Auden has not chosen a standard rhythmic pattern. Instead he shifts groups of stressed and unstressed syllables that effectively disrupt the poem's rhythm. This coupling of ordered and unordered patterns symbolizes the speakers efforts, and final failure, to reestablish order in his life after suffering the devastating loss of a loved one.

This mixture of traditional and nontraditional elements continues in the poem's overall structure as well as its rhyme scheme. "Funeral Blues" does incorporate a syncopated blues rhythm and melancholic tone, as its title suggests, but does not follow the traditional blues structure. Blues are characteristically short (three-line stanzas) and marked

by frequent repetition. Often the first line in each stanza is repeated in the second.

Historical Context

Modernism

Auden's early poetry was Modernist in style, but as Richard Johnson noted in his article on Auden in *The Dictionary of Literary Biography,* in the 1930s "he was creating something quite new to modern poetry, a civil style. His reputation at the time was for a certain casualness in his writing." The Modernist period in England is usually considered to have begun with World War I in 1914 and ended during the depression years in the 1930s. Modernist poets like T. S. Eliot and Ezra Pound revolted against traditional literary forms, replacing the standard flow of poetic language with fragmented phrases and broken lines. Modernists vowed, in Ezra Pound's terms, to "make it new." They created new poetic structures and styles as they introduced new and sometimes shocking subject matter. Writers employed this type of experimentation in order to reveal a truer reflection of the inner self. Their poems often protested the sterility of society in the early part of the twentieth century and expressed a sense of the speaker's alienation

---

from that society. Part of their goal was to disrupt poetic conventions and therefore readers' expectations in order to challenge the standards of bourgeois culture. Auden, along with Eliot, Pound, Yeats, and Hopkins helped create this new form.

The Auden Generation

English society in the 1930s became increasingly concerned with the political and economic realities of that decade, especially the rise of Fascism and the threat of another world war. Much of the poetry of this period reflected the culture's pessimism and turned back to the more realistic structures common in the first decade of the twentieth century. Themes often revolved around class division and sexual repression. The poets of what has come to be known as "The Auden Generation" (Auden along with C. Day-Lewis, Louis MacNeice, and Stephen Spender) or "The Oxford Group" addressed these themes with defiance. Each poet envisioned a new world order based on Marxist precepts. Their poetry is characterized by its variety—its use of different genres (like Auden's adoption of the blues ballad form) and quick shifts of tone, intermingling the colloquial and the obscure, the serious and the playful.

Critical Overview

The revised version of "Funeral Blues" appeared in Auden's collection of poetry, *Another Time,* published in 1940. Initial reviews of the volume were mixed. Richard Eberhart in the *Boston Transcript* stated, "These poems maintain Auden's reputation at its high level. There is scarcely a bad line in the book." Alfred Kreymborg in *Living Age* found that the poems reveal "a new note of tenderness, a mature appraisal of love in an otherwise crumbling world." Other critics, however, felt the poems confirmed their opinion that Auden, in T. C. Worsely's words in the *New Statesman and Nation,* "is and always will be an uneven poet." P. M. Jack writing for *The New York Times* insists that *Another Time* "might be called 'marking time,' in which many of the faults and few of the virtues of the author are seen. In particular there is a startling restriction of the imagination…. The imagery is humdrum."

A few comments specifically on "Funeral Blues" appeared later in scholarly books and articles. Monroe K. Spears in his *Poetry of W. H. Auden* praised the style of the poem, claiming that its

"blues rhythm and syncopation are expertly suggested." George T. Wright in his book on Auden commends the poem's "elegant polished expression of longing." Public response to the poem was overwhelmingly positive after John Hannah recited an excerpt in the hit film *Four Weddings and a Funeral.* Since the publication of *Another Time,* scholars' assessment of Auden's career has been quite strong. Sean O'Brien in London's *Sunday Times* notes "Auden is one of the few modern poets whose reputation has not dimmed in the years following his death…. There is a widening stream of critical and biographical writing, as well as Edward Mendelson's enormous labours on the gradually emerging Complete Works." Most scholars would agree with the appraisal of Auden's body of work made by the National Book Committee, which awarded him the National Medal for Literature in 1967: "[Auden's poetry] has illuminated our lives and times with grace, wit and vitality. His work, branded by the moral and ideological fires of our age, breathes with eloquence, perception and intellectual power."

Criticism

Wendy Perkins

Wendy Perkins, an Associate Professor of English at Prince George's Community College in Maryland, has published articles on several twentieth-century authors. In this essay she examines the revisions made in the final version of "Funeral Blues" and how those revisions reflected changes in tone and theme.

The first version of W. H. Auden's "Funeral Blues" appeared in his play *The Ascent of F6* in 1936 and was referred to by its first line, "Stop all the clocks, cut off the telephone." In 1940 Auden included a revised version of the poem in his collection of poetry, *Another Time.* The revision, which he titled "Funeral Blues," retained the original poem's first two stanzas and replaced the last three with two new stanzas. George T. Wright, in his book on the poet, noted that Auden "was a continual reviser, rearranger, and even discarder of his early poems." This revision, however, was one of his more drastic ones. When Auden turned "Stop all the clocks" into "Funeral Blues," he transformed a confused mixture of burlesque and sorrow into a stirring lament over the death of a loved one, creating what Sean O'Brien in London's *Sunday Times* called his most "accessible" poem.

> *Auden's revision of "Funeral Blues" removes the burlesque elements of the early version in its clear and honest presentation of an individual's desperate attempt to cope with a devastating loss."*

The Ascent of F6, written with Auden's long-time collaborator Christopher Isherwood, was a critical success when it was first presented by the Group Theatre in 1937, but the play's reputation has suffered over the years. The plot focuses on the quest to climb a mountain by a group of characters who all have personal reasons for the expedition. Michael J. Sidnell, in his article on Auden for the *Dictionary of Literary Biography,* argues that the play's main theme reveals "the authors' disenchantment with group worlds." Sidnell continues, "On the one hand it presents, in flat caricature, a group of English establishment cronies mixing sport and politics in a strong solution of cant; on the other, a group of high-minded mountaineers who, under stress, are revealed as ordinarily weak men." "Stop all the clocks" appears in the play as a song sung by two characters following the strange death of James Ransom, one of the leaders of the climb. The song is sung in an odd scene that Joseph Warren Beach, in his book *The Making of the Auden Canon,* called "a strange mixture of allegory and burlesque, at the same time that the dialogue continues to pursue a serious and somewhat mystifying psychological theme—musical comedy style." The last three stanzas reflect this odd mixture as they refer to the other members of the climbing party and the funeral of Ransom.

Beach argues that these stanzas are "inferior in quality and too monotonously lugubrious in tone." Their tone, however, also becomes frivolous and absurd, especially in the last stanza with its attention on racing the coffin to the gravesite. The hyperbole (an overstatement characterized by exaggerated language) in the fourth stanza turns the funeral ceremony into a burlesque. The "weeping" crowds listen to "a few words sad and kind" while another character employs "a powerful microscope" as he "searches their faces for a sign of hope." The comic tone at the end of the poem turns the first two stanzas into an exaggerated sentiment on the death of a loved one. The entire poem, then, becomes a parody of the traditional blues lyric.

After Auden revised the poem, it was set to music by Benjamin Britten and sung by soprano Hedli Anderson for the stage. John Fuller, in *W.H. Auden: A Commentary* noted, "The ironic effect of the hyperbole is much changed when the song is sung by a single singer lamenting the death of her lover." The new version becomes in Wright's words an "elegant polished expression of longing." Beach insists that the fragments of the old and revised version "are pieced together without any striking evidence of their separate origin. They make together a lively composition in a vein appealing to world-weary modern readers as well as sophisticated nightclub audiences."

In the new version, the first two stanzas strike a somber note as the speaker prepares for the funeral of a loved one. The first few lines introduce the poem's main theme: when death ends a relationship that affords life a sense of meaning and completeness, people often engage in a desperate struggle to restore order in the midst of the ensuing chaos. In an effort to reestablish the order provided by the relationship with the loved one, the speaker gives commands as to what must be done for the ceremony. John G. Blair, in *The Poetic Art of W. H. Auden* noted, "Auden frequently chooses the imperative to attract attention." Blair states that this technique brings the poem "closer to the dramatic immediacy of dialogue, for the speaking voice is usually directed not to the reader but to an audience or another character whose presence is implied by the framing of the poem." In these first lines the speaker directs others to alter the landscape so it will become symbolic of his/her emotional state. Clocks, telephones, dogs, and pianos must not make a sound in honor of the one who has died. Clocks must stop since time, in essence, has stopped for the speaker after the loss of love. Telephones must be cut off since no further communication is desired. Dogs, who often bark during play, must be quieted since the speaker does not feel playful. Not even the music from a piano can be appreciated. The only sound the speaker wants to hear is the somber and appropriate beat of a "muffled" drum as the funeral procession begins. Only after these careful preparations have been completed can the coffin be brought out and the mourners come. The speaker then orders the listeners to have "moaning" airplanes fly overhead, writing "He Is Dead," with unavoidable finality. The processional path must be appropriately decorated with "crepe bows round the white necks of the public doves" and black gloves must be worn by policemen.

In the third stanza, the speaker reveals the sense of order he/she experienced prior to the death of the loved one. The first three lines describe the completeness of their relationship in images of distance and time. The ninth line, "He was my North, my South, my East and West," suggests that he gave the speaker direction and a sense of constancy. The next line and a half, "my working week and my Sunday rest, / My noon, my midnight" describes him as an integral part of every moment of the speaker's daily life. He influenced the speaker's communication ("my talk") and mood ("my song"). These lines suggest that he was, in fact, the speaker's life. The final line of this stanza expresses the genuine sorrow the speaker experiences over his/her loss and points to a growing sense of disillusionment. The speaker had previously believed "that love would last for ever" but now admits, "I was wrong." Auden reinforces this sense of disillusionment with a caesura in the middle of this line, separating the speaker's previous romantic illusions from the harsh reality of the present.

The speaker's efforts to create order from chaos cannot alleviate the sense of disillusionment coupled with feelings of bitterness expressed in the poem's final stanza. The ceremony so carefully constructed by the speaker in the first two stanzas does not seem to be enough to express or reflect his/her intense grief. As a result, the speaker turns from the everyday objects (the telephones, clocks, and piano) to cosmic ones (stars, moon, sun), traditional subjects for ballads, and expresses a desire to alter the universe. Auden employs a caesura (a pause that breaks rhythm) in the middle of the thirteenth line to show the effects of the speaker's sorrow and his/her desire to recreate the universe in order to objectify that sorrow. The beauty of nature cannot be appreciated anymore. Since the stars "are not wanted now," the landscape must change. The speaker's "star" (the loved one) has been effectively "put out" and so the moon, the sun, the ocean, and the woods must be packed up, dismantled, poured away and swept up since they can no longer offer comfort. As in stanza two, the speaker here calls for all to recognize and echo his suffering. The world has changed after the death of his love, and as a result "nothing now can ever come

What Do I Read Next?

- Margaret Atwood wrote "Death of a Young Son by Drowning" in 1970. This poem, published in 1990 in her *Selected Poems,* focuses on the speaker's response to the death of her son.

- "Musee des Beaux Arts," written in 1938 and published in 1940 with "Funeral Blues" in his *Another Time,* is one of Auden's most famous poems. It presents a different type of statement on suffering.

- "Tonight I Can Write" by Pablo Neruda is another heartfelt expression of grief over the loss of a loved one. This poem was published along with other fine love poems in a collection of Neruda's poetry, *Twenty Love Poems and a Song of Despair* (1969).

- "The Weary Blues" by Langston Hughes was written in 1925 and can be found in *The Selected Poems of Langston Hughes.* "The Weary Blues" like "Funeral Blues" contains the specialized syncopated rhythm of a blues song.

to any good." There is no romantic sense in the finality of that statement of the transcendence of love or the possibility of regaining that love after death. Ultimately then, the speaker's efforts to restore order fail. The speaker's world has been shattered by a death that cannot be explained or resolved.

Hayden Carruth, in his article in *The Hudson Review,* commented on Auden's revision process: "And always his revisions were in the direction of simplicity and clarity, suppressing whatever was in the least inflated or mushy or unearned. For honesty he threw away the products of his rhetorical genius without a qualm." Auden's revision of "Funeral Blues" removes the burlesque elements of the early version in its clear and honest presentation of an individual's desperate attempt to cope with a devastating loss. The final version of the poem becomes a moving and powerful portrait of the effects that death can have on those who remain behind.

Source: Wendy Perkins, in an essay for *Poetry for Students*, Gale, 2001.

Jeannine Johnson

In the following essay, Johnson contends that the title "Funeral Blues" is a somewhat misleading one, since this poem's primary concern is not with death but with love.

Auden's poem "Funeral Blues" is better known by its first line, "Stop all the clocks, cut off the telephone," and perhaps for good reason. As he did with many of his poems over the course of his career, Auden made several changes to the language of "Funeral Blues" as he prepared it for republication. In addition to these revisions, Auden placed the poem in different contexts at different times, and these contexts affect its meaning almost as much as the words themselves. The poem first appeared in the 1936 play, *The Ascent of F6.* The poem was then significantly revised and published under the title "Funeral Blues" in Auden's 1940 collection, *Another Time.* This poem was also included in *Collected Shorter Poems* and *Collected Poems,* published in 1966 and 1976, respectively. Though the text of the poem remained the same as it was in *Another Time,* in both these later volumes it was presented with only the title "IX," as one poem in a sequence called "Twelve Songs."

Thus, over forty years, the poem underwent several transformations until it took on its final shape and title in *Collected Shorter Poems* and *Collected Poems.* It is significant that in the last volume of Auden's verse the poem appears exactly as it did in *Collected Shorter Poems* and that he continues to call it "IX," not "Funeral Blues." Although *Collected Poems* was published three years after Auden's death, the poet had nearly total control over its production, and the volume presents all the poems Auden wished to preserve, and in their final form. The other lyrics in the series "Twelve Songs" are various types of love poems. In replacing the title "Funeral Blues" with a number, Auden may have signalled that it, too, is a love poem of sorts. Thus, although a funeral provides the occasion for reflection and mourning, the impetus behind this poem is not to understand death, but to understand love.

Nevertheless, first and foremost "Funeral Blues" expresses the pain of loss. (Despite the questions I raise concerning the title, for the sake of convenience, I will continue to refer to this poem as "Funeral Blues.") The poet calls for quiet and for reverence: "Stop all the clocks, cut off the tele- phone, / Prevent the dog from barking with a juicy bone, / Silence the pianos and with muffled drum / Bring out the coffin, let the mourners come." The only sound the poet will allow is that of a "muf- fled drum" and, of course, of his own verse. Ac- cording to the literary critic John Fuller, Auden first wrote the poem for inclusion in the 1936 play, *The Ascent of F6,* an allegorical tale about power in which the hero is mountain climber Michael Ran- som. The poem is sung in response to what Fuller calls "the phantasmagoric death of James Ransom," Michael's brother (*W. H. Auden: A Commentary*). The poem in this drama is comprised of five stan- zas, and it is sung by two characters, Lord Stag- mantle and Lady Isabel. The first two stanzas are identical to those of the poem later published as "Funeral Blues," but the last three have nothing in common with the last stanzas of the later version of the poem. In them, Stagmantle and Isabel reflect on the fates of other people in their climbing party, and the purpose of the song is to chastise Michael for causing the death of his brother. However, the drama is based in fantasy, and James' death is not real, but only imagined. Therefore, the tone is rel- atively comic, or at least not as tragic as the poem in isolation might suggest.

When the poem appears as "Funeral Blues" in *Another Time,* the text is much changed. There it stands as the third of four poems in the sequence "Four Cabaret Songs for Miss Hedli Anderson." In these cabaret songs the singer is reflecting on the death of her lover, but they are contained in a sec- tion of the book called "Lighter Poems." The tone becomes slightly more serious when the poem ap- pears in *Collected Shorter Poems* and *Collected Poems.* In these later volumes, "Funeral Blues" is surrounded by eleven other poems, all written be- tween 1935 and 1938. The subject of loss is com- plemented by other themes, such as desire, secrecy, and love (and, specifically, homosexual love). Though these themes are more explicitly explored in the other eleven poems, they resonate impor- tantly in this one, and they disclose the motivation behind the poet's hyperbolic language.

The poet's grief is so great that he makes no attempt to comprehend death or to meditate upon it: he simply accepts it as the end of not one man's life but as the end of all life. The poem engages in hyperbole, or dramatic overstatement, closing with the astonishing proclamation that "The stars are not wanted now; put out every one, / Pack up the moon and dismantle the sun, / Pour away the ocean and sweep up the wood; / For nothing now can ever come to any good." In the face of this death, the poet claims, there is no need to go on living, so there is no need to preserve the sun or moon or anything else that sustains human existence.

The poet's exaggerations materialize in the form of the poem as well as in its content. The dominant line here is a ten-syllable line, as occurs in "Stop all the clocks, cut off the telephone" and "Bring out the coffin, let the mourners come." But many of the other lines extend to eleven or even twelve syllables, as in "Tie crepe bows round the white necks of the public doves" and "Let the traffic policemen wear black cotton gloves." These extra syllables may represent the excess of feeling which cannot be contained within the limits of language: the speaker's emotions spill out beyond ten syllables, requiring surplus beats to accommodate them. These longer lines may also symbolize how the speaker feels his loss extends beyond his private world into the public realm. The poet demands that airplanes moan and scribble "on the sky the message He Is Dead" for all to see. He believes that everyone will suffer as a result of his friend's death and that everyone and everything (including animals, machines, and objects in nature) should participate in his lament.

The speaker's distress is so vast because the deceased person was, in life, his lover: "He was my North, my South, my East and West, / My working week, and my Sunday rest, / My noon, my midnight, my talk, my song…." It might seem that the poet likens his lover to a compass and a calendar, as if to suggest how his lover helped him to define who he was and where he existed. But his lover was more the means by which to determine physical location or measure time: he *was* physical location, he *was* time. Because the lover was everything that verifies and constitutes life, geography and temporality no longer have any meaning for the poet. Even more than this, the lover was "my talk, my song," identifying him with speech, language, and poetry, which are all of immeasurable value to a poet. The lover was the tool by which the poet expressed and understood himself, and now that tool is gone.

If it is not evident from the language of "Funeral Blues," it is clear from the other lyrics in the sequence "Twelve Songs" that the speaker is male and that their passion did not meet with the approval of conventional society. In the fourth song, Auden speaks of kissing his lover, "Indifferent to those / Who sat with hostile eyes" directed toward the pair. In "Autumn Song," the sixth poem, "Whispering neighbours left and right / Daunt us from

> *… perhaps he is acknowledging that love, with all its anguish and all its joy, will renew itself perpetually, and that in the future the poet will experience it—and write about—again and again."*

our true delight…." In the poem immediately preceding "Funeral Blues," Auden refers to "a wicked secret" and confides that "There is always another story, there is more than meets the eye." All these comments point to the existence of what some people might consider an illicit love, that is, one between two men.

Auden only uses the word "love" once in this poem, and his tone is simultaneously sarcastic and despairing: "I thought that love would last for ever: I was wrong." The fact that "love" only becomes visible in a single instance might suggest that this topic is not of great importance to the poem. However, this is by far the most grave and deliberate line in the poem. It is composed of eleven words, only one of which contains more than one syllable. The monosyllabic words emphasize and protract each beat of the line until it arrives at the loud, deep, and irrevocable sound of "wrong." When the poet sees his mistake, when he understands that eternal love is impossible, he realizes that his calls in the first two stanzas were insufficient. It is not enough to stage a public procession of mourning in a single town on earth; instead, the entire planet and everything in the universe must come to an end.

Yet, though the poet seems to confirm that there is no such thing as everlasting love, his gesture to do away with the universe in response to love's passing indicates that in fact he equates the breadth of love with that of the universe. In other words, the infinitude of the universe makes no sense if love, too, is not infinite and eternal; thus if one is destroyed, they both are. Since the poet does not have the power to close down the universe, perhaps he is admitting that he may be similarly powerless to declare the end of love, regard-

The magic of Auden ... is how he is able to invoke his reader's emotions and have them share and grieve for the loss of someone who is never even named."

less of his sorrow. Or perhaps he is acknowledging that love, with all its anguish and all its joy, will renew itself perpetually, and that in the future the poet will experience it—and write about—again and again.

In some of the other "Twelve Poems" Auden addresses homosexual love, and in "Funeral Blues" the poet specifically identifies the deceased as male. Nevertheless, there is a universalizing gesture in this poem, as its voice changes several times. When it appeared in *The Ascent of F6,* "Funeral Blues" was to be sung by two people, one man and one woman. In *Another Time,* the "song" has a female singer, Hedli Anderson. In *Collected Poems,* Auden does not identify a particular speaker, further underscoring the flexibility of the poem. What literary critic James Fenton says of the fourth lyric in "Twelve Songs" is equally true of the ninth: "any reader can be the lover, the speaker of this poem," and the critic remarks that "there is generosity in this" ("Auden at Home"). What Fenton means is that Auden allows readers to use the poet's personal experience and apply it to their own lives, regardless of the gender of the reader or of the reader's beloved. In this Fenton substantiates what Auden's poem makes clear: that love, like poetry, is not only exceptionally resilient but also benevolently versatile.

Source: Jeannine Johnson, in an essay for *Poetry for Students,* Gale, 2001.

Aviya Kushner

Aviya Kushner, who is the poetry editor for New World Renaissance Magazine, earned an M.A. in creative writing from Boston University. In the following essay, Ms. Kushner discusses Auden's perspective on personal and public grief and how he parallels the two in his poem Funeral Blues.

During Auden's lifetime, Auden witnessed both World Wars and the deaths of many important public figures. Auden found himself writing many elegies, memorializing and capturing the impact these figures had on the public and their century. Auden's "In Memory of Sigmund Freud" remarks on the difficulty of writing an elegy when there are so many to mourn:

When there are so many we shall have to mourn,
when grief has been made so public, and exposed
to the critique of a whole epoch
the frailty of our conscience and anguish,

of whom shall we speak?

Thus, the poet's challenge, even when writing about a famous man, is to write something that distinguishes his subject from all the others who have recently died.

Here, in "Funeral Blues," Auden, through the voice of the speaker, seems to be writing an elegy for someone who meant a great deal to him personally. Although Auden does not clearly state about whom the poem is written, one can gather that speaker loved this person dearly. However, it is not clear that this is a conventional elegy: Auden may simply be mourning the end of a relationship, not a death. In either reading, Auden is wrestling with the realization that love does not always last. Auden uses some of his favorite images here to stress the fragility of love: clocks, midnight, ocean. With the "death" of this person in the speaker's world, time has stopped, and there is no reason for communication. All that is warranted now is quiet, to "silence the pianos," "cut off the telephone."

Although Auden wants this world to come to a halt, the death must be announced, as the next stanza details:

Let aeroplanes circle moaning overhead
Scribbling on the sky the message: He is Dead.
Put crepe bows round the white necks of the public
    doves
Let the traffic policemen wear black cotton gloves.

This stanza is about opening up this private grief for a public mourning. These images insist that everyone share in this person's loss because not only has the speaker lost someone very special, essentially, so has the world. Still, Auden is keeping a tight control on this stanza and about how this loss will be shared. The first line invoking the aeroplanes is a bold image. With the planes "moaning" overhead and the message being "scribbled" in the sky, large numbers of people are sure to note their significance. But then Auden seems to bring the loss back, emphasizing the loss of the speaker. The funeral messages get smaller, to the fine detail of the color of the policemen's gloves. These messages are more subtle and imply that only those very close to the deceased would note them. At the same time, it is interesting that very public figures (the policemen) wear the symbols. Auden carefully straddles that line between the public and private interpretations of grief.

Auden seems then to turn the poem, wanting the speaker to unequivocally claim this person, detailing his worth and value. The third stanza states:

> He was my North, my South, my East and West,
> My working week and my Sunday rest,
> My noon, my midnight, my talk, my song;

With nine uses of "my" in three lines, the speaker takes possession of his subject. Auden wanted to convey that this man was the central element of the speaker's life, that no matter the direction he turned, no matter the hour, this man was there. Auden also notes that the person was the speaker's "talk," his "song." Talk implies words and perhaps creations with words, such as poetry. What Auden is emphasizing here is that along with everything else, this man was the speaker's muse, the source of his artistic creation. These lines again stress the need to silence everything. Without this man, the speaker has lost his need to speak. With the loss of his core, there is nothing to sing about.

Auden then puts this private mourning back into the public sphere. With everything essential gone in the speaker's world, the obvious connection is to remove all that is essential in the world at large:

> The stars are not wanted now: put out every one,
> Pack up the moon and dismantle the sun,
> Pour away the ocean and sweep up the wood;
> For nothing now can ever come to any good.

The drastic actions suggested in this stanza signify on a larger scale what has happened in the speaker's life. The speaker has already lost his sun, his moon, his stars. Removing these objects would no longer have an impact on his life, but others would then be able to grasp the enormity of his sorrow.

Although Auden's elegies seem to express his personal bereavement at a particular person's passing, upon closer readings, one can see how he invites the public to share in the mourning process and really look at what has been lost with this death. With his elegies for more public figures like Sigmund Freud or W.B. Yeats, it is easier to share in Auden's sentiments because of his reader's famil-iarity with his subjects. The magic of Auden, however, is how he is able to invoke his reader's emotions and have them share and grieve for the loss of someone who is never even named.

Source: Aviya Kushner, in an essay for *Poetry for Students,* Gale, 2001.

Sources

Auden, W. H., and Christopher Isherwood, *The Ascent of F6,* Faber and Faber, 1936.

———, *Another Time,* Random House, 1940.

———, *Collected Poems,* edited by Edward Mendelson, Vintage, 1991.

———, *Collected Shorter Poems: 1927–1957,* Random House, 1966.

Beach, Joseph Warren, *The Making of the Auden Canon,* University of Minnesota Press, 1957.

Blair, John G., *The Poetic Art of W. H. Auden,* Princeton University Press, 1965.

Carruth, Hayden, review, in *The Hudson Review* Vol. 35, No. 2, Summer, 1982, pp. 334-40.

Eberhart, Richard, review, in *Boston Transcript,* March 27, 1940, p. 13.

Fenton, James, "Auden at Home," in *The New York Review of Books* April, 27, 2000, pp. 8-14.

Fuller, John, *W. H. Auden: A Commentary,* Princeton University Press, 1998.

Gritten, David, "A Look inside Hollywood and the Movies: W. H. Auden's Star Rises with 'Weddings,'" in *Los Angeles Times,* June 26, 1994, p. 25.

Jack, P. M., review, in *New York Times,* February 18, 1940, p. 2.

Johnson, Richard, *Dictionary of Literary Biography,* Volume 20: *British Poets, 1914–1945,* Gale, 1983, pp. 19-51.

Kreymborg, Alfred, review, in *Living Age,* Vol. 358, p. 195.

O'Brien, Sean, "The Auden Regeneration," in *Sunday Times* (London), July 31, 1994.

Sidnell, Michael J., "W. H. Auden," in *Dictionary of Literary Biography,* Volume 10: *Modern British Dramatists, 1900–1945,* Gale, 1982, pp. 12-24.

Spears, Monroe K., *The Poetry of W. H. Auden,* Oxford University Press, 1963.

Worsley, T. C., review, in *New Statesman and Nation,* Vol. 20, July 27, 1940, p. 92.

Wright, George T., "W. H. Auden: Chapter 11: Down Among the Lost People," in *Twayne's United States Authors Series Online,* G. K. Hall & Co., 1999.

For Further Study

Bogan, Louise, review, in *The New Yorker,* February 24, 1940, p. 76.
    This reviewer finds Auden's love poems in *Another Time* to be too "metaphysical."

Review, in *Times Literary Supplement,* July 6, 1940, p. 328.
    This review of Auden's *Another Time* praises Auden's verses "that spring from a deeper center without any loss of that closeness to the tumbled texture of modern life in which he has always excelled."

The Hiding Place

Jorie Graham
1989

"The Hiding Place" first appeared in the May 22 issue of *The New Yorker* in 1989. The poem is not one of Graham's most important or well known work, perhaps because it marks a departure from her typical style. Normally, Graham is known for her oblique lyrics, but "The Hiding Place" is one of her more narrative, more representational poems. Like all her other work, this poem is written in free verse in the first person singular.

A set interpretation of a Graham poem is next to impossible. The most one can hope for is a general impression while reading one of her poems. The occasion of this work is the famous Paris uprising that began in May of 1968. More precisely, Graham's memory of events surrounding the student demonstrations serves as the genesis of the poem. Like most postmodern poetry, the text of the poem wavers between imagination and reality. The poem might be grounded in a historical event, but it remains unclear which events actually happened and which are constructed memories.

A likely theme for "The Hiding Place" is the marriage of history and memory. Some aspects of the events are crystal clear, yet some may have never happened. Another possible reading would suggest that Graham advocates a kind of cultural revolution, just as her poems have engendered a sort of poetic revolution. The insistence not to give in, not to concede, may be a call to contemporary writers and artists to hold true to a creative vision. The poet seems to be empathizing with those students and workers struggling to make the world a better place.

Jorie Graham

Author Biography

Jorie Graham was born in New York City in May of 1951. When she was just three-months old, her family moved to Europe, where they settled in the South of France and then later in Italy. Because her mother was a well-known painter and her father a student of history and theology, Graham grew up with an appreciation for both sacred and secular concerns. Her interest in painting is reflected in her many poems about painters, and the frequency with which her poems deal with historical issues suggests her father's interests made an equal impact.

Graham began college in Paris at the Sorbonne where she became involved in the student uprising dramatized in "The Hiding Place." Eventually, she transferred to New York University, where she earned her bachelor of fine arts degree in 1973. In 1978, she took an MFA in creative writing from the prestigious Iowa Writer s Workshop at the University of Iowa, where she serves as a faculty member.

Unlike most contemporary poets, Graham achieved almost immediate success in the literary world. Early poems appeared in important publications like *The New Yorker, American Poetry Review* and *Georgia Review,* and Graham began winning awards that helped earn her recognition and helped get her books published. Her first two

books, *Hybrids of Plants and Ghosts* (1980) and *Erosion* (1983), were funded in part by grants awarded through Princeton University Press and established her as a poet transfixed by the matrix of language, history, art, and the machinations of the individual mind. Her next three collections, *The End of Beauty* (1987), *Region of Unlikeness,* (1991) and *Materialism* (1993) evinced a break in style toward a more disjunctive and indeterminate line and stanza, or phrases capable of multiple meanings expressed in free forms. Poems from each of these five books were collected in *Dream of the Unified Field: Selected Poems 1974-1994* (1995), an extremely important book for contemporary poetry in English and winner of the Pulitzer Prize for poetry in 1996. This book, along with attention from critic Helen Vendler, established Graham's reputation as one of the most important living American writers. In 1997, she published *The Errancy.*

Graham's *Swarm* (2000) is her most opaque work to date, and not surprisingly, reviews were mixed. In addition to her many awards, Graham was named the Boylston Professor at Harvard University, solidifying her importance to the world of contemporary poetry.

Poem Text

The last time I saw it was 1968.
Paris, France. The time of the *disturbances.*
    We had claims. Schools shut down.
A million *workers* and *students* on strike.

      Marches, sit-ins, helicopters, gas   5
They stopped you at gunpoint asking for papers.

    I spent 11 nights sleeping in the halls.
    Arguments. *Negotiations.*
Hurrying in the dawn looking for a certain leader
    I found his face above an open streetfire.
No he said, tell them no *concessions.*   10
    His voice above the fire as if there were no
    fire—

language floating everywhere above the sleeping
    bodies;
    and crates of fruit donated in secret;
and torn sheets (for tear gas) tossed down from
    shuttered windows;
    and bread; and blankets, stolen from the   15
    firehouse.

The ACRS (the government police) would swarm
    in around dawn
    in small blue vans and round us up.

Once I watched the searchbeams play on some
    flames.
    The flames push up into the corridor of
    light.

In the cell we were so crowded no one could sit or   20
    lean.
    People peed on each other. I felt a girl
vomiting gently onto my back.
    I found two Americans rounded up by
    chance,
their charter left that morning they screamed, what
    were they going to do?   25

    Later a man in a uniform came in with a
    stick.
Started beating here and there, found the girl in her
    eighth month.
    He beat her frantically over and over.
He pummeled her belly. Screaming aren't you
    ashamed?

    I remember the cell vividly   30
but is it from a photograph? I think the shadows as
    I
    see them still—the slatted brilliant bits
against the wall—I think they're true—but are they
    from a photograph?
    Do I see it from inside now—his hands, her
    face—or

is it from the news accounts?   35
    The strangest part of getting out again was
    streets.
The light running down them.
    Everything spilling whenever the wall
    breaks.
And the air—thick with dwellings—the air filled—
    doubled—
    as if the open   40

had been made to render—
    The open squeezed for space until the
    hollows spill out,
story upon story of them
    starting to light up as I walked out
How thick was the empty meant to be?   45
    What were we finding in the air?

    What were we meant to find?
I went home slowly sat in my rented room.
    Sat for a long time the window open,
    watched the white gauze curtain sluff this   50
    way that that
a bit—
    watched the air suck it out, push it back in
    Lung
of the room with streetcries in it. Watched until the
    lights
    outside made it gold, pumping gently.
Was I meant to get up again? I was inside. The   55
    century clicked by.

The woman below called down *not to forget
the*

loaf. Crackle of helicopters. Voice on a
    loudspeaker issuing
warnings.
    They made agreements we all returned to
    work.
The government fell but then it was all right again.   60
    The man above the fire, listening to my
    question,

the red wool shirt he wore: where is it? who has it?
    He looked straight back into the century: no
    concessions.
I took the message back.
    The look in his eyes—shoving out—into the   65
    open—

    expressionless with thought:
no—tell them *no*—

Poem Summary

Lines 1-6:

In the opening two stanzas, Graham provides
a time and a locale for the literal hiding place of
the title. The time is May of 1968, and the setting
is Paris. The uprisings of 1968 (called by the French
les evenements, the events) started with university
students at the Sorbonne on May 3, 1968. There
was confrontation between students and police at
the Sorbonne that led to a period of guerrilla warfare in the streets of the Latin Quarter in Paris. Graham, who was a student at the Sorbonne during the
disturbances, lets the reader know she was there
through the use of "I" and the unusual use of "you"
to represent herself, as opposed to "one." Though
she never says what the "it" is in the first stanza,
it can be assumed that she is referring to the hiding place, about which a great deal will be revealed.
Emphasis is placed on certain words through the
use of italics, perhaps to call attention to words or
terms that carried loaded public connotations at the
time.

Lines 7-10:

Graham moves from general descriptions of
the uprisings in the previous stanzas to a more autobiographical mode. A kind of narrative emerges
about how long she stayed in the hiding place, and
her search for a certain leader, a man who is always connected with fire, is introduced. Like the
notion of the hiding place, Graham will return to
the motif of the man and the fire.

Media Adaptations

- In 1991, Watershed Tapes out of Washington D.C. released an audiotape of Graham reading "The Hiding Place" and other poems.

- Graham reading her poem San Sepolcro and links to three other web sites featuring her work is available at the excellent Academy of American Poets, Jorie Graham exhibit, http://www.poets.org/lit/poet/jgrahfst.htm (June 22, 2000).

- Graham's collection of poems, *Region of Unlikeness* (1991), in which "The Hiding Place" appears, is an elegant, intellectual, and historical exploration of how personal visions and experience meshes with the sweep of history.

Lines 11-15:

In these four lines, Graham introduces an important motif in the poem, the motif of language and the open air. The freedom of the air (and of language) is contrasted to the cramped, confined space of the hiding place. She also returns to descriptions of the world outside the hiding place in an attempt to create alternate, but equally stark realities.

Lines 16-19:

In this stanza, Graham explains how the government secret police would round up student protesters. Again, she subtly lets the reader know that she was one of the people the police captured, and again, she focuses the reader's gaze away from the students and toward the fire, where the man's voice might be. Like a camera in a movie, the reader's eye is always being drawn from one scene to another.

Lines 20-28:

The poem takes a dramatic turn in the next few stanzas. Engaging in what poet Carolyn Forche would call a "poetry of witness," Graham describes some of the horrors of the cell into which she and the others found themselves squeezed. While deftly avoiding melodrama, the poet gives a stark account of people urinating and vomiting in the cell, as though the poem has turned into a documentary film. The most disturbing account tells of a policeman repeatedly striking the belly of a pregnant woman with a stick. These stanzas represent an usually realistic tone for Graham; thus, the circumstances seem particularly dire, lending the poem a rather remarkable tension.

Lines 29-34:

In yet another abrupt shift, the poet poses a shocking question to both herself and the audience: are the memories she's just recounted real, or did she make them up? In a classic postmodern gesture, Graham calls the certainty of memory and personal observation into question. She has a visual image of the cell, but is it an image she saw in a photograph? A common feature of postmodernism is the questioning of knowledge and the realization that there can never be one, singular truth. Here, Graham has no idea what is "true."

Lines 35-43:

Once more, the poet quickly jerks the reader back to the reality of the uprisings. It is difficult to tell whether or not events are imagined or are being reported. Either way, the poem turns from posing questions about truth to a descripton of the city after someone is released from jail. The motif of the open air recurs: space, openness, freedom seems to be squeezing out absence just as the bodies in the cell squeezed space out of the jail. Graham notes the sky seems to light up, perhaps referring to a fire lighting the dark Parisian sky.

Lines 42-47:

The poet muses on the theme of emptiness. What does someone find in the air once they are released from prison? Graham connects this kind of seemingly impossible searching with the student demonstrations: the question, "What were we meant to find?" becomes loaded with suggestion.

Lines 48-51:

Though there is no stanza break, there is a break in the flow of the poem. The shifts are becoming even more abrupt. The reader is transported now back to the poet's room, a rented room, where she sits, watching the exchange of inside and outside air. The notion of insides and outsides becomes yet another theme in the poem: is she an insider, or an outsider?

Lines 52-57:

In one of the most confusing sections of the poem, Graham conflates memory, voices from outside the window, sounds of helicopters, questions she asks herself, and historical information. When Graham says, "I was inside," the reader is left to wonder what, exactly, she is inside of: her room?; her memories?; history?; the twentieth century?; this poem?.

Lines 58-64:

Even though Graham assures that everyone went back to work and that the government survived the demonstrations, the poem continues. She has more questions for the mysterious man above the fire. Throughout the poem, there is reason to believe she is speaking of an actual man, but there is evidence here that the man, like the memory of the hiding place itself, might be fictitious. The red wool shirt seems to be a reference to Giuseppe Garibaldi's soldiers, known as the "Red Shirts," and the "*No* tell them *no*—" of the poem's final lines, mirror's a famous speech Garibaldi made to his men. Like the rest of the poem, the final lines are ambiguous. They could suggest a denial of violence. Or, Graham might be advocating a revolutionary spirit that refuses to compromise. Or, she could be talking to herself, telling herself the memories of such violence are simply not real.

Themes

History and the Present

While it is extraordinarily difficult to narrow in on anything as consistent as a "theme" in Jorie Graham's work, "The Hiding Place" does contain some ideas to unpack. Perhaps the most tenable theme in the poem is one of history and the present. The problems and burdens of history are always encroaching into the present day. The Chilean poet Pablo Neruda once wrote, "Love is so short. Forgetting is so long." In this poem, forgetting is long for Graham. In fact, she can't forget the memory of the beatings, of the cell, of the energy of the uprising, or the fervor for political justice. Towards the end of the poem, Graham writes, "I was inside. The century clicked by." Then, later, in referring to the man above the fire, she says, "He looked straight back into the century." History moves by at a rapid pace, and it brings memories with it. At one time, May of 1968 was the present. Now it is history. At some point, the poem will be history, as will the moment this essay is read.

Linked to the notion of history is the theme of seeking. Throughout the poem, Graham asks what she and the others who were revolting were supposed to find. What is one supposed to find by searching the historical past? What can one discover through memory? Through facts? Like most of Graham's poems, she provides no solid answers. When one examines history, when one examines one's memory, when one examines the present, all one gets is more questions. Facts tell only one side of the story, memory another. Perhaps history is the greatest hiding place of all. Graham might ultimately be suggesting that the secret to history is found in the present.

Public vs. Private

"The Hiding Place" dramatizes the tension between public and private worlds. The public world can be represented by streets, schools, history, events, buildings, and facts—items or occurrences that the public has knowledge of. The private world is a sphere hidden away from public scrutiny: memory, desire, fear, dreams, anxieties are private concerns that the public does not have access to. In this poem, public and private worlds collide, not only in terms of the hiding place or the cell but also in terms of what actually happened. In stanza eight, Graham is uncertain how reliable her memory of the cell actually is: "I remember the cell vividly / but is it from a photograph? I think the shadows as I / see them." Is her memory "vivid" because she actually experienced these events, or because she has seen these images in photographs in newspapers or magazines? Of course she was there, but are the specific images she remembers her own or constructed? In other words, are her memories, like the poem itself, publicly informed or privately informed?

The italicized words in the poem seem to carry a more public connotation than the non-italicized words. One can imagine seeing these words in the headlines of a newspaper, or hearing them spoken by countless people in Paris. Since the poem itself is an amalgamation of public and private language, Graham suggests that history, like poetry, is both a public and private facet of human life.

Places to Hide

After reading the poem, one might ask what the title has to do with a cell, a man above a fire, the uncertainty of memory, and political activism. Graham might argue that her poem explores events or memories people try to hide and the places in which they attempt to hide things from others and themselves. A good place to begin is to ask what, ex-

Topics for Further Study

- 1968 was a turbulent year in France, Germany, and America. Research what was going on around the world during 1968 and come up with some explanations as to why the political climate was so volatile during this period of recent history. Why were students so upset? Why aren't students rioting or protesting to this degree today?

- Graham is often cited as an important postmodern poet. Research postmodernism and look at some other postmodern poetry. Based on your findings, determine in what ways "The Hiding Place" may or may not be considered a postmodern text.

- Graham deliberately makes her poetry difficult. It would be much easier to write a short story about a memory of the 1968 uprisings in Paris. Consider why Graham would chose to write a lyric poem for an exploration of this memory. In what way is reading the poem similar to trying to make sense of a hazy memory?

- Graham is often compared to Wallace Stevens, John Ashbery, and Adrienne Rich. Read some poems by one or more of these poets and think about how and why her work mirrors theirs.

actly, is the hiding place? First of all, the hiding place is, literally, the place where the characters are holed up in the building; probably where she slept for eleven days. Figuratively, however, the hiding place is almost certainly the past. The speaker keeps harking back to the past, to May of 1968, posing questions about her actions and her motivations. One can never return, completely, to the past. The masks of experience, age, and priorities always hide its precise details. Additionally, the hiding place might be history itself. The individual experiences of the pregnant woman and the girl vomiting are hidden to most people behind the more objective, more public discourse of historical facts. And, lastly, the hiding place is human memory. How often do people (both intentionally and unintention-

ally) forget? Once a feeling or experience is forgotten, it is next to impossible to find again. So, there is tension in the poem between present, active language that may or may not be public, and past, public language that was intended to be active, both linguistically and politically. Given the potential reference to the revolutionary figure Guiseppe Garibaldi, it's possible that Graham is making a statement about the absence of political activism in contemporary society; perhaps that instead of standing up for what one believes, many choose to remain, forever, in their own hiding places.

Style

Like most postmodern poetry, "The Hiding Place" refuses to let the reader separate form and content. The jagged lines, the lack of symmetrical stanzas, the quick shifts from present to past and from public to private, underscore the thematic issues at work in the poem. Just as memory is chaotic, unpredictable, asymmetric, and always jumping from point to point, so is the poem itself.

Not only is the poem free of rhyme, meter, and any consistent stanzaic formation, it deliberately creates a sense of disarray. Furthermore, as the poem progresses, the poem's already tenuous order digresses. In stanzas 1-7, Graham employs enjambed lines fairly often, and each line contains similar numbers of words. After stanza 7, thoughts spill over into other lines, words spread out on the page, and lines may have only one or two words in them. Additionally, Graham occasionally makes the first word of a new sentence the final word in a line, so that the reader is always halting or pausing the reading process. For many postmodern writers and thinkers, history and knowledge are not fixed, uniform entities. Rather, they are fragmentary. Thus, the postmodern poem mirrors the postmodern view of history, culture, and knowledge.

Graham is famous for her difficult language, her obfuscating descriptions, and her non-linear lyrics. Oddly enough, "The Hiding Place" is one of her more narrative poems. Essentially, it is a complex short story. Techniques such as italicized words and non-transitional leaps puzzle the reader at first, but, ultimately, the form of the poem helps contribute to its theme of the uncertainty of memory.

Historical Context

"The Hiding Place" takes as its point of departure the infamous student uprising in Paris in the spring of 1968. The uprising of 1968 started with university students at the Sorbonne on May 3, 1968. There was confrontation between students and police at the Sorbonne that led to a period of guerrilla warfare in the streets of the Latin Quarter. Students and their sympathizers built barricades in the old Parisian revolutionary tradition. Armed police fought back. The government zigzagged between conciliation and repression. The conflict grew still worse and then spread to the provincial universities. Toward mid-May many workers began to join in. Strikes (usually of the sit-in variety) closed down factories and by 20 May at least 7 million workers had laid down their tools. Public services ground to a halt. Transportation broke down. In short, the country was paralyzed for a short time. In the Latin Quarter, the Sorbonne building was occupied and turned into a commune.

The students tried to reach out to industrial workers during this period by offering a broad critique of the present system. However, the workers really weren't interested in making common political cause with the students. In the end, the workers had different interests than the university students. Hence, students ended up settling for relatively limited concessions. So, what looked like revolution, turned out to be nothing more than a student-led uprising. It lasted only a few short months. But it did make clear that the university system needed a complete overhaul, and that students and faculty had to be involved in the changes. The result was that during the next several years, the Education Ministry carried out reforms. Among other things, it broke existing institutions into smaller units, with more local control over budgets and instructional methods. At the same time, though, student and faculty participation in institutional governance tended to politicize French universities. In fact, some of them became communist strongholds, others bastions of the right.

Graham was a young college student at the Sorbonne at the time. Her autobiographical account, oblique as it may be, dramatizes what it must have been like for students and political activists in Paris amidst the war-like conditions of revolution.

Critical Overview

"The Hiding Place" appears in Graham's 1991 collection *Region of Unlikeness,* probably Graham's least recognized book. Perhaps because of that and more ambitious poems in the collection, "The Hiding Place" has garnered virtually no critical atten-

tion. In fact, even the book reviewers of *Region of Unlikeness* avoided commenting on or even mentioning the poem. Similarly, recent book chapters by Helen Vendler, one of the two or three most important scholars of contemporary poetry, concentrate on Graham's more formally complex and experimental poems. Indeed, even though "The Hiding Place" might seem a bizarre poem, it is one of Graham's most traditional pieces.

However, while "The Hiding Place" may not be a magnet for literary criticism, Graham's poetry is. Aside from Helen Vendler's chapters on Graham in *The Breaking of Style* and *The Given and the Made: Recent American Poets,* influential critics such as Thomas Gardner, Bonnie Costello, and Mark Jarman have each written on Graham in the past few years. In a review of *Region of Unlikeness,* Costello notes the shift in Graham's poetry toward a more narrative energy, one that fuses plot and poetry as exemplified in "The Hiding Place": "Graham has taken it upon herself in her recent work to confront the power of plot and image head on. First she tested her metaphysics in a quiet, lyric space of nature and art, but lately she has plunged into the rush of history, memory, and contemporary life." In *The Given and the Made,* Vendler maps Graham's altered poetics in *Region of Unlikeness:* "Graham's tendency, in her first books, toward the exalted and the prophetic has been severely tempered, by the time she writes *Region of Unlikeness,* toward the material and the actual. Nonetheless, she remains determined not to let go of a principle of transcendent judgment, even in the presence of the unreliable and deniable chronicle we call history." For both Costello and Vendler, Graham's best poetry is that which sees the lyric as a meeting place for public and private concerns.

Other recent readers of Graham, such as Thomas Gardner, have compared her to John Ashbery in terms of both poet's use of language as a means of engaging the world, while William Olsen argues that Graham and Chase Twichell see the lyric as a way to disengage from the world. Vendler, Graham's best reader, sees her as following in the tradition of Gerard Manley Hopkins and Seamus Heaney as poets who break away from conventional modes of expression to create new worlds of experience.

Criticism

Dean Rader

Rader has published widely in the field of twentieth-century American poetry. In his essay he

> *For the poet, the hiding place is not only the literal space in which she and other students hid, but the hiding place is also, history, the past, and, ultimately, the poem itself.*"

discusses the various thematic possibilities of the title of Graham's poem, ultimately suggesting that all are linked.

Jorie Graham's poem "The Hiding Place" recalls another text bearing that same title, Corrie ten Boom's *The Hiding Place,* an autobiographical account of Boom's experiences hiding Jews from Nazi soldiers during World War II. Though the hiding place Graham explores in her poem is a vastly different kind of "place," Graham's poem seeks an intensity similar to that which ten Boom's book elicits. Like ten Boom's text, "The Hiding Place" is autobiographical, though to what degree is always up for debate. However, where ten Boom's text refers solely to the actual location in which Jews were hid, Graham's text is far more elusive. For the poet, the hiding place is not only the literal space in which she and other students hid, but the hiding place is also, history, the past, and, ultimately, the poem itself.

Oddly enough, Graham never mentions the hiding place specifically in her poem ("The last time I saw *it* was 1968"), a poetic move that suggests the title refers to more than one specific place. However, she does make reference to a literal hiding place where she and others stayed for 11 days during the student demonstrations in Paris in 1968: "I spent 11 nights sleeping in the halls." This line and the opening passage are the only real signs that the title denotes an actual place and not a mythical or symbolic place. Graham needs for the actual place to exist, however, so that she may dramatize the other hiding places her poem considers. The place in question is a room or building in which she and other students seek refuge. During the uprisings, the Parisian Police turned the area around the Latin Quarter in to a kind of war zone. Students

were beaten, arrested, harassed, and small bastions of student support groups sprouted throughout the city. Graham, who was 18 years old and a student at the Sorbonne in 1968, was in the middle of the action. Since she hid for 11 days, she must have felt that her safety was in jeopardy; apparently, it was, for she and a host of others were imprisoned in a cramped cell amid miserable conditions.

To write a poem about such a hiding place and to include in that poem a very realistic representation of women vomiting and urinating in a prison cell is to engage in what poet Carolyn Forche might call a "poetry of witness." In her introduction to her anthology *Against Forgetting: Twentieth Century Poetry of Witness,* published in 1991 (the same year as Graham's *Region of Unlikeness,* in which "The Hiding Place" appears), Forch claims that the poems in her anthology "will not permit us diseased complacency. They come to us with claims that have yet to be filled, as attempts to mark us as they themselves have been marked." Forch is correct: it is easier to forget than to remember. Graham's poem forces readers who do not know and readers who may have forgotten to remember the Paris demonstrations, the prison-like conditions, the mini-reign of terror. In her introduction to the *Best American Poetry 1990,* Graham implies that American poets have let the world off the hook, that they don't confront the difficult issues like they could or should. In "The Hiding Place," Graham reminds readers what was done to people and what poetry can do to those same people.

Because people forget, because history erases the past, people write. The implication of Graham's poem is that the hiding place under question in the poem is not just the geographical locale where she and others holed up, but history itself. The passing of time, the sweep of years, the accumulation of dates and facts and personal experience obliterates memories from the minds of the living. History successfully hides its more embarrassing moments simply by allowing people to forget.

Throughout her poetic career, Graham has used the lyric as means of forcing readers to remember by taking on history. In *Region of Unlikeness,* Graham has two poems with history in their titles, one called "Short History of the West," the other "The Phase after History," suggesting that how history is created and recreated is one of her more important themes. In "The Hiding Place," as in other of her poems, Graham posits that history is made, like a poem. It is not an objective, finite fact. It is a construct, and anything can be constructed to hide anything else.

In writing about *Region of Unlikeness,* Helen Vendler argues that by invoking historical moments in her work, Graham participates in the construction of new knowledge about history: "Language about history is as contingent as the 'beast' and its linked stories, but if uttered at the 'right' time will partake, however socially and historically constructed, of the shape of that historical moment." Thus, as is the case for most of Graham's lyrics, "The Hiding Place" does not offer any answers to the problems of history. Rather, by its very existence, it raises provocative questions.

Just as "The Hiding Place" evokes an interrogation of the public realm, so does it invite the reader into the uncharted waters of the private realm. Throughout the poem, Graham wonders how reliable the memory of her own past actually is: "I remember the cell vividly / but is it from a photograph?." A few lines later, she writes "Do I see it from the inside now—his hands, her face or / is it from the news accounts?" Here, Graham poses questions most readers have also posed. Are memories of the past accurate? A great deal of the poem dramatizes the tension between being inside and outside. Graham wonders if her memory of these events is from inside, that is, from her own experience or if an outside force, like a story or a photograph, has planted the images in her head. If history is unreliable and one's memory is unreliable, then on what can one rely? Graham might ultimately argue that like history, one's past is indeterminate. In the final analysis, all one has is interpretation.

Because all one has is interpretation, an exacting lyric poem provides the perfect medium for raising these questions. Readers unaccustomed to Graham's elusive thematics or her fragmentary lines may find her motives concealed behind these distancing gestures. Indeed, without question, the most satisfying reading of the title points to the real hiding place being the poem itself. Thus, the poem becomes a metaphor for the room in the Parisian building, history and one's past because it participates in each. Meaning, answers, formulas are hidden in the poem. It is difficult to determine what, exactly, the poet wants readers to take from her poem. In the final stanzas, Graham describes asking a man, a certain leader, a question: "The man above the fire, listening to my question, // the red wool shirt he wore: where is it? who has it? / He looked straight back into the century: no concessions. / I took the message back." If one replaces the word "it" with the words "the meaning of the poem 'The Hiding Place,' " then the "it" in the first

line and the "its" throughout take on an entirely different significance. Where is the meaning to the poem? Who has the meaning? Does the reader? Does Graham? Is the meaning lost in history? Is the meaning hiding in the hiding place that is the poem "The Hiding Place"

Graham is an important postmodern writer, and one tenet of postmodernism is the text's awareness that it is a text and not life itself. In other words, the poem is not a photograph; it is not reality, nor does it pretend to be. It is an interpretation of reality. It is one of many versions of reality, just as there are many versions of history, or, for that matter, of one's past. The poem, a participant in both the present and the past, reveals itself only a little, like life itself. Only over time, can people begin to understand the complexities of the present and the past, and how they converge.

Finally, it should be clear by now that the hiding place is not the past or history or the poem: it is all of them, and more. In fact, all are connected via the poem. Carolyn Forche claims that poems about events become events themselves, carriers of the events they refer to: "If, as [Walter] Benjamin indicates, a poem is *itself* an event, a trauma that changes both a common language and an individual psyche, it is a specific kind of event, a specific kind of trauma. It is an experience entered into voluntarily…. One has to read or listen, one has to be willing to accept the trauma." Readers of Graham's poem take on the trauma of the Parisian students, the burden of history, the ambiguity of interpretation. The message Graham refers to in the stanzas above, the message she brings back, is the experience of exchange, of expression, of listening and engaging. If readers and writers do this, there will be no need for a hiding place of any kind.

Source: Dean Rader, in an essay for *Poetry for Students,* Gale, 2001.

Greg Barnhisel

Barnhisel holds a Ph.D. in American literature. In this essay, he describes how Jorie Graham uses the powerful experience of being involved in the 1968 Paris student/worker strike to explore questions of being and the representation of the world.

Jorie Graham's poem "The Hiding Place" takes as its subject the student and worker uprisings in Paris in May of 1968, but as is the case with most of this very deep and complex poet's work, the poem also addresses more profound metaphysical issues. The volume in which the poem appears,

" *This is history seen from the ground level, not history told by a historian."*

Region of Unlikeness, takes its name from a passage from the *Confessions of St. Augustine.* Throughout the volume Graham, like Augustine, mediates on the difference between the physical world and the unknowable world of God. But where Augustine's jumping-off point is his own sensual experiences of the world, Graham's is the broader world of human experience and of history.

Graham's comfort in European settings is a essential element of the poems in *Region of Unlikeness* and of "The Hiding Place" in particular. Graham grew up in France and Italy and spent much of her childhood surrounded by the religious and artistic artifacts of those two countries. As a child, she says, she played in the churches of Rome; the churches' mosaics and sculptures and paintings were a part of her play. But "The Hiding Place," like a number of other poems in *Region of Unlikeness,* is less about that aspect of European culture than it is about the chaotic, often violent events of the 1960s and 1970s.

In the 1960s, Western Europe underwent many dramatic social transformations. World War II left Europe in shambles, but the two decades following the war brought the non-Communist half of the continent economic development almost unparalleled in its history. Countries such as Italy that had been poor and undeveloped at the end of the war were now prosperous. As a result, those countries' populations began to become accustomed to comforts they had never known. The young generation chafed under the old structures of family, religion, and government that had been put in place in the lean years after the war, and began to demand societal reforms.

1968 was the year in which the student-led unrest in Europe exploded. In Italy, Marxist students led strikes at universities and occupied the university of Rome. Even Communist Eastern Europe was affected, for in Czechoslovakia the "Prague Spring," a gradual loosening of the Communist strictures on expression, was in progress. But Paris was the location for the event that came to define "the 1960s" in European minds. In May of 1968,

students in Parisian universities went on strike to demand structural changes in the higher education system. Soon, they were joined in their strike by union members. The strikes turned violent and fighting in the streets of Paris ensued. In the end, the government of General Charles de Gaulle, who was the very representation of the French nation during World War II, fell. With the end of de Gaulle's government and the Gaullist party's dominance of French national life, France could now move beyond the aftermath of World War II.

Graham was in Paris for the strike, and the events and incidents of "The Hiding Place" come from her experiences there. Whether the "I" of the poem is actually her, whether the details she narrates are "true" in the strictest sense of the word, are not in themselves important. The details ring true, and the narrator—whether Graham or a stand-in for her—recounts her story in the breathless, sense-impression-laden way of someone who has lived through a traumatic, chaotic, and large-scale upheaval. This is history seen from the ground level, not history told by a historian. The poem draws two kinds of distinctions: the most important distinction is between the world of physical being and the unknowable "being" of God, whose nature cannot be expressed in human language. Graham introduces these themes in the book's foreword.

But in the poem, she also calls attention to registers of human language, and provides two kinds of voices. In the first stanza, Graham distinguishes the world as she saw it from the world as explained by those who stand apart from the events. Her personal impressions dominate the poem in sentences full of concrete nouns and adjectives. But the first stanza is in the language of one who is not involved; the description is abstract, bloodless. The poet uses italics to highlight the words of public rhetoric—negotiations, workers, students, disturbances, concessions. These are the words that newscasters and the leaders of each side would use, and Graham, interested in the complications inherent in using language to describe sensory impressions, alludes to "language floating everywhere above the sleeping bodies." Language, especially the language of abstract nouns, is separate from experience.

After the first three stanzas, though, this register of public rhetoric is lost, and the reader is immersed fully in the language of sensory impression for a while. The poem calmly and frankly describes the scene in a crowded jail cell, attempting to show the reader how such abstract nouns and concepts can end up determining people's physical circumstances—the bloodless word "disturbances" translates to the narrator, in a jail cell, being vomited on and seeing a pregnant woman beaten by police. In her descriptions of the sensory details of the scenes, she utterly omits her emotional or mental impressions; she is simply a "tabula rasa," a blank slate, recording impressions but not reacting to them.

For all of the vivid physical details of the poem, though, the narrator's mind is constantly drawn to a very abstract feature of the world—light. Like a painter, Graham's narrator notes the play of light and remarks on how the light feel even as she plainly and unadornedly describes the horrors of the jail cell. "Once I watched the searchbeams play on some flames. / The flames push up into the corridor of light." she says in the fifth stanza as she is in the process of describing the "swarm[ing]" police vans. Instead of giving her emotional impressions of this scene, she tells about the meeting of two sources of light. Where is the fear that she must have had? Where is the disgust and anger and terror that she must have felt in the jail cell? Instead, she tells about "the shadows as I / see them still— the slatted brilliant bits / against the wall."

The poet's concern with light and her detached attitude toward her experiences comes to a climax when she is released from the jail. As she leaves, she notes that "the strangest part of getting out again was *streets.* / The light running down them." Light now represents freedom, for it cannot be curbed, cannot be held. This stanza ends with a number of images of swelling and bursting, both of air and of light.

The stanza that follows is the heart of the poem. In it, Graham asks the unanswerable questions about the nature of the world that are always on her mind. Her use of abstract language is confusing, but can be pulled apart. She speaks of how "the air filled—doubled—as if the open had been made to render." "Render" here is an important word, with multiple meanings: it can mean to hand over, to give up, to give back, to cause to be or to make, to represent or depict, to prounounce or declare, or even to melt down. In addition, the word suggests another word, "rend," which means to tear apart. The open, or all that is outside the jail, is torn apart, and the air and light spill forth, and this physical sense of "to rend" or "to render" is the primary sense in which she is using the word. But she also suggests that the open is handed over to her, that it is pronouncing or declaring something, that it is depicting something. Like air, like light, the open is undefinable and cannot be captured or held.

Language works similarly. Using "render" for all of its multiple meanings, Graham emphasizes the tricky, inaccurate, but also open nature of language. If it cannot ever express exactly what one is trying to express, if it is insufficient to describe sensory or emotional experience, it also can open up infinite possibilities for meaning. Like the air, which is filling and doubling until its "hollows spill out," language is so filled with meaning that its richness must be explored for its own sake. "How thick was the empty meant to be?" Graham asks of space and of language. "What were we finding in the air?"

Graham's metaphysical concerns, omnipresent in much of this volume, are muted in "The Hiding Place," but still traceable. The poem is suffused in the physical details of a particular place and time, but at this point the narrator's mind slips into an oblique musing about the nature of physical space and of language—the kinds of thoughts expressed by Augustine in the book's foreword. Moreover, like Augustine, Graham is sent into her metaphysical musings by sensory input. In his *Confessions,* Augustine frankly and at times humorously describes the sensual pleasures of the world that he enjoyed before discovering the deeper and more perfect world of God: he talks of the pleasures he takes in tastes, in sights, and even in human touch. As the narrator is released from jail, she enters the narrow streets of Paris and observes "the light running down them./ Everything spilling whenever the wall breaks."

But, like Augustine, she is always aware of the inability of language to capture the nature of God, of the transcendent, of the infinite. Humans and God are far apart, "in a region of unlikeness" as Augustine says, and language, a human construct, by definition cannot sufficiently describe God. The physical world, the fact that objects have definite shapes and ends, underscores the world's separation from God. In the "things that are contained in space," Augustine writes, he "found no place to rest." As we are confined in space and in time we cannot understand the nature of God," he continues: "so it is with all things that make up a whole by the succession of parts; such a whole would please us much more if the parts could be perceived at once rather than in succession." And Augustine also notes the futility of language: he I imagines the Word of God comparing its nature to the nature of human language and saying that "it is far different. These words are far behind me. They do not exist." Language, working as it must by metaphor and metonym and analogy, can never

What Do I Read Next?

- Graham collected her best poems from her first five collections in *The Dream of the Unified Field: Selected Poems 1974-1994* (1995). Winner of the Pulitzer Prize for poetry, this book gives an excellent overview of Graham's poetry.

- Graham's introduction to *The Best American Poetry 1990* (1991) is a well-articulated statement of what she thinks contemporary American poetry should do and be.

- Poet, journalist and anarchist Angelo Quattrocchi was posted in France in 1968 and captures the tensions of the student uprisings in *Beginning of the End: France, May 1968.*

- *Postmodern American Poetry: A Norton Anthology* (1994) is the most comprehensive collection of Postmodern poetry in print. A helpful introduction and an immense menu of poets offers a panorama of perspectives on postmodernist verse.

capture God, because there exists nothing on the earth that can be compared with Him. "To whom then will ye liken me, or shall I be equal? saith the Holy One," Graham quotes, from the Book of Isaiah (40:25).

Source: Greg Barnhisel, in an essay for *Poetry for Students*, Gale, 2001.

Pamela Steed Hill

Pamela Steed Hill has had poems published in over 100 journals and has been nominated for a Pushcart Prize three times. Her first collection, In Praise of Motels, *was published in 1999 by Blair Mountain Press. She is an associate editor for University Communications at Ohio State University. In this essay, Hill examines the use of images of light and fire, which make us question whether there really is a place to "hide."*

One can read Jorie Graham's poem "The Hiding Place" and comprehend its general meaning and

sentiment without knowing the specific historical reference on which this work is based. It takes place in Paris in 1968, and it involves that turbulent time of student unrest and labor strikes. But a more thorough knowledge of the actual events that occurred during the "May 1968 revolution" in France enhances the understanding of the historical perspective and the ironies that Graham relies on in the poem.

The decade of the 1960s was a time of social upheaval all over the world. Young people, especially, wanted to bring about a change in practices and values not only social, but political, economic, and moral as well. While revolts against governments have been around since government itself, the rebellion that occurred in the universities and factories in France during the spring of 1968 was the first time a western capitalist government was nearly toppled by a mixture of organized revolution and outright anarchy. The Sorbonne, one of the world's most renowned universities, founded as a theology college in 1253, was at the heart of the uprising, and Jorie Graham was a seventeen-year-old high school graduate living in Paris at the time.

Graham was born in the United States but spent her first 17 years in both Italy and France. During the 1960s, working class citizens in France (and elsewhere) became more vocal about the injustices they felt they were suffering at the hands of a bourgeois government and unsympathetic management. University students took up the cause of the workers, as well as that of international students and workers who were supposedly treated even more unfairly than the French. As opinions, arguments, and tempers intensified, so did actions. In May 1968, a series of violent clashes between students and workers on one side and police and government forces on the other began to occur on a daily basis. The Sorbonne (and other schools) and several factories were taken over and occupied by students and workers. Unsympathetic university officials and factory managers were locked out. In response, French Prime Minister Charles De Gaulle sent in the police and the ACRS, the government police, to oust the rebels and restore the status quo. In the end, that is what occurred, but "The Hiding Place" presents a first-hand account of the violence and degradation that many suffered throughout the ordeal.

The major irony in this poem is the title itself. In the first line, the speaker states that the last time she saw "it [the hiding place] was 1968." After that, it is never mentioned again and it is unclear where or what it actually was. More importantly, it is unclear whether such a place even existed. Throughout the poem, it is clear that opportunities to "hide" are rare, if not impossible. On a literal level, there is nowhere to hide from the police. Inevitably, "The ACRS would swarm in around dawn / in small blue vans and round us up." On another level, there is no chance for privacy, no way even for the rebels to "hide" themselves from each other, for in the Sorbonne, they had to hold meetings "above the sleeping bodies" and in jail "no one could sit or lean. / People peed on each other." On a larger, more universal and abstract scale, there is no place to hide from history itself. Whenever one looks "straight back into the century," one cannot deny or be protected from the knowledge that humans have always been cruel to one another and the world has always been unbalanced by those who have and those who have not.

The poem is a straightforward account of events that occurred in the streets and in the jails of Paris at that time, but it is also interwoven with images of fire and light, implying some type of revelation, but never quite *revealing* the answer. The speaker runs from the university to look for one of the student leaders and finds "his face above an open streetfire" and his voice refusing to make concessions "above the fire as if there were no fire." Later, as the police vans arrive, the speaker watches "the searchbeams play on some flames. / the flames push up into the corridor of light." In the jail cell, shadows play off light like "slatted brilliant bits," and in the streets it is the "light running down them" that seems strange to those who have been imprisoned. At the end of the poem, the speaker sits in her room with the windows open and watches the white curtain blow in the breeze "until the lights / outside made it gold." The poem then returns to the image of the "man above the fire," still proclaiming "no concessions."

A run-through of the general premise of the poem helps place people and events in somewhat chronological order, but one can also examine how the fire/light imagery is incorporated into the undercurrent of irony of the idea of a "hiding place" where there is no place to hide. Graham paints a very vivid picture of Paris in 1968 in the poem's fifth line: "Marches, sit-ins, helicopters, gas." These four words describe the actions of both sides of the struggle, marches and sit-ins by the students/workers and helicopters and gas as used by the CRS. The "certain leader" for whom the speaker searches does not appear even to attempt to hide, for he stands near a fire in the street, ig-

> *Whenever one looks "straight back into the century," one cannot deny or be protected from the knowledge that humans have always been cruel to one another and the world has always been unbalanced by those who have and those who have not."*

noring its existence and all the turmoil and violence that the flames represent. He is determined not to give in to the authorities, nor to concede anything through negotiation. In a sense, this student reflects the more universal and historical perspective on hiding. He is the one at the end of the poem who looks "straight back into the century," seeming to recall all the atrocities that have occurred in the past and using that knowledge as an impetus to keep fighting, to refuse any concessions. Compare the description of him at the end of the poem ("The look in his eyes, shoving out, into the open") to a line in the tenth stanza describing the open air: "The open squeezed for space until the hollows spill out, / story upon story of them / starting to light up." What the student's eyes "light up" is perhaps the entire point of Graham's poem. There is no place to hide from history, and the only way to prevent any future *need* to is to continue to fight for human and civil rights.

Critic Peter Sacks, writing for the *New York Times Book Review*, calls *Region of Unlikeness*, Graham's collection containing "The Hiding Place," the poet's "darkest book," alluding to the number of poems that involve "a terrifying experience of crisis" and compulsions for release, for "the capacity to face and survive one's own implication in stories of entrapment and unredeemable pain." It is true, on one hand, that the people who find themselves in jail in this poem are there due to their "own implication" in the social uprising. If the speaker or any of the other students or workers had not chosen to riot, the police would not have arrested them. On the other hand, Graham implies that one should not be so quick to blame the students and workers exclusively for their troubles. She exposes guilt on the part of the authorities as well, addressing the "two Americans rounded up by chance" and the inexcusable beating of a pregnant girl in the jail cell. The vicious attack, exaggerated or not, implies an authority that would stoop to the lowest level possible to exert its power. Not only does the "man in a uniform" beat people indiscriminately, but, when he finds "the girl in her eighth month," he beats her "frantically over and over," aiming directly for her unborn child by *pummeling* her belly. Of course, the obvious irony in this stanza is the fact that the attacker is the one screaming "aren't you ashamed?" at the helpless mother-to-be. His question is not only ridiculous and hypocritical, but it is also ambiguous: should the girl be ashamed for her part in the student unrest or for being pregnant and (probably) unwed, or both? The point is that the answer doesn't matter. Any "guilt" the young student may bear is completely overshadowed by the atrocious cruelty of the uniformed man.

In stanzas 10 and 11 of "The Hiding Place," Graham asks three questions that ultimately have no answer, but that indicate there *is* something for the "light" to reveal, if only one can figure out what it is. "How thick was the empty meant to be?" refers to "the air thick, with dwellings, the air filled doubled" which the speaker encounters upon her release from jail. Freedom feels especially vibrant and thick after having lost it for a period, and the question is really asking how free human beings are meant to be. The other two questions that Graham poses are related in terms of how things are and how they should be. "What were we finding in the air?" and "What were we meant to find?" again examine the role of freedom in our lives, the "Everything spilling whenever the wall breaks." What one may actually find upon first release is the immediate rush of liberty and abandonment, a sense even of victory or complete autonomy. But these emotions are usually short-lived. Perhaps what one was *meant* to find is a way to maintain that freedom, so that when looking back into the past, one can do so without shame and without a need to hide from history. That the poet uses the word "meant" twice in these three questions implies the existence of a higher, or a designed, purpose in life and in the events people create for themselves. The hard part is in achieving that purpose and keeping it in the light.

The hiding place in this poem is just as elusive at the end as it is in the beginning. The contention here is that one does not actually exist. So why title a poem by a name that has no representation or explanation within it? Beyond the obvious "writers do it all the time" reply, Jorie Graham seems to want people to ponder more than the existence (or non-existence) of a place to hide. What is more pressing, and more indicative of human life and human history, is why one *needs* one. This is a question that has many centuries' worth of answers, but, at this point, no solution.

Source: Pamela Steed Hill, in an essay for *Poetry for Students,* Gale, 2001.

Sources

Costello, Bonnie, in *The New Republic,* Vol. 206, No. 4, January 27, 1992 pp. 36-40.

Forch, Carolyn, ed. *Against Forgetting: Twentieth Century Poetry of Witness,* Norton & Norton, Co., 1991.

Gardner, Thomas, Review of *Region of Unlikeness,* in *Contemporary Literature,* Vol. 33, No. 4, Winter 1992, pp. 712-34.

Graham, Jorie, *Region of Unlikeness,* Ecco Press, 1991.

Olsen, William, "Lyric Detachment: Two New Books of Poetry (Jorie Graham's *Region of Unlikeness,* Chase Twichell's *Perdido),*" in *Chicago Review,* Vol. 38, No. 3, 1991, pp. 76-89.

Sacks, Peter, "What's Happening," in *New York Times Book Review,* May 5, 1996, p.16.

Vendler, Helen, *The Breaking of Style,* Harvard University Press, 1995.

———, *The Given and the Made,* Faber and Faber, 1995.

For Further Study

Costello, Bonnie, review of *Region of Unlikeness,* in *The New Republic,* Vol. 206, No. 4, January 27, 1992, pp. 36-40.

   Intriguing reading of Graham's poetic journey until *Region of Unlikeness.* Although the review is not negative, it is less laudatory than most.

Gardner, Thomas, review of *Region of Unlikeness,* in *Contemporary Literature,* Vol. 33, No. 4, Winter, 1992, pp. 712-34.

   Gardner contextualizes Graham's poetry among that of three other contemporary poets, Phillip Booth, Linda Gregg, and John Ashberry, ultimately suggesting that for these four poets, language functions as both "wilderness and home."

Henry, Brian, "Exquisite Disjunctions, Exquisite Arrangements: Jorie Graham's 'Strangeness of Strategy,'" in *The Antioch Review,* Vol. 56, No. 3, Summer, 1998, pp. 281-94.

Intriguing article that argues that Graham is one of very few female poets to achieve success using the long line. Henry claims that Graham has developed three distinctive, significant styles in employing this poetic strategy.

Olsen, William, "Lyric Detachment: Two New Books of Poetry (Jorie Graham's *Region of Unlikeness,* Chase Twichell's *Perdido*)," in *Chicago Review,* Vol. 38, No. 3, 1991, pp. 76-89.

Olsen claims that both poets make a deliberate effort to distance themselves from life's experiences, yet it is this detachment that attracts the reader. For Olsen, Graham is more abstract and achieves a unity in conflicting ideas.

Spiegelman, Willard, "Jorie Graham's 'New Way of Looking,'" in *Salmagundi,* Fall, 1998, pp. 244-76.

Focusing on her constructs and interpretations of perception and description, Spiegelman explores Graham's use of painting as a metaphor for seeing the world.

Vendler, Helen, *The Breaking of Style,* Harvard University Press, 1995.

Vendler argues that Graham, like Seamus Heaney and Gerard Manley Hopkins evinces a break in style over her career. Focusing on the individual line, Vendler suggests that Graham find herself writing a poetry of excess via a move to longer, more disjunctive lines.

————, *The Given and the Made,* Faber and Faber, 1995.

Vendler considers Graham's poetry alongside that of Robert Lowell, John Berryman, and Rita Dove. Drawing on both biographical and thematic issues, Vendler argues that Graham's poetry seeks a resolution to numerous tensions, both personal and political.

————, review of *Region of Unlikeness,* in *The New York Times Review of Books,* Vol. 38, No. 19, November 21, 1991, pp. 50-57.

Though she doesn't mention "The Hiding Place," Vendler places *Region of Unlikeness* in the context of Graham's larger poetic project. Ultimately, Vendler's review of Graham's book is overwhelmingly positive.

How We Heard the Name

Alan Dugan

1956

Written in 1956, "How We Heard the Name" appeared in the multiple award-winning *Poems* of 1961. While Alan Dugan's verse had been published in magazines prior to 1961 (he received an award from *Poetry* magazine in 1946), it would be difficult to exaggerate the impact of his first collection. As Helen Chasin wrote in reviewing a later volume, *Poems 4:* "Never a promising young poet, Dugan showed what he could do, which was considerable, in his first book."

"How We Heard the Name" is typical Dugan. The poem concerns a chance encounter between a soldier and a group of shepherds in the aftermath of an ancient battle, but with Dugan the "aboutness" of a poem can never be reduced to subject matter alone. Its tone ironic, its language colloquial, "How We Heard the Name" is a mordant rumination on history, ambition, and identity. It is a deeply personal poem yet also a deeply impersonal one. It is, in short, a bundle of artful contradictions held together by an idiosyncratic sensibility. Writing in *The Dictionary of Literary Biography,* Thomas McClanahan stresses the "equivocal stance" adopted by Dugan toward his subject matter, his readers, and, most of all, himself: "He is in many respects both observer and participant, withdrawn and involved, writing from a distance about things that matter greatly to him."

Alan Dugan

the Pulitzer Prize, the National Book Award, and the Prix de Rome (awarded by the American Academy of Arts and Letters).

Thanks to the publicity and prize money attached to these awards, Dugan was able to devote himself more intensively to writing and traveling, supplementing his income with teaching stints at various colleges and universities. In 1963-64, for example, he lived in Paris on a Guggenheim Fellowship; in 1965-66, he was a guest lecturer in poetry at Connecticut College; and a Rockefeller Foundation grant staked him to a year of travel through Central and South America in 1967.

From 1967-1969, Dugan lived in Bronxville, New York, serving as poet-in-residence at Sarah Lawrence College. Since 1969, he has been associated with the Fine Arts Work Center in Provincetown, Massachusetts. He has continued to receive awards for his work: the Shelley Memorial Award in 1982, the Melville Cane award in 1984, and the American Academy award in 1985. His poetry appears frequently in the *American Poetry Review, Poetry,* and other journals.

Author Biography

Alan Dugan was born on February 12, 1923, in Brooklyn, New York. He attended school in Brooklyn and in Queens, then he entered Queens College, New York, in 1941. His studies were interrupted by service in World War II. Following the war, Dugan completed college first at Olivet College, Michigan, then at Mexico City College, Mexico, where he received his B.A. in English in 1949. He remained at Mexico City College for an extra year of graduate study before returning to New York City, where he spent the next ten years in a variety of non-academic jobs, including publishing, advertising, and as a model maker at a medical supply house. But he was writing poetry all the while, and in 1961 his first book, *Poems,* was published.

Poems was selected for publication by the prestigious Yale Series of Younger Poets. Reviewing the book in the April 27, 1961 issue of the *Christian Science Monitor,* critic Philip Booth enthused: "Alan Dugan' poems make up, clearly, the most original first book that has appeared on any publisher's poetry list in a sad long time. Poem by poem, he happily defies literary pigeonholing." What followed was a degree of commercial and critical success rarely matched by a first book of poems. In 1962, the book won three major awards:

Poem Text

The river brought down
Dead horses, dead men
And military debris,
Indicative of war
Or official acts upstream,   5
But it went by, it all
Goes by, that is the thing
About the river. Then
A soldier on a log
Went by. He seemed drunk   10
And we asked him Why
Had he and this junk
Come down to us so
From the past upstream.
"Friends," he said, "the great   15
Battle of Granicus
Has just been won
By all of the Greeks except
The Lacedaemonians and
Myself: this is a joke   20
Between me and a man
Named Alexander, whom
All of you ba-bas
Will hear of as a god."

Poem Summary

Lines 1-8:

The first 8 lines of the poem constitute a single long sentence written in everyday language. Its tone is conversational, musing, but also matter-of-fact. The narrator of the poem is reporting something to his listeners. As the poem's title suggests, it is the story of how the narrator and his friends happened to hear a certain name for the first time. The first two words and the last two words of the sentence are identical: "the river." This embeds a circular structure within the linear flow of the poem, like an eddy spinning in a direction opposite to the prevailing current of a river. Even as the poem runs on past the end of the first sentence, the echo of "the river" works in the reader's mind to return them to the beginning of the sentence.

Between the appearances of "the river" is a list of items carried downstream in the current: "Dead horses, dead men / And military debris, / Indicative of war / Or official acts upstream." The narrator and his fellows are standing on the bank of the river watching as the carnage of war drifts by. Their attitude is reflective, as if what they are seeing doesn't really involve them: "But it went by, it all / Goes by, that is the thing / About the river." Notice the juxtaposition of simple, direct language that conveys the grim reality of slaughter—"dead horses, dead men"—with abstract language that removes itself from the bloody reality of war: "Indicative of war / Or official acts upstream." Such stark juxtapositions of language and imagery are one of the primary ways that Dugan infuses his poem with irony. Poetic irony, according to the definition offered by Babette Deutsch in *Poetry Handbook: A Dictionary of Terms,* is "a statement that contradicts the actual attitude of the speaker or a situation that contrasts what is expected with what occurs and always having overtones of mockery."

Lines 8-14:

Suddenly, in the midst of this liquid conveyor belt of death, comes life: "Then / A soldier on a log / Went by." Curious, the narrator asks the drunken soldier what has happened: "Why / Had he and this junk / Come down to us so / From the past upstream." There is something comical in the image of a drunken soldier clinging to a log, yet this touch of the absurd is another ironic juxtaposition; it underscores, rather than erases, the impression of casual horror Dugan is carefully developing. Here, for the first time, the river is explicitly linked to time in the phrase "the past upstream." This phrase has a multitude of meanings. From the perspective of the narrator, upstream literally equals the past, not just in time but in space, for once something reaches him from there, whatever event set it in motion has already taken place. But

it also refers to time itself, and to history. If time is the river, then history is simply "this junk" carried downstream in the flow of time. Remember Dugan's artful suggestion in the first eight lines of the poem that the flow of the river may be circular as well as linear. If the river of time can also flow in a circle, then history will inevitably repeat itself. Dead horses, dead men, and drunken soldiers may go drifting by, but sooner or later, in some sense, they will return.

Lines 15-20:

From this point, the soldier seems to take over the poem. The narrator's voice is not directly heard again. Yet this is essentially an illusion; it should not be forgotten that the soldier's words are being recited by the narrator as they were originally spoken to him and his friends along the banks of the river. It should also be remembered that just as the narrator is concealed behind or within the voice of the soldier, so, too, is Dugan, the poet, hidden behind the voice of the narrator, and the voice of the soldier as well. Although the soldier addresses the narrator and his fellows as "Friends," it is clear that his attitude toward them is far from friendly. His words are fairly dripping with contempt and irony: "The great / Battle of Granicus / Has just been won / By all the Greeks except / The Lacedaemonians and / Myself." What can his listeners on the riverbank know of the Battle of Granicus, the Greeks, and the Lacedaemonians, let alone the identity and personal history of this soldier who refers to himself with such an air of embittered self-importance? Their knowledge or ignorance is irrelevant to the soldier, for he is primarily talking to himself here, as bitter, self-important people often do. But just as the soldier's audience may be mystified by these terms, so, too, might Dugan's contemporary audience be unfamiliar with the Battle of Granicus and the Lacedaemonians. In a sense, then, Dugan is addressing the readers of his poem with the same contempt and irony the soldier lavishes upon his audience. The difference, and it is an all-important one, is that Dugan's readers are free to educate themselves about these terms and the history to which they refer. In fact, Dugan provides the clues they need to do so and thus enter into a deeper understanding of the multiple ironies of his poem.

A quick check of any encyclopedia will reveal that the Battle of Granicus was fought in 334 B.C. between the armies of Alexander the Great and the Persian Empire. The meaning of the soldier's words is clarified by the fact that Alexander's forces were made up of soldiers drawn from all the Greek city-states, with the exception of Sparta, whose citizens also went by the name of Lacedaemonians.

Lines 20-24:

Only now, at the poem's end, is the name referred to in its title revealed, the riddle answered. True, that information is implicit in the information conveyed in the immediately preceding lines, but the name itself, Alexander, does not appear until line 22. The revelation comes in an almost offhand way, drenched in even more contempt and sarcasm than has heretofore characterized the soldier's speech: "This is a joke / Between me and a man / Named Alexander, whom / All of you babas / Will hear of as a god." The term "ba-bas"— an example of the poetic device known as onomatopoeia (a word whose meaning is indicated by its sound and which replicates the sound of the thing it represents)—shows that the narrator of the poem and his fellows are shepherds, and its use by the soldier demonstrates his sense of his own superiority to them.

That sense of superiority is also seen in the soldier's characterization of the outcome of the Battle of Granicus as a joke between him and Alexander the Great. Even as the soldier talks about Alexander with disdain, mocking his aspirations to godhood, he puts himself on a level with Alexander as if he, too, might have an equal claim to godhood if he cared to assert it. Encyclopedias inform readers that the Greek mercenaries who fought on the side of the Persians in that battle were led by a Greek named Memnon, and that Memnon escaped the slaughter of his troops at the close of the battle. Readers have ample evidence to assume that Dugan expects them to make the connection and identify the anonymous soldier as none other than General Memnon himself in the act of deserting his men in a decidedly ignominious fashion.

Yet the poem does not become mired in its dense underlay of history. On the contrary, just as General Memnon is being carried past the observers on the riverbank, shouting out private jokes and allusions his listeners cannot understand, so, too, Dugan seems to be saying, is the stuff of history ceaselessly flowing by daily lives, its warnings ignored or understood incompletely. Knowing that history repeats itself, and that Alexander the Great, for all his brilliant conquests, was dead at the age of 33, and proud Memnon remembered only because of his link to Alexander, Dugan finds little to emulate in the soldiers of the world. Nor does he cast his lot with the shepherds. Rather, Dugan

sees himself, in his poetic calling, as partaking of both, yet belonging to neither. By no means is this a source of solace or self-congratulation. Readers should bear in mind that Dugan, a veteran of World War II, was himself 33 years old when he wrote this deceptively slight poem, a poem distinguished as much by the unsparing ironies of its unfolding implications as by the rigorous intelligence and disciplined artistry evident in its every line.

Themes

"How We Heard the Name" tells the story of a brief meeting between a soldier of a defeated army and a group of shepherds. Floating down the river past the watching shepherds, the soldier makes mocking jokes at his own expense and theirs, and offhandedly mentions the name of the victorious general responsible for his defeat, Alexander the Great.

Human Condition

Dugan examines the place of human beings in history, and the place of history in time. What he sees causes him simultaneously to smile and wince, for while he perceives a kind of cosmic joke in the actions and aspirations of human beings (including himself). It is a joke at the expense of readers, and himself, just as the drunken soldier of the poem sees the result of the Battle of Granicus, with all its bloodshed, as a joke between himself and Alexander.

In the poem, Dugan presents soldiers and shepherds. The first group are men of action, driven by ambition, who seek to leave an enduring mark on history. Alexander the Great is the archetypal man of this type, for he set out while in his twenties to conquer the world. By the time of his death at the age of 33, he had succeeded to a remarkable extent in doing just that. Indeed, there are a mere handful of names in all of history as or more widely known than that of Alexander (one of them, Jesus Christ, also died at the age of 33). The second group of men, to which the poem's narrator belongs, are men of peaceful pursuits. They live humble lives, letting the events of history, set in motion by men of action, pass them by like the waters of a river or clouds in the sky.

Dugan finds little to choose between the drunken posturings of the soldier and the willful, even prideful, ignorance of the shepherds. Yet as a poet, he knows that he shares qualities with both.

Topics for Further Study

- Explain the difference between rhetorical line breaks and the use of enjambment. Illustrate using a different poem by Alan Dugan.

- Define the term "irony," and give an example of its use in another of Dugan's poems. Be sure to explain what makes your example ironic.

- Write a poem based on a famous historical event and narrated by an eyewitness to, or participant in, the event. Do not reveal the name of the event or the narrator anywhere in the poem.

- Prepare a report on the figure of Memnon, including his actions at the Battle of Granicus and his subsequent history. State whether or not you believe history has remembered him fairly, and why or why not.

Like the shepherd, he is a man of introspection and observation, marked by history, rather than marking it. Nevertheless, like the soldier, he seeks (albeit through poetry, rather than warfare) to leave a mark on history by creating a monument in words as enduring, if ultimately meaningless, as the reputation of Alexander the Great. For Dugan, the joke and the tragedy of existence is that no one, not the soldier, not the shepherd, not even a keen-eyed poet like himself who perceives the ironies of history, can escape from history, or irony.

Time

"How We Heard the Name" is a rumination in and about time. Specifically, Dugan examines the place of human beings, and of the history they make, in time. To do this, he utilizes a common metaphor, equating time with a river. Normally, time is thought of (in another common metaphor) as proceeding like an arrow in a straight line from the past, through the present, and into the future. But Dugan sees time differently. He perceives it as circular in nature, or consisting of circular eddies and counter-currents. The circular structure of the first eight lines of the poem, a sentence beginning and ending with the words "the river," is Dugan's

subtle way of alerting his readers to his unusual conception of time.

If time is circular, then whatever is carried downstream in its flow can come round again. In the poem, the river not only carries dead horses and dead men, as well as "military debris / Indicative of war / Or official acts upstream," it also carries live, drunken men who shout their self-important words at whoever happens to be watching them go by. History, says Dugan, is "junk." But that doesn't mean it can be ignored or escaped: certainly not by the soldier, swept along in time's river; nor by the shepherds lining the riverbank, despite their belief that "it all / Goes by, that is the thing / About the river."

Even though he is writing about events set in the distant past, Dugan is also writing about the present. Given the circularity of time, and the consequent repetitiveness of history, past and present are interchangeable, even identical. What seems a philosophical conceit is actually a practical truth for a man like Dugan, who fought in World War II to deny the ambitions of Nazi dictator Adolph Hitler, a man who saw himself as a modern-day Alexander. The attitude Dugan expresses toward humanity and the monuments it seeks to build to itself in time—the "junk" of war, history, and poetry—is marked by distance, irony, and resignation. The only solace Dugan provides his readers or himself is the beauty and order possible in language, in art. As Dugan said in an interview appearing in the fall, 1999 issue of *Compost* magazine, "Art is a very difficult thing. It doesn't necessarily improve people or ruin people, it just is." And for Dugan, it is all there is.

Style

"How We Heard the Name" consists of 24 lines of varying length and meter. As such, it belongs to the type of poetry known as free verse, a poem written without any set meter or rhyme scheme. Written as prose, these 24 lines translate into 4 complete sentences. And indeed, there is something prosaic about the language of the poem. Yet this seeming artlessness is carefully and artfully contrived. As Dugan explained in *Compost*, "A poet is a person who makes an assemblage of words that don't necessarily tell a story, but tries to transmit a powerful emotion verbally."

If there is no set meter or rhyme scheme, what determines where Dugan breaks his lines? In free verse, line breaks can come at the logical end of a thought or sentence, as, for example, in line 14. This is known as a rhetorical line break. More common, however, in this poem and in free verse generally, is the use of enjambment, in which lines are broken in mid-thought or sentence so as to break the rhythm, unsettle the reader, and act against, or react in interesting and unexpected ways with, the sound or sense of the poem's prevailing emotional thrust or logical argument. One example of enjambment occurs in lines 10-12: "He seemed drunk / And we asked him Why / Had he and this junk … " The word "Why" at the end of line 11 seems a natural stopping place, as if the narrator and his fellows are asking the soldier why he is drunk. But although the line breaks there, it does not end, and the reader is carried unexpectedly around the corner to what turns out to be a very different question—the question, in fact, on which the entire poem hinges. By using the technique of enjambment to vary the length, rhythm, and meaning of his lines, Dugan skillfully manipulates his readers' experience of those lines and of the poem itself in his quest to "transmit a powerful emotion verbally."

The effect of beginning and ending the first sentence of the poem (lines 1-8) with the words "the river" has already been discussed in detail. But that is by no means the only technique worth noting in that sentence. The second line, "dead horses, dead men," echoes Lewis Carroll's famous poem, "Humpty Dumpty." The allusion is ironic, juxtaposing readers' memories of a beloved rhyme from childhood with a scene of battlefield carnage. But the irony runs deeper still, for the events of "Humpty Dumpty" are not as innocent or childlike as readers may remember. That poem tells of a "great fall," after which "all the king's horses" and "all the king's men" could not restore the shattered Humpty Dumpty to wholeness and life. The same is true in the aftermath of the Battle of Granicus, and after World War II as well, when not even the words of poets like Dugan can mend what has been broken.

Although the poem is written in free verse, it does contain some rhymes. The rhymes are clustered in lines 10-16: "by" and "Why"; "drunk" and "junk"; "us" and "Granicus." They fall in the center of the poem, and are preceded and followed by unrhymed lines. Dugan uses these rhymes to inject a new element into his poem at the same time a new character, the soldier, appears. Just as the rhymes upset the established rhythms of the poem, so, too, does the arrival of the soldier upset the

rhythms of the shepherds' lives. Yet although the soldier continues speaking for the rest of the poem, the rhymes end at line 16. Dugan is suggesting that great events and personages of history, like the Battle of Granicus and Alexander should be seen as ephemera, neither more nor less meaningful than all the other, seemingly insignificant events surrounding them. In the *Compost* interview, Dugan speaks of his poems as a "meeting place between the unconscious, emotional flow of words and the conscious demand for an intelligent search for order in the universe. The two things being at war with each other. The war between the unconscious flow and the conscious desire, this is what makes the language of poetry."

Historical Context

"How We Heard the Name" was written in 1956. Since Dugan served in the military during World War II, the shadow of that global conflict hangs over the poem. The poem is concerned with and impacted by events subsequent to the end of World War II, just as the poem is "about" events taking place after the Battle of Granicus.

The United States emerged from World War II in a position of strength. Indeed, the conclusion of the war marked the beginning of a period of unprecedented cultural, political, economic, and military expansion for the United States. The Soviet Union, too, emerged from the war as a great power. By 1956, with the Soviets in possession of the same nuclear capability as the Americans, it was clear that the two countries, with their competing systems of government, were the most powerful rivals in the world. Because the consequences of a direct conflict between the U.S. and the U.S.S.R. were too risky to be purposefully provoked, the two antagonists waged a different kind of war, one that became known to history as the Cold War.

During the Cold War the two superpowers battled each other indirectly, sometimes entering into combat themselves but never face to face. When Communist North Korea, viewed by the United States as a Soviet satellite, invaded South Korea in June 1950, for example, the U.S. responded by sending General Douglas MacArthur, one of the great generals of World War II, to beat back the invaders. A stalemate was assured when Communist China sent their massive army into the war on the side of the North Koreans. In 1956, Hungary, an Eastern European country that had fallen behind

Compare & Contrast

- **1956:** Playing against the Brooklyn Dodgers, New York Yankee Don Larsen pitches the first perfect game in World Series competition. The Yankees ultimately take the Series 4 games to 3 and become World Champions.

  1958: The Brooklyn Dodgers break the hearts of thousands of fans by moving to Los Angeles.

  2000: Larsen's remains the only perfect game in World Series history. The Dodgers remain in Los Angeles. The Yankees are defending World Champions.

- **1956:** Martin Luther King, Jr., is arrested in protests associated with the Montgomery Bus Boycott.

  1968: Martin Luther King, Jr., is assassinated in Memphis, Tennessee. James Earl Ray is arrested and convicted for the killing.

1988: James Earl Ray dies in prison after years of protesting his innocence in the face of overwhelming evidence to the contrary. Before his death, Dexter King, Martin Luther King, Jr.'s son, affirms his belief that Ray is innocent and that his father was murdered as part of a larger conspiracy.

- **323 B.C.:** Alexander the Great dies in Babylon after drinking too much at a party. He is 33 years old.

  1956: 33-year-old poet Alan Dugan writes "How We Heard the Name."

  2000: Forensic examination of a skeleton found in a tomb in Vergina, Greece, leads archeologists to conclude that the occupant is Alexander's half-brother and successor, Philip III Arrhidaeus, raising the possibility that items discovered in the tomb once belonged to Alexander the Great.

---

the so-called Iron Curtain of Soviet influence following World War II, revolted against Soviet oppression. The United States, though sympathetic, could do nothing but watch and protest uselessly as Soviet tanks rolled in to crush the rebellion. A little more than a decade later, the same thing happened in Czechloslovakia. Similar scenarios were enacted in Vietnam, Afghanistan, and countless other hot spots around the world before the collapse of the Soviet Union in the 1980s and early 1990s.

On the domestic front in 1956, the President of the United States was Dwight D. Eisenhower, a hero of World War II. Dugan surely had Eisenhower, the recent conflict in Korea (ended by cease fire in June 1953), and current events in Hungary very much in mind while writing "How We Heard the Name." The quick expansion, and even quicker collapse, of Alexander's empire serves as a warning to Americans and Soviets who see their historical situation as unique, and the ultimate victory of their cause as inevitable.

Critical Overview

Despite the unusually enthusiastic critical response to Dugan's first poetry collection, *Poems* (1961), critics have since been far more stinting, in their praise. Poet Robert Pinsky says of Dugan that he writes "with great comedy and sensitivity" about ordinary things. Most critics agree. X. J. Kennedy, for example, describes Dugan's style as "a plain stodgy no-nonsense American prose, like that of your nearest bartender." Critics are also united in identifying a fierce and unapologetically pessimistic sense of irony as the driving force of Dugan's poetry. R. J. Mills writes that Dugan's strongest poetic effects are achieved "through mockery, invective, sudden reversal, and exposure." Other critics, such as Richard Ellman and Robert O'Clair, in *The Norton Anthology of Modern Poetry,* point to Dugan's lonely and idiosyncratic voice: "Alan Dugan is conspicuously unaffiliated—to other poets, to any affirmative creed, to life itself."

Many critics, like Thomas McClanahan, praise the proud dignity and relentless honesty of Dugan's work: "He faces the world precariously, unwilling to flatter his own ego at the expense of accurate description or truthful insight." McClanahan goes on to observe, however, that "Dugan's curious watching is at once his strength and his weakness as a poet." A number of critics argue that this weakness outweighs his strength. J.D. McClatchy, reviewing Dugan's *New and Collected Poems* in *Poetry* magazine, writes that "By his third book it was apparent, and by the fourth and fifth too obvious, that Dugan was plowing a very narrow field. It is not just that his misanthropic tone had hardened into a mannerism, but that it prevented access to larger, more complex areas of experience." McClatchy goes on to characterize Dugan as "another burnt-out case."

Dugan's work has fervent partisans and detractors, but his poetry is recognized by both as being at the fringes of the contemporary scene. This is not necessarily a valid judgment of the ultimate worth of his poetry, however. As McClanahan states, "Given the quality of his writing and the dearth of comment upon it, it is not wholly unrealistic to predict that Dugan might well become one of those enigmatic poets in American literature who is never really heard until he has stopped speaking." Dugan himself would surely appreciate the irony of that.

Engraved profile of Alexander the Great (356-323 B.C.), the Greek conqueror Dugan names at the end of his poem about the evolutionary impact of history.

Criticism

Paul Witcover

Paul Witcover is a novelist and editor in New York City with an M.A. in Creative Writing and Literature from the City University of New York. In the following essay, he discusses the use of irony and allusion in Alan Dugan's poem, "How We Heard the Name."

In the *Dictionary of Literary Biography*, Thomas McClanahan says of the poet Alan Dugan, "If he can be said to write from any one vantage point, it is that of objective alienation, a perspective that allows him to stand apart from situations and comment like an old man who has seen and heard it all." This quality of objective alienation, which might also be called ironic detachment, is the predominant tone of Dugan's early poem, "How We Heard the Name," written in 1956, when the poet was thirty-three. It is somewhat counter-intu-

itive that a poem as rigorously objective and emotionally reserved as this one can nevertheless speak to readers in a moving and personal way. Yet such is the case.

The title of the poem, "How We Heard the Name," promises readers an account of an event or series of events. Its tone is colloquial, as if the story, whatever it may be, is about to be related over a glass of beer at a local bar. Like all good storytellers, the nameless narrator of this poem—who speaks not just for himself but on behalf of a group of people, hence the "we"—is very much aware of the expectations of his audience. Storytelling, after all, is a kind of public performance, as is poetry, for that matter. Recall that the earliest epic poetry, like that of Homer, was an art of the spoken and chanted word. Although written on the page, this is a poem readers are to imagine being spoken by a fictional character who is relating certain events to a fictional audience. Robert Browning and, more recently, Robert Frost, were masters of this type of poem, which falls into the category of dramatic poetry.

Imagine, then, that this poem, this story, is being told in a tavern (the precise identity of the set-

> *As will become apparent, in this poem irony itself is riven by splits, giving rise to a kind of double or even triple irony that must have been both dizzying and exhilarating to readers in 1956.*

ting, as well as of the narrator and the audience, is not that important, although the poem ultimately does provide some of this information). Whoever the audience is, they already know the name to which the title refers. If they did not, it is likely that the narrator would mention the name in prefacing the story. Why is this important? Because it introduces right from the outset a split between the world of the poem and the world of the reader. Of course this split is always there, in every poem. Some poets labor mightily to disguise it; others brazenly call attention to it. Dugan does neither. He creates a world and steps aside, or seems to, letting his readers find their own way into it and through it even at the risk of losing their way. Yet while seemingly absent from the poem, Dugan is actually very much present, giving his readers clues to help them along, if only they have the wit to recognize them. Poetry of this sort demands a reader's full attention and intelligence.

At first glance such poems may seem to reflect a degree of contempt on the part of the poet for his readers, and with some poets that is doubtless the case. But if Dugan's poetry is difficult, it is not to trumpet his superiority; on the contrary, he is simply paying his readers the compliment of assuming they are at least as intelligent and insightful as he is. Which may or may not be true, but it's nice to get the benefit of the doubt! Here Dugan gently teases his readers with two riddles: who are the "we," and what is "the name" they hear? Again, these riddles are not present within the context of the poem itself, the fictional world of the narrator and his audience; they are only apparent to those who approach the poem from outside, seeking to gain entrance.

The language of the poem, like that of its title, is of the everyday sort. Yet as the reader progresses line by line, it becomes clear that something relatively unusual is being talked about. "The river brought down / Dead horses, dead men / And military debris, / Indicative of war / Or official acts upstream." The disjunction between the subject of this first sentence—which meanders through eight lines very much like the river that is its literal beginning and end—and the language employed therein, constitutes a second split, adding to the effect of the split referred to above between the respective worlds of the poem and its readers, as well as between the poet, the narrator, and their respective audiences. Indeed, the poem, despite its apparently smooth and seamless surface, is shot through with cracks and splits of all kinds: of identity, of time, of structure and rhythm.

They are present not because Dugan is a sloppy writer. On the contrary, it's through the purposeful and artful manipulation of such fissures that Dugan gives his poem its pervasive and quietly devastating tone of irony. Babette Deutsch, in her indispensable *Poetry Handbook: A Dictionary of Terms*, defines irony as "a statement that contradicts the actual attitude of the speaker or a situation that contrasts what is expected with what occurs and always having overtones of mockery." The phrase "official acts," for example, used by the narrator as a euphemism for war, is ironic (it also reveals something about the narrator that he would choose to employ such a phrase). As will become apparent, in this poem irony itself is riven by splits, giving rise to a kind of double or even triple irony that must have been both dizzying and exhilarating to readers in 1956. It is less so now, after nearly half a century. In fact, some postmodern literary critics and philosophers, such as Jean-Francois Lyotard, would argue that this sense of multiply nested ironies, like the overlapping windows of a computer screen, has come to characterize all aspects of contemporary culture.

The overt subject of the poem, then, is a war; or, more specifically, the aftermath of a battle. To paraphrase, the narrator (and his fellows) are standing along the bank of a river and watching detritus suggestive of a clash of armies being carried downstream. Among this detritus, finally, is a soldier clinging to a log. The narrator asks him why "Had he and this junk / Come down to us so / From the past upstream." Note how Dugan establishes an almost drowsy rhythm by the measured repetition of words (in line 2, "Dead horses, dead men," with its eerie echo of Lewis Carroll's "Humpty Dumpty") and phrases ("the river" begins and ends the first sentence of the poem). Another example is to be found in lines 6 and 7: "But it went by, it all / Goes by" echoes a final time in line 10, then suddenly, unexpectedly, breaks that rhythm by the introduction of rhymes—"junk" and "drunk," "by" and "Why," "us" and "Granicus." He does this to underscore the importance of the soldier: just as the rhythm of the poem is jarringly broken by the use of rhyme, so, too, will the rhythm of the narrator's life, and the lives of those he speaks for, be broken by the soldier's arrival, which heralds the arrival of another.

To appreciate this aspect of the poem, it is necessary to know a little history. The soldier refers to the Battle of Granicus. In 334 B.C., the armies of Alexander the Great attacked and defeated the Persian forces on the plains of Adrasteia after fording the river Granicus. The soldier relates that the battle "Has just been won / By all the Greeks except / The Lacedaemonians and / Myself." Alexander's armies were drawn from all the city-states of Greece, with one exception—the Lacedaemonians. The Lacedaemonians, better known as the Spartans, refused to fight under any but a Spartan general. In truth, their refusal was politically rather than militarily motivated; the Spartans feared (quite rightly) the loss of their independence in Alexander's empire. But who is this mysterious, self-important soldier who states that the battle has been won by all the Greeks except the Spartans and himself, and goes on to explain, "This is a joke / Between me and a man / Named Alexander." Surely, no common soldier would speak with such bitterness and intimacy of the great Alexander. The fiercest fighting in the Battle of Granicus was between Alexander's men and Greek mercenary troops in the pay of the Persians. The mercenaries were led by a Greek general named Memnon. History records that Memnon escaped the slaughter of his mercenaries that ended the battle; thus, readers may reasonably conclude that the nameless soldier is none other than General Memnon himself, in the act of fleeing the vengeance of Alexander in a rather undignified fashion. Alexander, then, is "the name" referred to in the title of the poem.

But what about the "we"? That riddle, too, is soon solved. Memnon scornfully refers to his audience as "ba-bas." This is an example of the poetic device known as onomatopoeia: that is, the use of a word whose meaning is indicated by its sound, which replicates the sound of the thing it represents.

What Do I Read Next?

- Dugan's *New [and] Collected Poems, 1961–1983,* published in 1985, is an indispensable resource for anyone interested in Dugan's development as a poet.

- Readers interested in Alexander the Great will find Robin Lane Fox's 1994 biography, *Alexander the Great,* an engrossing read, almost more like a novel than a history book.

- A classic study of Alexander from a military standpoint is J.F.C. Fuller's *The Generalship of Alexander the Great,* reissued in 1989. The author's account of the Battle of Granicus is especially well done.

- An amusing and moving interview conducted by J.C. Ellefson and Belle Waring with Dugan appeared in the May 1990 issue of the *American Poetry Review*

Here, "ba-ba" suggests the bleating of sheep. Memnon is addressing a group of shepherds. They become the targets of the bitterness and contempt he feels both toward himself, as a defeated general who has abandoned his men, and toward Alexander, the victor and would-be god. And in fact, just as Memnon predicts, Alexander declared himself to be divine soon after the Battle of Granicus, though this self-proclaimed apotheosis did not prevent his death just over ten years later, in 323 B.C. It is worth noting that Alexander was thirty-three years old when he died, the same age as Dugan when he wrote this poem.

Memnon's attitude to the shepherds is plainly one of superiority. Even though he has been defeated by Alexander, Memnon is still better than those lining the river and watching him drift by. Memnon is a man of action, used to being at the center of things, possessing knowledge that, he believes, will forever change the world of the shepherds. Even as Memnon disparages Alexander, he takes pains to assert his closeness to the would-be god, as though he, too, is a god.

But is he correct in this attitude? The shepherds are not quite as unsophisticated as Memnon believes. This fact is revealed in the first sentence of the poem, when the narrator uses the ironic phrase "official acts" as a euphemism for war. Far from being naive or stupid, these shepherds possess a wisdom that comes of long experience with the "official acts" of men such as Alexander and Memnon. The shepherds are like the river itself, timeless and enduring: " it all / Goes by, that is the thing / About the river." Would-be gods and conquerors are ephemeral events in the lives of these men. Alexander's invasion may temporarily upset the flow of their lives, just as the detritus of war upsets the flow of the river, but this effect is not likely to be a permanent one. Dugan had introduced rhymes to show how the soldier's arrival broke the rhythm of the river and the lives of the shepherds. Those rhymes do not continue through the remainder of the poem. On the contrary, they disappear almost at once, like the ripples of a stone tossed into a stream will spread out for a while only to vanish as if they had never existed at all.

The narrator speaks for more than just the shepherds, however. Note that he does not ask Memnon why he has come floating down from upstream. Instead, he asks, "Why / Had he and this junk / Come down to us so / From the past upstream." That is a curious phrase, "the past upstream." Many poets have likened the flow of a river to the flow of time, and Dugan is availing himself of this common metaphor. In a sense, it is literally true, for the events that have taken place upstream have happened in the immediate past of the shepherds. But Dugan is also talking about the way in which the past flows down through time to influence the present and the future. Even more specifically, he is talking about how Alexander the Great set out to conquer the world and wound up dead at the age of thirty-three.

Dugan, himself thirty-three, is reminding himself (and his readers) of the perils of vanity. One of the intentional ironies here is that simply by writing his poem, Dugan sets himself apart from the shepherds and aligns himself with Alexander. A poem is, in a sense, like a monument erected to withstand the ravages of time, and few figures from ancient history were more determined to raise enduring monuments to themselves than Alexander the Great.

Source: Paul Witcover, in an essay for *Poetry for Students*, Gale, 2001.

Erica Smith

Erica Smith is a writer and editor. In the following essay Smith examines the poem's depiction of warfare and the idea of individual conscience.

Alan Dugan's poem "How We Heard the Name," from his volume *Poems* (1961), begins with a startling image: "The river brought down / Dead horses, dead men / And military debris." In these few terse lines the speaker has successfully situated himself in a precise place (near a river) and moment (after some kind of battle or other military event). Furthermore, the allusion to dead horses suggests that the poem takes place sometime in the past, when mounted soldiers were common in warfare.

In the next lines the speaker offers an interpretation of what he sees: that the debris is "Indicative of war / Or official acts upstream." Although he is witnessing horrific sights, including decaying carcasses, the speaker does not display great emotion regarding this apparent destruction. Instead, he keeps a detached and ironic tone, drolly wondering about "official acts"—presumably of those in government. He seems cynical regarding the actions of those in power. The reader is left to wonder whether the speaker sees himself as impacted by, or accountable to, those who govern him.

The speaker's subsequent comments summarize his feelings regarding the ravages he sees. His mood is more of resignation than of pure indifference: "But it all went by, it all / Goes by, that is the thing / About the river." The speaker's concerns seem to be cosmic, rather than mundane. He is suggesting that whatever comes to pass, no matter how catastrophic, is ultimately impermanent. The river takes on a greater meaning, too: it stands for the passage of time. A river, like time, is always moving. A river has literally washed away the remnants of a battle, and over time the emotional impact of the battle will diminish. The speaker's intuitive knowledge that all things are fleeting can be seen as a sign of maturity and insight. It may also indicate hardship, for these sights of death are not considered unusual by the speaker.

The action of the poem moves on when the speaker notices a soldier drifting down the river on a log. For the first time in the body of the poem the speaker suggests that there are companions with him, citing "we": "we asked him Why / Had he and this junk / Come down to us so / From the past upstream." The soldier, like the speaker, is in the midst of the wreckage of war. Yet he too seems unaffected. In fact, he is so nonchalant the speaker wonders if the soldier is drunk. Despite these circumstances, the soldier offers a cogent reply:

> "Friends," he said, "the great
> Battle of Granicus
> Has just been won
> By all of the Greeks except
> The Lacedaemonians and
> Myself: this is a joke
> Between me and a man
> Named Alexander, whom
> All of you ba-bas
> Will hear of as a god."

This section of the poem firmly plants it within a specific historical period. The reference to Alexander is of Alexander the Great (356–323 B.C.), son of Philip, King of Macedon and conqueror of the civilized world. After his father's assassination in 336 B.C., Alexander ascended the throne while suppressing his rivals in Greece and razing the city of Thebes. Then, setting out from Ilium (formerly Troy)—a choice deliberately made as a romantic nod to the Homeric epic—Alexander began a campaign to conquer the Mediterranean front of the Persian Empire. By his death in 323 B.C., Alexander had succeeded in conquering land as far east as India. He also founded several towns, most notably the city of Alexandria. Alexander is credited with extending Greek civilization to the East, and his reign is considered to have ushered in the Hellenistic Age of territorial kingdoms.

The soldier's reference to the Battle of Granicus identifies the first battle (334 B.C.) in Alexander's Persian campaign. At the time he crossed the Dardanelles, Alexander commanded about 30,000 foot soldiers and over 5,000 cavalry, of whom nearly 14,000 were Macedonians and about 7,000 Greek allies. At the Granicus (modern Kocabas) River Alexander encountered Persian troops, and after nearly falling prey to the Persian attempt to lure him across the river and kill him, Alexander was victorious. However, the battle resulted in a slaughter of Greek mercenaries and an incarceration of 2,000 other soldiers who were then returned to Macedonia.

It is likely that, making reference to the battle being a victory for "all of the Greeks except the Lacedaemonians and myself," the soldier is referring to this massacre of Greeks. The soldier does not elaborate on the circumstances; however, he presents himself as being in a private joke with Alexander and that the fate of others hung in the balance. Consequently the reader is led wonder if the soldier is Darius, leader of the mercenaries.

> *A river, like time, is always moving. A river has literally washed away the remnants of a battle, and over time the emotional impact of the battle will diminish."*

This interpretation would explain the soldier's wry attitude regarding Alexander, especially as Alexander would continue to pursue his Persian campaign. After prevailing at Granicus Alexander was greeted with open arms by many cities, and tyrants were thrown out and replaced by democracies. As a result Alexander's fame and legend continued to grow.

Further illustrating his wry attitude, the soldier calls the speaker and his companions "ba-bas", implying that they are somehow naive (even the sound "ba-bas" echoes the sound made by a sheep, and by extension suggests the "sheep mentality"of conformity). It is already expected that Alexander's fame will spread, that he will be described as god-like, and will be revered by the masses: but the soldier knows the more complicated realities of war.

In the context of the speaker, the assumptions of the soldier cannot go unchallenged. The soldier's view of the speaker may be that of a naive man in the countryside. Yet the speaker has already proven himself to be skeptical. He is decidedly unimpressed by the "official acts" of those in power. The speaker is more likely to share the soldier's sardonic view of Alexander's victories, and probably would not revere Alexander as others would. Even the title of the poem, "How We Heard the Name" has a detached quality to it, for Alexander is not even cited directly; his is just a name like any other. However, the mention of "the name" also has a larger-than-life, even foreboding, quality to it.

The reader is left to wonder how the speaker did, in fact, come to know "the name" and what it meant to him. More likely than not, the speaker's life was altered irrevocably by being absorbed into Alexander's growing empire. Therefore, the speaker would have been directly affected by the

The poem takes its most stinging shot at the historical hero in the last two lines, which tell that those ignorant enough to believe the heroic tales of embellished history are little more than fools, or 'babas.'"

outcomes of the battle despite his seeming indifference to it.

A reader can also shed light on "How We Heard the Name" by considering it in light of Dugan's body of work. Specifically, critics have noted that it is characteristic for Dugan to comment on of society using restrained language and wry humor. In this instance, he filters a historical event through the voice of a speaker who is indeed unsentimental, who looks warily upon the "official acts" of government. Compounding the matter, the speaker then encounters one who is downright embittered, the soldier who presents himself to the speaker not quite straightforwardly, but rather through a riddle ("this is a joke / Between me and a man / Named Alexander"). Moreover, the reader is witnessing a historical event unfold from the outside in, a kind of reversal typical in Dugan's poetry.

"How We Heard the Name" is also quite possibly a commentary on certain events of the twentieth century. One could imagine a similar situation unfolding, for example, in China under Mao, the Soviet Union under Stalin, or quite possibly in an earlier America. Those who inhabit remote regions are on the fringe of the great social upheavals, and do not necessarily ask for them, yet feel their impact nonetheless. It is dubious that the speaker in "How We Heard the Name" was craving to be absorbed by Alexander's empire. However, the events of history go by as the river does. As the speaker declares "that is the thing about the river," the reader could imagine that through this poem Dugan is making a similar statement.

Source: Erica Smith, in an essay for *Poetry for Students*, Gale, 2001.

Pamela Steed Hill

Pamela Steed Hill has had poems published in over 100 journals and has been nominated for a Pushcart Prize three times. Her first collection, In Praise of Motels, *was published in 1999 by Blair Mountain Press. She is an associate editor for University Communications at Ohio State University. In this essay, Hill discusses how "How We Heard the Name" uses allusions to Alexander the Great to warn against the human tendency to make heroes of battle leaders and to force readers to look at the evils of war, no matter how glorious history has made it out to be.*

Dugan's first collection, *Poems,* contains several works in which war plays a major role, including "How We Heard the Name." Dugan spent World War II in the Army Air Corps, and that experience inspired much of his early poetry's themes, especially the notion of humankind's blind acceptance of the evils of battle. As in most of his work, the characters in "How We Heard the Name" are fairly flat, and the language is conversational and unadorned. Lacking the flash of unusual imagery and explicit descriptions, though, does not lessen the poignancy of this poem. Instead, its strength lies in the searing sarcasm that Dugan employs to take a shot at one of history's most renowned heroes: Alexander the Great. However, it isn't just the ancient warrior and leader himself that comes under the poet's critical tongue, but all those who have made a "god" of him and who only perpetuate evilness by remaining ignorant of its human source. "How We Heard the Name" is essentially an extended metaphor that is both cautionary and chastising: it warns that people should give second thought to whom they call "great."

To fully appreciate the poem, it is necessary to understand its historical references. The Battle of Granicus, fought in May 334 B.C., was Alexander the Great's first of four major battles he would fight and win in his military career. It was also the one in which he came closest to failure and death. Alexander ascended to the throne of Macedonia, in Greece, at the age of twenty, after the death of his father, King Philip II. Being schooled in the ways of military tactics since he was a young boy, he quickly proved himself a fierce and capable leader going into battle. This was most evident when he led his troops across the Granicus River in Asia Minor and surprised the Persians who had expected the Macedonians to take a different route. Although

Alexander came close to losing his head, literally, in a tangle with the Persian military leaders, he was victorious in the end, opening the way for further advances into Asia Minor. Alexander the Great became noted for his remarkable insights into fighting a battle, including anticipating his enemies' moves, having a keen sense of timing, and coordinating heavy infantry, heavy cavalry, light infantry, and light cavalry in a single attack.

"Lacedaemonians" is another name for the Spartans of ancient Greece. The city-state of Sparta became very powerful and its men were known for their military prowess. For years, Sparta ruled Greece, but it was eventually defeated by the city-state of Macedonia, leading the way for Alexander the Great's father to become king. This, of course, led the way for Alexander himself.

With this brief rundown of historical events, Dugan's "How We Heard the Name" is more accessible, but perhaps still partly ambiguous. The first few lines are clear enough, describing "military debris," including dead horses and dead soldiers, floating down a river. We are not sure who is standing along the bank watching this grisly parade, but the persona is a plural "we" and, whoever they are, they know that the scene is "indicative of war." But Dugan throws in what may be considered a touch of sarcasm by adding "or official acts." Often, the true horror of war is disguised in euphemisms, such as "official acts" or "conflict." One of the most recent examples of this practice that caused outrage among many Americans was the refusal by some government and military officials to acknowledge that a "war" was going on in Vietnam. Because war had not been officially declared, some people called it the conflict in Vietnam. While Dugan's personal experience was with World War II—a war that many find more justified than others—he was still confronted with the atrocities of violence and bloodshed and, likely, some questionable actions by his own leaders. And while bad memories may remain with people throughout their lives, they may seek a little comfort in knowing "it all goes by" in spite of recollections. Lines 6 and 7 in "How We Heard the Name" can be taken both literally and figuratively. The words "but it all went by" refers to the debris floating on downstream out of sight of those watching, but in adding "it all / goes by," Dugan means that time passes and all the events of our lives pass with it, even monumental events such as war.

The occurrence of the "soldier on a log" drifting by is a bit ambiguous, in that the reader is not sure whether he represents a certain historical military man or is more of an everyman figure representing the task of carrying out the orders that others have created. Regardless of the specific reference, the presence of the soldier allows an opportunity for a voice from the past to make a connection with the present—a present not unlike ancient times, with wars, conflicts, and official acts. In the conversation with the soldier, who "seemed drunk," the reader learns that he has transcended centuries on the river, having started out some 300 years before the birth of Christ. When asked why he and the military "junk" had made such a long journey, he reveals that he has just come from fighting in the Battle of the Granicus. His answer implies that he was on the losing side (the war was won by "all of the Greeks except / The Lacedaemonians and / Myself") and is, therefore, a Persian. But since his actual identity is not disclosed, this is only an assumption, and one based on logic. Logic of course, is not a necessary component of good poetry, so it can be speculated that the soldier could be a disgruntled Macedonian who fought on Alexander the Great's side. In making his statement, he claims it is a "joke" between him and Alexander, but it is a joke full of cynicism and mockery, not humor and good will.

Why would the soldier claim that all but a part of the nation of Greece was a winner in this war; why not all of Greece? To answer this it is helpful to recall that Lacedaemonia (Sparta) once ruled the entire area and was proud of its military and political power. The Spartan glory days, however, ended when the Greek state of Macedonia challenged and defeated the Lacedaemonians, paving the way for Alexander the Great's father to take over.

The poems takes its most stinging shot at the historical hero in the last two lines, which tell that those ignorant enough to believe the heroic tales of embellished history are little more than fools, or "ba-bas." In reality, Alexander came close to losing both the Battle of the Granicus and his life, and yet he came out of it politically and socially unscathed. No one recalled the near-deadly mishaps, for only the good things made good stories. And while it is true that Alexander would go on to earn his moniker "the Great" by continuing to score unlikely victories, even when his army was outnumbered, it is also true that he did so at the cost of much human life. And there lies the point of "How We Heard the Name."

As a veteran of World War II, Dugan knows not only the names but the deeds and stories that surround the actions of heroes. He also knows that battle victories and medals of honor are not all that heroes share in common, but that a trail of blood-shed and devastation also follows each one. In selecting the historical lauding of Alexander the Great as an example of the world's human source of evilness, the poet attempts to showcase the epitome of heroism-gone-bad. The poem states that the greater the battle stories—and, therefore, the greater the number of casualties—the more likely the winner will become known as a "god." But something is wrong, Dugan warns, with glossing over the loss of life that occurs in wars in favor of tales of glory and heroic acts. It is not the warriors themselves who are the source of wrongness; they are, rather, a product of the real problem. And that real problem is the unexplainable, pervasive force of human nature that glorifies war and perpetuates its existence.

Source: Pamela Steed Hill, in an essay for *Poetry for Students,* Gale, 2001.

Sources

Birkerts, Sven, "But Does It Rhyme?," in *Washington Post,* August 2, 1998.

Deutsch, Babette, *Poetry Handbook: A Dictionary of Terms: Fourth Edition,* Harper Perennial, 1974.

Ellman, Richard, and Robert O'Clair, eds., *The Norton Anthology of Modern Poetry: 2nd Edition,* W. W. Norton, 1988, pp. 1089-1090.

McClanahan, Thomas, *Dictionary of Literary Biography,* Volume 5: *American Poets since World War II, First Series,* Gale, 1980.

"The Poetry of Things: An Interview with Alan Dugan," in *Compost,* Fall, 1999, pp. 42-45.

For Further Study

Bradley, George, ed., *The Yale Younger Poets Anthology,* Yale University Press, 1998.
    This collection gives some comparative sense of the distinctiveness of Dugan's poetry when it first appeared by placing it in the context of the work of other Yale Younger Poets, such as George Starbuck and Adrienne Rich.

Forche, Carolyn, ed., *Against Forgetting: Twentieth-Century Poetry of Witness,* W. W. Norton, 1993.
    Dugan's poetry is collected along with the work of others, all of it wrestling with the obligations of poets to bear witness to the darkest truths of history.

Howard, Richard, *Alone with America: Essays on the Art of Poetry in the United States since 1950,* Atheneum, 1969, pp. 99-106.
    A helpful start in placing Dugan's early work in a historic and poetic contextt.

Stepanchev, Stephen, *American Poetry since 1945,* Harper, 1965.
    Another useful guide to placing Dugan's early work in its historic and poetic context, but its tone, and its judgments, may seem dated to contemporary students.

Landscape with Tractor

Henry Taylor
1983

Originally published in the Summer, 1983 issue of *Ploughshares,* "Landscape with Tractor" is the opening poem in Henry Taylor's Pulitzer Prize winning collection of poems, *The Flying Change,* published in 1985. Included in a section titled "Heartburn," the poem is a meditative narrative framed by rhetorical questions the speaker asks. The "you" to whom he addresses his questions, however, is as much a part of himself as it is the reader. Like many of the poems in the collection, this one deals with themes of memory, loss, and change, specifically the ways in which human beings are able (or not) to accommodate change, and to integrate traumatic memories into their lives. In twelve quatrains (units of four lines) the poem's introspective speaker describes a scenario in which he discovers the body of a woman while mowing his field. The speaker is changed forever by the experience and haunted by the image of the woman and the meaning of her life. The speaker's tone shows indignation at having his peaceful life interrupted as well as frustration at what the event will mean to his life. The landscape is both physical (the speaker's field) and psychological (the speaker's consciousness). The physical landscape of the poem is a familiar one in Taylor's poetry and his life. He was born and raised on a farm in rural Virginia and knows intimately the ways of the country. The psychological landscape is one of a person who has been changed forever by an event but is unable to grasp the significance of that change.

Henry Taylor

Author Biography

Henry Splawn Taylor's knowledge of rural life and the natural world is rooted in his own experience. Born in Lincoln, Virginia, in 1942 to Thomas Edward and Mary Splawn Taylor, Taylor grew up on a large farm with his parents and three sisters. His father was an educator, farmer, and horse trainer, and Taylor himself developed an early love for riding horses. This passion is evident in many of Taylor's poems, especially those in *The Flying Change,* his 1986 Pulitzer Prize winning volume. Taylor sometimes refers to his childhood in the country as "Edenic."

Taylor was also blessed to grow up in a culturally rich environment. Neighbors of the Taylors included the painter Arshile Gorky, the guitarist Carlos Montoya, and the photographer Marion Post Wolcott, all of whom socialized with Taylor's family. He not only learned about music and art from these neighbors but he developed a positive image of what an artist was as well. Taylor's parents, whom Taylor referred to as Tom and Mary even when he was a child, were passionate about the arts. His father introduced him to the poems of Edward Arlington Robinson, and in the ninth grade Taylor became absorbed in the stories of Ambrose Bierce. Perhaps more than anyone, though, Taylor has been influenced by the storytelling and conversation of his grandfather, Henry B. Taylor.

Taylor attended public schools until the ninth grade, when he switched to George School, a Quaker facility his grandmother, sisters, and cousins also attended the school at one time or another. It was at George School that Taylor developed his desire to be a writer. After graduating high school, Taylor enrolled at the University of Virginia. There he became fast friends with Richard Diller and Kelly Cherry, who have themselves gone on to become well-respected writers. He also met the writer George Garrett, who joined the University of Virginia's faculty in 1962. Garret is both mentor and friend to Taylor, and one of his strongest admirers. Upon graduating with a bachelor's degree in English in 1965, Taylor enrolled in the M.A. program in creative writing from Hollins College, from which he graduated in 1966. For most of his professional life Taylor has worked as an editor and teacher, serving as associate editor of *Magill's Literary Annual,* and teaching at a number of universities, including Roanoke College, the University of Utah, and the American University in Washington, D.C., where he is currently Professor of English.

Poem Text

How would it be if you took yourself off
To a house set well back from a dirt road,
With, say, three acres of grass bounded
By road, driveway, and vegetable garden?

Spring and summer you would mow the field,   5
Not down to lawn, but with a bushhog,
Every six weeks or so, just often enough
To give grass a chance, and keep weeds down.

And one day—call it August, hot, a storm
recently past, things green and growing a bit,   10
And you're mowing, with half your mind
On something you'd rather be doing, or did once.

Three rounds, and then on the straight
alongside the road, maybe three swaths in
From where you are now, you glimpse it. People   15
Will toss all kinds of crap from their cars.

It's a clothing-store dummy, for God's sake.
Another two rounds, and you'll have to stop,
Contend with it, at least pull it off to one side.
You keep going. Two rounds more, then down   20

Off the tractor, and Christ! Not a dummy, a corpse.
The field tilts, whirls, then steadies as you run.
Telephone. Sirens. Two local doctors use
     pitchforks
To turn the body, some four days dead, and
     ripening.

And the cause of death no mystery: two bullet 25
  holes
In the breast of a well-dressed black woman
In perhaps her mid-thirties. They wrap her,
Take her away. You take the rest of the day off.

Next day, you go back to the field, having
To mow over the damp dent in the tall grass 30
Where bluebottle flies are still swirling,
But the bushhog disperses them, and all traces.

Weeks pass. You hear at the post office
That no one comes forward to say who she was.
Brought out from the city, they guess, and dumped 35
like a bag of beer cans. She was someone,

and now is no one, buried or burned
or dissected; but gone. And I ask you
again, how would it be? To go on with your life,
putting gas in the tractor, keeping down thistles, 40

and seeing, each time you pass that spot
the form in the grass, the bright yellow skirt,
black shoes, the thing not quite like a face
whose gaze blasted past you at nothing

when the doctors heaved her over? To wonder, 45
from now on, what dope deal, betrayal,
or innocent refusal, brought her here,
and to know she will stay in the field till you die?

Poem Summary

Stanza 1:

The title of the poem "Landscape with Tractor" suggests that the composition will be descriptive. Titles with "Landscape" in them are more popular with paintings, and the title suggests the poem will be in that tradition. The poem opens with a question about a supposedly hypothetical situation. This "what if?" scenario, addressed to the second person "you," asks readers to picture a house off a dirt road with "three acres of grass bounded / By road, driveway, and vegetable garden." This pastoral setting evokes a feeling of rural calm and self sufficiency. It is a paradise of sorts that the speaker asks readers to imagine themselves in.

Stanza 2:

A character, the "you," is put into motion. The details that follow suggest that the speaker, not the reader, is being addressed. The speaker is addressing an imagined part of himself. He describes the rituals of maintaining the piece of land around his house, "to give grass a chance, and keep weeds down." By using a bushhog, which is the name for a tractor that can cut large areas of grass, the speaker is not cutting the grass "down to lawn," but leaving it a little bit wild, perhaps to remind him-

self of nature's capacity to grow, and to distinguish his field from suburban lawns.

Stanza 3:

The speaker describes a man daydreaming while in the midst of cutting grass. The man is the poet, and the landscape is as much a mental landscape of someone habituated to routine as it is a physical landscape. The language is informal. "Call it August" suggests that it could be any month, that the exact time doesn't matter. Such a device allows the speaker to distance the description of the event while simultaneously clueing the reader that he is talking about himself. As in most of this poem Taylor uses various poetic devices, including alliteration ("green and growing") and internal rhymes ("growing" and "mowing"), to provide texture to his description, to create the verbal landscape in which his physical and mental landscape is embodied.

Stanza 4:

Into this well-ordered and ordinary physical landscape and the distracted, but ordinary mental landscape of the speaker something appears that needs to be made sense of. Rather than say what this thing is, Taylor has the speaker discover it at the same time as the reader, heightening anticipation. His tone becomes agitated when he says that "People / Will toss all kinds of crap from their cars." And the opening question of the poem now sounds more like a complaint, similar to when someone says, "How would you like it if … ?."

Stanza 5:

The intrusion into the speaker's world of a "clothing-store dummy" surprises him, but does not deter him from his routine, which he continues. The tone of disgust in the previous stanza is continued, as the speaker must "contend" with the dummy. To heighten the suspense of the unfolding story Taylor uses a run-on line to end a stanza for the first time in the poem.

Stanza 6:

The sense that this is a hypothetical story is now abandoned as more details are provided. The true nature of the object is revealed to the reader at the same time it is discovered by the narrator, who is shocked by his find. Instead of describing his emotions, he speaks of his perceptions of the landscape: "The field tilts, whirls, then steadies as you run." The fragments "Telephones. Sirens." of

Media Adaptations

- Watrershed Tapes distributes Taylor's 1985 audiocassette, Landscape with Tractor. Watershed Tapes can be ordered online at http://www.watershed.winnipeg.mb.ca/

dressed simultaneously to readers and to himself. He has had a life-shattering experience yet must continue with his life. He questions how he will be able to accommodate this experience into his routine, especially when he is reminded of it on a regular basis. The more he thinks about the woman's absence, the more present she becomes, as he adds details to his previous description of her. Readers know what she was wearing and the effects of decomposition on her body. His obsession with the woman grows, and the poem's ends with his realization, posed in the form of a question, that it will be with him until he dies.

the third line underscore the breathlessness of the speaker, and his description of the doctors turning over the body with pitchforks shows us the narrator's disgust with the scene.

Stanza 7:

The description reads almost like a crime report. We are provided with more details of the corpse's identity, although no name is attached. The parallelism of the last two sentences emphasizes the speaker's reaction to the body. His routine is interrupted, and he stops work for the day.

Stanza 8

Rather than telling readers how he has been affected, the speaker shows the effect through imagery. Now, however, it is the imagery of absence, the "damp dent" where the body had been, and the "bluebottle flies … swirling" above the space. The bushhog takes on symbolic importance here, as it removes all evidence of the death, of the intrusion of the outside world into the orderliness and routine of the speaker's life.

Stanza 9

In small towns the post office is often the place where neighbors meet and news is disseminated. This stanza contrasts with stanza seven, where the reader is told that the woman's death was "no mystery." In this stanza the woman's life *is* a mystery. Her identity remains unknown. This stanza begins a series where sentences run over into the next stanza, creating a rhythmic urgency that will continue until the end of the poem.

Stanzas 10-12

The fleetingness of life and identity is addressed. The speaker asks a rhetorical question, ad-

Themes

Order and Disorder

"Landscape with Tractor" illustrates how the ways in which humans think about the world and themselves can be drastically changed by a single incident. Such incidents often come as a surprise and remain in a person's consciousness, altering it forever. The first third of Taylor's poem describes the setting of the speaker's home and his routine of mowing the field. It is a pastoral setting, and the "grass bounded / By road, driveway, and vegetable garden" suggests an orderliness to the speaker's existence, boundaries which demarcate his life and activities. This orderliness is also underscored through the speaker's capacity to do his work without really thinking about it, "with half your mind / On something you'd rather be doing, or did once." This doing without thinking is also evident when he first sees an object in his field and thinks it's a mannequin. The idea that it might be a human body doesn't enter into the speaker's mind because it is not part of his expectations. When he discovers the mannequin is actually a corpse, his world is changed forever; he is thrust into the present. The sixth stanza shows the torrent of emotion the speaker experiences, and the succeeding stanzas detail the way in which the image of the woman's body grows in the speaker's imagination unchecked. With each stanza something new about the woman is revealed to the speaker, but each piece of information only makes the woman's death more mysterious. Both her identity and the motivation behind her killing remain unknown. The disorder that the memory of the woman's body introduces into the speaker's life, a disorder that emerges each time the speaker mows over the "damp dent" where the body once was, changes his world, but the effect is unclear to the reader and the speaker. The poem, which reads as an attempt to come to grips with this experience, whether it was actual or imagined, serves as a metaphor for any such experience. By ending the poem with the question "How would it be?" Taylor thrusts the speaker's experience into readers' minds, asking them to imagine how such an event would change their own lives.

Death

"Landscape with Tractor" relates a story of experience encroaching on innocence. The poem echoes the story of the Garden of Eden. The speaker's field represents a contemporary version of the garden. It is isolated, with plenty of land and a vegetable garden. The speaker does not have to work very hard, mowing the grass infrequently (every six weeks). Into this paradise comes death in the form of what appears to be "a clothing-store dummy." This interruption into the dreamy world of the speaker and his country home jolts the speaker. He must now "contend" with death as real and human, and present, rather than thinking about it as a seasonal thing that happens to his garden and field. The knowledge that death brings to the speaker changes him irrevocably, and changes his relationship to his field, nature. Although his bush-hog can eliminate all physical traces of the body, the speaker cannot get the image of the woman out of his mind. Details about her death flood him whenever he thinks of her. She reminds him of the possibility of his own death. When he says that "she will stay in that field" until he dies, he is using "field" not only to denote the physical field that he tends, but his own field of consciousness as well. In his consciousness an awareness of mortality has been planted and continues to grow. By wondering about the circumstances of the dead woman's life and the way in which she went from being "Someone" into "no one," the speaker implicitly wonders about the meaning of his own existence and the inevitability of his death.

The title "Landscape with Tractor" suggests that it will be in the tradition of landscape paintings. Such paintings as Bruegel's "Winter Landscape with the Bird Trap" are meditations on place that ask viewers to look more closely at a familiar scene, or to look at a scene in a new way. Taylor's poem is a meditation *and* a narrative: that is, it tells a story of a particular event while simultaneously exploring the meaning of that event. Characters in the story include country doctors, the dead woman, townspeople, and the speaker himself. Although the speaker addresses the second person "you" throughout the

Topics for Further Study

- Brainstorm in writing or discussion about a time when a particular event changed the way that you experienced a part of your daily routine, then write a "Before and After" essay detailing that change and its consequences.

- Taking the position of the "you" in "Landscape with Tractor," write an essay answering the questions that the speaker poses.

- Compose a description of a rural Garden of Eden as it would look in the twentieth century, and then compose one of an urban Garden of Eden. Discuss the similarities and differences in your descriptions and what these tell you about your own conception of paradise.

poem, the way in which he relates details and the poem's tone suggests that he is also addressing a part of himself. In doing this, he is attempting to understand the impact of this event on his life.

Explaining the use of his persona in the poem, Taylor wrote in an email to this critic stating, "My not having had the actual experience is the main reason for the poem's slightly unusual use of second- and first-person narration. For most of the way, the second-person narration is not noticeably different from that of many poems where 'I' seems to have been changed to 'you' for no better reason than to avoid 'I.' Near the end, though, the narrator suddenly intrudes in the first person, saying "And I ask you again, how would it be?" By that time I was interested not only in trying to avoid claiming the experience too fully for myself, but also in trying to make a small comment on the tendency to use 'you' for 'I.'"

The speaker's tone is one of a measured bewilderment and growing resignation. He has enough emotional distance from the event to recall it in some detail, yet he has not yet been able to integrate its impact into his life. By using a steady rhythmic base and quatrains (four line stanzas), the most common stanza form in English versification,

Compare & Contrast

- **1985:** Cellular phones are introduced into automobiles.

  Today: Due to the increase in accidents caused by people driving while talking on their cellular phones, some states and cities are considering making it a crime to drive and talk.

- **1970:** The rate for murder and non-negligent manslaughter in the United States is 7.9 per one hundred thousand people.

  1980: The rate for murder and non-negligent manslaughter in the United States is 10.2 per one hundred thousand people.

  1990: The rate for murder and non-negligent manslaughter in the United States is 9.4 per one hundred thousand people.

  1995: The rate for murder and non-negligent manslaughter in the United States is 8.2 per one hundred thousand people.

- **1980:** A mentally ill fan, Mark Chapman, fatally shoots former *Beatle* John Lennon outside his apartment in New York City.

  1981: A mentally ill man, John Hinkley, Jr., shoots President Reagan and three others. All survive.

  1995: Former football star, O.J. Simpson is acquitted after being accused of murdering his wife, Nicole Simpson, and her friend. The trial is marked by racial tension.

- **1980:** Reagan names Elizabeth Dole as his Secretary of Transportation.

  1984: Walter Mondale names Geraldine Ferraro as his running mate for president of the United States, the first time a woman is nominated for a national office by a major party.

  1999: Elizabeth Dole runs in the presidential primaries, faring poorly before she bows out.

Taylor underscores the inherent tension in the speaker's voice. This tension is underscored by the repeated use of the speaker's rhetorical question, "How would it be?" Rhetorical questions are questions used for effect and are not asked in order to be answered.

Historical Context

In 1980 Americans elected as president Ronald Reagan, a conservative Republican and former actor best known for his strident anti-communism and telegenic presence. Reagan appealed to both traditional conservative Republicans as well as working-class Democrats, who saw in him a no-nonsense leader committed to limiting the federal government's interference with state government and the individual. Republicans also captured control of the Senate for the first time since 1952. The economic policies of Reagan's administration, sometimes derisively called "Reaganomics," in-

cluded massive tax cuts, which in turn led to a ballooning federal budget deficit. The administration acted to speed up deregulation of such industries as airlines, banking, and domestic oil production to foster competition and lower prices for consumers. Claiming that federal programs for the needy sapped their initiative, Reagan instituted "welfare reform." In 1984 the country re-elected Reagan, who soundly defeated Walter Mondale and his running mate, Geraldine Ferraro, the first woman to be nominated for a national office by a major party.

Though Taylor wrote and published the poem in the 1980s, the event on which "Landscape with Tractor" is based occurred in the late 1960s or early 1970s, according to the poet. However, it wasn't Taylor who found the body on his land, but an employee of Taylor's father who worked on the Taylor family farm. Until this day, the woman's identity remains unknown, as do the exact circumstances of her death. Taylor recalled hearing the story from his father while he was still teaching at the University of Utah, where he was on the faculty from 1968-1971. The line between fact and fiction is often blurred in poetry, and poets often take "poetic license," "borrowing" events from other people's lives or inhabiting other voices. In an essay about his own life in the *Contemporary Authors Autobiography Series* Taylor wrote: "When I was in my twenties and early thirties, I felt no obligation to be faithful to autobiographical fact, and wrote several far-fetched poetical fictions in which the speaker was not readily distinguishable from that person who, as I see it, is me." In an email to the critic, Taylor notes, "The voice and manner of the poem are, I think, influenced by my reading of Robert Penn Warren's poems, which I came to love in the 1970s, having previously felt no more for them than respectful admiration. For a little while there in the 70s, I read his poems more avidly than I read any others." Warren, perhaps best known for his novel *All the Kings Men,* was also a southern writer. He died in 1989.

Critical Overview

"Landscape with Tractor," which was initially published in a 1983 issue of *Ploughshares,* has been reprinted a number of times, appearing in *The Morrow Anthology of Younger American Poets* (1985) and *The Ploughshares Reader* (1987). Watershed Tapes of Washington, D.C., released an audio-cassette *"Landscape with Tractor,"* which features the poet reading 22 other poems as well as the title piece. Reviewing Taylor's Pulitzer-prize winning collection, *The Flying Change,* in which "Landscape with Tractor" appears, David Shapiro claimed in *Poetry* that Taylor crafts his poems, "as house, as space, as dwelling." Citing the first stanza of the poem, Shapiro noted that "Taylor's poems concern boundaries and the pride of boundaries." Though he had been writing and publishing poetry for twenty years before he won the prize, Taylor was not well known to the public, but then few poets are. In the introduction to his bibliographic chronicle of Taylor's published work from 1961-1987, Stuart Wright stated that most "poets and critics alike, felt that this recognition had been far too long in coming." Writing for the *Dictionary of Literary Biography,* Taylor's mentor and friend George Garret, seconded that sentiment, claiming that Taylor's formalism has often worked against his poetry becoming better known: "If Taylor's work has received some recognition from poets of an older generation and some serious and favorable

attention from some of the poets of his own age, his work is not nearly so well known, yet, as it might be. In forms and content, style and substance, he is not so much out of fashion as deliberately, determinedly unfashionable. His love of forms is (for the present) unfashionable."

Criticism

Chris Semansky

Chris Semansky's essays and poems regularly appear in literary journals and magazines. He is currently working on an anthology of poems and stories about Eve, titled "The Lady and Her Snake." In this essay, Semansky examines how Taylor's poem is both a description of a traumatic event and a psychological portrait of the speaker.

Henry Taylor draws on the landscape tradition associated with painting in his poem, "Landscape with Tractor." Historically, landscape paintings have often been considered meditations on a place. An artist's use of color, light, texture, and perspective is intended to show the place in a new way, or perhaps in a manner that is thoroughly familiar. In Taylor's poem, however, *place* is as much a psychological landscape as it is a physical one. In recounting an event that changed his life, the speaker of the poem creates an emotional terrain that tells readers about his fears and desires and, in the process, asks readers to reflect on their own.

The poem's first stanza describes a place and asks readers how it would be if they took off to that place, "a house set well back from a dirt road, / With ... three acres of grass bounded / By road, driveway, and vegetable garden." This image of well-ordered isolation dominates the poem. It is not only a physical isolation (readers are not told of any other people at the house) but an isolation of the speaker's psyche. The borders of the speaker's land are also, symbolically, the borders of his mind. He tends both, cultivating familiarity and routine in his actions and thinking. His work structured according to the seasons, the speaker appears content in the first few stanzas to mow his field just enough to keep it maintained.

The tractor is the other term in the poem's title and appears in the second stanza as a symbol of seemingly benign technology. However, the tractor is also the means by which the speaker orders his land. While he sits on the tractor, the speaker's mind can wander; he doesn't have to pay close attention to his work. The tractor, then, as symbol of

> *A painting might depict the scene of the first three stanzas in watercolor grays, light blues, and greens of a man mowing his field, his features undefined, maybe facing away from the viewer. In the foreground of the painting is the image of the body in stark relief, red and black.*

modern technology, not only saves labor for the speaker, but frees his mind from the details of daily work. It is into this kind of hazy, daydreaming, unfocused, yet routinized mind that the image of the "clothing-store dummy" intrudes. A painting might depict the scene of the first three stanzas in watercolor grays, light blues, and greens of a man mowing his field, his features undefined, maybe facing away from the viewer. In the foreground of the painting is the image of the body in stark relief, red, and black.

The landscape of the speaker's mind contains images of human beings in general and of city people in particular. These images are rooted in generalizations that often approach stereotype. They show a mind comfortable thinking "inside the box," inured to new ideas or ways of seeing the world. When the speaker first spots the corpse he doesn't know what it is, saying "People / will toss all kinds of crap from their cars." The word choice here underscores the speaker's irateness of having his routine interrupted and of people in general. It suggests he's had his pastoral home sullied before by the rudeness of people in cars, presumably from the city. That he continues mowing instead of stopping and that he says he has to "contend" with the dummy, underscores his attitude towards this interruption in his day.

The image of the country doctors comes close to caricature. They move the body by pitchfork, a farming tool, something city people don't expect of doctors, but might of "country" practitioners. The doctors' action is disturbing: it suggests a casual, if not disrespectful, attitude towards the human body. The woman is black, a fact introduced a few lines later. Although the race of the speaker isn't mentioned, readers can reasonably infer that he is white by the simple fact that he includes the detail of the woman's race in his description. The image also has symbolic resonance. The ripening corpse is like a fertilizer, which the doctors are turning, helping the break in the speaker's routine grow into an event that will obsess him. The removal of the corpse only increases his inability to resume his life, as he is reminded of her by "the damp dent in the tall grass/ where bluebottle flies are still swirling." The mystery of her life and death only deepens.

The speaker attempts to make sense of the woman's death. His own distrust of city people is shared by other town folk:

> Weeks pass. You hear at the post office
> That no one comes forward to say who she was.
> Brought out from the city, they guess, and dumped
> like a bag of beer cans. She was someone,
> and now is no one, buried or burned
> or dissected; but gone....

The suddenness by which a person can lose their life and whatever meaning it held hits the speaker. Though intimately aware of the cycles of growth and death in nature, the speaker is shocked by the woman's death, by the way her body is treated like trash by those who dumped her (though he shows no such shock at how the doctors treated her). This shock also carries a degree of indignation, as the intrusion of the city and its ugliness into his pastoral paradise prevents him from continuing his own well-ordered and predictable life in the country. In the tenth stanza he asks how it would be if "you" could not get the image of the corpse out of your mind. In doing so, he is in effect registering his frustration at the degree to which the intruding image is engulfing his consciousness. He is also wondering what this will do to his life from now on.

The question implies that this experience has changed the speaker and will change him further. His relationship to his field has changed, as he will no longer be able to complete his work mindlessly. And his relationship to his own mind has changed, as he must work to regulate his growing awareness of death and its inherent mysteries. His constant questioning underscores the tumult of his consciousness. The more he questions, however, the deeper the mystery. When the speaker initially encounters the woman he doesn't even recognize her humanity; she looks like a mannequin. But the more he thinks about her, in her absence, the more human she becomes, until in the penultimate stanza he describes her as "the form in the grass, the bright yellow skirt,/ black shoes, the thing not quite like a face/ whose gaze blasted past you at nothing." Curiously, the addition of these details curiously give the woman more presence in the speaker's mind *and* in readers' minds.

In the final stanza the speaker returns to the image of the doctors turning her over. He is left "To wonder, / from now on, what dope deal, betrayal, / or innocent refusal, brought her here." The speaker elaborates on the kind of presence by listing possible reasons for her death. The only specific reason in the list is the "dope deal," which reverberates in readers' minds because of his previous description of the woman as being from the city. The presence of such a reason illustrates the way the speaker thinks in stereotypes. His inability to think about or describe anyone in the poem in a positive manner feeds readers' sense of the speaker as a disillusioned person who finds it difficult to participate in the human community in any emotionally meaningful way.

Discovering the woman, however, has given him reason not only to think about other people's lives but to think about his own death. Though the end of the poem suggests that this woman's death will forever haunt the speaker in his country paradise, on a larger scale it argues for the idea that no human is an island, and that no matter how much humans may try to separate themselves from other human beings, connection and responsibility remain.

Source: Chris Semansky, in an essay for *Poetry for Students,* Gale, 2001.

Jonathan N. Barron

Jonathan N. Barron is associate professor of English at the University of Southern Mississippi. He has co-edited Jewish American Poetry *(University Press of New England),* Roads Not Taken: Rereading Robert Frost *(University of Missouri Press) as well as a forthcoming collection of essays on the poetic movement,* New Formalism. *Beginning in 2001 he will be the editor in chief of* The Robert Frost Review.

Race, perhaps the most difficult and necessary topic to beset contemporary American literature, manifests itself in Taylor's poem, "Landscape with Tractor," and becomes its main subject and theme. Rather than claim that race is an essential determining characteristic of people, the poem instead

What Do I Read Next?

- "Landscape with Tractor" is included in Taylor's Pulitzer-Prize winning collection, *The Flying Change,* published in 1985. Many of these poems are formal (about one fourth are sonnets) and address the ordinariness of country life and the nature of change.

- For an understanding of Taylor's own critical sensibilities, read his 1992 collection of essays *Compulsory Figures: Essays on Recent American Poets.* In this collection Taylor trains his critical eye on poets such as Louis Simpson, William Stafford, and Louis Simpson.

- Dan Johnson interviews Henry Taylor in the 1976 issue of *Window* magazine. Taylor discusses his own approach towards writing and his thoughts on contemporary poetry.

reveals the problematic thoughts and guilty associations that arise by the mere presence of a black woman's corpse on a white man's farm. In telling this story, Taylor's poem blends two literary genres, southern literature and pastoral poetry.

To understand this poem, then, one needs to know a bit about both of these genres. To begin with the ancient pastoral tradition, one need only know that it takes as its central characters, shepherds or, in this case, farmers. In the conventional pastoral poem, the shepherd meditates on the relationship between nature and the city. Usually, these meditations lead to speculations and critiques of various social institutions: the best most representative example of such pastorals are Virgil's *Eclogues.* Indeed, it is just such Eclogues that Taylor invokes in his own "Landscape with Tractor." This poem, in the first person voice of a farmer, is typical of the genre because it maintains the conventions of a rural man who depicts social institutions and the conflict between the country and the city by invoking nature. It departs from pastoral conventions because it is so modern. Instead of an ancient shepherd, this farmer is a contemporary

> *Rather than claim that race is an essential determining characteristic of people, the poem instead reveals the problematic thoughts and guilty associations that arise by the mere presence of a black woman's corpse on a white man's farm.*"

man who drives a "bushhog" to cut the grass of his three acre field. Still, his meditation on the grass ends up being as much about the social world of the city as any classical eclogue. Another departure from the conventional form is the fact that Taylor's farmer, instead of speaking to another farmer, speaks directly to the reader. At first, one thinks the speaker is merely discussing the merits of a particular method of cutting grass. In fact, however, he is asking how the reader would have reacted had the reader discovered the body he has found. By introducing a plot about the discovery of a dead African-American woman on a white farmer's land, Taylor summons the poem's second dominant literary genre, the themes and conventions of southern literature.

Specifically, southern literature is said to consist of the "tragic sensibility." Ever since the Civil War, southern literature has developed its own thematic concerns both in poetry and in fiction. To summarize, southern writers depict their mostly rural, agrarian region as a place lost, defeated, isolated, and forgotten by the ongoing history of 20th century industrial life. Linked to this tragic sensibility, however, is a focus on tradition, family, heritage, and place. The sensibility is "tragic" in the classical sense because it claims for the south the moral, ethical truth of American society. Southern literature, in other words, laments the tragic fact that the real moral center of place, heritage, family has been lost and will not soon, if ever, return to dominate American life. Southern writers usually insist that these qualities make the south stronger, morally better than the United States'

more industrialized regions. Southern literature, then, is tragic because it accepts as final the loss of faith in tradition, family, and the importance of place to one's sense of self.

By the 1940s, just when Taylor was born, this tragic sensibility came to dominate southern fiction. Eventually, southern writers in the 1940s developed a particular subset of southern literature, the Southern Gothic. Like southern literature generally, it incorporated a great deal of symbolism and myth into its fictions, but it also emphasized the grotesque, strange, and bizarre events and characters that populate what is a predominantly rural region. In turn, the emphasis on the grotesque and the bizarre went hand in hand with a focus on the problem of evil in human affairs.

In this same decade, another event that was not necessarily literary but did help to shape and announce what would be the dominant concern of post World War II America occurred. In 1944, one of the more important sociological studies to effect American life was published: Gunner Myrdal's *An American Dilemma: The Negro Problem and Modern Democracy*. That book made the problem of race in America, specifically legalized discrimination in the south, a new and urgent political issue. Ultimately, this book would be a major source of evidence for the Supreme Court's ruling on desegregation in 1954. *An American Dilemma*, however, merely told in scientific prose what the southern novelists had long been depicting. For the most part, in other words, the southern novel was an anti-racist, anti-segregationist affair. Whatever the stance of the particular writer, though, southern literature made it quite clear that to write about the south was to write about race relations: their depiction was as fundamental to southern literature as were the new focus on the gothic and the grotesque that came to such prominence in the 1940s.

Therefore, when Taylor, already in his forties, published his third book in 1985, *The Flying Change*, the book from which "Landscape with Tractor" is taken, he was already participating both in the continuation of the ancient pastoral form, and in the revival of poetry as a major form for southern literature. As a poet in the south, Taylor could not help but know that southern literature had distinguished itself not through its poetry but through its prose: fiction writers like William Faulkner, Flannery O'Conner, and Eudrora Welty had far surpassed in literary influence their poetic peers. He knew this in part because he was born and educated in Virginia where he was initiated through his family and his own interests into southern literature and its concerns. According to the writer George Garrett, however, Taylor had a unique perspective on the southern themes of heritage, place, and family, since he came from a family and a community of Quakers dating back to eighteenth-century Virginia. In other words, Taylor may have come from the south and been educated into its literary traditions, but his community had always been opponents to both war and slavery on moral, religious grounds.

Perhaps this dissenting heritage explains Taylor's attraction to the poetry of James Dickey. Another southerner, but also a generation older than Taylor, Dickey was critical of some of the region's literary conventions. In fact, Dickey was the first poet significantly to change the assumption that southern literature ought to consist solely of fiction. When he burst on the scene with his narrative poetry, he incorporated into the forms of pastoral poetry the themes and plot lines of southern fiction.

Thanks to Dickey's precedent, then, Taylor had a place, stylistically speaking, already waiting for him when he began to publish. It was as if Dickey had given him permission to write his stories in verse instead of in prose. Unlike Dickey, though, Taylor extended his narrative thrust: his poetry is often far more willing even then Dickey to spin a yarn. In fact, Taylor's use of narrative has often been somewhat controversial because, ever since the 1960s, American poets have preferred poems that avoid too much story and plot. But taking his cue from Dickey, Taylor has told story after story in each of his books.

The story told in "Landscape with Tractor" is particularly notable because it links the narrative tradition of southern literature (particularly its gothic variant) to the structure of a pastoral poem. The play of genres, however, is not what makes this an important poem. Rather, it is the thematic result of this combination that matters. For thanks to his manipulation of the conventions of both genres, Taylor is able to sharpen his own focus on race, the real subject of his poem. Both southern literature and the pastoral require, as part of their structure, that the writer deal with, and engage, social themes. Both southern literature and the pastoral are incredibly social genres. By definition, they both require writers to examine the people who live in specific well defined rural communities. By contrast, if one were to focus in one's poem only on an individual or only on a pure description one would not be writing either the conventional pas-

toral, or conventional southern literature. Therefore, Taylor's "Landscape with Tractor" becomes one of the key documents in contemporary American literary discussions about race and racism precisely because it so successfully blends the southern literary tradition and the ongoing tradition of pastoral poetry. It is precisely because Taylor blends two fundamentally social genres together that he is able to get inside the story of race in America.

That this social element of Taylor's poem has been well understood is clear from perhaps the best reading of the poem so far. That reading, interestingly enough, does not come from an essay but rather from a poem, "On the Turning Up of Unidentified Black Female Corpses" by the African American poet, Toi Derricotte. In her poetic response to Taylor, she implicitly comments on Taylor's racial theme. But before explaining Derricotte's critique, a more detailed glance at Taylor's poem is in order.

The poem, in twelve stanzas of four lines each, relies on meter for its rhythm. Usually, four-line stanzas indicate a ballad. This would make sense since the ballad is the most common English language form for telling stories in poetry. But ballads depend on a particular rhyme (*abab*) and a particular meter (four beats, tetrameter, alternating with three beats, trimeter). Although this poem does have a ballad's four line stanza it does not have either its rhyme or its meter. In other words, the poem is not a simple country tale about the common folk, low subjects fit for a low form. It may be possible to say that these lines are in three beats. But to do this one would have to know that, already by his third book, Taylor himself was known for his use of the anapestic foot, something he learned, so George Garrett tells us, from James Dickey. The anapest, two unstressed syllables followed by a stress, would allow one to read Taylor's lines as trimeter, a common meter for ballads. But, to my ear at any rate, these lines scan better as pentameter. In other words, even the ghost of a reference to the ballad in the form of a three beat line is less likely than the more conventional, more serious five beat line, (pentameter). This means that the poem is more serious than a ballad. Because ballads are not the pastoral genre's most impressive form, because ballads are considered low and often anti-intellectual, it ought not to be surprising that this poem would look like a ballad even though it actually scans in the same meter as Shakespeare's sonnets and Wordsworth's great period poems.

Ultimately, the fact that it is so difficult to determine the exact meter of these lines tells us even more about its theme: in America, when it comes to race, nothing is simple, nothing is easily deciphered. To clue readers into the ambiguity of race that this poem will explore, Taylor makes his own meter fundamentally ambiguous as well.

Also, he is equally deceptive in his word choice and language. The poem seems so simple, there is virtually no need to look up any word in the dictionary, for example. But this simple diction is as ambiguous as the meter. For what seems to be so straightforward is, in fact, a mystery so deep that, by the end of the poem, no language can adequately explain it.

Turning now to the poem itself one notices that from the very first, Taylor invites us into his speaker's mind. We are not just a witness to what he discovers, but we are also made to undergo the same shock and moral crisis that he undergoes as well. The poem begins:

> How would it be if you took yourself off
> To a house set well back from a dirt road,
> With, say, three acres of grass bounded
> By road, driveway, and vegetable garden?

In these lines the reader is offered an invitation. Why not go to a pleasant three acre farm? Small and compact it might offer an attractive meal and a fine time of conversation and fun. Invited into this farm, Taylor's speaker then continues to ask what the reader would do. In the second and third stanza, he tells how the reader would mow the field. He brings the reader into the visceral experience of riding the "bushhog." In the fourth stanza, after the readers have been asked to become this farmer, he introduces the gothic, grotesque element into the poem. At first neither he nor first time readers know what he's talking about. The fourth stanza merely tells that "we glimpse it." The farmer's first reaction is, therefore, meant to be the same as the reader's, and then to think as he thinks: "People / Will toss all kinds of crap from their cars."

The first encounter with the corpse, then, is annoyance. Typical of pastoral poetry, the farmer signals his disgust with city folk who have no concern for the fields that gives them the food they eat and much of the clothes they wear. Angry that passersby would throw "crap" from their cars, Taylor's speaker, in the next stanza, gets a closer look. He thinks what he sees is "a clothing-store dummy." He cannot believe how rude, how amazingly weird, city folk are. That they would throw a dummy on his field! Knowing, as the reader does

after finishing the poem, however, that this is, in fact, a dead woman, the initial response of Taylor's speaker is not only upsetting, but, because the body is of a black woman, it is also potentially racist. Blacks as mere property; blacks as mere dummies, blacks as cast off goods. Are not these the same sentiments that have had such a powerful and enduring reality in the south? To this speaker's horror, although he knows himself not to be racist, his first reaction to the body was, in terms of race in America, classically racist. At this point, guilt, always a moral emotion, enters into the poem. It explains why he had to make his readers literally share in his experience as if it were happening to them for the very first time. He needs his readers to feel as he feels in order to prove that his first thoughts about this woman are not racist thoughts.

Exactly half way through the poem, Taylor realizes just what has been left on his field: "the field tilts, whirls, then steadies as you run." Here, Taylor captures the delirium of his discovery. What follows likens the corpse to what, in her famous song, Billie Holiday called, a strange fruit. The harvest of this field is a "four days dead, and ripening" "well-dressed black woman." In the next stanza, the reader learns that the cause of death is "no mystery: two bullet holes / In the breast."

But rather than enter into the experience or imagined life of this woman, the poem then returns its focus back to the speaker and away from the woman. By returning to the speaker, the urgency of the opening question, "How would it be?" becomes all the more poignant and difficult. For now that the reader has been invited into this man's life the reader must respond as he does to this discovery.

In the second half of the poem, the final six stanzas, he reports his response as a psychological and social dilemma, precisely the American dilemma Gunner Myrdal wrote of in his famous 1944 report. In the ninth stanza, "weeks pass." Clearly still upset, the speaker seeks whatever news he can find about the woman. At the post office, he learns that she was brought out "from the city, they guess, and dumped / like a bag of beer cans." Here the typical pastoral critique of the city joins an endemic racism common to the rural south. In the country, the white locals associate city folk with a cold, dispassionate lack of concern even as they are not surprised to see that black folk are no better than garbage. Taylor's speaker does not share such racist views but he reports what he hears and adds a wonderful enjambment that breaks his thought not only across a line but over a stanza as well, as if to indicate his profound disagreement with his neighbors. The stanza concludes: "She was someone." That line does not end the sentence, however, which continues in the tenth stanza:

> and now is no one, buried or burned
> or dissected; but gone. And I ask you
> again, how would it be? To go on with your life,
> putting gas in the tractor, keeping down thistles ...

Taylor's speaker, unlike the men in the post office, understands that this body was a woman and that, despite her many connections and associations, the body has gone unclaimed. Whether her body went to science, to a crematorium, or to a grave the sad truth is that no one ever claimed her. By asking his opening question again, Taylor transforms the woman into a haunting presence that now inhabits his speaker's land. For better or worse this woman is now part of his identity, his land, his place, his heritage. Could you, he asks his readers, go on with your life after seeing her? Even though, weeks later, there is only "that spot" where she once lay, her presence remains. The final lines of the final stanza ask:

> ... To wonder,
> from now on, what dope deal, betrayal,
> or innocent refusal, brought her here,
> and to know she will stay in the field till you die?

Because her presence is unresolved, unexplained, he conjures up three explanations. She was involved in drugs, she was involved in some shady deal where she betrayed someone and paid for it with her life, or, perhaps, she was truly an innocent victim whose refusal to do whatever she had been asked to do got her killed. The fact that she is black and that she has been shot immediately brings the drug and betrayal connection to the speaker's mind. Would he have had the same thoughts if a well-dressed white woman in her mid-thirties had been discovered, or, for a white woman, would only the last scenario present itself? This, too, is part of the poem's sub-text of guilt. It hides beneath the more obvious social dimension of race. And it is that social dimension—the fact that this murdered woman is black—that matters most. Her presence on this white man's farm, particularly in the southern context of the poems of *The Flying Change*, resonates symbolically. For in symbolic terms the black woman who has come back, as if from no where, to haunt him represents the black bodies of the south. They will and must haunt the southern landscape in order to challenge its claim to honor, integrity, and truth. No pastoral ideal of the land can dare deny or pretend that the black victims of the south do not exist. Typical of his Quaker, non-con-

formist background, Taylor asserts the typical themes of southern literature—community, history, place—but he does so, at the end, by asking just how much responsibility this seemingly innocent white farmer owes to the tragic history of the land he farms. Yes, the woman will stay with him until he dies, as much a part of his farm as he.

The reaction to Taylor's third book was intense, so much so that it won the Pulitzer Prize for the best book of poetry published in 1985. Of all the reactions to this collection, however, none is more compelling than the poem by Toi Derricotte that retells Taylor's story. But Derricotte makes a significant change. She asks her readers to sympathize with the victim not the farmer:

> Mowing his three acres with a tractor,
> a man notices something ahead—a mannequin
> —he thinks someone threw it from a car. Closer
> he sees it is the body of a black woman.

Rather than ask how readers would feel had they found her, she asks how it feels to be like her; how it feels, to be, yourself, a black woman in a majority white country. She asks what it says about American culture that such events are so typical anyway: "How many black women / have been turned up to stare at us blankly" she asks. After meditating on this grim reality, she admits, in her concluding stanza, that "part of me wants to disappear," but rather than disappear she instead asserts her affiliation with her African American community and heritage:

> Then there is this part
> that digs me up with this pen
> and turns my sad black face to the light.

Facing the light of her identity, Derricotte uncovers what too many readers will be likely to want to ignore, or avoid, in Taylor's poem. Her poem, in effect, says that it matters fundamentally and absolutely that the woman Taylor's farmer discovers is black. Both poets, beginning with Taylor, turn their attention to the ongoing American dilemma that is race relations. As fit a subject for poetry as for prose.

Source: Jonathan N. Barron, in an essay for *Poetry for Students,* Gale, 2001.

Adrian Blevins

Adrian Blevins, a poet and essayist who has taught at Hollins University, Sweet Briar College, and in the Virginia Community College System, is the author of The Man Who Went Out for Cigarettes, *a chapbook of poems, and has published poems, stories, and essays in many magazines, journals, and anthologies. In this essay, Blevins*

... as the study of any number of writers who take a significant interest in the details of their own homelands will tell us, human universals always rise from specific details the color of the mountain and the odd, cool texture of the fishing stream."

explores the psychological implications in Henry Taylor's poem and argues that Taylor uses the details of his homeland as a backdrop to more internal meditations.

"Landscape with Tractor" is one of the most memorable poems in *The Flying Change*. It reveals, as many of Tayor's poems do, the poet's consciousness of the rift between the idyllic surface of the country landscape and the darker and more violent essence sometimes contained within that landscape and sometimes brought out from the city and dumped there. Despite the harsh aspects of the story told by "Landscape with Tractor," the poem does not simply imply that the picturesque countryside has been invaded by the horrors of the more "civilized" world. The speaker's more comprehensive realization is that humans must first learn to carry and then somehow bear all their eyes take in. Thus, there are psychological implications inherent in this poem implications about the enduring nature of experience and memory and about how each might work to inform, instruct, and appall the human psyche.

"Landscape with Tractor" is a fairly straightforward narrative poem. It tells a story in the present tense about a day at some point in the speaker's past when he comes across the dead body of a "well-dressed black woman" in a field, that, "bounded / by road, drive way, and vegetable garden," he often mowed with his tractor. In addition to relating the gruesome details of his discovery, saying that "Two local doctors use pitchforks / To turn the body, some four days dead, and ripening,"

the speaker also expresses his initial reaction to it. He says that "the field tilts, whirls, then steadies as [he] runs," and that the next day "bluebottle files are still swirling." These details work to reveal that the experience the speaker is relating is in fact an authentic one there are no flights of imagination here, no make-believe murder-mystery or pretend foul-play. The poem then leaps to the speaker's realization that the dead woman's body will stay with him forever; the experience, he understands, has become a constant part of him, a knowledge and weight he must bear, as he says, to his own death.

"Landscape with Tractor" is filled with a range of glorious tensions. Although his work in forms can place Taylor among the contemporary American poets associating themselves with what is called The New Formalism, such a placement would be dreadfully reductive. Taylor, unlike some of the poets associated with this movement, is not merely concerned with the political and/or reactionary act of reviving traditional poetic forms. Rather, he is interested in exploring all possible methods for expressing his take on the human adventure, a project which sometimes leads him to marry both traditional and less well-known forms. The effect is a well-crafted tonal strain that is original and haunting.

"Landscape with Tractor" is written in well-controlled quatrains, or four-line-stanzas. The regularity of Taylor's line and the order of his stanzas produces a tone of reserve; it is what American poet and critic Richard Dillard calls a "well-modulated voice." But the speaker's use of slang (as in "People / Will toss all kinds of crap from their cars") as well as his use of a whole variety of idiomatic expressions (as in "it's a clothing-store dummy, for God's sake") produces a tension that makes the speaker's voice at once intimate and aloof. Thus, the speaker achieves, by way of his tone, the storyteller's authority, which comes in part from his ability to appear to stand back from the events he is narrating. He also attains the poet's authority, which comes from his ability to use any means necessary in this case narrative suspense, exacting details, heightened diction, a relatively consistent rhythm, and a final and surprising turn inward in order to express outrage and sorrow.

The speaker's use of the second person, because it contains the power of direct address and approximates the pitches of everyday conversation, also helps him to achieve a tone of intimacy:

How would it be if you took yourself off
To a house set well back from a dirt road,

With, say, three acres of grass bounded
By road, driveway, and vegetable garden?

Taylor also addresses the reader explicitly toward the end of "Landscape with Tractor" when he states, "And I ask you / again, how would it be?" After this line, in a nice turn, the speaker seems to move inward, appearing in this greatest moment of emotional intensity to be talking to himself. Thus, one of the poem's psychological progressions can be recognized—a movement from public to private utterance:

> or dissected; but gone. And I ask you
> again, how would it be? To go on with your life,
> putting gas in the tractor, keeping down thistles,
> and seeing, each time you pass that spot
> the form in the grass....

Taylor moves in this most organic fashion away from the historian's act of recording moments in telling detail to the poet's act of exploring the ambiguities and complexities inherent in the more emotive realms of human experience. The fact that the poem begins and ends on unanswerable questions reinforces the unresolvable nature of the experience the speaker narrates. "Landscape with Tractor" strives not to answer questions about the fragility of human life or the violent essence of human nature; it seeks, instead, and perhaps in small memorial, to pose or submit the facts of a sad story in as straightforward a manner as possible, uncovering one of the most absolute of human truths. The speaker's final realization reminds that violent or unacceptable experiences are psychologically permanent.

References to the significance of the region of many of Henry Taylor's poems or to what American critic Peter Stitt calls "Mr. Taylor's sense of nostalgia for his home territory" are not in and of themselves erroneous. Nevertheless, because it is possible for certain readers to over-emphasize the poetic significance of Taylor's love and knowledge for Virginia farmland and folk (especially those contemporaries "bunched up in several urban areas," as American writer and critic George Garrett calls them), it seems important to point out that the Taylor landscape is often as much scenery and setting as it is topic. Since Taylor works so beautifully in the narrative mode, his interest in atmosphere and background should not be surprising. Besides, as the study of any number of writers who take a significant interest in the details of their own homelands will tell us, human universals always rise from specific details the color of the mountain and the odd, cool texture of the fishing stream.

Source: Adrian Blevins, in an essay for *Poetry for Students*, Gale, 2001.

Sources

Derricotte, Toi, "On the Turning Up of Unidentified Black Female Corpses," in *Captivity*, University of Pittsburgh Press, 1989.

Dillard, R. H. W., "The Flying Change," in *The Hollins Critic*, Vol. XXIII, No 2, April, 1986, p. 15.

Garrett, George, "Henry Taylor," in *Dictionary of Literary Biography*, Vol. 5: *American Poets Since World War II, First Series*, Part II, Gale, 1980, pp. 322-27.

Horowitz, David, Peter N. Carroll, and David D. Lee, eds., *On the Edge: A New History of 20th-century America*, West Publishing Co., 1990.

Johnson, Dan, "An Interview With Henry Taylor," in *Window*, Spring, 1976, pp. 1-21.

Meyers, Jack, and David Wojahn, eds. *A Profile of Twentieth-Century American Poetry*, Southern Illinois University Press, 1991.

Shapiro, David, "A Review of Henry Taylor's *The Flying Change*," in *Poetry*, March, 1987, pp. 348-350.

Stitt, Peter, "Landscapes and Still Lives," in *New York Times Book Review*, May 4, 1986, pp. 22-3.

Taylor, Henry, *Compulsory Figures: Essays on Recent American Poets*, Louisiana State University Press, 1992.

———, *Contemporary Authors Autobiography Series*, Vol. 7, Gale, 1988. pp. 171-89.

———, *The Flying Change*, Louisiana State University Press, 1985.

———, *Understanding Fiction: Poems, 1986–1996*, Louisiana State University Press, 1996.

For Further Study

Broughton, Irv, ed., *The Writer's Mind: Interviews with American Authors*, University of Arkansas Press, 1990.
    Broughton interviews a number of American authors, both poets and fiction writers, including Paul Zimmer, Colleen McElroy, and Fred Chappell. He also interviews Henry Taylor, who talks about his childhood and those who influenced his writing.

Jarman, Mark, and David Mason, eds., *Rebel Angels: 25 Poets of the New Formalism*, Story Line Press, 1996.
    Rebel Angels is an anthology presenting poets aligned with or sympathetic to New Formalism, a movement in American poetry reviving rhyme, meter, and narrative in innovative ways.

Wright, Stuart, "Henry Taylor: A Bibliographic Chronicle, 1961-1987," in *Bulletin of Bibliography*, Vol. 45, No. 3, 1988, pp. 79-91.
    Wright provides a thorough checklist of work published by Taylor from 1961-1987, including poems which have yet to appear in a collection. A short critical introduction accompanies the bibliography.

The Negro Speaks of Rivers

Langston Hughes

1921

"The Negro Speaks of Rivers" was the first poem published in Langston Hughes's long writing career. The poem first appeared in the magazine *Crisis* in June of 1921 and was subsequently published in Hughes's first volume of poetry, *The Weary Blues,* in 1926. Written when he was only 19, "The Negro Speaks of Rivers" treats themes Hughes explored all his life: the experiences of African Americans in history and black identity and pride. Hughes claimed that 90 percent of his work attempted "to explain and illuminate the Negro condition in America." Through images of rivers, African civilizations, and an "I" who speaks for the race, Hughes argues for the depth, wisdom, and endurance of the African soul. The form of the poem reinforces these themes. Using a collective, mythic "I," long lines, and repeated phrases, Hughes invokes the poetry of Walt Whitman, another bard who "sang" America. Onwuchekwa Jemie notes in his book *Langston Hughes: An Introduction to the Poetry,* however, that unlike Whitman, Hughes "celebrates not the America that is but the America that is to come."

Author Biography

Hughes was born in in 1902 in Joplin, Missouri, to James Nathaniel and Carrie Mercer Langston Hughes, who separated shortly after their son's birth. Hughes' mother had attended college, while

his father, who wanted to become a lawyer, took correspondence courses in law. Denied a chance to take the Oklahoma bar exam, Hughes' father went first to Missouri and then, still unable to become a lawyer, left his wife and son to move first to Cuba and then to Mexico. In Mexico, he became a wealthy landowner and lawyer. Because of financial difficulties, Hughes' mother moved frequently in search of steady work, often leaving him with her parents. His grandmother Mary Leary Langston was the first black woman to attend Oberlin College. She inspired the boy to read books and value an education. When his grandmother died in 1910, Hughes lived with family friends and various relatives in Kansas. In 1915 he joined his mother and new stepfather in Lincoln, Illinois, where he attended grammar school. The following year, the family moved to Cleveland, Ohio. There he attended Central High School, excelling in both academics and sports. Hughes also wrote poetry and short fiction for the *Belfry Owl,* the high school literary magazine, and edited the school yearbook. In 1920 Hughes left to visit his father in Mexico, staying in that country for a year. Returning home in 1921, he attended Columbia University for a year before dropping out. For a time he worked as a cabin boy on a merchant ship, visited Africa, and wrote poems for a number of American magazines. In 1923 and 1924 Hughes lived in Paris. He returned to the United States in 1925 and resettled with his mother and half-brother in Washington, D.C. He continued writing poetry while working menial jobs. In May and August of 1925 Hughes's verse earned him literary prizes from both *Opportunity* and *Crisis* magazines. In December Hughes, then a busboy at a Washington, D.C., hotel, attracted the attention of poet Vachel Lindsay by placing three of his poems on Lindsay's dinner table. Later that evening Lindsay read Hughes's poems to an audience and announced his discovery of a "Negro busboy poet." The next day reporters and photographers eagerly greeted Hughes at work to hear more of his compositions. He published his first collection of poetry, *The Weary Blues,* in 1926. Around this time Hughes became active in the Harlem Renaissance, a flowering of creativity among a group of African American artists and writers. Hughes, Zora Neale Hurston, and other writers founded *Fire!,* a literary journal devoted to African American culture. The venture was unsuccessful, however, and ironically a fire eventually destroyed the editorial offices. In 1932 Hughes traveled with other black writers to the Soviet Union on an ill-fated film pro-

Langston Hughes

ject. His infatuation with Soviet Communism and Joseph Stalin led Hughes to write on politics throughout the 1930s. He also became involved in drama, founding several theaters. In 1938 he founded the Suitcase Theater in Harlem, in 1939 the Negro Art Theater in Los Angeles, and in 1941 the Skyloft Players in Chicago. In 1943 Hughes received an honorary Doctor of Letters from Lincoln University, and in 1946 he was elected to the National Institute of Arts and Letters. He continued to write poetry throughout the rest of his life, and by the 1960s he was known as the "Dean of Negro Writers." Hughes died in New York on May 22, 1967.

Poem Text

I've known rivers:
I've known rivers ancient as the world and older
　　than the flow of human blood in human
　　veins.
My soul has grown deep like rivers.

I bathed in the Euphrates when dawns were young.
I built my hut near the Congo and it lulled me to　　5
　　sleep.
I looked upon the Nile and raised the pyramids
　　above it.

Media Adaptations

- *Langston Hughes: Poet,* a 1994 release by Schlessinger Video Productions, blends biographical information with a discussion of Hughes' art.

- "The Negro Sings of Rivers" is one of several poems included on *Langston Hughes: The Poet in Our Hearts,* a 1995 video from Chip Taylor Communications.

- The 1992 Waterbearer video, *A Meditation on Langston Hughes and the Harlem Renaissance,* dramatizes Hughes' role in the Harlem of the 1930s.

- *Langston Hughes: The Dream Keeper* includes photographs, readings, criticism and biographical information about Hughes, a 1988 release by Intellimation.

- The Harper Collins 1992 audiocassette, *Langston Hughes Reads,* includes "The Negro Speaks of Rivers."

I heard the singing of the Mississippi when Abe
    Lincoln went down to New Orleans, and
    I've seen its muddy bosom turn all golden in
    the sunset.

I've known rivers:
Ancient, dusky rivers.

My soul has grown deep like the rivers.   10

Poem Summary

Lines 1–4:

Speaking for the African race ("negro" was the preferred term in 1921), the "I" of this poem links people of African descent to an ancient, natural, life-giving force: rivers. By asserting that he has "known rivers ancient as the world," the speaker asserts that he, and people of African descent, have an understanding of elemental forces in nature that precede civilization. The repetition of "rivers" and

"human" lends these lines a wise, resonant tone, like that found in Biblical passages. In the first two lines, the speaker refers to rivers as a natural force outside himself. Line 3 likens the human body to earth by comparing rivers to "human blood in human veins." Line 4 personalizes that comparison as the speaker compares the depth of his soul to the depth of rivers. In the space of four lines the speaker moves from historically and symbolically associating himself and his people with rivers to metaphorically imagining rivers as part of his blood and soul. Rather than one human relationship to rivers emerging as true or primary, each of these associations intertwine.

Lines 5–7:

Line 5 lets the reader know that the "I" is no mortal human speaker, but the mythic, timeless voice of a race. To have "bathed in the Euphrates when dawns were young," in prehistory, the speaker must be millions of years old. In lines 5 through 7, the speaker establishes the race's ties to great, culturally rich civilizations along famous rivers in the Middle East and Africa. The Euphrates River was the cradle of ancient Babylonia. It flows from Turkey through Syria and modern Iraq. The Congo originates in central Africa and flows into the Atlantic. The Nile, which runs from Lake Victoria in Uganda in Africa through Egypt to the Mediterranean, was the site of ancient Egyptian civilization. The speaker's actions show that he reveres the river and depends on it for multiple purposes. He bathes in the water, builds his hut next to it, listens to its music as he falls asleep, and is consoled or inspired by the river when, as a slave in Egypt, he builds the great pyramids.

These actions reinforce the notion (from lines 1-3) that peoples of African descent have ancient spiritual and physical ties to nature. When Hughes wrote this poem in 1921, ideas and images of primitive, tribal cultures were very chic in American art and literature. After Hughes visited Africa in 1923, he no longer viewed Africa as a mythic, exotic land where black identity was rooted, but instead as a land ravaged by Western imperialism, a symbol of lost roots. In his later writing, Hughes steered away from images of African primitivism, for he saw such depictions of African and African-American culture as impeding rather than advancing the cause of racial equality.

Lines 8–10:

Here Hughes draws an analogy between the ancient rivers alongside which Africans founded civilizations, and the Mississippi, the river on which several American cities were built, including St. Louis (Hughes's birthplace) and New Orleans. Onwuchekwa Jemie, writing in *Langston Hughes: An Introduction to the Poetry,* notes that "the magical transformation of the Mississippi from mud to gold by the sun's radiance is mirrored in the transformation of slaves into free men by Lincoln's Proclamation." In *The Life of Langston Hughes,* Arnold Rampersad views this transformation as "the angle of a poet's vision, which turns mud into gold." The sun's transformation of muddy water to gold provides an image of change. The change may represent the improved status of African Americans after the Civil War, hope for future changes, or the power of the poet to transform reality through imaginative language. Line 8 personifies the river by giving it the human capacity to sing. The river's singing invokes both the slave spirituals and songs of celebration after the slaves were freed. Line 9 also personifies the river by endowing it with a "muddy bosom." The Mississippi river is known for its muddiness. The term "bosom" is associated with women and so connotes fertility and nurturing. Through this personification, Hughes associates the ceaselessness of the mighty river with the eternal, life-affirming endurance of Africans and African Americans.

Lines 11–13:

The poem closes with the phrases that opened it. The speaker's language completes a cycle that mirrors the river's eternal cycling of waters around the earth and the African race's continuing role in human history. By enacting the circling of time and rivers, the speaker again associates himself with those elemental forces. The phrase "dusky rivers" refers literally to rivers that appear brown due to mud and cloudy skies. Figuratively, the phrase again likens rivers to peoples of African descent, whose skin is often called "dusky" or dark. The final line reaffirms the speaker's sense of racial pride, of continuity with ancient, advanced civilizations, and of connection to life-giving, enduring forces in nature.

Themes

Heritage

"The Negro Speaks of Rivers," Hughes' first published poem, introduces a theme which would recur in several other works throughout his career.

Many critics have classified this group as the "heritage" poems. Amazingly, although it was composed very quickly when he was only seventeen, it is both polished and powerful. In fact, in *Langston Hughes: An Introduction to the Poetry,* Onwuchekwa Jemie labels it the most profound of this group.

The poem utilizes four of the world's largest and most historically prominent rivers as a metaphor to present a view, almost a timeline in miniature, of the African-American experience throughout history. The opening lines of the poem introduce the ancient and powerful cultural history of Africa and West Asia, with the mention of the Euphrates and the dawn of time. Next the Congo, mother to Central Africa, lulls the speaker, to sleep. The world's longest river, the powerful and complex Nile with its great pyramids, follows. Last, the poem moves to more recent times, with the introduction of the Mississippi. Even though the Mississippi and Congo both hold bitter connotations of the slave trade, each of the four has contributed to the depth of the speaker's soul. The poem stresses triumph over adversity as the "muddy bosom" of the Mississippi turns golden.

The speaker clearly represents more than Langston Hughes, the individual. In fact, the "I" of the poem becomes even more than the embodiment of a racial identity. The poem describes, underlying that identity, an eternal spirit, existing before the dawn of time and present still in the twentieth century. The different sections of the poem emphasize this: the speaker actually functions on two levels. One is the human level. The first words of lines five through eight create a picture of the speaker's ancestors: bathing, building, looking, hearing. However, the poem also discusses a spiritual level where the soul of the speaker has been and continues to be enriched by the spirit of the river, even before the creation of humanity. Thus, the second and third lines of the poem develop an eternal, or cosmic, dimension in the poem.

Wisdom and Strength

The poem's cosmic dimension adds an additional theme making the poem more than a tribute to the heritage of the past. It honors the wisdom and strength which allowed African-Americans to survive and flourish in the face of all adversity, most particularly the last few centuries of slavery. Hughes associates this strength with the spirit of these rivers which Jemie describes in *Langston Hughes: An Introduction to the Poetry* as "transcendent essences

Topics for Further Study

- Rivers were vital to early civilizations, yet today many suffer from a variety of types of pollution. Choose one of the rivers mentioned in the poem and report on its current condition.

- Research the importance of the Harlem Renaissance in giving voice to the soul of the African-American community.

- Investigate Abraham Lincoln's role in abolishing slavery.

- Hughes connects the African-American soul with rivers. Write an extended metaphor connecting your spirit to some aspect of nature.

---

so ancient as to appear timeless, predating human existence, longer than human memory." Jemie continues by noting that as the black man drank of these essences, he became endowed with the strength, the power and the wisdom of the river spirit. Thus Hughes stresses the ancient cultural heritage of the African-American, the soul which existed even before the "dawns were young." The poem then makes clear that through all of the centuries, the speaker—or in other words, the collective soul—has survived indomitable, like the rivers. The poem exalts the force of character, the wisdom and strength, which created this survival.

This tribute developed out of Hughes' personal life. He describes the inspiration for the poem in his autobiography, *The Big Sea.* While he was crossing the Mississippi on a visit to his father, a man who baffled and frustrated Hughes because of his prejudice, he began "thinking about my father and his strange dislike of his own people." Hughes contrasts this attitude with his own admiration for the "bravest people possible—the Negroes from the Southern ghettoes—facing tremendous odds." The Mississippi suddenly seemed to be a graphic symbol of that bravery. He notes that being sold down the river literally meant being torn violently from one's own family. Yet even after centuries of brutal inhumanity in bondage, the African-American

spirit has emerged triumphant. This poem became Hughes' tribute to the strength and the wisdom of his people.

Rivers

Rivers have been a powerful force throughout human history. Many early mythologies made the river—or the river god—a symbol of both life and death. It is easy to understand the reason for this since most of the great early civilizations grew up in river valleys. The Euphrates, which is the first of the rivers mentioned in the poem, helps to form Mesopotamia. Even today, world history textbooks refer to the area using the symbolic phrase, the cradle of civilization, because of the number of ancient kingdoms which flourished there: Ur, Sumer, Babylon. The Nile, too, played a central role in early civilization. It ensured Egyptian prosperity. Thus the river was worshipped as the god, Khnum, who made the earth fruitful. Central African tribes also believed in the powerful river spirits who were sources of life, wisdom, and purification. Even, today, Christian baptism, which originated when John the Baptist anointed Jesus Christ in the River Jordan, represents both a symbol of purification and the entrance to new life.

S. Okechukwu Mezu discusses the importance of rivers in both mythology and poetry in his study *The Poetry of Leopold Sedar Senghor:* "The river in most societies is considered a source of life, of new life in particular: a source of ablution and purification." He then mentions several poets who absorb this view into their work, such as Hughes and Whitman, whose "personification of the river … is not far removed from the anthropomorphism and pantheism that characterize certain elements in African traditional religion."

Style

"The Negro Speaks of Rivers" is spoken in first person point of view. However, the "I" represents neither a persona nor the author. Rather, the "I" speaks as and for people of African descent. "The Negro" of the title represents an archetype rather than an actual individual. There is a precedent for this collective "I" in the poetry of Walt Whitman, who spoke as and for America in his poem, "Song of Myself." Hughes adopts two other elements in this poem that show the influence of Whitman: long lines and repetition of phrases. The long, free verse lines of this poem signal the speaker's attempt to encompass the world with his words. Hughes repeats several phrases ("I've known rivers," "my soul has grown deep like rivers"), to make the poem sound like an incantation, or magical spell. Some critics remark that these repetitions echo the tone and rhythm of black spirituals. Hughes became famous for his use of other African American musical forms in his poetry, particularly jazz and blues.

In addition to repeating phrases, Hughes repeats syntactic units in a catalog or list: "I've known," "I bathed," "I built," "I looked," etc. The Bible catalogs who begot whom, and who boarded the ark; the poet Virgil cataloged all the ships and heroes going into the Trojan War. Catalogs, like the technique of long lines, represent vast numbers and magnitude. In "The Negro Speaks of Rivers," the catalog of the speaker's actions testifies to his (and the race's) vast worldly experience and importance in human history.

Historical Context

During the period of Reconstruction which followed the American Civil War, Northern troops remained in the South in order to help eradicate the lingering effects of slavery. In spite of much opposition, the Freedman's Bureau was established; its purpose was, in large part, to protect the rights of the black population. In addition, branches of a political organization, known alternately as the Union or Loyalty League, were established to ensure voting rights for former slaves. As a result of this, many African Americans held political office at the local, state, and federal level; two black senators and several congressmen were elected from the South during those years. In fact, one of the senators, Hiram R. Revels, was elected to complete the term of Jefferson Davis, former president of the Confederacy.

However, when the Northern troops left the region in 1877, state and local governments quickly returned to white domination. Local authorities began to set up a series of statutes aimed at disenfranchising black citizens. Poll taxes and literacy tests were mandated; laws requiring segregation were passed. The federal government in Washington looked the other way, ignoring the problem. Thus by the beginning of the twentieth century, the South was once again firmly under white control. Blacks were summarily denied rights they had previously held. In Alabama, for example, the number of blacks on the voting rolls went from 181,470 in 1900 to 3000 in 1901.

The denial of political and civil rights was, however, only a part of the problem which blacks faced in the United States. Once the Reconstruction era ended, blacks had little protection against a rising wave of violence directed against them. Lynching became part of the southern way of life. In "Blood at the Root," an article on lynching in *Time* magazine, Richard Lacayo noted that "lynching evolved into a semiofficial institution of racial terror against blacks. All across the former Confederacy, blacks who were suspected of crimes against whites—or even 'offenses' no greater than failing to step aside for a white man's car or protesting a lynching—were tortured, hanged and burned to death by the thousands." The NAACP collected statistics which indicated that during the years between 1889 and 1918 over 2572 blacks were lynching victims.

Several prominent African-American leaders attempted to address these issues. One was Booker T. Washington, perhaps the most dominant figure in African-American political and social thought at the time and the founder of the Tuskeegee Institute in Alabama. He did not believe in directly challenging the unjust southern system. Instead, he felt that vocational and technical training, which would improve the economic status of blacks, would encourage a gradual change. The primary educational goal of his Tuskeegee Institute, therefore, was industrial education, the preparation for jobs. While academic subjects were not ignored, they also were not emphasized.

Several other noted black figures of the time, however, rejected Washington's non-aggressive policy, calling his views accomodationist. One prominent critic was W.E.B. DuBois, a teacher and intellectual who had received a doctoral degree from Harvard. DuBois was joined by William Monroe Trotter, editor of the *Boston Guardian*, a newspaper which regularly attacked Washington's views. Both of these men felt that Washington's approach, which was very popular with white politicians, was actually harmful to blacks. In 1905, the two organized a meeting at Niagara Falls to protest discrimination. The "Niagara Movement" called for active protest against injustice. This eventually led to the founding of the National Association for the Advancement of Colored People (NAACP) in 1909.

Cedric Robinson in *Black Movements in America* describes the weaknesses, problems, and victories of the NAACP during its early years: "Despite its contradictions, its frequent political timidity, and the active hostility of presidents, congresses, and

Compare & Contrast

- **1921:** Nicola Sacco and Bartolomeo Vanzetti were convicted of murder and sentenced to be executed; several observers felt the men were judged because of their anarchist politics rather than because they were truly guilty.

  1997: Governor Michael Dukakis of Massachusetts, a liberal Democrat, posthumously pardoned Sacco and Vanzetti.

  2000: Governor Dan Ryan of Illinois, imposed a moratorium on executions in the state since it was proved that since 1977 thirteen people who were sentenced to death were later declared innocent.

- **1921:** Eubie Blake's *Shuffle Along* was produced on Broadway, one of the first black musicals to receive widespread public acclaim.

  1948: Harry Truman uses one of the songs from *Shuffle Along,* "I'm Just Wild About Harry," as his theme song in the Presidential campaign.

  1999: The NAACP mounted protests against the television and movie industries for not employing enough black personnel, both on and off the screen.

government agencies like the Federal Bureau of Investigation, the NAACP managed from it earliest years to mount powerful propaganda and legal challenges to lynching; racist courts and juries; the exclusion of Blacks from the armed services; apartheid in public transportation, education, and housing."

In spite of these successes of the NAACP, the black population in the United States was increasingly under attack. Woodrow Wilson, who was born in the South, proved hostile to black requests for equality, and soon segregation became official government policy in offices in Washington, D. C. When Monroe Trotter led a protest group to meet with Wilson, the two men became involved in an exceedingly angry confrontation. Mob violence was also on the increase. During the years from 1906 to 1920, race riots occurred in cities throughout the United States. In fact, the summer of 1919 was labeled the "Red Summer" by the poet, James Weldon Johnson, since riots took place in 25 different cities, leaving over 100 dead and many more injured. The NAACP organized marches to protest the violence.

This became another important part of the NAACP's role: to publicize the issues facing blacks. In order to accomplish this, DuBois founded *Crisis* magazine, which also provided a fo-

rum for the artistic expression of black writers. For several decades, it provided a voice of protest, celebration, and opportunity. *Crisis* magazine first published Hughes' "The Negro Speaks of Rivers" in 1921.

Critical Overview

As Hughes's first published poem, critics view "The Negro Speaks of Rivers" as the first indication of the poet's lifelong themes and concerns. Although most critics now praise his ongoing dedication to racial struggle, when *The Weary Blues,* was published in 1926, critical reactions were mixed. A number of reviewers, including black intellectuals, questioned whether Hughes's colloquial language and racial themes constituted propaganda or "real art," oversimplification or clear vision. Critics do not claim that "The Negro Speaks of Rivers" is particularly propagandistic, though it heralds a moralizing tendency in Hughes's poetry. This poem, moreover, is sometimes considered one of his lyrics, and lyrics are often considered non-political.

Critics regard this poem as a lyric because it has a first person speaker who expresses a strongly felt emotion and appears to exist outside of time. These critics note, however, that the "I" in the poem represents less an individual persona or Hughes himself than a mythic, collective persona. Several critics suggest that the lyric speaker of this poem begins with personal memory but moves steadily toward collective memory. Raymond Smith, in his essay, " *Hughes: Evolution of the Poetic Persona*," argues that in both early and later poems, Hughes "transforms personal experience and observations into distillations of the Black American condition." In his essay, "The Origins of Poetry in Langston Hughes," Arnold Rampersad similarly argues that "personal anguish has been alchemized by the poet into a gracious meditation on his race, whose despised ("muddy") culture and history ... changes within the poem from mud into gold." Rampersad also finds in the poem a traditional lyric concern with time and death. In *The Life of Langston Hughes, Vol. I,* Rampersad writes, "With its allusions to deep dusky rivers, the setting sun, sleep and the soul, "The Negro Speaks of Rivers" is suffused with the image of death and, simultaneously, the idea of deathlessness."

Critics often attribute the personal anguish Rampersad mentions to Hughes's anxieties about his father. Hughes wrote the poem on a train he took to visit his estranged father in Mexico. Crossing the Mississippi outside St. Louis, Missouri, his birthplace, Hughes recalled, "I looked out the window ... [and] began to think what that [muddy] river, the old Mississippi, had meant to Negroes in the past—how to be sold down the river was the worst fate that could overtake a slave ... Then I remembered reading how Abraham Lincoln had made a trip down the Mississippi on a raft, ... seen slavery at its worst, and had decided within himself that it should be removed from American life. Then I began to think of other rivers in our past ... " In this record of the poem's composition, Hughes reveals how a personal meditation was transformed through his associations into a meditation on collective racial identity and history, and how a lyric became an ars poetica, or artistic statement, for his career.

Criticism

Chloe Bolan

Chloe Bolan teaches English as an adjunct at Columbia College of Missouri extensions in Lake County and Crystal Lake, IL. She writes plays, *short stories, poems and essays and is currently working on a novel. In "The Negro Speaks of Rivers" by Langston Hughes, she interprets the poem as not only a black history lesson, but as a deeply felt and dignified tribute to those of African heritage.*

"The Negro Speaks of Rivers" is probably the most anthologized of Langston Hughes' poems. Although Hughes brought rhythmic innovations from jazz and the blues to his future poetry, this classic poem, written when he was only 18 years old, stands at the gateway of his entire body of work. In it is the beginning of his "affirmation of blackness," as critic Raymond Smith states in "Hughes: Evolution of the Poetic Persona" from *Modern Critical Views: Langston Hughes.*

The black man had been brought to American shores as a slave and his presence preceded the birth of the United States, but in those years of forced illiteracy when a slave was forbidden to read and write, no work of note dealt with his history. After being freed by Abraham Lincoln in the Emancipation Proclamation of 1863, his rights were squashed in the South under the Jim Crow laws. These blatant injustices dealt with separate but unequal drinking fountains, blacks sitting at the back of the bus, not being allowed into hotels except through the back door as employees, and innumerable other humiliations. In particular, the act of voting was made into such an obstacle course for black voters, most were discouraged from the ordeal. Those that weren't found themselves physically threatened. The liberal North harbored less but subtler prejudices that stifled black initiative. When Langston Hughes began writing, he devised his own emancipation proclamation, quoted in "The Black Aesthetic in the Thirties, Forties, and Fifties" by Dudley Randall in *Modern Black Poets:*

We younger Negro artists who create now intend to express our individual dark-skinned selves without fear or shame. If white people are pleased, we are glad. If they are not, it doesn't matter. We know we are beautiful. And ugly too. If colored people are pleased we are glad. If they are not, their displeasure doesn't matter either. We build our temples for tomorrow, strong as we know how, and we stand on top of the mountain, free within ourselves.

Despite this thrust toward individual black pride, pride of black heritage was a necessary element to "stand on top of the mountain." Hughes knew this on a personal level, since his father, of mixed race but always identified as black, despised the Negro and left the United States to become highly successful in Mexico. In fact, Hughes was

In the end, after a life of cruel hardship, the heavenly rewards come at death, at sunset. The black mother and her progeny, who never abandoned their spirituality but refined it into music, poetry, and dance, are now seen for their true value, revealed in the light as golden.

on his way there to ask his father for college tuition when he wrote this poem. Although Hughes would soon hate his father for his views, when he wrote this, his hatred had not surfaced yet. This poem was most likely an anticipated reply to his father's criticism. In that case, out of anxiety and suppressed anger, a positive and stately poem emerged.

"The Negro Speaks of Rivers" begins with the speaker's claim: "I've known rivers." Rivers suggest to us places of travel, exploration, discovery, and even settling down beside one. Then he expands the idea: he has "known rivers ancient as the world and older than the flow of human / blood in human veins." Now we are being transported back in time, not to man's ancient history, but to a time before man even existed, when the rivers alone existed. Yet these rivers mirror man because the water that flows in their channels is similar to the blood that flows in man's veins. Also, our speaker is giving us a sweeping overview, suggesting possibly the beginnings of life by presenting a picture of water, one of the essentials for life. At this point, also, we understand the speaker is not only speaking for himself, but for all Negroes.

In the second stanza, which is only a line, Hughes compares his soul to the rivers, saying it has the depth of a river. Decades after this poem was published, during the 1960s, "soul" became a term used to describe black music and black food. The implications were that this music and food

came from the deprivations the black man had to endure in an oppressive white society and, therefore, came from the soul.

In the third stanza, the speaker traces Negro history through rivers intimately connected with the evolution of those with African roots. He tells us he "bathed in the Euphrates River when dawns were young." The Euphrates and the Tigris in present day Iraq comprise a two-river system that creates what is known as the fertile crescent, land between these rivers that benefits from the waters overflowing their banks. Millennia ago, "when dawns were young," and the country was called Mesopotamia, this fertile soil allowed its people not merely to survive, but to flourish, and western civilization began here along with western writing. Also, according to Muslims, Jews, and Christians, the Garden of Eden existed nearby, a beautiful spot believed to be the Al-Qurah of today. Although the Negro race did not begin in the Middle East, due to Africa's proximity, an African could have bathed in the Euphrates in ancient times. Besides, African slaves were sold to countries in the Americas populated by Judeo-Christian Europeans, products of this Mesopotamian-born, Western civilization. So, by force, this background became the Negroes' background.

The next river mentioned is the Congo, the second longest river in Africa, which runs through the center of the continent. Hughes states in *A Pictorial History of Black Americans,* "that Africa not only gave the world its earliest civilizations, it gave the world *man.*" Africa has long been considered the birthplace of man, since the human bones excavated there are the oldest found. Here the speaker "built [his] hut" and was "lulled … to sleep," suggesting the idealized beauty and peace the Negro enjoyed in this earliest of Edens. Here, too, rich civilizations rose up in a world where man lived beside the lion and the elephant. Ironically, though, in the more recent past, tribes living along the Congo, and the Kongo tribe in particular, helped feed the slave trade. This kind of betrayal can only happen to those who are "lulled … to sleep" and unable to take action. The second interpretation does not contradict the first, but puts events into sequence and deepens the poetry.

The third river is the Nile, the longest river in Africa and one that flows through many African nations. But the speaker is referring to those places along the river where he "raised the pyramids above it." Those Africans who helped build the pyramids were the Nubians who had a respected role in Egyptian society as soldiers and traders. More importantly, Hughes states in *A Pictorial History of Black Americans,* that "[b]lack Pharaohs ruled Egypt for centuries and black Queen Nefertete [was] one of the most beautiful women of all time." Although Hughes might have wished to emphasize the Nile's glamour, the fact is, the whole of ancient Egyptian religion lauded death over life and focused on the pharaohs and their comfortable survival in the next world. Because of the pyramids, the Egyptians needed as much manpower as possible and enslaved those they captured to build their gigantic tombs. Still, this knowledge does little to detract from the glamour and, if anything, balances it with reality.

The last river mentioned is the Mississippi, the longest river in the United States, and one intimately connected to slavery. A slave sold down the river in Mark Twain's Missouri was doomed to an even worse fate than he was already living: Slavery was more entrenched in the deep South, escape to the free states was even farther away, and any slave sent down the river was not only leaving a familiar place, but family as well. However, the speaker "heard the singing of the Mississippi when Abe Lincoln went down to New /Orleans"; the river was "singing" because, according to legend, when the future president saw the horrors of slavery, he vowed to eliminate that institution from the country.

In the last half of that line, the speaker has seen the Mississippi's "muddy bosom turn golden in the sunset." On a physical level, the speaker as Hughes most likely saw that phenomena as he wrote the poem on a train crossing the river from Illinois to St. Louis, Missouri. Its muddy bosom connects it to the Negro mother who nurtured her babies despite the fact that they could be taken away from her at any time and despite the fact that some of their fathers were the white masters. In the end, after a life of cruel hardship, the heavenly rewards come at death, at sunset. The black mother and her progeny, who never abandoned their spirituality but refined it into music, poetry and dance, are now seen for their true value, revealed in the light as golden.

In the fourth stanza the speaker repeats the phrase that he has "known rivers," but now he broadens the image to include "[a]ncient, dusky rivers." This concludes our history tour and ties these rivers to the color of dusk, the magical color of twilight, and the color of the Negro. The Negro encompasses the African in Africa or on any other continent, and especially the African-American, Hughes' first audience.

What Do I Read Next?

- *The Crisis Reader: Stories, Poetry and Essays from the NAACP's Crisis Magazine* not only includes some of Hughes' work but also provides insights into the political, cultural, social thought of Black America in the first part of this century.

- This 1999 release of W. E. B. DuBois' *The Souls of Black Folk: Authoritative Text, Contexts, Criticism,* edited by Henry Louis Gates, Jr., provides an informative perspective for viewing DuBois' classic work.

- The 1958 Brazilier collection, the *Langston Hughes Reader,* includes some of Hughes' best work in all genres.

- *Let Nobody Turn Us Around: Voices of Resistance, Reform and Renewal, An African American Anthology* contains Hughes' "The Negro Artist and the Racial Mountain" as well as works by W. E. B. DuBois, Marcus Garvey, and several writers of the Harlem Renaissance.

- Hughes admired Carl Sandburg's poetry for its populist stance; Sandburg's *Complete Poems* are available in a Harcourt Brace edition.

- The *Portable Harlem Renaissance Reader* collects essays, memoirs, poetry, and fiction of the period, along with a brief but informative history.

The last stanza repeats the second stanza: "My soul has grown deep like the rivers." Now we understand more profoundly what the speaker means, for each of these rivers has nurtured the Negro and some have transported him as a slave. The final repetitions also add a rhythm to the poem, as if, after the flow of the first and third stanzas, like the river, this poem has arrived at its mouth, its place of proclamation to the world. These people, these Negroes, have come out of Africa, and later out of slavery, and they have flourished in the fertile crescent of their spirituality and contributed much to

> *Like Whitman in "Song of Myself," Hughes constructs a poem that not only connects the individual to the land, to particular geographical places but also to history and to a distinctive culture, making the poem, like the river itself, a vehicle by which one flows through one space into another."*

world civilization. Let them look back on a golden heritage, Hughes seems to say; let them speak of these rivers that are so much a part of that heritage.

Source: Chloe Bolan, in an essay for *Poetry for Students,* Gale, 2001.

Dean Rader

Dean Rader has published widely in the field of twentieth-century poetry. In his essay he explores the connections between Hughes and Walt Whitman.

In his poem, "I, Too," Hughes both implicitly and explicitly responds to the great poet of freedom and democracy, Walt Whitman. Hughes' opening lines recalls Whitman's "I Hear America Singing," "Still Though the One I Sing" and even *Song of Myself.* Hughes' poem suggests that he, the Negro, the "Other," can also sing of and for America. A similar notion is at work in Hughes' famous poem, "The Negro Speaks of Rivers." In this poem, Hughes invokes the technique and spirit of Whitman yet again in an attempt to write a lyric that carries both public and private significance. Like Whitman in "Song of Myself," Hughes constructs a poem that not only connects the individual to the land, to particular geographical places but also to history and to a distinctive culture, making the poem, like the river itself, a vehicle by which one flows through one space into another.

Perhaps the first formal signpost to Whitman is Hughes' use of the first person singular. Of course, poets have been using the first person for centuries, but Whitman and Hughes both use the lyric "I" in ways unlike other poets. For one thing, the "I" in the poems does not really stand for the literal, biographical human beings Walt Whitman and Hughes. In *Song of Myself,* for instance, Whitman writes early on that he is in "perfect health," but we know now that he was not always in particularly good health. In fact, he was often in poor health. And, it is unlikely that he literally sent his barbaric yawp over the roofs of the world, though he might have done a good deal of yelling. Similarly, the biographical figure, Hughes, did not build his hut near the Congo, as he says in the poem, nor did he participate in the construction of the pyramids in Egypt. In both poems, the poets use the lyric persona to let the individual stand for many, or, to be more precise, to stand for everyone. In line two of *Song of Myself,* Whitman writes, "And what I assume you shall assume / For every atom belonging to me as good belongs to you." In this poem, Whitman lays the groundwork for Hughes; he establishes the ability for the lyric "I" to stand for both the individual and society. So, in "The Negro Speaks of Rivers," when Hughes writes, "I bathed in the Euphrates," or "I heard the singing of the Mississippi when Abe Lincoln went down to New Orleans," he is not speaking autobiographically, he is speaking metaphorically. He has not done these things himself; he has done them through others. Through a poetic and cultural connection to these places and to history, he has participated in important events for African and African-American citizens.

This African and African-American thematic in "The Negro Speaks of Rivers," distinguishes Hughes' poem from Whitman's water poems and, for that matter, *Song of Myself.* Where Whitman's texts aggressively attempt to subsume all readers and certainly all Americans, Hughes' trajectory is more narrow. His poem rises out of a decidedly African-American concern. At no point in the poem does he mention Boston or England or Plymouth Rock. Instead, he positions the poem amidst an overtly African and African-American landscape, in particular, the rivers of Africa and the deep South. Hughes uses the metaphor of the river, of a river's origin, to comment on his own origin and the origin of black experiences across the globe. It is possible that Hughes is suggesting a kind of shared cultural memory—N. Scott Momaday, the great American-Indian writer, claims he has a memory of crossing the Bering Strait centuries ago—but more likely, he posits that he is part and parcel of every man from the Congo or every woman from Mississippi who has come before him. In other words, all past African and Africa American history has flowed and emptied into him, just as a river empties into the sea. He is the repository of their hopes, their dreams, their struggles, their pride, and their cultural heritage. Just because these individuals or even these societies no longer exist, does not mean that they are dead. They live on through the poet, through his voice and through his poetry. Additionally, the poem stands as a provocative testament to African-American culture-like the Mississippi, it will continue moving, progressing, growing.

This notion of growing, of thriving is important for Hughes, because he wants his poem to carry the same invigorating power as rivers themselves. In his important book *Structuralist Poetics,* Jonathan Culler discusses the importance of performative language on ancient and contemporary cultures. According to Culler, performative language is expression that makes things happen, that is performance itself. A great deal of early Native American poetry is an excellent example of performative language. For Native Americans, there was no distinction between poetry, spells, rituals and songs. All were one singular expression that animated the world and the gods. Many scholars have commented on how Whitman's long lists, his catalogs, resemble a chant or an incantation, emblematic of many Native-American songs. In "The Negro Speaks of Rivers," Hughes enacts a similar mode of communication. The repetition of "I've known rivers" gives the poem an otherworldly feel, as though it were a sacred text, perhaps biblical. Indeed, the "I've known rivers" refrain, and the chant-like list in the third stanza recall a psalm or a Christian litany or a gospel song. In his book *The Weary Blues,* the collection in which "The Negro Speaks of Rivers" appears, Hughes includes a section of poems called "The Feet of Jesus," which imitate gospel songs and Sunday morning preaching. Thus, his poem not only echoes the incantatory orality of pre-literate African cultures, but it also mirrors the incantatory orality of contemporary African American worship services, prayers, and songs. In both instances, and in the poem itself, the individual speaker participates in communal discourse, and mere language is transformed into something transcendent.

While Hughes' poem works on a cultural or spiritual level, it also works on a political level, just as many of Whitman's do. Also like Whitman, Hughes' poems are deceptively complex. On the surface, they seem easily accessible, perhaps even simple. But, in almost every instance, the poems carry a subtext of anger or resistance or outrage, yet, Hughes is able to make his vision palatable to white audiences. In an early review of *The Weary Blues,* Alain Locke claims that in this collection, there is "a mystic identification with the race experience which is, I think, instinctively deeper and broader than any of the poets has yet achieved." More than any other poem in the book, "The Negro Speaks of Rivers" embodies Locke's argument. In this poem, dedicated to the great African-American writer W. E. B. DuBois, Hughes grounds contemporary African-American culture in its regal culture of African history. Without question, whites and blacks are the target audience. He wants to remind both black and white readers of the rich and regal history of African Americans, and he wants to inform his black audience that his soul and their souls have been nourished by these experiences. That they, like each of the major rivers referred to in the poem will persist and endure, is one of Hughes' main themes for the piece.

Through his poetry, particularly *Song of Myself,* Whitman turns America into a kind of myth. He says in his introduction to *Song of Myself* that America is itself the greatest poem. Similarly, Hughes elevates the experiences and history of African Americans to the level of myth. The speaker, a sort of bard-like figure, constructs a worldview that offers a spiritual, physical, historical, and personal narrative, a timeless reading of the union of past and present realities. Through this poem, Hughes suggests that African Americans are themselves a great poem, a masterful epic, more sweeping, more powerful than the mere two hundred years informing the poem that is America. Without question, Hughes links the scope of the epic with the steadiness and vitality of the river with African American experiences, suggesting, in the final analysis, that all are connected. Water flows through Africa, through America, and as Hughes suggests in the first stanza, water courses through these lands as blood through the veins, linking both physical and spiritual humanity. According to R. Baxter Miller, Hughes creates a kind of myth that speaks to the generative force of black persistence: "Whether north or south, east or west, the rivers signify in concentric half-circles the fertility as well as the dissemination of life." Indeed, throughout the poem, through the anagogic river and metaphors of flowing and connection, Hughes reclaims America through its origins in Africa.

> *Part of him denies the relevance of Africa at all. The central force of the question in his refrain is rhetorical—"one three centuries removed" from his original homeland, how can Africa mean anything to him? But within Cullen's poem lies a different answer—for imaginings of Africa inhabit him, almost haunting him."*

Source: Dean Rader, in an essay for *Poetry for Students*, Gale, 2001.

Sarah Madsen Hardy

Sarah Madsen Hardy has a doctorate in English literature and is a freelance writer and editor. In the following essay, she compares Hughes' "The Negro Speaks of Rivers" to "Heritage," a poem by Hughes' Harlem Renaissance contemporary Countee Cullen.

Poets often use their poems to speak to each other across centuries and continents—and sometimes, just across town. Hughes and Countee Cullen were part of the same literary generation. Born within a year of each other, both poets found their way to Harlem, which was, in the 1920s, beginning to rise to fame as the vital and fashionable center of African-American art and culture. Both men are remembered as representatives of one of the most important American literary and arts movements, the Harlem Renaissance, which reached its height in the 1930s. However, these two black poets had very different views of race and art. While both promoted racial equality and progress for blacks through their art, Cullen drew on the largely British tradition of his formal schooling when he wrote. Hughes was also well educated, but he drew inspiration for his poetry largely from folk forms, in-

cluding, most notably, the African-American musical tradition of the blues. In this essay, I will compare two of their poems as part of a literary dialogue between the poets about the significance of Africa to African Americans—Hughes' first publication, "The Negro Speaks of Rivers" and one of Cullen's best known poems, "Heritage." The poems take up a remarkably similar theme, but their interesting differences in form and philosophy highlight the complexity of the question both poets pose: in Cullen's famous words, "What is Africa to me?"

In their poems, Hughes and Cullen take up the issue of the place of Africa in the mind and soul of the African-American poet. This was an important question during the Harlem Renaissance because, up until this point in American history, the only African Americans who were given any credit for serious artistic talent were those—like Phyllis Wheatley—who were adept at making use of white, European forms, despite their limited access and experiential connection to this tradition. The Harlem Renaissance actually began as an artistic movement of *white* artists who provocatively drew inspiration from supposedly primitive African and African-American art forms. Later in the movement, blacks began to claim these sources for their own artistic expression and use them toward more political ends. But in the early-and mid-1920s, when these poems were written, the status of black artists drawing on Africa for inspiration was still quite tentative. The poems present conflicting visions of Africa as a part of the African-American self and as a source of inspiration for the black poet.

"The Negro Speaks of Rivers" uses the central metaphor of the river to speak of a black history that flows fluidly from Africa to America. The speaker does not reflect Hughes as an individual, but rather his connection to a mythic and collective black soul. What makes such a collectivity possible is the powerful force of *shared* history. "Heritage" also addresses the relationship between Africa and America within the African-American self, but Cullen's vision is far less peaceful and continuous. He speaks individually and personally of a self divided, *cut off* from Africa by the forces of history. Part of him denies the relevance of Africa at all. The central force of the question in his refrain is rhetorical—"one three centuries removed" from his original homeland, how *can* Africa mean anything to him? But within Cullen's poem lies a different answer—for imaginings of Africa inhabit him, almost haunting him. Africa exists as a chaotic, passionate shadow force within his "civilized" poet's soul.

The idea of civilization is important to both Cullen and Hughes. In the Harlem Renaissance, whites celebrated the supposedly "primitive" (that is, natural, basic, and uncivilized) qualities of black culture because they were seen as rejuvenating a depleted, *over*-civilized Western culture. This put black artists in an awkward position, for they needed to prove themselves as artists capable of mastering the "sophisticated" European styles associated with civilization, but they at once wanted to draw on and bring value to their own cultural influences and traditions. Hughes' poem claims civilization from its most ancient as the birthright of the African American. He claims for blacks a proud legacy that dwarfs any achievements of the United States' one-hundred-fifty-year history, and even those of Europe. "I bathed in the Euphrates when dawns were young. / I built my hut near the Congo and it lulled me to sleep. / I looked on the Nile and raised the pyramids above it." In contrast, Cullen is torn by a familiar—and racist—dichotomy between (white/Western) civilization and (black/African) nature. There is a fascinating tension in his poem between its formal meter and rhyme scheme—which demonstrate the author's "civilized" discipline and respect for European literary tradition—and the powerful imagery of an imaged Africa, which speaks to the "wildness" in his soul: "So I lie, who all day long / Want no sound except the song / Sung by wild barbaric birds / Goading massive jungle herds, / Juggernauts of flesh that pass / Trampling tall defiant grass / Where young forest lovers lie, / Plighting troth beneath the sky." Hughes denies any such tension between civilization and nature. The river, a symbol of nature, has a dignity that makes small even the collective efforts of human civilization; it is "older than the flow of human blood in human veins." But the river is at once part of human history and civilization, carrying the speaker from ancient times to a chapter in American history that was, at the time Hughes wrote, still within individual memory. His form reflects this confidence and harmony. The poem uses repetition of phrases and structures in a manner similar to a song. Rather than adapting a European style to his own devices as does Cullen, Hughes draws on an oral culture that is both ancient African and contemporary African American. In doing so, he redefines what it means to be civilized to include the cultural traditions of Africa.

Closely associated with the question of the African-American's claim to civilization is the issue of the his relationship to a collective past. The relevance of history to African Americans was one of the issues debated among participants in the Harlem Renaissance. Some promoted the image of the New Negro, one that left behind the ignorance and humiliation of slavery and reinvented himself. The idea of a new man, one who leaves his history behind, is part of an American tradition dating from the Pilgrims and encompassing the many immigrant groups who came to the United States to start anew. In the case of African Americans, the history left behind is the ignoble past of slavery, wherein blacks were treated as animals in an ultimate stripping away of claims to civilization and selfhood. Cullen speaks from the position of the New Negro, asking, "What is last year's snow to me? / Last year's anything? The tree / Budding yearly must forget / How its past arose or set." The irony of the title "Heritage" is that it debates whether heritage really exists for African Americans and questions the extent to which it is a source of power.

The image of the New Negro was at odds, however, with the re-valuation of indigenous African and African-American art forms that also characterized the Harlem Renaissance. Once whites took an interest in jazz and African sculpture, they earned new cache as Culture. Though Hughes, like Cullen, studied British poetry, its influence is little in evidence in "The Negro Speaks of Rivers" or much of his other poetry. He both reclaims and redefines history for African Americans by turning away from European traditions and derogatory definitions of Africanness, instead valuing oral forms such as the blues. Admitting to none of the conflict over heritage that Cullen expresses, Hughes looks grandly upon a past that transcends the moment of slavery, referring to its horrors only as they came to an end, "when Abe Lincoln went down to New Orleans."

Both poets use water imagery to express the African-American's relationship to the past. Hughes speaks of rivers, and Cullen describes the primal beat of rain falling to evoke a primitive African self lurking within. Hughes' river flows strongly *forward,* carrying hope for the future, "its muddy bosom turn[ing] all gold in the sunset," but the sound of rain agitates Cullen, as it threatens to pull him *backward* into an obscure, imagined time before history: "From the unremittant beat / made by cruel padded feet / Walking through my body's street./ Up and down they go, and back / Treading out a jungle track. // ... In an old remembered way / Rain works on me night and day." Hughes proudly claims Africans as a historical people—a radical assertion in light of the predominant view of them as primitive and "timeless" propagated by Europeans. Cullen, in contrast, shows how this racist view has divided his consciousness and hindered his ability to draw power from his heritage. For him, Africa is "a book one thumbs"—one written by Europeans. The African heritage that Cullen portrays so ambivalently in his poem is ahistorical, while Hughes argues forcefully for the African-American's claim to a historical tradition—one that is not dependent on the Westernized mediation of book learning, but instead relies on a form of knowledge intrinsic to the black soul.

Though they address remarkably similar questions and concerns, the two poems can be understood as having different goals and, therefore, offering different visions. Hughes offers a representation of the black soul as strong and unified, despite the injuries done to it by the racism of the American context. Though his poem speaks of the past, Hughes's vision is focused on the future, when the devastation of slavery can begin to seem small in relationship to a long and proud historical tradition. "The Negro Speaks of Rivers" can be understood as a utopian vision, one that is located in an ideal and mythic "no place." Cullen's "Heritage," in contrast, offers a vision of the human struggle of his present context. The African-American soul that he portrays is not ideal, but real. It is torn and pained by racism, though not destroyed by it. Cullen is bent on using his art to show the struggle, while Hughes creates a poem in which the struggle has been overcome.

Source: Sarah Madsen Hardy, in an essay for *Poetry for Students,* Gale, 2001.

Sources

Baldwin, James, "Sermons and Blues," in *The New York Times Book Review,* March 29, 1959, p. 6.

Hughes, Langston, *The Big Sea,* Knopf, 1940, reprinted Hill and Wang, 1993.

Hughes, Langston, Milton Meltzer, and C. Eric Lincoln, "First, We Were Africans," in *A Pictorial History of Black-americans,* Crown Publishers, Inc., 1983, p. 7.

Jemie, Onwuchekwa, *Langston Hughes: An Introduction to the Poetry,* Columbia University Press, 1976.

Lacayo, Richard, "Blood at the Root," in *Time,* April 10, 2000, pp. 122-123.

Locke, Alain, review of *The Weary Blues,* 1927.

Mezu, S. Okechukwe, *The Poetry of Leopold Sedar Senghor,* Fairleigh Dickinson University Press, 1973.

Miller, R. Baxter, "Some Mark to Make": The Lyrical Imagination of Langston Hughes, *Critical Essays on Langston Hughes,* edited by Edward J. Mullen, G. K. Hall &, Co., 1986, p. 160.

Rampersad, Arnold, *The Life of Langston Hughes: I, Too, Sing America, Vol. I, 1902–1941,* Oxford University Press, 1986, 468 p.

———, "The Origins of Poetry in Langston Hughes," in *Langston Hughes,* Edited by Harold Bloom, Chelsea House Publishers, 1989, pp. 179-189.

Randall, Dudley, "The Black Aesthetic in the Thirties, Forties, and Fifties," in *Modern Black Poets,* edited by Donald B. Gibson, Prentice-Hall, Inc., 1973, p. 35.

Robinson, Cedric J, *Black Movements in America,* Routledge, 1997.

Smith, Raymond, "Hughes: Evolution of the Poetic Persona," in *Langston Hughes,* edited by Harold Bloom, Chelsea House Publishers, 1989, pp. 45-60.

For Further Study

Berry, Faith, *Langston Hughes: Before and Beyond Harlem,* Wings Books, 1996.
    An insightful portrait which traces the development of Hughes' literary career.

Gates, Henry Louis, Jr., and K. A. Appiah, *Langston Hughes: Critical Perspectives Past and Present,* Amistad, 1993.
    The collection includes a wide range of essays discussing Hughes' use of many different genres.

Hornsby, Alton, Jr., *Milestones in 20th Century African-American History,* Visible Ink Press, 1993.
    This work provides a brief yet clear picture of recent African American history.

Miller, R. Baxter, *The Art and Imagination of Langston Hughes,* University of Kentucky Press, 1986.
    Miller provides a detailed analysis of Hughes' poetry, discussing the theme of African heritage and its use in "The Negro Speaks of Rivers."

Mullane, Deirdre, ed., *Words to Make My Dream Children Live: A Book of African American Quotations,* Anchor Books, Doubleday, 1995.
    Quotes from Hank Aaron to Andrew Young are affirmations on achieving dreams.

Rampersad, Arnold, *The Life of Langston Hughes,* 2 vols., Oxford University Press.
    This very detailed biography discusses literary and social influences on Hughes' writing.

Out, Out—

Robert Frost
1916

"Out, Out—" was first published in the 1916 collection *Mountain Interval.* Both the description of a terrible accident and a comment on the human need to resume one's life after a tragedy, "Out, Out—" is one of Frost's most shocking and disturbing performances. Like many of Frost's poems, "Out, Out—" is written in blank verse, with the events described by an unnamed (yet characterized) speaker.

The poem is based upon a real incident. In 1901, Michael Fitzgerald, one of Frost's friends and neighbors, lost his son Raymond during an accident with a buzzsaw; after accidentally hitting a loose pulley, the saw descended and began cutting his hand. He bled profusely and was rushed into the house; a doctor was called, but the young man went into shock and died of heart failure.

According to Jeffery Meyers (author of *Robert Frost: A Biography*), Frost thought that the poem was "too cruel to read in public." For those readers who associate Frost with folksy, homespun philosophers observing the beauties of rural New England, "Out, Out—" will be something of a surprise—for the poem *is,* in a sense, cruel: the boy dies a terrible death and all the speaker can say is, "No more to build on there." Even more shocking is Frost's depiction of the adults who watch the boy take his final breaths. After his death, they "turned to their affairs" since "they / Were not the one dead." Ultimately, Frost suggests, this "turning away" from death is, sometimes, the only possible reaction.

Robert Frost

Author Biography

Robert Frost was born in San Francisco in 1874; his father, William, was a journalist and his mother, Isabel, was a schoolteacher. After William's death (from tuberculosis) in 1885, Frost's mother moved herself, Robert, and his sister, Jeanie, to the east, eventually settling in Salem, Massachusetts in 1886. Frost graduated as co-valedictorian of his high school class in 1892. (He shared this auspicious title with Elinor White, who he courted and eventually married.) Frost enrolled in Dartmouth College but did not complete his first semester. (The school eventually awarded him two honorary degrees.) After dropping out, he tried to persuade Elinor to marry him, but she wanted to first finish her studies at St. Lawrence University. Distraught, Frost left New England and roamed about Virginia's Dismal Swamp for a short time; Elinor managed to graduate in three years and married Frost in 1885. The couple had five children, although their lives were marked by tragedy: Elliott, their first son, died of cholera at the age of four; Marjorie, their youngest daughter, died after giving birth at the age of twenty-nine; Elinor died in 1938; their son Carol committed suicide in 1940; and their daughter Irma was committed to a psychiatric hospital in 1947.

The history of Frost's career as a poet is much more a story of success and triumph. His first published poem was "My Butterfly: An Elegy," collected in a little book of five poems called *Twilight* (1894) which Frost had privately printed. (He had only two copies made—one for Elinor and one for himself.) After an unsuccessful attempt at farming and struggling to have his poems read by a wider audience, Frost moved his family to England in 1912. It was there that Frost published his first two "real" books of poetry: *A Boy's Will* (1913) and *North of Boston* (1914). These books showed tremendous promise and were reviewed favorably by the American poet Ezra Pound.

In part because of World War I, Frost moved back to the United States in 1915 and continued to fulfill the promise of his first two books. In 1916 he published *Mountain Interval*, containing "Birches," "The Road Not Taken," and "Out, Out–." 1923 saw the publication of *West Running Brook* and *New Hampshire*, containing "Stopping By Woods on a Snowy Evening," and in 1924 Frost won the first of his four Pulitzer Prizes. Other collections followed: *A Further Range* (1936), *A Witness Tree* (1942), *Steeple Bush* (1947), and *In The Clearing* (1962).

Frost cultivated a public persona that his students, critics, and biographers have found, by turns, irritable, fascinating, and impenetrable—as the number of books on Frost's life and work makes clear. His most notable moment in the public eye was when he read "The Gift Outright" at the inauguration of John F. Kennedy in 1961. Frost died in 1963 two months before his eighty-ninth birthday. As household a name as any poet could hope to become, Frost enjoyed universal fame for both his cheerful observations and his dark, often disturbing, ambiguities. His *Complete Poems* appeared in 1967.

Poem Text

The buzz saw snarled and rattled in the yard
And made dust and dropped stove-length sticks of
      wood,
Sweet-scented stuff when the breeze drew across it.
And from there those that lifted eyes could count
Five mountain ranges one behind the other   5
Under the sunset far into Vermont.
And the saw snarled and rattled, snarled and
      rattled,
As it ran light, or had to bear a load.
And nothing happened: day was all but done.
Call it a day, I wish they might have said   10
To please the boy by giving him the half hour

That a boy counts so much when saved from work.
His sister stood beside them in her apron
To tell them "Supper." At the word, the saw,
As if to prove saws knew what supper meant,   15
Leaped out at the boy's hand, or seemed to leap—
He must have given the hand. However it was,
Neither refused the meeting. But the hand!
The boy's first outcry was a rueful laugh,
As he swung toward them holding up the hand   20
Half in appeal, but half as if to keep
The life from spilling. Then the boy saw all—
Since he was old enough to know, big boy
Doing a man's work, though a child at heart—
He saw all spoiled. "Don't let him cut my hand   25
            off—
The doctor, when he comes. Don't let him, sister!"
So. But the hand was gone already.
The doctor put him in the dark of ether.
He lay and puffed his lips out with his breath.
And then—the watcher at his pulse took fright.   30
No one believed. They listened at his heart.
Little—less—nothing!—and that ended it.
No more to build on there. And they, since they
Were not the one dead, turned to their affairs.

Poem Summary

Lines 1-3:

The poem begins with a description of the buzz saw that later "attacks" the unnamed boy. Frost personifies the saw, saying it "snarled and rattled." He also contrasts the harsh noise of the saw with the "sweet" scent of the wood that the saw cuts into pieces. This is the first of the poem's several contrasts (including serenity and violence, youth and adulthood, panic and calm, speech and silence, and, of course, life and death).

Lines 4-8:

Frost clarifies the setting in these lines: the action is occurring in rural Vermont, and from where the boy is working one can see five mountain ranges. This peaceful and picturesque sight, like the "sweet-scented" wood mentioned earlier, contrasts the horrors that are about to occur. The sun is setting and day is ending—as the boy's life will end at the conclusion of the poem. Frost reminds the reader of the saw's power by repeating the words "snarled and rattled."

Lines 9-12:

The speaker expresses his wish that someone—presumably an adult—would have told the boy to "Call it a day"; doing so would have prevented the accident. The speaker's wish raises the issue of the boy behaving (and eventually dying)

like a man, an issue that becomes more pronounced as the poem proceeds. A boy loves to gain a half hour and be "saved from work," but this boy did not (as the speaker hints) receive such a lucky reprieve.

Lines 13-18:

The section describes the accident as well as the speaker's attempt to make sense of why it happened in the first place. The image of the girl in an apron yelling, "Supper!" recalls the idea of the boy behaving like an adult—like her brother, she is helping with the chores and, in doing so, entering the world of adulthood. After her announcement, the speaker first suggests that the saw, in an attempt to show its intelligence, "Leaped out at the boy's hand." Again, personification is used to imply that the saw has a mind of its own. However, the speaker realizes that this is simply impossible, and qualifies his initial description of the saw's "leap" with the phrase, "or seemed to leap." His confusion over *why* such a thing happened increases in the next lines: "He must have given the hand. However it was, / Neither refused the meeting." Ultimately, all the speaker can conclude is that both the boy *and* the saw had a "meeting," which itself is an odd term, since "meeting" usually describes a meeting of people with other people, not inanimate objects. Thus, the speaker cannot wholly abandon the notion of the personified saw and, although he has already discounted such an idea (with "or seemed to leap"), he clings to it as one possible way to explain the boy's otherwise meaningless death.

Lines 19-22:

As the previous lines depict the speaker's reaction to the accident, these lines depict the boy's reaction. The reader learns that the boy's "first outcry was a rueful laugh"—a decidedly adult reaction combining immense sorrow, disbelief, and an ironic commentary on the situation. The image of the boy trying to keep his hand balanced on his arm "to keep / The life from spilling" contrasts that of the "Five mountain ranges one behind the other" first presented to the reader.

Lines 22-27:

After his initial panic, the boy becomes prophetic. (According to many old legends and mythologies, dying people could suddenly have visions of the future.) Since the boy is about to die a "man's" death, he is "old enough to know" that nothing will save him after losing so much blood.

Media Adaptations

- A double audiocassette set titled *Robert Frost Reads* was released in 1997 by HarperCollins Publishers.

- Another audio edition of Frost reading his work is *The Robert Frost Poetry Collection*, released in 2000 by Harper Audio.

- *The Poetry of Robert Frost* is an audiocassette featuring poems read by Carl Reiner and Susan Anspach. It was released in 1996 by Dove Audio.

The speaker recalls the idea of the boy's entering the world of adulthood when he calls him a "big boy / Doing a man's work, though a child at heart." The boy's pleadings to his sister—his only spoken words in the poem—reflect his age and create a sense of the pathetic nature of his death. The reader is moved, but the speaker seems cold: his reaction to the boy's plea is, "So. But the hand was gone already." This decidedly detached response reflects the speaker giving up his search for explanations for the accident. All he can say is, "So" (for the boy's expression of terror needs no explanation) and "But the hand was gone already." While the speaker earlier dwelled on the possibility of personification, he has now retreated into the world of facts. There is, ultimately, *nothing to say* about the boy's death other than the facts that led up to it.

Lines 28-32:

These lines describe the doctor's attempts at saving the boy and the boy's final breaths. The "dark of ether" into which the doctor guides the boy is like the underworld to which many mythological heroes journey—another of the poem's ironies. When told that the boy "puffed out his lips with his breath," the reader is invited to contrast this image with the earlier one of the boy running and yelling to his sister. Like all living things, he has moved from a world of noisy action to one of quiet stillness. Like the earlier statement, "But the

hand was gone already," the description of the boy's final moments is shocking because of the detached tone in which it is described: "Little—less—nothing!—and that ended it."

Lines 33-34:

The final lines reflect the speaker's turning wholly toward an attitude of detachment and seeming indifference. His final remark of how both the doctor and the family "turned to their affairs" seems callous and almost offensive (especially with he word "affairs," implying that they all began riffling through their social calendars)—but one must keep in mind that the language here is more figurative than literal. *Eventually* they "turned to their affairs," since there is simply nothing else for them to do. Since there is "No more to build on there" and "they / Were not the one dead," the adults must continue their lives, bereft of both the boy and any solid explanation for why he had to die such a terrible death.

Themes

Childhood versus Adulthood

"Out, Out—" concerns a boy who loses his hand—and then his life—in an accident involving a buzz saw with which he is working on a rural Vermont farm. The boy is initially portrayed as a "big boy / Doing a man's work." He is using the buzz saw in an attempt to behave in a grown-up way, as children will often become their parents' "little helpers" in an attempt to assert their independence and maturity. (This is what his sister is doing by wearing an apron and announcing "Supper" as if she is the matriarch of the family.) The fact that he is cutting wood with a buzz saw—truly a dangerous and "adult" piece of machinery—attests to his desire to be a "big boy," helping with the chores. Despite that fact, the boy would be pleased with having been given "the half hour / That a boy counts so much when saved from work," he continues sawing the wood for his family's stove, willingly contributing to the literal and figurative warmth of his home.

However, once the accident occurs, the boy begins figuratively "Doing a man's work" by *dying* like a man. In the second it takes the saw to "leap" at his hand, the boy enters an adulthood marked by violence, fear, and death. Although the boy wanted to behave like a "big boy," once the accident occurs, he betrays his age by crying like a terrified child:

"Don't let him cut my hand off— The doctor, when he comes. Don't let him, sister!"

His subsequent death is met with shock, for "No one believed" that such a random accident could so quickly snuff out the life of a boy. But these same adults eventually view the death in a way that shocks the reader: "And they, since they / Were not the one dead, turned to their affairs." This "turning away" from the boy is not literal, but metaphorical—adults know that grief must be controlled, lest it consume one's life. According to "Out, Out—," adulthood demands this kind of eventual response. A conclusion in which Frost described the sorrow of the parents, for example, would imply that their grief could never be abated—and although Frost is not implying that the parents' grief will only be a temporary feeling, he does suggest that, ultimately, all people "turn to their affairs" to some degree after a tragedy in order to resume their lives.

The Meaninglessness of Life

Upon learning of the death of his wife, Shakespeare's Macbeth remarks, "Out, out, brief candle" and compares human life to

> a tale Told by an idiot, full of sound and fury, Signifying nothing.

Macbeth sees life as a series of events tumultuous in themselves but not leading up to any greater theme or ideal. A tale literally "told by an idiot" would be contradictory and illogical—which is exactly how he views all human endeavor when he speaks these lines.

Frost's poem evokes Macbeth's pessimistic philosophy through its descriptions of the buzz saw, the boy's terror, and the adults when faced with the boy's death. The saw is, indeed, "full of sound" from the very first lines of the poem:

> The buzz saw snarled and rattled in the yard And made dust and dropped stove-length sticks of wood.

—and the personification is repeated when the speaker states

> And the saw snarled and rattled, snarled and rattled, As it ran light, or had to bear a load.

The "fury" of the saw, of course, is seen in its "attack" upon the boy, when it "Leaped out at the boy's hand, or seemed to leap." Similarly, the boy is full of "sound and fury," offering first a "rueful laugh" and then a series of pleas as he tries to prevent "The life from spilling" out of his arm.

All of this noise and motion, however, ultimately builds to no great event or insight on the part of the characters. The boy dies in a noticeably quiet moment ("They listened at his heart") and all the

Topics for Further Study

reader is told of this death is that there is "No more to build on there." Flights of angels do not sing the boy to his rest, nor do any of the adults pause to consider the tenuous nature of human life. The boy dies for *no reason at all* (for surely a self-aware saw is no real reason), and his death leaves the adults silent. The "sound and fury" of both the boy and the saw have "signified nothing," which accounts for the chilling effect of the poem's final lines.

Style

"Out, Out—" is written in blank verse: unrhymed iambic pentameter, which is five feet of one iamb (an unstressed followed by a stressed syllable) each. Of course, Frost varies the accented syllables throughout the poem to avoid having his speaker's voice become too regular and stilted; thus the poem is still in blank verse, but blank verse that is highly modulated to emphasize the importance of particular words and ideas. (The best examples of modulated blank verse are Shakespeare's plays.) An example of Frost altering the strict iambic pentameter to make the sound echo the sense occurs in the boy's pleadings to his sister:

> He saw all spoiled. "Don't let him cut my hand off—
> The doctor, when he comes. Don't let him, sister!"
> So. But the hand was gone already.

In the fist line above, Frost substitutes a spondee (two stressed syllables) in the second foot to emphasize the gravity of the boy's sudden recognition of his own death. Frost also dangles an extra syllable at the end of the line; the rhythm is therefore somewhat uneven, reflecting the boy's panic. The next line is regular blank verse (again with an extra syllable at the end); Frost lulls the reader back into the expected meter, only to upset him again with the next line, which begins with a trochee, adding more shock value to the speaker's comment ("So") before again resuming the expected meter. A reader with a sensitive ear can detect this kind of metrical variation in almost every line of the poem.

Frost also uses personification when describing the saw. Phrases like "snarled and rattled" emphasize the saw's apparent ferocity; the lines, "the saw, / As if to prove saws knew what supper meant, / Leaped out at the boy's hand, or seemed to leap—" reinforce the idea that the saw is a sentient machine, suddenly tempted into revealing its intelligence by "eating" the boy's hand. Ironically, the poem as a whole depicts a personified *thing* attacking a living boy—who, at the end of the poem, becomes as inanimate as the thing that seemed to attack him.

The poem's final couplet features a number of important metrical maneuvers. "No more to build on there" is strictly iambic, which creates the sense of the speaker citing some adage or easily-remembered piece of wisdom. The repetition of "they" reinforces the idea that the family is considering what to do with themselves now that the boy is dead—a major issue of the poem. In the poem's final line, Frost substitutes a spondee in the third foot, emphasizing the "one dead" about whom nobody seems to know what to say, as well as the verb "turned," which suggests a physical and emotional retreat from the horror at hand.

Historical Context

The assassination of Archduke Francis Ferdinand of Austria by a Serbian nationalist on July 28, 1914, was a shocking enough event—but no one alive at that time could have predicted the immense and terrible ramifications of this single act of violence. Ferdinand's assassination sparked World War I, a conflict so complex, bloody, and demoralizing that historians still debate some of its causes and long-term ramifications. The tensions leading to the war had been brewing for years, and when the war finally broke out, the Central Powers (Germany, the Ottoman Empire, Austria-Hungary, and Bulgaria) battled the Allies (England, France, Russia, Italy, and the United States) until the armistice was declared on November 11, 1918. (In total, thirty-two nations participated in the War.) The four years of fighting brought with them over thirty-seven million casualties, the deaths of approximately ten million civilians, terrible economic ruin for a number of nations, and, most ironically, the sparks (in the Treaty of Versailles) that would later ignite World War II.

The devastation brought by the war had an understandably large effect on European and American values and assumptions. Many people (artists and writers among them) saw the war as the end of an era—the end of a time where the world, for all its mystery, still made sense in fundamental ways. The scale of death that people witnessed during the war caused them to question their long-held beliefs about government, religion, and the horrors of which the human race is capable. England, for example, no longer seemed the Edwardian paradise many believed it to have been—now it was a ravaged nation, mourning the deaths of almost a million of its soldiers. (As William Butler Yeats wrote in "The Second Coming" (1919), "Things fall apart, the center cannot hold.") This doubting and questioning of "old world" values gave birth to the artistic movement known as *Modernism* a movement whose practitioners explored the decay of authority and the often-fragmentary nature of modern life. Modernist poets created new forms and broke with longstanding literary traditions. For example, T. S. Eliot's *The Waste Land* (1922) is a free-verse examination of hopelessness and despair; this wildly experimental poem is, in part, Eliot's portrayal of life after World War I. Other Modernist poets who employed experimental forms and techniques were Ezra Pound (whose *Cantos* were first published in 1917), Edgar Lee Masters (whose *Spoon River Anthology* appeared in 1915), D. H. Lawrence (whose *New Poems* appeared in 1918), and e.e. cummings (whose *Tulips and Chimneys* appeared in 1923).

Not all poets, however, embraced Modernist ideas and forms—the reading public was still en-

Compare & Contrast

- **1916:** World War I continues, with Germany declaring war on Portugal and Italy declaring war on Germany. The war will continue until 1918.

  1939: World War II begins when Germany invades Poland and Britain and France declare war on Germany. President Franklin Delano Roosevelt initially declares that the Unites States will remain neutral, but the U.S. enters the war in 1941 after the Japanese attack on Pearl Harbor. The war will continue until 1945.

  1990: Iraq invades Kuwait, prompting President George Bush to begin Operation Desert Storm and defeat the Iraqi Army in less than a year.

- **1915:** Robert Frost publishes *A Boy's Will* and *North of Boston,* his two groundbreaking books of verse.

  1943: Frost publishes *A Witness Tree* and is awarded the Pulitzer Prize.

  1961: Frost reads "The Gift Outright" at the inauguration of President John F. Kennedy.

  1963: Frost publishes *In the Clearing* and dies later this year.

- **1916:** Democrat Woodrow Wilson continues the first of his two terms as President; a Democrat will not be reelected to the White House again until 1933, when Franklin Delano Roosevelt begins his three terms.

  1963: Democrat Lyndon B. Johnson is elected President; his administration will be marked by the outbreak of the Vietnam War.

  1993: Democrat William ("Bill") Clinton elected President: after he completes two terms in office, his Vice President, Albert Gore, will run for President against Republican George W. Bush in one of the nation's most intense and explosive political contests.

- **1929:** "Black Friday" occurs on October 28 when the U.S. stock market collapses and ushers in the Great Depression, the worst economic disaster in U.S. history.

  1941: With the U.S. entrance into World War II, industry expands at great speeds, and the country is pulled out of the depression.

  1991: With the end of the Cold War and the subsequent phasing down of military spending, the U.S. enters a sustained period of prosperity.

---

amored with many "old-style" poets, such as Thomas Hardy, Rupert Brooke, Carl Sandburg, and Edwin Arlington Robinson. Poetry in English was thus at a turning point, with several of its practitioners demanding that a poet must (in Ezra Pound's words) "Make it new," while other poets focused on a world that seemed to exist only in their verse. It was in the midst of this artistic "Great War" that Frost entered the literary scene. He was forty years old when World War I began and had just published *A Boy's Will* (1913) and *North of Boston* (1914) in England. (These were published in the United States in 1915.) A reader who skims the surface of Frost's poetry may find him far from experimental, since many of his poems recall a seemingly idyllic life in rural New England—a pas-

toral paradise free from the terrors that had just gripped the globe. Such an opinion, however, falls flat when one considers that Frost's poetry is often a *combination* of traditional verse forms and the dark, ironic sentiments often found in Modernist works. In other words, Frost was able to explore modern fears with deceptively "traditional" settings, perhaps best seen in his conclusion to "Stopping by Woods on a Snowy Evening" (1923):

> The woods are lovely, dark and deep, But I have promises to keep, And miles to go before I sleep, And miles to go before I sleep.

As history would reveal, the modern world did, indeed, have "miles to go" before it took the rest it needed after the even greater war which was to begin in 1939.

Critical Overview

Since the publication of his first book (*A Boy's Will*) in 1913, Frost's reputation and worldwide fame grew tremendously, and his death in 1963 has done nothing to lessen the number of admirers his verse gains every year. When his poetry first began to be noticed, many readers and critics thought of Frost as a gruff Yankee philosopher—an image that Frost was very much responsible for cultivating. However, by the mid-1960s, critics began reassessing Frost's work and finding it much less simple than they first assumed. According to William Pritchard, author of *Robert Frost: A Literary Life Reconsidered,* "The popular view of [the poems] as essentially spirit-warming tributes to man and nature had been replaced by a presumably more sophisticated view of them as 'dark' parables rather, ironic meditations played out behind deceptively simple surfaces." Today, Frost is admired for his ambiguities and ironies more than for poems like "The Road Not Taken" and "Birches," which, although among his most famous, are generally thought to pale in comparison with darker poems such as "Home Burial," "Acquainted with the Night," and "My Desert Places."

"Out, Out—" has fared very well in the opinions of modern scholars. Pritchard praises it as "one of Frost's grimmer poems" not so much because of its subject as much as "the way its narrator provides no guiding tone of response—tragic or otherwise—to the event." Jeffrey Meyers, in his book *Robert Frost: A Biography,* calls "Out, Out—" "one of his greatest poems" but feels that its ending is not a figurative depiction of resuming one's life after tragedy; instead, he calls it a "bitter comment on the callous indifference to human suffering." Finally, in his book *Robert Frost: A Life,* Jay Parini calls "Out, Out—" one of Frost's "most affecting poems" because he "allows the poem to open into a complex and suggestive ambiguity" and "leaves a good deal of interpretive work for the reader to accomplish."

Criticism

Daniel Moran

Daniel Moran is a secondary-school teacher of English and American Literature. He has contributed several entries and essays to the Gale series Drama for Students. In the following essay, Moran examines the ways in which "Out, Out—" dramatizes, in an American setting, the ideas of the Shakespearean passage from which Frost took his poem's title.

The title of Frost's poem is an allusion to Shakespeare's *Macbeth,* the tragedy of a man who—prompted by his insatiable ambition—murders his king and several others who threaten his tenuous rule. Near the end of the play, Macbeth learns from a servant that the queen, his wife, is dead. After all of his scheming and surrendering to the most base and evil parts of his own nature, this news prompts Macbeth to utter one of Shakespeare's most sobering and pessimistic soliloquies:

> She should have died hereafter;
> There would have been time for such a word.
> Tomorrow, and tomorrow, and tomorrow
> Creeps in this petty pace from day to day
> To the last syllable of recorded time;
> And all our yesterdays have lighted fools
> The way to dusky death. Out, out, brief candle!
> Life's a walking shadow, a poor player
> That struts and frets his hour upon the stage
> And then is heard no more. It is a tale,
> Told by an idiot, full of sound and fury,
> Signifying nothing.

The death of his wife suggests to Macbeth the ultimate meaninglessness of his ambition and the folly of all ambition everywhere. Experience teaches us nothing, since the past only lights "fools / The way to dusky death." And although time seems to crawl for the duration of one's life, that same life can be snuffed out in an instant, as the flame of a candle burns brightly for hours but is extinguished in a second. This paradox causes Macbeth to ruminate on the meaningless of all human endeavor: ultimately, despite its "sound and fury," human life signifies "nothing." She "should have died hereafter"—in her old age—but has instead died now and reduced all of their ambition to dust.

The achievement of Frost's "Out, Out—" is that he replicates not the situation of Shakespeare's play, but the *feeling* of Macbeth when he learns about the death of his wife. Using his trademark locale (rural New England), Frost dramatizes Macbeth's manifesto of hopelessness in a distinctly American setting to explore the ways in which the thoughts of a defeated and solitary Scottish king are equally at home in a story of a Vermont boy who dies from a bizarre accident. While completing this difficult task, Frost also explores the way in which an innocent boy steps into the world of experience and adulthood, only to find that this world is a cruel and unjust place.

The poem begins with the saw having, literally, the first word—as it will figuratively have the last:

> The buzz saw snarled and rattled in the yard
> And made dust and dropped stove-length sticks of
> wood,
> Sweet-scented stuff when the breeze drew across it.

This saw is no mindless tool; instead, it attacks the wood like a pit bull, snarling and rattling as the boy feeds it. This hint of malice, however, is downplayed in these lines, since the saw is in the service of the family (making wood for their stove) and the sticks it creates are "sweet-scented stuff"; the alliteration adds to the "sweetness" of the wood (for the repeated *s* is sweet-sounding) and a word like "stuff" belongs in the mouth of a rustic observer, rather than a Shakespearean king.

The poem's setting also serves to downplay the initial ferocious sounds of the saw: "Five mountain ranges, one behind the other / Under the sunset far into Vermont" are not a besieged Scottish castle, but generic elements of an American pastoral. Still, the saw continues its steady barking:

> And the saw snarled and rattled, snarled and
> rattled,
> As it ran light, or had to bear a load.

The boy—the saw's master, in a sense—decides how hard the saw will work, and the saw keeps at its work. The repetition of "snarled and rattled, snarled and rattled," however, hints to the reader that everything can change—like Macbeth's marriage—in an instant. The mountain ranges are a beautiful sight, but the snarling of the saw adds a touch of menace.

The speaker's regret about the events he is about to describe colors his descriptions of what he *wishes* had happened moments before the accident:

> Call it a day, I wish they might have said
> To please the boy by giving him the half hour
> That a boy counts so much when saved from work.

These lines emphasize the boy's innocence: although he was using a buzz saw (a dangerous piece of "adult" machinery), he was, the speaker stresses, still a boy. "Call it a day" is a phrase used by adults to tell other adults to stop working; all the boy (any boy) really wants is another half hour in which to play. Later, the boy is described as a "big boy / Doing a man's work, though a child at heart," and the above passage underscores the boy's youth to make his eventual death more shocking and inexplicable. (Note that the boy's sister is also a child playfully pretending to belong to the world of adults, announcing "Supper" in her apron). While kids pre-

> *Using his trademark locale (rural New England), Frost dramatizes Macbeth's manifesto of hopelessness in a distinctly American setting to explore the ways in which the thoughts of a defeated and solitary Scottish king are equally at home in a story of a Vermont boy who dies from a bizarre accident."*

tending to be adults (by doing adult chores or wearing adult clothes, for example) are often viewed as cute, this boy's dabbling with adulthood proves deadly because adults *die* more often than children as part of the natural order of things.

When the accident occurs, the speaker cannot rationalize or even describe it in definitive terms. Frost replicates this observer's struggle to put the accident in a logical sequence of cause-and-effect:

> At the word, the saw,
> As if to prove it knew what supper meant,
> Leaped out at the boy's hand, or seemed to leap—
> He must have given the hand. However it was,
> Neither refused the meeting. But the hand!

The speaker can only offer an explanation of the accident based on the premise that the saw gained a moment of sentience and attacked the boy—but the speaker also knows that this is impossible, so he qualifies his explanation with "or *seemed* to leap" before admitting, "He must have given the hand" and that "Neither refused the meeting." The speaker is, in effect, doing with his description of the accident what humans often do when faced with an inexplicable event or an unexpected death: trying to find a reason, a cause, for what has occurred. The poem as a whole, however, suggests that for something like this accident there *is* no reason. All a person can say is, "But the hand!"—all an observer can do is proclaim his own shock. Thus, the initial personification of the saw

What Do I Read Next?

- Like "Out, Out—," Frost's poem "Birches" (1915) also explores the tension between the worlds of childhood and adulthood.

- Frost's poem "Nothing Gold Can Stay" (1923) explores the issue of transient beauty and (like "Out, Out—") the fleeting nature of all earthly things.

- "Home Burial" (1923), one of Frost's dramatic poems, depicts an argument between a husband and wife about the appropriate response to the death of their son.

- William Wordsworth's poem "A Slumber Did My Spirit Seal" (1800) depicts a man who once thought his lost love beyond "the touch of earthly years" and who attempts to grapple with her mortality.

- Dylan Thomas's poem "A Refusal to Mourn the Death, by Fire, of a Child in London" (1945) toys with the issues raised in "Out, Out—"; in it, Thomas explains the reasons for his *not* offering (what he calls) an "Elegy of innocence and youth."

- "Infant Innocence," a short poem by the late Victorian English poet A. E. Housman, treats the theme of an innocent youth figuratively devoured by the adult world.

- Naturally, a reader of "Out, Out—" will find a reading of Shakespeare's *Macbeth* (c. 1606) useful in understanding the forces that prompt Macbeth to make the statement Frost uses as the title for his poem.

- J. D. Salinger's novel *The Catcher in the Rye* (1951) has as its protagonist a teenager unable to cope with the death of his younger brother and, in a larger sense, with the encroachment of adulthood upon his innocent self.

---

is, in a sense, a lie—an attempt (as above) to offer some rationale for the boy's death.

Unlike the speaker, momentarily entangled in explanations, the boy reacts in a childlike and frantic manner that reflects his youth and inexperience in a world where things happen for no reason at all:

> The boy's first outcry was a rueful laugh,
> As he swung toward them holding up the hand
> Half in appeal, but half as if to keep
> The life from spilling. Then the boy saw all—
> Since he was old enough to know …

In this one instant, the boy crosses into the realm of adulthood, where he is no longer innocent of the world's random cruelty. His "rueful laugh" is a fleeting attempt at self pity, his balancing of his hand on his arm is a fleeting attempt at self-preservation, but still the boy "saw all." He knows what is to come, but retreats back into childhood for a final plea:

> "Don't let him cut my hand off—
> The doctor, when he comes. Don't let him, sister!"

The boy's biggest problem here is not saving his hand but saving his life; symbolically, he is also begging his sister to let him stay in the realm of childhood.

By this point, the tone of the speaker has changed from one of outrage to one of seemingly cold objectivity:

> So. But the hand was gone already.
> The doctor put him in the dark of ether.
> He lay and puffed his lips out with his breath.

The "So" signals a change in the speaker's attitude toward his subject—for what *can* an observer say about the boy's pleadings? "He pleaded well?" "His cries made me feel sorry for him?" Perhaps—but ultimately, all that one *can* say is "So," just as all Macbeth can say is, "Out, out, brief candle!" "The hand was gone already" reflects the speaker's succumbing to the reality of what is happening, as the boy is about to succumb to the effects of his "life … spilling." Entering "the dark of ether" is like a journey to the underworld, and the boy's earlier frantic cries are contrasted by his inability to speak: all he can do is puff "his lips out with his breath." Once "full of sound and fury," the boy's voice is now "signifying nothing."

The poem ends with the speaker growing more indifferent, although this indifference is more philosophical than literal:

> And then—the watcher at his pulse took fright.
> No one believed. They listened at his heart.
> Little-less-nothing!—and that ended it.
> No more to build on there. And they, since they
> Were not the one dead, turned to their affairs.

The boy's death is described in the most generic and unadorned language: his pulse slows, "and that ended it. / No more to build on there." One might expect the speaker to evoke the passion of Dylan Thomas's "Do Not Go Gentle Into That Good Night," in which he commands his dying father to

> Rage, rage, against the dying of the light!

—but Frost's mission here is to replicate the *lack* of passion felt by Macbeth upon learning of his wife's death. "That ended it" and "No more to build on there" are phrases in which the speaker stands slowly shaking his head with his palms upturned and his eyebrows raised. The speaker, an adult, has already learned about the inability of any words to explain why this boy had to die. As with, "However it was, / Neither refused the meeting," the speaker can only fall back on indifference—but this indifference is more of a philosophical stance than a literal lack of concern: the doctor and the boy's family (collected under "they" in the last sentence) return to their lives, "since they / Were not the one dead." This may strike readers as uncaring and cold, but only if these same readers do not realize that Frost is describing an *eventual* "turning" to their affairs. Over time, "they" return to their own lives, since there is nothing they can say or do to bring the boy back or even explain why he had to be snatched from them in the first place. The endorsement of this attitude—that the world is a place where random events sometimes destroy the innocent for no good reason—is a part of growing up, which is why, after finishing the poem (and even dwelling on it for a long, long time), the adult reader himself will, eventually, turn to *his* affairs as well.

Frost's achievement, therefore, is manifold: he applies the philosophy of a fictional Scottish king to a fictional Vermont boy, suggests that the acceptance of such a philosophy is part of growing up, and finally illustrates the philosophy's truth

through the reaction of the very reader to whom he is presenting these ideas. "You are shocked, I know," thinks Frost. "But eventually, your shock will subside, you'll stop trying to rationalize the event, and see that, in a very real way, Macbeth was right." "Out, Out—," both the phrase and the poem, are about all there is to say about a death for which there is no explanation.

Source: Daniel Moran, in an essay for *Poetry for Students*, Gale, 2001.

Bill Wiles

Bill Wiles teaches and writes in the shadow of Vermont's Green Mountains. He has sat in the very chair from which Robert Frost taught scores of students at the Bread Loaf School of English. In this essay, Wiles explores the tension between the pastoral landscape and the realities of rural life.

The state of Vermont publishes a quarterly magazine known as *Vermont Life*. On either its front or back cover, readers will invariably find a photograph of a farm scene. The house is almost always white, the barn almost always red. If the season is winter, readers see a field of untrammeled snow. If the scene is autumn, the path filled with fallen leaves appears untrodden. Spring or summer photos usually portray immaculate fields or breathtaking sunsets. Rarely will the reader be treated to depictions of rutted roads, rusted pickup trucks, or manure piles. The reality is that visitors to Vermont farms are more likely to see those scenes that do not make the cover of *Vermont Life*. In many of his poems, Robert Frost tackles this tension between the perfect world of the magazine photographer and the hard-bitten reality of life on a rural New England farm.

In "Out, Out—," Frost places the action in what might be termed a picture postcard setting worthy of *Vermont Life*, but suggests that the people who live on this farm may be just too busy with the day-to-day business of survival to admire the view. The visual brilliance of the sunset and the five mountain ranges contrasts with the drab, common dust and sticks of the boy's chore of cutting wood for the stove. The pleasing odor of the newly sawn wood as it is borne by the breeze clashes with the onomatopoetic snarling and rattling, snarling and rattling, snarling and rattling of the buzz saw. The work of the day, uneventful as it is, has intruded on the idyllic rural scene. But, even here, the day's labor is coming to an end; the boy's sister calls "them" (suggesting others besides the boy are doing necessary chores) to the evening meal. It

> *The pleasing odor of the newly sawn wood as it is borne by the breeze clashes with the onomatopoetic snarling and rattling, snarling and rattling, snarling and rattling of the buzz saw."*

looks as though the next scene will be the large family gathered around the sturdy table sharing a meal of simple yet hearty fare.

Frost is unwilling to continue this pastoral scene, and uses one of his more confusing transitional lines: " … the saw / … / Leaped out at the boy's hand, or seemed to leap—" Jay Parini in *Robert Frost: A Life* states that "perhaps the saw was animate and malicious." Also, Parini suggests that Frost has made the world of technology "ominous, even rapacious," a reaction against the industrialization of farming.

This contrast between the postcard view of the opening six lines outlines the tension the romantic notion of living in the country at the beginning of the twentieth century and the harsh realities of farm life before rural electrification, radio, paved roads, telephone, and other modern conveniences. Livestock died from a variety of ailments and problems. So too did many of the human inhabitants as well, young and old. Disease, sickness, and accidents took their toll. Communicable diseases, such as influenza, hit rural pockets of New England very hard. Children were especially vulnerable. Entire families perished. It would be easy for a lesser poet to surrender to despair.

Frost, however, turns his attention to those who remain, even as the boy's blood spills onto the rocky New England soil. Frost notes the sister, the doctor, the "watcher at [the boy's] pulse," and they who "were not the one dead." Frost is sometimes taken to task for this seeming indifference on the part of the survivors, but the idea fits squarely with the way of life on the farm. Cows have to be milked; animals have to be fed and watered; wood still has to be cut for the stove. Donald Grenier in

Robert Frost: The Poet and His Critics mentions the observations of Radcliffe Squires from *The Major Themes of Robert Frost:* "'Out, Out—' show[s] the human watchers experiencing normal griefs and yet convinced that life's more important task is to keep living …"

It is the boy's immediate reaction to the accident that piques the reader's interest. Parini describes the "rueful laugh" as a "familiar Frostian note" where both the reader and the boy see the irony of the boy's fate. Everything—the boy's life, the family unit, as well as the boy's hand—is ruined ("spoiled"). There is little room for a boy who cannot "pull his weight" in the subsistence economy of a rural farming, "circumstances are such," Parini states, "that an extra 'hand' is essential for survival."

Another personage haunts the entire poem— the speaker of the title words, Macbeth. Frost appears to compare Macbeth's expression of futility to the boy's rueful laugh. There are, however, marked differences in the two views of existence. Macbeth sees only the "sound and the fury" of life. His own "vaunting ambition" clouds his ability to accept responsibility for the present death of Lady Macbeth, the deaths of Duncan, Banquo, and the family of Macduff, and his own impending death. The boy, on the other hand, sees his own value to the family and community plummet to nothing when he loses his hand. He can no longer contribute; his role shifts in an instant from worker to liability. His death, in a practical way, saved the family and small community from carrying a nonproductive member. "No more to build on there …" Macbeth lives in a universe where nothing is what it seems. ("Fair is foul; foul is fair / Hover through the fog and filthy air.") What appears beautiful on the surface has a center filled with ugliness. The boy inhabits a world where the natural beauty of the New England mountains and the hazards of farm work exist side by side. One has a reality that is carefully hidden and concealed; the other exhibits a painful reality cheek by jowl with sweet-scented breezes and a mountain sunset.

Source: Bill Wiles, in an essay for *Poetry for Students*, Gale, 2001.

Aviya Kushner

Aviya Kushner discusses Robert Frost's poem "Out, Out—"and how its often subtle references to the Bible *and Shakespeare's* Macbeth *inform the reading of this poem, emphasizing its more serious and darker tones.*

Although Robert Frost would later in his life become a farm owner, a husband and father, and a four-time winner of the Pulitzer Prize in poetry, his life was often marked by struggle, beginning with the early death of his father and the untimely deaths of his own children. Frost achieved wide acclaim and popularity not only with academic critics, but with the American public. Frost was even honored as the nation's Poet Laureate, reading at the inauguration of John F. Kennedy. When Frost died, Kennedy said: "His death impoverishes us all; but he has bequeathed his nation a body of imperishable verse from which Americans will forever gain joy and understanding."

Several decades after Frost's death, one notes in his work the dueling influences of success and hardship. On the surface, Frost's poems are about apple-picking, birches, and putting up fences—the daily activities of a peaceful country existence. But there is a darkness rumbling beneath the lines, and the ugly side of the human heart is well-chronicled in Frost's seemingly bucolic, quintessentially American poems.

"Out, Out—" is one of Frost's most chilling poems. The title is a quotation from the last act of Shakespeare's *Macbeth,* when Macbeth says:

> To-morrow, and to-morrow, and to-morrow
> Creeps in this petty pave from day to day
> To the last syllable of recorded time,
> And all our yesterdays have lighted fools
> The way to dusty death. Out, out, brief candle!
> Life's but a walking shadow, a poor player
> That struts and frets his hour upon the stage
> And is then heard no more. It is a tale
> Told by an idiot, full of sound and fury,
> Signifying nothing.

Readers familiar with *Macbeth* can immediately catch Frost's hint at inevitable death and the swiftness of human life.

Frost's poem begins ominously. They saw "snarls and rattles, snarls and rattles," alluding to both the sounds of anger and the sounds of a snake. "Rattle" may recall the snake in the Garden of Eden, who was a main cause for the ejection from Paradise and the loss of initial innocence. What's more, the snake in the Biblical story is the instrument of betrayal, and thus the poem's first line subtly introduces the idea of callousness toward humans' fates.

The second line's mention of "dust" again brings up the Biblical idea of originating from dust and returning to dust. The opening three lines are memorable also thanks to Frost's mastery of the music of English. These lines have a distinctive sound that mimics the objects they describe.

The word "So," all alone in a sentence captures the hopelessness of the situation. The doctor merely walks in and numbs the boy. But suddenly—and this is a poem about sudden twists of fate—something changes ... "

"The buzz saw snarled and rattled" uses the "s" and "r" sounds of a saw cutting wood, and shaving the strips to dust. The alliteration continues with "dust" and "dropped," followed by "stove-length sticks" and "sweet-scented stuff."

While the opening three lines focus on sound and smell, the fourth line finally addresses sight. The "and from there" emphasizes that the visual description is coming last:

> And from there those that lifted eyes could count
> Five mountain ranges one behind the other
> Under the sunset far into Vermont.

This juxtaposition of "lifted eyes" and "mountain" recalls the Psalms:

> I lift mine eyes unto the mountain
> From whence will come my help?

After the depiction of the mountain ranges and the sunset, the original sawing sound returns. "And the saw snarled and rattled, snarled and rattled." The ominous tone of the poem returns too, tempered by: "Nothing happened." The speaker then interjects:

> Call it a day, I wish they might have said
> To please the boy by giving him the half-hour
> That a boy counts so much when saved from work.

This line hints that disaster is on its way instead of the respite for which the boy might so appreciate. Here is where the speaker shows an understanding of the ways of the country—a half-hour means so much to a child.

The sister—a new character—comes out in an apron and announces that supper is ready, as she might have done countless times before. But on this day everything changes. Instead of the boy and the other men coming home to a nice meal, the day quickly changes because "the saw leaps out." Here again the Bible peeks through, as the sudden leap of a sharp object recalls Abraham's attempted sacrifice of his own son, or in the prophetic writings, Yiftach's actual sacrifice of his own daughter.

The saw jumps. There is some confusion, and the speaker admits it with "however it was." It is unclear to the reader what is happening, which parallels the confusion of the characters in the poem. The jagged grammar mimics that confusion, particularly with:

"But the hand!"

The boy's first response is a "rueful laugh," but then the boy holds up the injured hand, both for help, and to prevent the massive loss of blood. The boy suddenly realizes what has happened, and what will happen:

Then the boy saw all—
Since he was old enough to know, big boy
Doing a man's work, though a child at heart—
He saw all spoiled.

With "all spoiled," it may appear that the boy is about to live life as a cripple. He then speaks for the first and only time in the poem:

Don't let him cut my hand off—
The doctor, when he comes. Don't let him, sister!"

This disjunction in language—first "him," then the explanation of doctor, mirrors the confusion of the actual accident, when what exactly happened was unclear. The sister is begged to prevent the inevitable. And then the speaker explains:

So. But the hand was gone already.

The word "So," all alone in a sentence captures the hopelessness of the situation. The doctor merely walks in and numbs the boy. But suddenly—and this is a poem about sudden twists of fate—something changes:

And then—the watcher at his pulse took fright.
No one believed. They listened at his heart.
Little—less—nothing! And that ended it.

"That ended it."—the boy's life ends with that phrase. The preceding description—"little, less, nothing"—neatly and frighteningly sums up the life lived. The boy was a child, or "little." With his hand gone, he was "less." And then, with his pulse gone, he was "nothing."

No more to build on there. And they, since they
Were not the one dead, turned to their affairs.

The last lines return to the manual labor and construction tone of the poem's opening. This time,

though, there is nothing left to build in that spot. While the final line suggests that there are other "affairs" to turn to, it is also a condemnation, with no separation between the behavior of relatives and strangers. Living is what people continue to do after a death. The only ones who truly stop are the dead themselves. Frost may have realized that despite the ending of some lives, the survivors must go on. The living can only "build on" from there.

Source: Aviya Kushner, in an essay for *Poetry for Students*, Gale, 2001.

Sources

Frost, Robert, *The Poetry of Robert Frost*, Holt, Rinehart and Winston, 1969.

———, *Robert Frost's Poems, with an Introduction and Commentary by Louis Untermeyer*, Washington Square Press, 1971.

Grenier, Donald J., *Robert Frost: The Poet and His Critics*, American Library Association, 1974.

Meyers, Jeffrey, *Robert Frost: A Biography*, Houghton Mifflin Company, 1996.

Parini, Jay, *Robert Frost: A Life*, Henry Holt and Company, 1999.

Pritchard, William H., *Frost: A Literary Life Reconsidered*, Oxford University Press, 1984.

For Further Study

Frost, Robert, *Poetry, Plays, and Prose*, The Library of America, 1995.
This is the definitive edition of Frost's work, featuring all of his individual books of poetry plus ninety-four uncollected poems (seventeen published for the first time). The volume also contains a generous sampling of Frost's letters and forty-five pages of notes concerning publication dates and textual variations.

Parini, Jay, *Robert Frost: A Life*, Henry Holt and Company, 1999.
Of the many biographies of Frost, Parini's is the most recent and certainly one of the most accessible, having been praised by numerous critics for its readability and insight into an often misrepresented figure.

Pritchard, William, *Lives of the Modern Poets*, University Press of New England, 1980.
Pritchard's book is a collection of studies of poets ranging from Thomas Hardy to William Carlos Williams. The chapter on Frost, while not dealing with "Out, Out—" specifically, is still an engaging overview of Frost's career and poetry.

The Phoenix

Howard Nemerov
1950

"The Phoenix" concludes Howard Nemerov's second collection of poetry, *Guide to the Ruins.* Its plainspoken and flat tone, its short lines, and its subject matter of death and rebirth perfectly suit an end poem. It is not only the final poem in this book; Nemerov felt so strongly about the poem's tone of finality that he also used it to close his popular 1960 collection *New and Selected Poems.* "The Phoenix" is sparse, ominous, and frightening, calling forth a dead world of mythological beasts and powers of which humans no longer are able to conceive. Ironically, for a poem that conjures up such a sense of foreboding and finality, the poem is one of the few in the book that does not end with a period—it just fades away, letting its final utterance (the word "Word") resonate in the reader's mind.

Author Biography

Born in 1920 in New York City, Howard Nemerov lived his early life in the city, and attended the exclusive Fieldston School—where he was a fine student and an excellent athlete—before matriculating at Harvard. After graduating from Harvard in 1941, Nemerov enlisted in the Royal Canadian Air Force, then in the Eighth U.S. Army Air Force in England. He was discharged in 1945. Immediately after the war, Nemerov and his English wife lived in New York City, where Nemerov wrote *The Image and the Law,* his first collection of poems, but they

Howard Nemerov

Poem Text

The Phoenix comes of flame and dust
He bundles up his sire in myrrh
A solar and unholy lust
Makes a cradle of his bier

In the City of the Sun   5
He dies and rises all divine
There is never more than one
Genuine

By incest, murder, suicide
Survives the sacred purple bird   10
Himself his father, son and bride
And his own Word

soon found themselves in need of money and Nemerov took a job teaching English at Hamilton College in upstate New York. In 1948, Nemerov left Hamilton and began teaching at Bennington College in Vermont, where he stayed until 1966, at which point he moved to Brandeis University near Boston. In 1969, Nemerov began teaching at Washington University in St. Louis, and made St. Louis his home for much of the rest of his life.

By 1948, Nemerov had begun writing in earnest. After *The Image and the Law* in 1947, he published a novel, *The Melodramatists,* in 1949, and then *Guide to the Ruins,* the collection in which "The Phoenix" appears, in 1950. Over the next decades, Nemerov continued to teach, to write poetry, fiction, and criticism, and to win the respect of his peers. He has won numerous prizes, grants, and fellowships, most notably the Consultancy in Poetry at the Library of Congress in 1963-1964, a Guggenheim Fellowship in 1968-69, an Academy of American Poets Fellowship in 1970, election to the American Academy of Arts and Letters in 1976, and the Pulitzer Prize for his *Collected Poems of Howard Nemerov* in 1978. In 1988, he was named Poet Laureate of the United States. Nemerov died in 1991. His papers are housed at Washington University.

Poem Summary

Stanza 1:

In the first stanza of the poem, the narrator introduces the topic of the phoenix. The phoenix is a mythical bird, originally appearing in Egyptian mythology but taken from that tradition by the Greeks and then the Romans. The bird, as described in the first stanza, "comes of flame and dust." According to the myth, the phoenix is born out of the funeral pyre of its father, and in this stanza Nemerov's narrator notes that it "bundles up his sire in myrrh" and "makes a cradle of his bier," or resting place.

Stanza 2:

The second stanza continues the description of the phoenix, and places the phoenix in a metaphysical context. The bird rises "all divine" "in the City of the Sun." The reader does not know what this means—what and where is the City of the Sun? What does it mean, specifically, that the bird is "divine?" He is also "genuine," a word that has come to be attached almost exclusively to commercial products. What, the reader asks, does it mean that the bird is "genuine?" Is the poet somehow being ironic?

Stanza 3:

The final stanza portrays the phoenix as an entirely self-sufficient being. He is his own primary cause—"himself his father, son and bride"—and the continuance of his race is ensured through means that humans consider abhorrent—"incest, murder, suicide." At the end of the poem, the narrator compares the phoenix to God Himself, for like God, the phoenix is self-sufficient. The doctrine of the Trinity holds that God the Father and God the Son are of one substance, and many theologians argue that the Holy Spirit—the third constituent of the Trinity—is in fact the Word: as the Gospel of John says, "In the beginning was the Word, and the Word was with God, and the Word was God." Although many commentators have remarked on the similarity between the myth of the phoenix and the story of God and Jesus, here Nemerov brings the idea of the Word into this equation—and, by omitting the period at the end of the stanza, he also suggests the illimitable, atemporal nature of God.

Themes

Myth

"The Phoenix" is based largely on the Egyptian myth of the phoenix. In that myth, the phoenix is a bird that lives for hundreds of years, only to sacrifice itself in fire at the end of its lifespan. From that fire, a new phoenix is born. Only one phoenix can exist on earth at a time. The phoenix has traditionally represented rebirth, because it self-propogates. The myth of the phoenix also manifests humans' ongoing fascination with fire—like another mythological beast, the salamander, the phoenix is actually comfortable in fire.

In addition, Nemerov emphasizes the self-sufficiency of the bird—it does not need a mate in order to reproduce. In this, the bird is like God, who created his own son out of his own substance. Nemerov emphasizes this aspect of the bird's life cycle in his line, "Himself his father, son and bride." He also notes that the bird "bundles up his sire in myrrh," and myrrh, a type of incense popular in the Middle East in ancient times, is often associated with the story of Jesus' nativity. In this, Nemerov melds the Christian myths of the Trinity and immaculate conception with the Egyptian and Classical myth of the phoenix.

Cruelty/Violence

In "The Phoenix," Howard Nemerov emphasizes the cruel and violent nature of ancient myths. The phoenix has always represented a frightening aspect of nature, born out of fire and dying in self-generated fire. But Nemerov focuses on the more primal themes of the phoenix myth: the violence of the bird's birth and death and the autosexuality of its regeneration. Using such language as "unholy lust," "incest, murder, suicide," and "cradle of his bier," the poet underscores how the terms of human morality do not apply to the phoenix.

Topics for Further Study

- What other literary or artistic works make use of the image of the phoenix? Research the history of this mythological bird. What has it symbolized over history? How has it been used?

- Egyptian culture first used the image of the phoenix. How did the phoenix function in Egyptian mythology? What are other elements of Egyptian mythology? Research the pantheon of Egyptian gods and on the creation myths of Egypt.

- Howard Nemerov takes the form, line, and rhyme scheme of this poem partially from the well-known American poet Emily Dickinson. Who was Emily Dickinson? What did she write about? What elements of her poetry are discernible in Nemerov's own poetry? You will have to read more of Nemerov's poetry to answer this question.

Style

"The Phoenix" is written in three stanzas in a fairly regular rhythmic pattern. Each stanza contains four lines; the first and third lines and the second and fourth lines rhyme. Moreover, each line is a self-contained entity. Although the poem has no punctuation, most of the lines are grammatically complete sentences and could end with a period: "The Phoenix comes of flame and dust," for example, or "There is never more than one." Unlike the free-verse forms that dominated American poetry in the 1940s and 1950s, the regular lines in this poem do not spill over, grammatically or conceptually, to the next line. Instead, the lines each make a complete statement and express a complete idea.

Nemerov uses the rhythm of each line, as well as the structure of the stanzas, to establish the meaning of the poem. The lines are based on iambic tetrameter—each line containing four iambs, or poetic "feet," that consist of one unstressed and one stressed syllable. Iambic pentameter (five iambs per line) has traditionally been the preferred line in

Compare & Contrast

- **1950:** U.S. President Harry S Truman is embroiled in the Korean War. This conflict, sparked when Communist-led North Korean troops invaded South Korea, was never an "official" war, only a "police action." An armistice was signed by the belligerents in 1953.

  2000: The armistice between North and South Korea is still in effect, but North Korea, led by the dictator Kim Jong Il, continues to behave erratically and unpredictably. Although a famine has gripped the nation for years, the North Korean government continues to spend a great deal of its money on armaments. In addition, the country is the only Stalinist-style totalitarian state left on the planet today. American officials fear Kim's unpredictability and suspect that he is attempting to acquire nuclear weapons.

- **1950:** Spurred by the massive industrial production needed at the end of World War II, the American economy is booming. Returning soldiers share in this prosperity, and as a result of government programs and a healthy private sector, more families are able to own homes, own cars, and go to college than ever before.

  2000: The American economy is entering its tenth consecutive year of rapid growth, and largely as a result of the burgeoning computer industry (a field in which the U.S. leads the world), prosperity seems endless.

- **1950:** Joseph Stalin, the Soviet premier, rules his country with an iron fist and challenges the U.S. for world cultural and military supremacy. After his death, his successor, Nikita Kruschev, will let the world know of the extent of Stalin's brutality.

  2000: Russian leader Boris Yeltsin retires, and his hand-picked successor Vladimir Putin takes over. Russia's transition from a state-run communist economy to a "free-market" capitalist economy has been difficult, and the Russian people have suffered great economic hardships. At the same time, a small group of people have enriched themselves by purchasing state-owned properties at bargain prices. The U.S. fears for Russia's stability.

English for long poems, verse dramas, and epics—Renaissance sonnets, Milton's *Paradise Lost,* Wordsworth's *The Prelude,* and of course most of Shakespeare's drama is in iambic pentameter. Iambic tetrameter, by contrast, has been a popular line in short lyric poetry for centuries. Alternating rhymed lines of iambic tetrameter and iambic trimeter (three feet) create a sing-song effect—Emily Dickinson and Wordsworth both wrote in this form, and many popular songs (think "The Yellow Rose of Texas") use the form.

Stanzas exclusively of iambic tetrameter, however, give poems a slow, contemplative feeling. Iambic pentameter is approximately the length of most English sentences, and thus iambic pentameter sounds like "real" speech. Iambic tetrameter, though, is slower and shorter than "real" speech. It makes the poem sound careful, precise. With the subject matter here, it also makes the poem sound ominous and foreboding. The rhymes (in an ABAB CDCD EFEF pattern) are not emphasized; some, such as "myrrh" and "bier," are less direct rhymes than they are "slant," or almost, rhymes. However, the rhymes work to tighten the stanzas, to link the lines together, and in this they counteract the isolating, slowing rhythm of the iambic tetrameter.

Historical Context

In 1950, poetry was a major issue in the public arena. Ezra Pound, one of the most famous English-language poets in the world, was confined to a Washington, D.C. mental hospital, having been found mentally unfit to stand trial on treason charges. During World War II, Pound had made broadcasts on Italian state radio, and many people felt that this was a treasonous act. (Pound argued that the content of his broadcasts was never determined by the Fascist authorities.) Disgraced, depressed, and shamed, Pound seemed to have departed the public eye, perhaps for good.

But that year, Pound published the latest installment of his long poem, *The Cantos.* This book, called *The Pisan Cantos,* because much of it had been written while Pound was incarcerated in an Army detention camp in Pisa, Italy, won the first Bollingen Prize for Poetry, an award sponsored by the Library of Congress. Immediately a furor was sparked. How could Pound be given an award for a book of poetry that, on its first page, mourns Mussolini? How could a traitor be given an award by the same government that had so recently wanted to execute him?

The controversy soon stopped focusing on Pound and became a debate about the proper way to look at poetry, or art in general, and about what the relationship of art and politics should be. The Bollingen judges defended their decision, saying that the aesthetic value of the book was their only criteria. Others, such as the poet and critic Robert Hillyer, shot back that it was impossible for vile political sentiments not to detract from a book's aesthetic value. Hillyer, writing in the *Saturday Review of Literature,* argues that a new poetic orthodoxy, epitomized by T.S. Eliot, wanted to make poetry hermetic, closed, and to take it out of public life by drowning it in obscurity. Hillyer's "common-sense" approach to poetry came under fire by both leftists and right-wingers, who felt that art must be given leeway to examine and express all political opinions.

In the midst of this controversy Nemerov began his career as a poet. Nemerov's early reviewers notes how his work demonstrates the influence of Eliot and, to a lesser extent, of Pound, but at this time it would have been hard to find a poet who was not influenced by these poets. Nemerov was as much influenced by Allen Tate or W.H. Auden as he was by Eliot. Nemerov's poetry, seen in retrospect, was actually rejecting the modernist models set forth by Pound and Eliot and the school of criticism (known as the New Criticism) that argued for the superiority of modernism. Instead, Nemerov looked to the past for his inspirations. Using rhyme (which was almost unknown among the modernists) and regular stanza form, Nemerov rebels against the orthodoxy of the avant-garde.

The Pound-Eliot orthodoxy ruled the American poetry scene for decades, largely because the most influential cultural critics and literature pro-fessors had grown up in the era when Pound and Eliot were revolutionizing the literary world. Nemerov, who has never gained the respect that other, more modernist-influenced poets have enjoyed, combined many of the innovations of modernism with a look back to traditional forms of verse. In this, he prefigures many poets of today, such as John Ashbery, Charles Wright, and W.S. Merwin.

Critical Overview

Although he had a great deal of success and became a very prominent poet, Howard Nemerov never has been a great favorite of academics, and as a result today he is not much read. Part of the problem is that Nemerov bucked trends: at a time (the 1940s and 1950s) when T.S. Eliot's and Ezra Pound's brand of literary modernism and experimentation dominated the world of English poetry, Nemerov looked back to traditional forms and regular rhythms. Nemerov did not reject modernism in the way that other poets—Peter Viereck, for instance, or Philip Larkin—did. However, neither did Nemerov fully embrace modernism's allusiveness, difficulty, and radical experimentation.

"The Phoenix" appeared in Nemerov's second collection of verse, *Guide to the Ruins.* Critics have responded to Nemerov's poetry with appreciation but rarely with eagerness or enthusiasm. The prominent reviewer Vivienne Koch, writing on *Guide to the Ruins* in the *Sewanee Review,* remarked on Nemerov's extensive poetic ambitions and said that he "is diligent, and explores with considerable ingenuity the possibilities of a great many traditional forms." "I should guess that Mr. Nemerov will eventually prove a worthy contender for high honors among the poets of his generation," Koch added. But she is not entirely positive about his book: "he has not entirely mastered his influences," she feels. But ultimately, she sees Nemerov as a talented, if limited, poet. "While I do not think," she concludes, "we can expect any enlargement of the capacity for sensuous appreciation … his sincerity and his sharp intellectual control will, no doubt, reap their proper increments."

I.L. Salomon, writing for the *Saturday Review of Literature,* is even less positive about Nemerov, and echoes, in harsher terms, some of Koch's criticisms. Nemerov "suffers from poetic schizophrenia," he says, because Nemerov imitates not the best aspects but the worst that his "masters ([T.S.] Eliot, [W.H.] Auden, [Allen] Tate) have imposed on a generation of poets." Salomon criticizes Ne-

> *It is a disturbing story, really, rooted in the violence and foreignness of the ancient world. Like the ancient gods, the phoenix "comes of flame and dust" and is both born out of and consumed in fire."*

merov for a lack of discipline: "too many [poems] lack the discipline of the writer's art. Good pieces are marred by a slovenly intrusion of slang and awkward phrase, and fail, since Mr. Nemerov's ear dares not be true to an authentic impulse. He slights accent and rhythm for the sake of being fashionable." Nemerov's "schizophrenia," according to Salomon, derives from the fact that he "must be modern and his modernity consists also of a studied carelessness of expression … it is incredible that a skillful poet would knowingly obtrude such haphazard writing on the public. In the name of modernity, it is done by design."

Other critics share Salomon's and Koch's ambivalent attitude about *Guide to the Ruins*. The *Hartford Courant's* Morse Allen remarks that "Mr. Nemerov in his disorder has produced these poems, and anyone who wishes to share in his disgruntledness should read them." In the New Haven *Register*, J.P. Brennan notes that "Nemerov is too often carried away by his subject matter." The poet and critic David Daiches, writing for the *Yale Review*, finds "a curious emptiness … generalized imagery which does not appear to be wedded together by a dominating vision … Too many of the poems lack a burning core to mould the pattern and imagery of the whole into a compelling shape." Will Wharton of the St. Louis *Post-Dispatch* deplores the poems' "uniformly querulous and carping tone," and in the *New Leader*, Harry Smith admonishes Nemerov for "an academic mastery of the superficial techniques of modernism does not insure good or interesting poetry."

"The Phoenix" itself has not received a great deal of attention. However, one critic, Julia Bartholomay, writing in her 1972 study of Ne-

merov entitled *The Shield of Perseus*, argues that the poem is about "the idea that words, besides being denotative and connotative, are also reflexive, being about themselves." She compares the poem to Shakespeare's "The Phoenix and the Turtle" and concludes that "the two visions of the universe [Nemerov's and Shakespeare's] are able to correspond, despite the differences in the poets' lenses, because of the bifocal nature of imagination."

Criticism

Greg Barnhisel

Greg Barnhisel holds a Ph.D. in American literature. In this essay, he discusses how Nemerov frames his depiction of the phoenix so as to emphasize the transcultural nature of the myth.

Originating in the mythology of ancient Egypt, the figure of the phoenix was adopted by the Greeks and the Romans, and as a consequence became a part of the Western cultural tradition. In his short, simple poem about "The Phoenix," Howard Nemerov retells the story of the phoenix, but in his retelling he emphasizes the paradoxical nature of the story. Although this story has persisted for millenia, Nemerov suggests, and although the story has been transmogrified into other, similar stories (especially the Christ story), it is in fact a terrifying story, profoundly other to our tradition and to the values that our culture holds. Nemerov even uses the form of his poem—its rhythm, construction, and rhyme—to allude to one of his predecessor poets who, like the figure of the phoenix, brought forth the strangeness and foreignness at the roots of our beliefs.

According to the *Encyclopedia Britannica*, the mythical phoenix was a bird, as large as an eagle, with a brilliant gold plumage and a beautiful cry. Only one phoenix existed on earth at any one time, and the bird had a tremendously long lifespan of no less than five hundred years. When its death came near, the bird built a bier, or a funeral pyre, of aromatic branches, spices, and other precious combustibles. It then threw itself on the fire and was consumed. From the ashes a new phoenix arose, which would embalm its father/predecessor in myrrh and bring the ashes to Egypt's 'Heliopolis,' or the City of the Sun, where the ashes would be placed on the altar of the sun. (The bird, not coincidentally, was associated with sun worship.) The *Encyclopedia Britannica* notes, as well, that "a variant of the story made the dying bird fly to He-

What Do I Read Next?

- In the first century A.D., the great Roman poet Ovid compiled an anthology of retellings of myths that he entitled *The Metamorphoses.* This book contains renditions of almost every famous myth known to the classical world, and does include, albeit in passing, a mention of the phoenix myth. Even though the book does not feature the phoenix prominently, it eminently merits reading.

- Nemerov discusses his own poetic practice and the ideas behind it in *Figures of Thought: Speculations on the Meaning of Poetry and Other Essays.* In this collection, Nemerov discusses, in his characteristically prickly prose, the philosophical and conceptual bases of his poetry. Particularly interesting in this anthology is the domination of the figure of Wallace Stevens, a poet who, by the 1970s, had displaced Eliot and Pound as the most influential American poet of the twentieth century.

- Nemerov won the Pulitzer Prize for his 1977 *Collected Poems of Howard Nemerov.* The book brought together all of the major works of a poet who had, by that time, been practicing for thirty years, and forced many readers to confront this difficult-to-pigeonhole writer as a major force in postwar American poetry.

- Nemerov is at times associated with a group of earlier poets known as the Objectivist school. Although he cannot be securely categorized as an Objectivist, he does share many of their concerns—most specifically, a belief that poetry must be grounded in the objective material reality of the real world and a concern with the complications inherent in sensory perception of the world. Other poets who are often called Objectivist include William Carlos Williams (a good collection of his is the *Selected Poems*), George Oppen, and Louis Zukofsky.

---

liopolis and immolate itself in the altar fire, from which the young phoenix then arose."

As well as being associated with sun worship (a cult that was very powerful in ancient Egypt as well as in Greece, where it was associated with the god Apollo), the phoenix was associated with immortality. Romans and the Roman state religion during the Imperial period compared the bird, arising from the ashes, to the myth of Rome's founding by Aeneas, who fled the ruin of Troy. The phoenix's immortality also appealed to Roman mythmakers, and consequently the phoenix appeared on Roman coins.

Nemerov's poem recounts these traditional attributes of the phoenix almost verbatim. The bird "comes of flame and dust," being born in a fire. "He bundles up his sire [i.e., father] in myrrh," the narrator continues. "In the City of the Sun" the bird "dies and rises all divine." The bird has no other parentage than himself: "himself his father, son and bride." In Nemerov's version, the bird is purple, not gold, however; the poet perhaps does this to emphasize both the phoenix's regalness (purple is

the traditional color of royalty) and bring it closer to Christian color symbolism, in which purple is one of the five colors prescribed by the early church, used especially during Lent, Advent, and at funerals.

Because of its connotations of immortality and its presence in late Roman culture, the phoenix came into the Christian iconological tradition. Like Christ, the phoenix is reborn from an apparently ignominious and irretrievable death. Also like Christ, the phoenix partakes of the mystery of the Trinity, for he is both the same as and different from his Father. Where the Trinitarian doctrine holds that Christ and God (and the Holy Spirit) are of one substance and are separate, the phoenix both is and is not constituted of his father—he is born from his father's ashes but is somehow separate from them. The fact that the phoenix's birth is accompanied by myrrh, a fragrant tree resin used by ancient Middle Easterners to make perfume, also connects it with the Christ narrative: at the Nativity, the Magi brought the infant Jesus gold, frankincense, and myrrh.

Nemerov, by combining language that alludes to the Christian tradition with the details of the story that are most violent and pagan, underscores to the reader the strangeness of the phoenix myth. It is a disturbing story, really, rooted in the violence and foreignness of the ancient world. Like the ancient gods, the phoenix "comes of flame and dust" and is both born out of and consumed in fire. The worship of the sun and the reverence of fire permeate the myth, and are entirely other to the monotheistic mind. The bird, the third line of the poem tells us, is motivated by "a solar and unholy lust." This line could not be a more explicit rejection of the Christian tradition, evoking sun worship and the "unholy." Moreover, in the final stanza the frightening actions of the phoenix—"incest, murder, suicide"—are noted as the very means by which the bird survives.

But as we have seen, the bird just as aptly represents many facets of the Christian narrative, and the language Nemerov chooses echoes the simple, Anglo-Saxon-derived vocabulary of the King James Bible. Such words as "cradle," "myrrh," "he dies and rises," "himself his father, son, and bride," and the mysterious mention of the "Word," all point to the story of Jesus as different from and consubstantial with the Father. But, the poet asks us to consider, how can we reconcile these profoundly different worldviews? The original phoenix myth centered on sun worship, immortality, and the power of fire, whereas Christianity emphasizes the worship of a single omnipotent God, who grants immortality. As we look at the poem more closely, the strangeness and residual paganism of Christianity comes clear. If the Phoenix "comes of flame and dust," does not God do so, as well, when he appears in the form of a burning bush to Moses in the desert? The linking of cradle and bier in the final line of the first stanza suggest the teleological nature of the Christ story—he really is born solely to die in order to bear sins away. The Trinitarian resonances of the phoenix story are clear, as well.

Subtly, then, Nemerov wishes to draw out the pagan roots of Christianity by telling this profoundly disconcerting story and sing the kind of language and images that readers familiar with the Christian tradition cannot help but catch. In this, Nemerov's poem has some important similarities with the work of another poet who delved into the strangeness at the heart of Christianity. The nineteenth-century American poet Emily Dickinson wrote hermetic, off-kilter, and immensely deep and resonant poems that were suffused with the language of the King James Bible. Her verse explored questions of death, of holiness, and of humans' relationship to the divine, but did so obliquely and quietly.

Unlike a religious poet such as Gerard Manley Hopkins who exhorted, pled, and extensively questioned in his work, Dickinson pared down her religious thought, loading up small words with extraordinary amounts of meaning in much the way that Nemerov does here. Nemerov takes Dickinson's emblematic line—the iambic tetrad—and uses it to explore the same questions that preoccupy Dickinson. He even goes so far as to imitate one of her most typical stanzaic constructions: a four-line rhymed stanza in which the final line is significantly shorter than the previous three (which have, generally, either been alternating iambic triads and tetrads or all iambic tetrads). These stanzas drift off disturbingly, for the rest of the lines give us a sense of rhythm that is betrayed in the final line, and Nemerov uses his final lines for precisely the same effect—the final words hang in space. Much as Dickinson does when she uses the language of "old-fashioned religion" to talk about the strangeness of life and the omnipresence of death, Nemerov uses Biblical language and structural allusions to Emily Dickinson to evoke the links and disjunctures between Christianity and the pagan tradition that preceded it.

Source: Greg Barnhisel, in an essay for *Poetry for Students,* Gale, 2001.

Jeannine Johnson

In the following essay, Jeannine Johnson outlines Nemerov's unique theories about poetry and examines his rather routine treatment of the phoenix as a general symbol of renewal.

Howard Nemerov was a much celebrated poet, winning the National Book Award and the Pulitzer Prize for his 1978 *Collected Poems* and receiving the Bollingen Prize, awarded by Yale University, in 1981. He also served, from 1988 to 1990, as the third poet laureate of the United States. Nemerov has been praised by some critics for his commitment to aesthetic perfection and for his insights into the ways that poetry links observation (or "seeing") and knowledge (or "saying"). However, since his first volume of verse, he has also been dismissed by others as unoriginal, unspontaneous, and unfeeling, an example of the worst type of the so-called "academic" poet.

Critical reaction to *Guide to the Ruins* (his second verse collection and the text in which "The

Phoenix" first appeared) is indicative of the controversy that followed Nemerov throughout his career. Vivienne Koch, in her review "The Necessary Angels," applauded Nemerov's "ingenuity" and "sharp intellectual control." I. L. Salomon, on the other hand, was less generous in "Corruption and Metaphysics," calling Nemerov "A university wit [who has] stifle[d] his considerable gifts by exploiting not the excellence but the defects his masters (Eliot, Auden, Tate) have imposed on a generation of poets."

Whatever professional readers might have believed, for Nemerov, thinking and feeling were not so easily distinguished, and in poetry, at least, they were not independent operations. He opens his essay "Poetry and Meaning" with a definition of poetry: "What I have to say to you is very simple; so simple that I find it hard to say. It is that poetry is getting something right in language, that this idea of rightness in language is in the first place a feeling, which does not in the least prevent it from existing." Nemerov implies that poetry reveals fundamental truths, and he argues that we intuit poetry's accuracy about these truths rather than consciously recognize them.

Nemerov was himself more successful in his mature poems than in his earlier ones at getting something right in language. Most, though by no means all, critics agree that Nemerov's skills as a poet improved markedly over the first two decades of his career. Part of his improvement came as he began to explore an ever-increasing range of subjects, forms, and emotions. However, even though he was more than what the title "academic poet" would suggest, Nemerov was at his best when he remained true to his philosophical roots, allowing sensation to arrive through intellectual inquiry. For instance, in "The Measure of Poetry," a prose poem from 1975, Nemerov compares poetry to an ocean wave and confides that "It is the power, not the material, which is transmitted."

"Because You Asked about the Line between Prose and Poetry" stands as an even more compelling reflection on the nature of poetry. In this poem, published in 1980, Nemerov likens sparrows to snowflakes and snowflakes to poems, and he identifies the boundary between prose and verse as follows: "There came a moment that you couldn't tell. / And then they clearly flew instead of fell" (*Sentences*). Although Nemerov wrote novels as well as poetry, he still found it difficult to name the difference between the literary genres. Instead, he offers through his metaphor the idea that poetic lan-

> " *Nemerov's delicate use of rhyme anchors the elusive concept which he tries to articulate, and the rhyme also provides an example of the way in which poetry does not tumble forth passively like prose, but instead is arranged more actively and deliberately.* "

guage "flies" while prose "falls," and declines to elaborate further. Nemerov's delicate use of rhyme anchors the elusive concept which he tries to articulate, and the rhyme also provides an example of the way in which poetry does not tumble forth passively like prose, but instead is arranged more actively and deliberately.

Some of the rhymes in "The Phoenix"—such as "myrrh" / "bier"—are similarly elegant and provocative; but some—like "Sun" / "one" and "bird" / "Word"—are more remarkable for their predictability. Perhaps this is appropriate, in so far as the predictable rhymes may parallel the regular cycle of the life and death of the phoenix. This legendary creature and its deeds are detailed in a particularly useful account composed by the ancient Greek historian Herodotus. In his *Histories,* written in the fifth-century B.C., Herodotus provides documentation of a "sacred bird ... the phoenix; I have not seen a phoenix myself, except in paintings, for it is very rare and visits the country (so they say at Heliopolis) only at intervals of 500 years, on the occasion of the parent-bird. To judge by the paintings, its plumage is partly golden, partly red, and its shape and size is exactly like an eagle. There is a story about the phoenix which I do not find credible; it brings its parent in a lump of myrrh all the way from Arabia and buries the body in the temple of the sun. To perform this feat, the bird first shapes some myrrh into a sort of egg as big as it finds, by testing, that it can carry; then it hollows the lump out, puts its father inside and smears some more myrrh over the hole. The egg-shaped lump is then just of the same weight as it was originally. Finally it is carried by the bird to the temple of the Sun in Egypt. Such, at least, is the story."

As he often does, Herodotus honors the stories of his ancestors and does his best simply to relay information passed on to him from previous sources. However, he cannot resist commenting on the story's credibility, and, though he refuses to say that the bird is an imaginary being, he nevertheless manages to reveal his doubts as to the reported activities of the phoenix. Of course, what is most important for poets such as Nemerov is not whether the bird ever existed but what it symbolizes. For thousands of years, authors have written about this mythical bird of Arabia that represents self-sacrifice, destruction, and renewal. The phoenix consumes itself in flames, and then rises from its own ashes. As Nemerov puts it, the bird "Makes a cradle of his bier," or creates from the place on which his coffin lies (his "bier) a site for his birth (his "cradle"). When he has come to life, the poet tells us, echoing Herodotus, that the phoenix "bundles up his sire in myrrh." The bird anoints its father with this fragrance and carries him to the "City of the Sun," or Heliopolis.

Nemerov's treatment of this old myth is not terribly original, but, in context, it is purposeful. "The Phoenix" is the last poem in the collection *Guide to the Ruins*, published in 1950. The volume opens with the title poem in which Nemerov introduces the idea of reconstructing myths which have been "broken" and "dishonored" by time and disuse. In this poem he suggests that in order to make our way through the present, we should revisit the past. However, we can never return to a previous time, and what comes to us as history is always incomplete, corroded, and even corrupted. Nemerov continues through other poems to investigate a variety of themes, but his interest lies primarily in ancient stories and legendary figures, and the issue of decay recurs, especially in so far as it is brought about by conflict and war.

The backdrop of war is important, for when Nemerov arrives at the end of his book, we are thereby prepared for the renewal that the phoenix's self-sacrifice makes possible. The "solar and unholy lust" refers to the bird's encounter with the sun: in most versions of the phoenix myth, it kills itself by flying too close to this solar orb, immolating itself in the heat and flames. This deed is "unholy" because it involves self-injury. But it is also necessary, and from this act the phoenix "dies

and rises all divine." Nemerov adds that "There is never more than one / Genuine," which is to say that the new bird is only born when its parent dies. The bird is "Himself his father," confirming a fundamental connection between disintegration and regeneration: for it is only when one phoenix dies that another can live. The promise of rebirth makes death less fearsome, and, though Nemerov does not emphasize this, the fact that the phoenix is reborn renders it a symbol of immortality.

Though the traditional colors of the phoenix are red and gold, Nemerov refers to the bird's plumage as "purple." This is the color of royalty, and, more importantly, it is the color of sacrifice. Christian imagery seems to resonate in the final stanza when Nemerov speaks of the phoenix as "Himself his father, son and bride / And his own Word." However, Nemerov, who was Jewish, is likely suggesting a more broad application of these ideas. The phoenix is itself a pre-Christian figure, and the "Word" may signify poetic language in general. Furthermore, the bird "By incest, murder, suicide / Survives." In other words, there is no single kind of suffering that it represents, and thus the phoenix offers hope for recovery without limits and, by extension, hope for discovery of the sort made possible by poetry.

Source: Jeannine Johnson, in an essay for *Poetry for Students,* Gale, 2001.

Sean K. Robisch

Sean Robisch is an assistant professor of ecological and American literature at Purdue University. In the following essay, he focuses on Nemerov's use of the mythological in "The Phoenix."

Every five hundred years, according to the myth, a great bird rises from the ashes of its dead progenitor. Maybe the sire of the bird was its mother or father; maybe the bird gives birth to itself; in some versions of the myth, both are true. It was called *semenda* in ancient India, *bennu* in ancient Egypt, and was represented by a great blue heron. Its name means "purple" or "palm leaf" in the Greek, and so it may have been connected with royalty (purple being a rare and difficult dye and therefore worn largely by the wealthy in the West; the palm frond holding a number of significant symbolic values). In some myths its rise and fall is associated with the rising and setting of the sun. But in all of the myths, the ashes are important, because they represent the ruins out of which something new is built. The myth is of resurrection, which means it is simultaneously about death and birth, and so it has remained one of the most famous and powerful stories of the ages. The story of the phoenix so ingrained itself in European consciousness that from the fifteenth to the seventeenth centuries it appeared in bestiaries; religious leaders declared it to be a real bird.

In *Howard Nemerov and Objective Idealism,* Donna L. Potts writes, "Language is for Nemerov what language once was for the alchemists—the means for transforming the base elements of this world into gold." Nemerov's assumption that language could have magical qualities was partly influenced by the philosophy of objective idealism. Language could be "magical" in the sense that it serves as a mediator between us and the physical world. This means that our imaginations participate in how the world works. Based on this assumption, myths are "real," and the mythic images of Nemerov's poems therefore have metaphoric power for him. If in ancient Egypt the bennu was a heron, then the actual bird and the imagined or magical bird—The Phoenix—are both necessary for stories, myths, and religions to exist. This may be one reason why Nemerov so consistently uses words we often associate with holiness and spiritual iconography in "The Phoenix." Each line carries some reference to the fundamental material of the world in connection to a kind of scriptural belief.

Nemerov frequently turns to myth in his writing, even in his speeches, which are peppered with references to past literatures, quotes in ancient languages, and applications of religion and belief to methods of writing. As an objective idealist, one who believes in the negotiation of imagination and fact, Nemerov in his work often attempts to cope with this negotiation, and his subject matter in *Guide to the Ruins* —especially ancient myth and war—give him the opportunity. Much of the collection (an early work of the poet's that comes before, in the view of many critics, his poetry fully matured) is devoted to ancient myths, juxtaposed with the experiences of war in the modern world and the structures of poetry. Such character-based poems as Nicodemus, "Virgin and Martyr," "Mars," and "Antigone" give "The Phoenix" a context necessary to our appreciation of its meanings. In fact, the title of the collection implies that the poet is taking us through the remnants of history, whether the ruins of old myths (the last—or first—of which in the book is "The Phoenix"), the ruins of war, or the inscriptions of sonnets on pages. Nemerov is certainly a referential poet, to the extent that some critics have accused him of being derivative.

> *If in ancient Egypt the bennu was a heron, then the actual bird and the imagined or magical bird—The Phoenix—are both necessary for stories, myths, and religions to exist."*

The formal rhyme scheme (abab) also gives the poem a kind of age; it reads like a nineteenth-century elegy, an epitaph worn thin on a stone. It is an explanation of the phoenix, a definition of it that retells the myth through the poet's characterization of the bird, rather than through a story form or an encyclopedic account of what a phoenix is. Nemerov chooses to focus on the character rather than the narrative perhaps because, as in many myths, the character is the narrative. The stories of the phoenix that most remember in the modern era focus primarily on what the creature is, rather than on what it does. The flooding of the Nile, for instance, and the beginning of a season in Egypt, is hardly the resonant myth of the phoenix in the western world. A more general cyclical myth adheres; there is birth and death, the rising and setting of the sun, but we have many other myths that represent such events. The individuality of the phoenix is in the nature (or magical metaphor of nature) of its rise and fall. It appears from its own ashes, and is the icon of fire. This distinguishes it from other resurrection myths (such as Christ from the tomb) by its elements, but, as we will see, the separation of mythologies is seldom complete.

Nemerov has been called "unromantic" in his treatment of nature, and frequently cited as employing "science" in his material. He is acutely romantic in many of his poems—practically an anachronism in his view of science and spirituality, especially as they meet on fairly simple terms in formalist poems. In a poem such as "The Phoenix," he joins the ranks of the seventeenth-century bestiary writers. It doesn't get much more romantic and unscientific than to construct a rhyming three-stanza poem to a mythic bird. We might say then, that Nemerov, like most poets, defies easy categorization. He writes about the material that moves him, and lets the philosophy work out itself. The myth is important enough to merit the poem. One thing we may find, however, seeping up through the characterization of the phoenix, is how Nemerov is enamoured with language as the mediator among the poet's imagination, religion, and objective reality. The final line, where we might start the explication of this poem, capitalizes "Word."

In the Bible, the word, logos, is represented physically by Christ. Nemerov connects the Christian and Egyptian myths in the poem by using his last two lines to articulate the resurrection of the phoenix in terms of the trinity and the immaculate conception. The mythic bird is the Word, the son, but it is also its own father and mother (because of rising from its ashes). This unity of myth is foreshadowed in the poem's second line, in which the preparation for burial of the father is made. Myrrh is an aromatic gum resin from a tree that grows in the Middle East and Africa. It was used in mummification, and was also a gift brought by one of the wise men to Christ's cradle (the image mentioned at the end of stanza one). Myrrh may have been one of the phoenix's foods. R. Van Den Broek, in his study *The Myth of The Phoenix,* explains that the mythic bird subsisted on many aromatics.

The cradle and bier (a funeral pyre) are the birth and death images, but the "solar" nature of the myth is called by Nemerov "unholy lust." But at the beginning of stanza two, the "City of the Sun" is capitalized, valorized, much like the Augustine "City of God." This could be a reference to the necessity of polarity, of the binary in belief that to have good one must have evil, and the phoenix, by its cyclical nature, accounts for both. He indicates this again in the final stanza, by casting the story in its darkest terms. The Phoenix lives by committing a sin, and continues through its life toward the moment of committing that sin again. In conjunction with the last lines of the poem, this implies that all myths have some element of the evil in their goodness, and vice-versa.

The "sacred, purple bird" is a Christ figure with which we might not be comfortable, but, in keeping with Nemerov's philosophy, it is "Genuine"—a myth as the real thing, and is still "divine." As in much of Nemerov's work; the simplicity of polarized images often belies itself; it makes us question how simple that split between good and evil, holy and unholy, birth and death,

actually is. Perhaps the magic of the phoenix is the way in which it casts doubt on the distinctions we make between how certain subjects are best raised again over the ages in our poems, and demands that we bring our imaginations to the world of objective reality. That way, we choose carefully the stories that most need to be retold, reborn.

Source: Sean K. Robisch, in an essay for *Poetry for Students,* Gale, 2001.

Sources

Bowers, Neal, and Charles L.P. Silet, "An Interview with Howard Nemerov," *Massachusetts Review,* Spring, 1981, pp. 43-57.

Brennan, J.P., Review of *Guide to the Ruins,* New Haven *Register,* June 19, 1950, sec. 4 p. 8.

Broek, R. Van Den, *The Myth of the Phoenix: According to Classical and Early Christian Traditions,* E. J. Brill, 1972.

Daiches, David, Review of *Guide to the Ruins* by Howard Nemerov, *Yale Review,* Winter, 1951, p. 356.

Duncan, Bowie, ed., *The Critical Reception of Howard Nemerov,* The Scarecrow Press, 1971.

Herodotus, *The Histories,* Translated by Aubrey de Selincourt, revised with introductory matter and notes by John Marincola, Penguin, 1996.

Koch, Vivienne, "The Necessary Angels of the Earth," in *The Critical Reception of Howard Nemerov: A Selection of Essays and a Bibliography,* edited by Bowie Duncan, Scarecrow Press, 1971.

———, Review of *Guide to the Ruins, Sewanee Review,* Autumn, 1951, p. 674.

Meinke, Peter, "Twenty Years of Accomplishment" in *The Critical Reception of Howard Nemerov,* edited by Bowie Duncan, The Scarecrow Press, 1971, pp. 29-39.

Nemerov, Howard, *The Collected Poems,* University of Chicago Press, 1977.

———, "Poetry and Meaning," in *Figures of Thought: Speculations on the Meaning of Poetry and Other Essays,* David R. Godine Publishers, 1978.

———, *Sentences,* University of Chicago Press, 1980.

———, "The Swaying Form: A Problem in Poetry," Nicholas Delbanco, editor, *Speaking of Writing: Selected Hopwood Lectures,* University of Michigan Press, 1990, pp. 163-176.

Potts, Donna L., *Howard Nemerov and Objective Idealism: The Influence of Owen Barfield,* University of Missouri Press, 1994.

Salomon, I.L., "Corruption and Metaphysics," *Saturday Review of Literature,* July 1, 1950, p. 33.

Smith, Harry, Review of *Guide to the Ruins,* New Leader, Nov. 13, 1950, p. 22.

Warden, Will, Review of *Guide to the Ruins,* St. Louis *Post-Dispatch,* May 18, 1950, E22.

For Further Study

Bartholomay, Julia A., *The Shield of Perseus: The Vision and Imagination of Howard Nemerov,* University of Florida Press, 1972.

> This early study of Nemerov focuses on such issues as the role of the imagination in poetic composition, the place of art in the world, and questions of intellectual and sensory perception.

Mills, William, *The Stillness in Moving Things: The World of Howard Nemerov,* Memphis State University Press, 1975.

> This book, a close reading of many of Nemerov's poems throughout his career (at least up to 1975), focuses on Nemerov's philosophical concerns and his attitudes toward artistic perception and the question of what to portray in poetry.

Potts, Donna L., *Howard Nemerov and Objective Idealism,* University of Missouri Press, 1994.

> Potts concentrates on the philosophical issues raised by Nemerov's poetry, using the epistemologist Owen Barfield (an acknowledged source for Nemerov's ideas) to read the verse.

Glossary of Literary Terms

A

Abstract: Used as a noun, the term refers to a short summary or outline of a longer work. As an adjective applied to writing or literary works, abstract refers to words or phrases that name things not knowable through the five senses.

Accent: The emphasis or stress placed on a syllable in poetry. Traditional poetry commonly uses patterns of accented and unaccented syllables (known as feet) that create distinct rhythms. Much modern poetry uses less formal arrangements that create a sense of freedom and spontaneity.

Aestheticism: A literary and artistic movement of the nineteenth century. Followers of the movement believed that art should not be mixed with social, political, or moral teaching. The statement "art for art's sake" is a good summary of aestheticism. The movement had its roots in France, but it gained widespread importance in England in the last half of the nineteenth century, where it helped change the Victorian practice of including moral lessons in literature.

Affective Fallacy: An error in judging the merits or faults of a work of literature. The "error" results from stressing the importance of the work's effect upon the reader—that is, how it makes a reader "feel" emotionally, what it does as a literary work—instead of stressing its inner qualities as a created object, or what it "is."

Age of Johnson: The period in English literature between 1750 and 1798, named after the most prominent literary figure of the age, Samuel Johnson. Works written during this time are noted for their emphasis on "sensibility," or emotional quality. These works formed a transition between the rational works of the Age of Reason, or Neoclassical period, and the emphasis on individual feelings and responses of the Romantic period.

Age of Reason: See *Neoclassicism*

Age of Sensibility: See *Age of Johnson*

Agrarians: A group of Southern American writers of the 1930s and 1940s who fostered an economic and cultural program for the South based on agriculture, in opposition to the industrial society of the North. The term can refer to any group that promotes the value of farm life and agricultural society.

Alexandrine Meter: See *Meter*

Allegory: A narrative technique in which characters representing things or abstract ideas are used to convey a message or teach a lesson. Allegory is typically used to teach moral, ethical, or religious lessons but is sometimes used for satiric or political purposes.

Alliteration: A poetic device where the first consonant sounds or any vowel sounds in words or syllables are repeated.

Allusion: A reference to a familiar literary or historical person or event, used to make an idea more easily understood.

Amerind Literature: The writing and oral traditions of Native Americans. Native American literature was originally passed on by word of mouth, so it consisted largely of stories and events that were easily memorized. Amerind prose is often rhythmic like poetry because it was recited to the beat of a ceremonial drum.

Analogy: A comparison of two things made to explain something unfamiliar through its similarities to something familiar, or to prove one point based on the acceptedness of another. Similes and metaphors are types of analogies.

Anapest: See *Foot*

Angry Young Men: A group of British writers of the 1950s whose work expressed bitterness and disillusionment with society. Common to their work is an antihero who rebels against a corrupt social order and strives for personal integrity.

Anthropomorphism: The presentation of animals or objects in human shape or with human characteristics. The term is derived from the Greek word for "human form."

Antimasque: See *Masque*

Antithesis: The antithesis of something is its direct opposite. In literature, the use of antithesis as a figure of speech results in two statements that show a contrast through the balancing of two opposite ideas. Technically, it is the second portion of the statement that is defined as the "antithesis"; the first portion is the "thesis."

Apocrypha: Writings tentatively attributed to an author but not proven or universally accepted to be their works. The term was originally applied to certain books of the Bible that were not considered inspired and so were not included in the "sacred canon."

Apollonian and Dionysian: The two impulses believed to guide authors of dramatic tragedy. The Apollonian impulse is named after Apollo, the Greek god of light and beauty and the symbol of intellectual order. The Dionysian impulse is named after Dionysus, the Greek god of wine and the symbol of the unrestrained forces of nature. The Apollonian impulse is to create a rational, harmonious world, while the Dionysian is to express the irrational forces of personality.

Apostrophe: A statement, question, or request addressed to an inanimate object or concept or to a nonexistent or absent person.

Archetype: The word archetype is commonly used to describe an original pattern or model from which all other things of the same kind are made. This term was introduced to literary criticism from the psychology of Carl Jung. It expresses Jung's theory that behind every person's "unconscious," or repressed memories of the past, lies the "collective unconscious" of the human race: memories of the countless typical experiences of our ancestors. These memories are said to prompt illogical associations that trigger powerful emotions in the reader. Often, the emotional process is primitive, even primordial. Archetypes are the literary images that grow out of the "collective unconscious." They appear in literature as incidents and plots that repeat basic patterns of life. They may also appear as stereotyped characters.

Argument: The argument of a work is the author's subject matter or principal idea.

Art for Art's Sake: See *Aestheticism*

Assonance: The repetition of similar vowel sounds in poetry.

Audience: The people for whom a piece of literature is written. Authors usually write with a certain audience in mind, for example, children, members of a religious or ethnic group, or colleagues in a professional field. The term "audience" also applies to the people who gather to see or hear any performance, including plays, poetry readings, speeches, and concerts.

Automatic Writing: Writing carried out without a preconceived plan in an effort to capture every random thought. Authors who engage in automatic writing typically do not revise their work, preferring instead to preserve the revealed truth and beauty of spontaneous expression.

Avant-garde: A French term meaning "vanguard." It is used in literary criticism to describe new writing that rejects traditional approaches to literature in favor of innovations in style or content.

B

Ballad: A short poem that tells a simple story and has a repeated refrain. Ballads were originally intended to be sung. Early ballads, known as folk ballads, were passed down through generations, so their authors are often unknown. Later ballads composed by known authors are called literary ballads.

Baroque: A term used in literary criticism to describe literature that is complex or ornate in style or diction. Baroque works typically express tension, anxiety, and violent emotion. The term "Baroque Age" designates a period in Western European literature beginning in the late sixteenth century and ending about one hundred years later.

Works of this period often mirror the qualities of works more generally associated with the label "baroque" and sometimes feature elaborate conceits.

Baroque Age: See *Baroque*

Baroque Period: See *Baroque*

Beat Generation: See *Beat Movement*

Beat Movement: A period featuring a group of American poets and novelists of the 1950s and 1960s—including Jack Kerouac, Allen Ginsberg, Gregory Corso, William S. Burroughs, and Lawrence Ferlinghetti—who rejected established social and literary values. Using such techniques as stream-of-consciousness writing and jazz-influenced free verse and focusing on unusual or abnormal states of mind—generated by religious ecstasy or the use of drugs—the Beat writers aimed to create works that were unconventional in both form and subject matter.

Beat Poets: See *Beat Movement*

Beats, The: See *Beat Movement*

Belles-lettres: A French term meaning "fine letters" or "beautiful writing." It is often used as a synonym for literature, typically referring to imaginative and artistic rather than scientific or expository writing. Current usage sometimes restricts the meaning to light or humorous writing and appreciative essays about literature.

Black Aesthetic Movement: A period of artistic and literary development among African Americans in the 1960s and early 1970s. This was the first major African American artistic movement since the Harlem Renaissance and was closely paralleled by the civil rights and black power movements. The black aesthetic writers attempted to produce works of art that would be meaningful to the black masses. Key figures in black aesthetics included one of its founders, poet and playwright Amiri Baraka, formerly known as LeRoi Jones; poet and essayist Haki R. Madhubuti, formerly Don L. Lee; poet and playwright Sonia Sanchez; and dramatist Ed Bullins.

Black Arts Movement: See *Black Aesthetic Movement*

Black Comedy: See *Black Humor*

Black Humor: Writing that places grotesque elements side by side with humorous ones in an attempt to shock the reader, forcing him or her to laugh at the horrifying reality of a disordered world.

Black Mountain School: Black Mountain College and three of its instructors—Robert Creeley, Robert Duncan, and Charles Olson—were all influential in projective verse. Today poets working in projective verse are referred to as members of the Black Mountain school.

Blank Verse: Loosely, any unrhymed poetry, but more generally, unrhymed iambic pentameter verse (composed of lines of five two-syllable feet with the first syllable accented, the second unaccented). Blank verse has been used by poets since the Renaissance for its flexibility and its graceful, dignified tone.

Bloomsbury Group: A group of English writers, artists, and intellectuals who held informal artistic and philosophical discussions in Bloomsbury, a district of London, from around 1907 to the early 1930s. The Bloomsbury Group held no uniform philosophical beliefs but did commonly express an aversion to moral prudery and a desire for greater social tolerance.

Bon Mot: A French term meaning "good word." A *bon mot* is a witty remark or clever observation.

Breath Verse: See *Projective Verse*

Burlesque: Any literary work that uses exaggeration to make its subject appear ridiculous, either by treating a trivial subject with profound seriousness or by treating a dignified subject frivolously. The word "burlesque" may also be used as an adjective, as in "burlesque show," to mean "striptease act."

C

Cadence: The natural rhythm of language caused by the alternation of accented and unaccented syllables. Much modern poetry—notably free verse—deliberately manipulates cadence to create complex rhythmic effects.

Caesura: A pause in a line of poetry, usually occurring near the middle. It typically corresponds to a break in the natural rhythm or sense of the line but is sometimes shifted to create special meanings or rhythmic effects.

Canzone: A short Italian or Provencal lyric poem, commonly about love and often set to music. The *canzone* has no set form but typically contains five or six stanzas made up of seven to twenty lines of eleven syllables each. A shorter, five- to ten-line "envoy," or concluding stanza, completes the poem.

Carpe Diem: A Latin term meaning "seize the day." This is a traditional theme of poetry, especially lyrics. A *carpe diem* poem advises the reader or the person it addresses to live for today and enjoy the pleasures of the moment.

Catharsis: The release or purging of unwanted emotions—specifically fear and pity—brought about by exposure to art. The term was first used by the Greek philosopher Aristotle in his *Poetics* to refer to the desired effect of tragedy on spectators.

Celtic Renaissance: A period of Irish literary and cultural history at the end of the nineteenth century. Followers of the movement aimed to create a romantic vision of Celtic myth and legend. The most significant works of the Celtic Renaissance typically present a dreamy, unreal world, usually in reaction against the reality of contemporary problems.

Celtic Twilight: See *Celtic Renaissance*

Character: Broadly speaking, a person in a literary work. The actions of characters are what constitute the plot of a story, novel, or poem. There are numerous types of characters, ranging from simple, stereotypical figures to intricate, multifaceted ones. In the techniques of anthropomorphism and personification, animals—and even places or things—can assume aspects of character. "Characterization" is the process by which an author creates vivid, believable characters in a work of art. This may be done in a variety of ways, including (1) direct description of the character by the narrator; (2) the direct presentation of the speech, thoughts, or actions of the character; and (3) the responses of other characters to the character. The term "character" also refers to a form originated by the ancient Greek writer Theophrastus that later became popular in the seventeenth and eighteenth centuries. It is a short essay or sketch of a person who prominently displays a specific attribute or quality, such as miserliness or ambition.

Characterization: See *Character*

Classical: In its strictest definition in literary criticism, classicism refers to works of ancient Greek or Roman literature. The term may also be used to describe a literary work of recognized importance (a "classic") from any time period or literature that exhibits the traits of classicism.

Classicism: A term used in literary criticism to describe critical doctrines that have their roots in ancient Greek and Roman literature, philosophy, and art. Works associated with classicism typically exhibit restraint on the part of the author, unity of design and purpose, clarity, simplicity, logical organization, and respect for tradition.

Colloquialism: A word, phrase, or form of pronunciation that is acceptable in casual conversation but not in formal, written communication. It is considered more acceptable than slang.

Complaint: A lyric poem, popular in the Renaissance, in which the speaker expresses sorrow about his or her condition. Typically, the speaker's sadness is caused by an unresponsive lover, but some complaints cite other sources of unhappiness, such as poverty or fate.

Conceit: A clever and fanciful metaphor, usually expressed through elaborate and extended comparison, that presents a striking parallel between two seemingly dissimilar things—for example, elaborately comparing a beautiful woman to an object like a garden or the sun. The conceit was a popular device throughout the Elizabethan Age and Baroque Age and was the principal technique of the seventeenth-century English metaphysical poets. This usage of the word conceit is unrelated to the best-known definition of conceit as an arrogant attitude or behavior.

Concrete: Concrete is the opposite of abstract, and refers to a thing that actually exists or a description that allows the reader to experience an object or concept with the senses.

Concrete Poetry: Poetry in which visual elements play a large part in the poetic effect. Punctuation marks, letters, or words are arranged on a page to form a visual design: a cross, for example, or a bumblebee.

Confessional Poetry: A form of poetry in which the poet reveals very personal, intimate, sometimes shocking information about himself or herself.

Connotation: The impression that a word gives beyond its defined meaning. Connotations may be universally understood or may be significant only to a certain group.

Consonance: Consonance occurs in poetry when words appearing at the ends of two or more verses have similar final consonant sounds but have final vowel sounds that differ, as with "stuff" and "off."

Convention: Any widely accepted literary device, style, or form.

Corrido: A Mexican ballad.

Couplet: Two lines of poetry with the same rhyme and meter, often expressing a complete and self-contained thought.

Criticism: The systematic study and evaluation of literary works, usually based on a specific method or set of principles. An important part of literary studies since ancient times, the practice of criticism has given rise to numerous theories, methods, and "schools," sometimes producing conflicting, even contradictory, interpretations of literature in general as well as of individual works. Even such basic issues as what constitutes a poem or a novel have been the subject of much criticism over the centuries.

D

Dactyl: See *Foot*

Dadaism: A protest movement in art and literature founded by Tristan Tzara in 1916. Followers of the movement expressed their outrage at the destruction brought about by World War I by revolting against numerous forms of social convention. The Dadaists presented works marked by calculated madness and flamboyant nonsense. They stressed total freedom of expression, commonly through primitive displays of emotion and illogical, often senseless, poetry. The movement ended shortly after the war, when it was replaced by surrealism.

Decadent: See *Decadents*

Decadents: The followers of a nineteenth-century literary movement that had its beginnings in French aestheticism. Decadent literature displays a fascination with perverse and morbid states; a search for novelty and sensation—the "new thrill"; a preoccupation with mysticism; and a belief in the senselessness of human existence. The movement is closely associated with the doctrine Art for Art's Sake. The term "decadence" is sometimes used to denote a decline in the quality of art or literature following a period of greatness.

Deconstruction: A method of literary criticism developed by Jacques Derrida and characterized by multiple conflicting interpretations of a given work. Deconstructionists consider the impact of the language of a work and suggest that the true meaning of the work is not necessarily the meaning that the author intended.

Deduction: The process of reaching a conclusion through reasoning from general premises to a specific premise.

Denotation: The definition of a word, apart from the impressions or feelings it creates in the reader.

Diction: The selection and arrangement of words in a literary work. Either or both may vary depending on the desired effect. There are four general types of diction: "formal," used in scholarly or lofty writing; "informal," used in relaxed but educated conversation; "colloquial," used in everyday speech; and "slang," containing newly coined words and other terms not accepted in formal usage.

Didactic: A term used to describe works of literature that aim to teach some moral, religious, political, or practical lesson. Although didactic elements are often found in artistically pleasing works, the term "didactic" usually refers to literature in which the message is more important than the form. The term may also be used to criticize a work that the critic finds "overly didactic," that is, heavy-handed in its delivery of a lesson.

Dimeter: See *Meter*

Dionysian: See *Apollonian and Dionysian*

Discordia concours: A Latin phrase meaning "discord in harmony." The term was coined by the eighteenth-century English writer Samuel Johnson to describe "a combination of dissimilar images or discovery of occult resemblances in things apparently unlike." Johnson created the expression by reversing a phrase by the Latin poet Horace.

Dissonance: A combination of harsh or jarring sounds, especially in poetry. Although such combinations may be accidental, poets sometimes intentionally make them to achieve particular effects. Dissonance is also sometimes used to refer to close but not identical rhymes. When this is the case, the word functions as a synonym for consonance.

Double Entendre: A corruption of a French phrase meaning "double meaning." The term is used to indicate a word or phrase that is deliberately ambiguous, especially when one of the meanings is risque or improper.

Draft: Any preliminary version of a written work. An author may write dozens of drafts which are revised to form the final work, or he or she may write only one, with few or no revisions.

Dramatic Monologue: See *Monologue*

Dramatic Poetry: Any lyric work that employs elements of drama such as dialogue, conflict, or characterization, but excluding works that are intended for stage presentation.

Dream Allegory: See *Dream Vision*

Dream Vision: A literary convention, chiefly of the Middle Ages. In a dream vision a story is presented as a literal dream of the narrator. This device was commonly used to teach moral and religious lessons.

E

Eclogue: In classical literature, a poem featuring rural themes and structured as a dialogue among shepherds. Eclogues often took specific poetic forms, such as elegies or love poems. Some were written as the soliloquy of a shepherd. In later centuries, "eclogue" came to refer to any poem that was in the pastoral tradition or that had a dialogue or monologue structure.

Edwardian: Describes cultural conventions identified with the period of the reign of Edward VII of England (1901–1910). Writers of the Edwardian Age typically displayed a strong reaction against the propriety and conservatism of the Victorian Age. Their work often exhibits distrust of authority in religion, politics, and art and expresses strong doubts about the soundness of conventional values.

Edwardian Age: See *Edwardian*

Electra Complex: A daughter's amorous obsession with her father.

Elegy: A lyric poem that laments the death of a person or the eventual death of all people. In a conventional elegy, set in a classical world, the poet and subject are spoken of as shepherds. In modern criticism, the word elegy is often used to refer to a poem that is melancholy or mournfully contemplative.

Elizabethan Age: A period of great economic growth, religious controversy, and nationalism closely associated with the reign of Elizabeth I of England (1558–1603). The Elizabethan Age is considered a part of the general renaissance—that is, the flowering of arts and literature—that took place in Europe during the fourteenth through sixteenth centuries. The era is considered the golden age of English literature. The most important dramas in English and a great deal of lyric poetry were produced during this period, and modern English criticism began around this time.

Empathy: A sense of shared experience, including emotional and physical feelings, with someone or something other than oneself. Empathy is often used to describe the response of a reader to a literary character.

English Sonnet: See *Sonnet*

Enjambment: The running over of the sense and structure of a line of verse or a couplet into the following verse or couplet.

Enlightenment, The: An eighteenth-century philosophical movement. It began in France but had a wide impact throughout Europe and America. Thinkers of the Enlightenment valued reason and believed that both the individual and society could achieve a state of perfection. Corresponding to this essentially humanist vision was a resistance to religious authority.

Epic: A long narrative poem about the adventures of a hero of great historic or legendary importance. The setting is vast and the action is often given cosmic significance through the intervention of supernatural forces such as gods, angels, or demons. Epics are typically written in a classical style of grand simplicity with elaborate metaphors and allusions that enhance the symbolic importance of a hero's adventures.

Epic Simile: See *Homeric Simile*

Epigram: A saying that makes the speaker's point quickly and concisely.

Epilogue: A concluding statement or section of a literary work. In dramas, particularly those of the seventeenth and eighteenth centuries, the epilogue is a closing speech, often in verse, delivered by an actor at the end of a play and spoken directly to the audience.

Epiphany: A sudden revelation of truth inspired by a seemingly trivial incident.

Epitaph: An inscription on a tomb or tombstone, or a verse written on the occasion of a person's death. Epitaphs may be serious or humorous.

Epithalamion: A song or poem written to honor and commemorate a marriage ceremony.

Epithalamium: See *Epithalamion*

Epithet: A word or phrase, often disparaging or abusive, that expresses a character trait of someone or something.

Erziehungsroman: See *Bildungsroman*

Essay: A prose composition with a focused subject of discussion. The term was coined by Michel de Montaigne to describe his 1580 collection of brief, informal reflections on himself and on various topics relating to human nature. An essay can also be a long, systematic discourse.

Existentialism: A predominantly twentieth-century philosophy concerned with the nature and perception of human existence. There are two major strains of existentialist thought: atheistic and Christian. Followers of atheistic existentialism believe that the individual is alone in a godless universe and that the basic human condition is one of suffering and loneliness. Nevertheless, because there are no fixed values, individuals can create their own characters—indeed, they can shape themselves—through the exercise of free will. The atheistic strain culminates in and is popularly associated with the works of Jean-Paul Sartre. The Christian existentialists, on the other hand, believe that only in God may people find freedom from life's anguish. The two strains hold certain beliefs in common: that existence cannot be fully understood or described through empirical effort; that anguish is a universal element of life; that individuals must bear responsibility for their actions; and that there is no common standard of behavior or perception for religious and ethical matters.

Expatriates: See *Expatriatism*

Expatriatism: The practice of leaving one's country to live for an extended period in another country.

Exposition: Writing intended to explain the nature of an idea, thing, or theme. Expository writing is often combined with description, narration, or argument. In dramatic writing, the exposition is the introductory material which presents the characters, setting, and tone of the play.

Expressionism: An indistinct literary term, originally used to describe an early twentieth-century school of German painting. The term applies to almost any mode of unconventional, highly subjective writing that distorts reality in some way.

Extended Monologue: See *Monologue*

F

Feet: See *Foot*

Feminine Rhyme: See *Rhyme*

Fiction: Any story that is the product of imagination rather than a documentation of fact. Characters and events in such narratives may be based in real life but their ultimate form and configuration is a creation of the author.

Figurative Language: A technique in writing in which the author temporarily interrupts the order, construction, or meaning of the writing for a particular effect. This interruption takes the form of one or more figures of speech such as hyperbole, irony, or simile. Figurative language is the opposite of literal language, in which every word is truthful, accurate, and free of exaggeration or embellishment.

Figures of Speech: Writing that differs from customary conventions for construction, meaning, order, or significance for the purpose of a special meaning or effect. There are two major types of figures of speech: rhetorical figures, which do not make changes in the meaning of the words; and tropes, which do.

Fin de siecle: A French term meaning "end of the century." The term is used to denote the last decade of the nineteenth century, a transition period when

writers and other artists abandoned old conventions and looked for new techniques and objectives.

First Person: See *Point of View*

Folk Ballad: See *Ballad*

Folklore: Traditions and myths preserved in a culture or group of people. Typically, these are passed on by word of mouth in various forms—such as legends, songs, and proverbs—or preserved in customs and ceremonies. This term was first used by W. J. Thoms in 1846.

Folktale: A story originating in oral tradition. Folktales fall into a variety of categories, including legends, ghost stories, fairy tales, fables, and anecdotes based on historical figures and events.

Foot: The smallest unit of rhythm in a line of poetry. In English-language poetry, a foot is typically one accented syllable combined with one or two unaccented syllables.

Form: The pattern or construction of a work which identifies its genre and distinguishes it from other genres.

Formalism: In literary criticism, the belief that literature should follow prescribed rules of construction, such as those that govern the sonnet form.

Fourteener Meter: See *Meter*

Free Verse: Poetry that lacks regular metrical and rhyme patterns but that tries to capture the cadences of everyday speech. The form allows a poet to exploit a variety of rhythmical effects within a single poem.

Futurism: A flamboyant literary and artistic movement that developed in France, Italy, and Russia from 1908 through the 1920s. Futurist theater and poetry abandoned traditional literary forms. In their place, followers of the movement attempted to achieve total freedom of expression through bizarre imagery and deformed or newly invented words. The Futurists were self-consciously modern artists who attempted to incorporate the appearances and sounds of modern life into their work.

G

Genre: A category of literary work. In critical theory, genre may refer to both the content of a given work—tragedy, comedy, pastoral—and to its form, such as poetry, novel, or drama.

Genteel Tradition: A term coined by critic George Santayana to describe the literary practice of certain late nineteenth-century American writers, especially New Englanders. Followers of the Genteel

Tradition emphasized conventionality in social, religious, moral, and literary standards.

Georgian Age: See *Georgian Poets*

Georgian Period: See *Georgian Poets*

Georgian Poets: A loose grouping of English poets during the years 1912–1922. The Georgians reacted against certain literary schools and practices, especially Victorian wordiness, turn-of-the-century aestheticism, and contemporary urban realism. In their place, the Georgians embraced the nineteenth-century poetic practices of William Wordsworth and the other Lake Poets.

Georgic: A poem about farming and the farmer's way of life, named from Virgil's *Georgics*.

Gilded Age: A period in American history during the 1870s characterized by political corruption and materialism. A number of important novels of social and political criticism were written during this time.

Gothic: See *Gothicism*

Gothicism: In literary criticism, works characterized by a taste for the medieval or morbidly attractive. A gothic novel prominently features elements of horror, the supernatural, gloom, and violence: clanking chains, terror, charnel houses, ghosts, medieval castles, and mysteriously slamming doors. The term "gothic novel" is also applied to novels that lack elements of the traditional Gothic setting but that create a similar atmosphere of terror or dread.

Graveyard School: A group of eighteenth-century English poets who wrote long, picturesque meditations on death. Their works were designed to cause the reader to ponder immortality.

Great Chain of Being: The belief that all things and creatures in nature are organized in a hierarchy from inanimate objects at the bottom to God at the top. This system of belief was popular in the seventeenth and eighteenth centuries.

Grotesque: In literary criticism, the subject matter of a work or a style of expression characterized by exaggeration, deformity, freakishness, and disorder. The grotesque often includes an element of comic absurdity.

H

Haiku: The shortest form of Japanese poetry, constructed in three lines of five, seven, and five syllables respectively. The message of a *haiku* poem usually centers on some aspect of spirituality and provokes an emotional response in the reader.

Half Rhyme: See *Consonance*

Harlem Renaissance: The Harlem Renaissance of the 1920s is generally considered the first significant movement of black writers and artists in the United States. During this period, new and established black writers published more fiction and poetry than ever before, the first influential black literary journals were established, and black authors and artists received their first widespread recognition and serious critical appraisal. Among the major writers associated with this period are Claude McKay, Jean Toomer, Countee Cullen, Langston Hughes, Arna Bontemps, Nella Larsen, and Zora Neale Hurston.

Hellenism: Imitation of ancient Greek thought or styles. Also, an approach to life that focuses on the growth and development of the intellect. "Hellenism" is sometimes used to refer to the belief that reason can be applied to examine all human experience.

Heptameter: See *Meter*

Hero/Heroine: The principal sympathetic character (male or female) in a literary work. Heroes and heroines typically exhibit admirable traits: idealism, courage, and integrity, for example.

Heroic Couplet: A rhyming couplet written in iambic pentameter (a verse with five iambic feet).

Heroic Line: The meter and length of a line of verse in epic or heroic poetry. This varies by language and time period.

Heroine: See *Hero/Heroine*

Hexameter: See *Meter*

Historical Criticism: The study of a work based on its impact on the world of the time period in which it was written.

Hokku: See *Haiku*

Holocaust: See *Holocaust Literature*

Holocaust Literature: Literature influenced by or written about the Holocaust of World War II. Such literature includes true stories of survival in concentration camps, escape, and life after the war, as well as fictional works and poetry.

Homeric Simile: An elaborate, detailed comparison written as a simile many lines in length.

Horatian Satire: See *Satire*

Humanism: A philosophy that places faith in the dignity of humankind and rejects the medieval perception of the individual as a weak, fallen creature. "Humanists" typically believe in the perfectibility of human nature and view reason and education as the means to that end.

Humors: Mentions of the humors refer to the ancient Greek theory that a person's health and personality were determined by the balance of four basic fluids in the body: blood, phlegm, yellow bile, and black bile. A dominance of any fluid would cause extremes in behavior. An excess of blood created a sanguine person who was joyful, aggressive, and passionate; a phlegmatic person was shy, fearful, and sluggish; too much yellow bile led to a choleric temperament characterized by impatience, anger, bitterness, and stubbornness; and excessive black bile created melancholy, a state of laziness, gluttony, and lack of motivation.

Humours: See *Humors*

Hyperbole: In literary criticism, deliberate exaggeration used to achieve an effect.

I

Iamb: See *Foot*

Idiom: A word construction or verbal expression closely associated with a given language.

Image: A concrete representation of an object or sensory experience. Typically, such a representation helps evoke the feelings associated with the object or experience itself. Images are either "literal" or "figurative." Literal images are especially concrete and involve little or no extension of the obvious meaning of the words used to express them. Figurative images do not follow the literal meaning of the words exactly. Images in literature are usually visual, but the term "image" can also refer to the representation of any sensory experience.

Imagery: The array of images in a literary work. Also, figurative language.

Imagism: An English and American poetry movement that flourished between 1908 and 1917. The Imagists used precise, clearly presented images in their works. They also used common, everyday speech and aimed for conciseness, concrete imagery, and the creation of new rhythms.

In medias res: A Latin term meaning "in the middle of things." It refers to the technique of beginning a story at its midpoint and then using various flashback devices to reveal previous action.

Induction: The process of reaching a conclusion by reasoning from specific premises to form a general premise. Also, an introductory portion of a work of literature, especially a play.

Intentional Fallacy: The belief that judgments of a literary work based solely on an author's stated or implied intentions are false and misleading. Critics who believe in the concept of the intentional fallacy typically argue that the work itself is sufficient matter for interpretation, even though they may concede that an author's statement of purpose can be useful.

Interior Monologue: A narrative technique in which characters' thoughts are revealed in a way that appears to be uncontrolled by the author. The interior monologue typically aims to reveal the inner self of a character. It portrays emotional experiences as they occur at both a conscious and unconscious level. Images are often used to represent sensations or emotions.

Internal Rhyme: Rhyme that occurs within a single line of verse.

Irish Literary Renaissance: A late nineteenth- and early twentieth-century movement in Irish literature. Members of the movement aimed to reduce the influence of British culture in Ireland and create an Irish national literature.

Irony: In literary criticism, the effect of language in which the intended meaning is the opposite of what is stated.

Italian Sonnet: See *Sonnet*

J

Jacobean Age: The period of the reign of James I of England (1603–1625). The early literature of this period reflected the worldview of the Elizabethan Age, but a darker, more cynical attitude steadily grew in the art and literature of the Jacobean Age. This was an important time for English drama and poetry.

Jargon: Language that is used or understood only by a select group of people. Jargon may refer to terminology used in a certain profession, such as computer jargon, or it may refer to any nonsensical language that is not understood by most people.

Journalism: Writing intended for publication in a newspaper or magazine, or for broadcast on a radio or television program featuring news, sports, entertainment, or other timely material.

K

Knickerbocker Group: A somewhat indistinct group of New York writers of the first half of the nineteenth century. Members of the group were linked only by location and a common theme: New York life.

Kunstlerroman: See *Bildungsroman*

L

Lais: See *Lay*

Lake Poets: See *Lake School*

Lake School: These poets all lived in the Lake District of England at the turn of the nineteenth century. As a group, they followed no single "school" of thought or literary practice, although their works were uniformly disparaged by the *Edinburgh Review*.

Lay: A song or simple narrative poem. The form originated in medieval France. Early French *lais* were often based on the Celtic legends and other tales sung by Breton minstrels—thus the name of the "Breton lay." In fourteenth-century England, the term "lay" was used to describe short narratives written in imitation of the Breton lays.

Leitmotiv: See *Motif*

Literal Language: An author uses literal language when he or she writes without exaggerating or embellishing the subject matter and without any tools of figurative language.

Literary Ballad: See *Ballad*

Literature: Literature is broadly defined as any written or spoken material, but the term most often refers to creative works.

Lost Generation: A term first used by Gertrude Stein to describe the post-World War I generation of American writers: men and women haunted by a sense of betrayal and emptiness brought about by the destructiveness of the war.

Lyric Poetry: A poem expressing the subjective feelings and personal emotions of the poet. Such poetry is melodic, since it was originally accompanied by a lyre in recitals. Most Western poetry in the twentieth century may be classified as lyrical.

M

Mannerism: Exaggerated, artificial adherence to a literary manner or style. Also, a popular style of the visual arts of late sixteenth-century Europe that was marked by elongation of the human form and by intentional spatial distortion. Literary works that are self-consciously high-toned and artistic are often said to be "mannered."

Masculine Rhyme: See *Rhyme*

Measure: The foot, verse, or time sequence used in a literary work, especially a poem. Measure is often used somewhat incorrectly as a synonym for meter.

Metaphor: A figure of speech that expresses an idea through the image of another object. Metaphors suggest the essence of the first object by identifying it with certain qualities of the second object.

Metaphysical Conceit: See *Conceit*

Metaphysical Poetry: The body of poetry produced by a group of seventeenth-century English writers called the "Metaphysical Poets." The group includes John Donne and Andrew Marvell. The Metaphysical Poets made use of everyday speech, intellectual analysis, and unique imagery. They aimed to portray the ordinary conflicts and contradictions of life. Their poems often took the form of an argument, and many of them emphasize physical and religious love as well as the fleeting nature of life. Elaborate conceits are typical in metaphysical poetry.

Metaphysical Poets: See *Metaphysical Poetry*

Meter: In literary criticism, the repetition of sound patterns that creates a rhythm in poetry. The patterns are based on the number of syllables and the presence and absence of accents. The unit of rhythm in a line is called a foot. Types of meter are classified according to the number of feet in a line. These are the standard English lines: Monometer, one foot; Dimeter, two feet; Trimeter, three feet; Tetrameter, four feet; Pentameter, five feet; Hexameter, six feet (also called the Alexandrine); Heptameter, seven feet (also called the "Fourteener" when the feet are iambic).

Modernism: Modern literary practices. Also, the principles of a literary school that lasted from roughly the beginning of the twentieth century until the end of World War II. Modernism is defined by its rejection of the literary conventions of the nineteenth century and by its opposition to conventional morality, taste, traditions, and economic values.

Monologue: A composition, written or oral, by a single individual. More specifically, a speech given by a single individual in a drama or other public entertainment. It has no set length, although it is usually several or more lines long.

Monometer: See *Meter*

Mood: The prevailing emotions of a work or of the author in his or her creation of the work. The mood of a work is not always what might be expected based on its subject matter.

Motif: A theme, character type, image, metaphor, or other verbal element that recurs throughout a single work of literature or occurs in a number of different works over a period of time.

Motiv: See *Motif*

Muckrakers: An early twentieth-century group of American writers. Typically, their works exposed the wrongdoings of big business and government in the United States.

Muses: Nine Greek mythological goddesses, the daughters of Zeus and Mnemosyne (Memory). Each muse patronized a specific area of the liberal arts and sciences. Calliope presided over epic poetry, Clio over history, Erato over love poetry, Euterpe over music or lyric poetry, Melpomene over tragedy, Polyhymnia over hymns to the gods, Terpsichore over dance, Thalia over comedy, and Urania over astronomy. Poets and writers traditionally made appeals to the Muses for inspiration in their work.

Myth: An anonymous tale emerging from the traditional beliefs of a culture or social unit. Myths use supernatural explanations for natural phenomena. They may also explain cosmic issues like creation and death. Collections of myths, known as mythologies, are common to all cultures and nations, but the best-known myths belong to the Norse, Roman, and Greek mythologies.

N

Narration: The telling of a series of events, real or invented. A narration may be either a simple narrative, in which the events are recounted chronologically, or a narrative with a plot, in which the account is given in a style reflecting the author's artistic concept of the story. Narration is sometimes used as a synonym for "storyline."

Narrative: A verse or prose accounting of an event or sequence of events, real or invented. The term is also used as an adjective in the sense "method of narration." For example, in literary criticism, the expression "narrative technique" usually refers to the way the author structures and presents his or her story.

Narrative Poetry: A nondramatic poem in which the author tells a story. Such poems may be of any length or level of complexity.

Narrator: The teller of a story. The narrator may be the author or a character in the story through whom the author speaks.

Naturalism: A literary movement of the late nineteenth and early twentieth centuries. The movement's major theorist, French novelist Emile Zola, envisioned a type of fiction that would examine human life with the objectivity of scientific inquiry. The Naturalists typically viewed human beings as either the products of "biological determinism," ruled by hereditary instincts and engaged in an endless struggle for survival, or as the products of "socioeconomic determinism," ruled by social and economic forces beyond their control. In their works, the Naturalists generally ignored the highest levels of society and focused on degradation: poverty, alcoholism, prostitution, insanity, and disease.

Negritude: A literary movement based on the concept of a shared cultural bond on the part of black Africans, wherever they may be in the world. It traces its origins to the former French colonies of Africa and the Caribbean. Negritude poets, novelists, and essayists generally stress four points in their writings: One, black alienation from traditional African culture can lead to feelings of inferiority. Two, European colonialism and Western education should be resisted. Three, black Africans should seek to affirm and define their own identity. Four, African culture can and should be reclaimed. Many Negritude writers also claim that blacks can make unique contributions to the world, based on a heightened appreciation of nature, rhythm, and human emotions—aspects of life they say are not so highly valued in the materialistic and rationalistic West.

Negro Renaissance: See *Harlem Renaissance*

Neoclassical Period: See *Neoclassicism*

Neoclassicism: In literary criticism, this term refers to the revival of the attitudes and styles of expression of classical literature. It is generally used to describe a period in European history beginning in the late seventeenth century and lasting until about 1800. In its purest form, Neoclassicism marked a return to order, proportion, restraint, logic, accuracy, and decorum. In England, where Neoclassicism perhaps was most popular, it reflected the influence of seventeenth-century French writers, especially dramatists. Neoclassical writers typically reacted against the intensity and enthusiasm of the Renaissance period. They wrote works that appealed to the intellect, using elevated language and classical literary forms such as satire and the ode. Neoclassical works were often governed by the classical goal of instruction.

Neoclassicists: See *Neoclassicism*

New Criticism: A movement in literary criticism, dating from the late 1920s, that stressed close textual analysis in the interpretation of works of literature. The New Critics saw little merit in historical and biographical analysis. Rather, they aimed to examine the text alone, free from the question of how external events—biographical or otherwise—may have helped shape it.

New Journalism: A type of writing in which the journalist presents factual information in a form usually used in fiction. New journalism emphasizes description, narration, and character development to bring readers closer to the human element of the story, and is often used in personality profiles and in-depth feature articles. It is not compatible with "straight" or "hard" newswriting, which is generally composed in a brief, fact-based style.

New Journalists: See *New Journalism*

New Negro Movement: See *Harlem Renaissance*

Noble Savage: The idea that primitive man is noble and good but becomes evil and corrupted as he becomes civilized. The concept of the noble savage originated in the Renaissance period but is more closely identified with such later writers as Jean-Jacques Rousseau and Aphra Behn.

O

Objective Correlative: An outward set of objects, a situation, or a chain of events corresponding to an inward experience and evoking this experience in the reader. The term frequently appears in modern criticism in discussions of authors' intended effects on the emotional responses of readers.

Objectivity: A quality in writing characterized by the absence of the author's opinion or feeling about the subject matter. Objectivity is an important factor in criticism.

Occasional Verse: Poetry written on the occasion of a significant historical or personal event. *Vers de societe* is sometimes called occasional verse although it is of a less serious nature.

Octave: A poem or stanza composed of eight lines. The term octave most often represents the first eight lines of a Petrarchan sonnet.

Ode: Name given to an extended lyric poem characterized by exalted emotion and dignified style. An ode usually concerns a single, serious theme. Most odes, but not all, are addressed to an object or individual. Odes are distinguished from other lyric poetic forms by their complex rhythmic and stanzaic patterns.

Oedipus Complex: A son's amorous obsession with his mother. The phrase is derived from the story of the ancient Theban hero Oedipus, who un-

knowingly killed his father and married his mother.

Omniscience: See *Point of View*

Onomatopoeia: The use of words whose sounds express or suggest their meaning. In its simplest sense, onomatopoeia may be represented by words that mimic the sounds they denote such as "hiss" or "meow." At a more subtle level, the pattern and rhythm of sounds and rhymes of a line or poem may be onomatopoeic.

Oral Tradition: See *Oral Transmission*

Oral Transmission: A process by which songs, ballads, folklore, and other material are transmitted by word of mouth. The tradition of oral transmission predates the written record systems of literate society. Oral transmission preserves material sometimes over generations, although often with variations. Memory plays a large part in the recitation and preservation of orally transmitted material.

Ottava Rima: An eight-line stanza of poetry composed in iambic pentameter (a five-foot line in which each foot consists of an unaccented syllable followed by an accented syllable), following the *ababababcc* rhyme scheme.

Oxymoron: A phrase combining two contradictory terms. Oxymorons may be intentional or unintentional.

P

Pantheism: The idea that all things are both a manifestation or revelation of God and a part of God at the same time. Pantheism was a common attitude in the early societies of Egypt, India, and Greece—the term derives from the Greek *pan* meaning "all" and *theos* meaning "deity." It later became a significant part of the Christian faith.

Parable: A story intended to teach a moral lesson or answer an ethical question.

Paradox: A statement that appears illogical or contradictory at first, but may actually point to an underlying truth.

Parallelism: A method of comparison of two ideas in which each is developed in the same grammatical structure.

Parnassianism: A mid nineteenth-century movement in French literature. Followers of the movement stressed adherence to well-defined artistic forms as a reaction against the often chaotic expression of the artist's ego that dominated the work of the Romantics. The Parnassians also rejected the moral, ethical, and social themes exhibited in the works of French Romantics such as Victor Hugo. The aesthetic doctrines of the Parnassians strongly influenced the later symbolist and decadent movements.

Parody: In literary criticism, this term refers to an imitation of a serious literary work or the signature style of a particular author in a ridiculous manner. A typical parody adopts the style of the original and applies it to an inappropriate subject for humorous effect. Parody is a form of satire and could be considered the literary equivalent of a caricature or cartoon.

Pastoral: A term derived from the Latin word "pastor," meaning shepherd. A pastoral is a literary composition on a rural theme. The conventions of the pastoral were originated by the third-century Greek poet Theocritus, who wrote about the experiences, love affairs, and pastimes of Sicilian shepherds. In a pastoral, characters and language of a courtly nature are often placed in a simple setting. The term pastoral is also used to classify dramas, elegies, and lyrics that exhibit the use of country settings and shepherd characters.

Pathetic Fallacy: A term coined by English critic John Ruskin to identify writing that falsely endows nonhuman things with human intentions and feelings, such as "angry clouds" and "sad trees."

Pen Name: See *Pseudonym*

Pentameter: See *Meter*

Persona: A Latin term meaning "mask." *Personae* are the characters in a fictional work of literature. The *persona* generally functions as a mask through which the author tells a story in a voice other than his or her own. A *persona* is usually either a character in a story who acts as a narrator or an "implied author," a voice created by the author to act as the narrator for himself or herself.

Personae: See *Persona*

Personal Point of View: See *Point of View*

Personification: A figure of speech that gives human qualities to abstract ideas, animals, and inanimate objects.

Petrarchan Sonnet: See *Sonnet*

Phenomenology: A method of literary criticism based on the belief that things have no existence outside of human consciousness or awareness. Proponents of this theory believe that art is a process that takes place in the mind of the observer as he or she contemplates an object rather than a quality of the object itself.

Plagiarism: Claiming another person's written material as one's own. Plagiarism can take the form of direct, word-for-word copying or the theft of the substance or idea of the work.

Platonic Criticism: A form of criticism that stresses an artistic work's usefulness as an agent of social engineering rather than any quality or value of the work itself.

Platonism: The embracing of the doctrines of the philosopher Plato, popular among the poets of the Renaissance and the Romantic period. Platonism is more flexible than Aristotelian Criticism and places more emphasis on the supernatural and unknown aspects of life.

Plot: In literary criticism, this term refers to the pattern of events in a narrative or drama. In its simplest sense, the plot guides the author in composing the work and helps the reader follow the work. Typically, plots exhibit causality and unity and have a beginning, a middle, and an end. Sometimes, however, a plot may consist of a series of disconnected events, in which case it is known as an "episodic plot."

Poem: In its broadest sense, a composition utilizing rhyme, meter, concrete detail, and expressive language to create a literary experience with emotional and aesthetic appeal.

Poet: An author who writes poetry or verse. The term is also used to refer to an artist or writer who has an exceptional gift for expression, imagination, and energy in the making of art in any form.

Poete maudit: A term derived from Paul Verlaine's *Les poetes maudits* (*The Accursed Poets*), a collection of essays on the French symbolist writers Stephane Mallarme, Arthur Rimbaud, and Tristan Corbiere. In the sense intended by Verlaine, the poet is "accursed" for choosing to explore extremes of human experience outside of middle-class society.

Poetic Fallacy: See *Pathetic Fallacy*

Poetic Justice: An outcome in a literary work, not necessarily a poem, in which the good are rewarded and the evil are punished, especially in ways that particularly fit their virtues or crimes.

Poetic License: Distortions of fact and literary convention made by a writer—not always a poet—for the sake of the effect gained. Poetic license is closely related to the concept of "artistic freedom."

Poetics: This term has two closely related meanings. It denotes (1) an aesthetic theory in literary criticism about the essence of poetry or (2) rules prescribing the proper methods, content, style, or diction of poetry. The term poetics may also refer to theories about literature in general, not just poetry.

Poetry: In its broadest sense, writing that aims to present ideas and evoke an emotional experience in the reader through the use of meter, imagery, connotative and concrete words, and a carefully constructed structure based on rhythmic patterns. Poetry typically relies on words and expressions that have several layers of meaning. It also makes use of the effects of regular rhythm on the ear and may make a strong appeal to the senses through the use of imagery.

Point of View: The narrative perspective from which a literary work is presented to the reader. There are four traditional points of view. The "third person omniscient" gives the reader a "godlike" perspective, unrestricted by time or place, from which to see actions and look into the minds of characters. This allows the author to comment openly on characters and events in the work. The "third-person" point of view presents the events of the story from outside of any single character's perception, much like the omniscient point of view, but the reader must understand the action as it takes place and without any special insight into characters' minds or motivations. The "first person" or "personal" point of view relates events as they are perceived by a single character. The main character "tells" the story and may offer opinions about the action and characters which differ from those of the author. Much less common than omniscient, third person, and first person is the "second-person" point of view, wherein the author tells the story as if it is happening to the reader.

Polemic: A work in which the author takes a stand on a controversial subject, such as abortion or religion. Such works are often extremely argumentative or provocative.

Pornography: Writing intended to provoke feelings of lust in the reader. Such works are often condemned by critics and teachers, but those which can be shown to have literary value are viewed less harshly.

Post-Aesthetic Movement: An artistic response made by African Americans to the black aesthetic movement of the 1960s and early 1970s. Writers since that time have adopted a somewhat different tone in their work, with less emphasis placed on the disparity between black and white in the United States. In the words of post-aesthetic authors such as Toni Morrison, John Edgar Wideman, and Kristin Hunter, African Americans are portrayed as looking inward for answers to their own questions, rather than always looking to the outside world.

Postmodernism: Writing from the 1960s forward characterized by experimentation and continuing to apply some of the fundamentals of modernism, which included existentialism and alienation. Postmodernists have gone a step further in the rejection of tradition begun with the modernists by also rejecting traditional forms, preferring the antinovel over the novel and the antihero over the hero.

Pre-Raphaelites: A circle of writers and artists in mid nineteenth-century England. Valuing the pre-Renaissance artistic qualities of religious symbolism, lavish pictorialism, and natural sensuousness, the Pre-Raphaelites cultivated a sense of mystery and melancholy that influenced later writers associated with the Symbolist and Decadent movements.

Primitivism: The belief that primitive peoples were nobler and less flawed than civilized peoples because they had not been subjected to the corrupt influence of society.

Projective Verse: A form of free verse in which the poet's breathing pattern determines the lines of the poem. Poets who advocate projective verse are against all formal structures in writing, including meter and form.

Prologue: An introductory section of a literary work. It often contains information establishing the situation of the characters or presents information about the setting, time period, or action. In drama, the prologue is spoken by a chorus or by one of the principal characters.

Prose: A literary medium that attempts to mirror the language of everyday speech. It is distinguished from poetry by its use of unmetered, unrhymed language consisting of logically related sentences. Prose is usually grouped into paragraphs that form a cohesive whole such as an essay or a novel.

Prosopopoeia: See *Personification*

Protagonist: The central character of a story who serves as a focus for its themes and incidents and as the principal rationale for its development. The protagonist is sometimes referred to in discussions of modern literature as the hero or antihero.

Proverb: A brief, sage saying that expresses a truth about life in a striking manner.

Pseudonym: A name assumed by a writer, most often intended to prevent his or her identification as the author of a work. Two or more authors may work together under one pseudonym, or an author may use a different name for each genre he or she publishes in. Some publishing companies maintain "house pseudonyms," under which any number of authors may write installations in a series. Some authors also choose a pseudonym over their real names the way an actor may use a stage name.

Pun: A play on words that have similar sounds but different meanings.

Pure Poetry: poetry written without instructional intent or moral purpose that aims only to please a reader by its imagery or musical flow. The term pure poetry is used as the antonym of the term "didacticism."

Q

Quatrain: A four-line stanza of a poem or an entire poem consisting of four lines.

R

Realism: A nineteenth-century European literary movement that sought to portray familiar characters, situations, and settings in a realistic manner. This was done primarily by using an objective narrative point of view and through the buildup of accurate detail. The standard for success of any realistic work depends on how faithfully it transfers common experience into fictional forms. The realistic method may be altered or extended, as in stream of consciousness writing, to record highly subjective experience.

Refrain: A phrase repeated at intervals throughout a poem. A refrain may appear at the end of each stanza or at less regular intervals. It may be altered slightly at each appearance.

Renaissance: The period in European history that marked the end of the Middle Ages. It began in Italy in the late fourteenth century. In broad terms, it is usually seen as spanning the fourteenth, fifteenth, and sixteenth centuries, although it did not reach Great Britain, for example, until the 1480s or so. The Renaissance saw an awakening in almost every sphere of human activity, especially science, philosophy, and the arts. The period is best defined by the emergence of a general philosophy that emphasized the importance of the intellect, the individual, and world affairs. It contrasts strongly with the medieval worldview, characterized by the dominant concerns of faith, the social collective, and spiritual salvation.

Repartee: Conversation featuring snappy retorts and witticisms.

Restoration: See *Restoration Age*

Restoration Age: A period in English literature beginning with the crowning of Charles II in 1660 and running to about 1700. The era, which was characterized by a reaction against Puritanism, was the first great age of the comedy of manners. The finest literature of the era is typically witty and urbane, and often lewd.

Rhetoric: In literary criticism, this term denotes the art of ethical persuasion. In its strictest sense, rhetoric adheres to various principles developed since classical times for arranging facts and ideas in a clear, persuasive, appealing manner. The term is also used to refer to effective prose in general and theories of or methods for composing effective prose.

Rhetorical Question: A question intended to provoke thought, but not an expressed answer, in the reader. It is most commonly used in oratory and other persuasive genres.

Rhyme: When used as a noun in literary criticism, this term generally refers to a poem in which words sound identical or very similar and appear in parallel positions in two or more lines. Rhymes are classified into different types according to where they fall in a line or stanza or according to the degree of similarity they exhibit in their spellings and sounds. Some major types of rhyme are "masculine" rhyme, "feminine" rhyme, and "triple" rhyme. In a masculine rhyme, the rhyming sound falls in a single accented syllable, as with "heat" and "eat." Feminine rhyme is a rhyme of two syllables, one stressed and one unstressed, as with "merry" and "tarry." Triple rhyme matches the sound of the accented syllable and the two unaccented syllables that follow: "narrative" and "declarative."

Rhyme Royal: A stanza of seven lines composed in iambic pentameter and rhymed *ababbcc*. The name is said to be a tribute to King James I of Scotland, who made much use of the form in his poetry.

Rhyme Scheme: See *Rhyme*

Rhythm: A regular pattern of sound, time intervals, or events occurring in writing, most often and most discernably in poetry. Regular, reliable rhythm is known to be soothing to humans, while interrupted, unpredictable, or rapidly changing rhythm is disturbing. These effects are known to authors, who use them to produce a desired reaction in the reader.

Rococo: A style of European architecture that flourished in the eighteenth century, especially in

France. The most notable features of *rococo* are its extensive use of ornamentation and its themes of lightness, gaiety, and intimacy. In literary criticism, the term is often used disparagingly to refer to a decadent or overly ornamental style.

Romance:

Romantic Age: See *Romanticism*

Romanticism: This term has two widely accepted meanings. In historical criticism, it refers to a European intellectual and artistic movement of the late eighteenth and early nineteenth centuries that sought greater freedom of personal expression than that allowed by the strict rules of literary form and logic of the eighteenth-century Neoclassicists. The Romantics preferred emotional and imaginative expression to rational analysis. They considered the individual to be at the center of all experience and so placed him or her at the center of their art. The Romantics believed that the creative imagination reveals nobler truths—unique feelings and attitudes—than those that could be discovered by logic or by scientific examination. Both the natural world and the state of childhood were important sources for revelations of "eternal truths." "Romanticism" is also used as a general term to refer to a type of sensibility found in all periods of literary history and usually considered to be in opposition to the principles of classicism. In this sense, Romanticism signifies any work or philosophy in which the exotic or dreamlike figure strongly, or that is devoted to individualistic expression, self-analysis, or a pursuit of a higher realm of knowledge than can be discovered by human reason.

Romantics: See *Romanticism*

Russian Symbolism: A Russian poetic movement, derived from French symbolism, that flourished between 1894 and 1910. While some Russian Symbolists continued in the French tradition, stressing aestheticism and the importance of suggestion above didactic intent, others saw their craft as a form of mystical worship, and themselves as mediators between the supernatural and the mundane.

S

Satire: A work that uses ridicule, humor, and wit to criticize and provoke change in human nature and institutions. There are two major types of satire: "formal" or "direct" satire speaks directly to the reader or to a character in the work; "indirect" satire relies upon the ridiculous behavior of its characters to make its point. Formal satire is further divided into two manners: the "Horatian," which

ridicules gently, and the "Juvenalian," which derides its subjects harshly and bitterly.

Scansion: The analysis or "scanning" of a poem to determine its meter and often its rhyme scheme. The most common system of scansion uses accents (slanted lines drawn above syllables) to show stressed syllables, breves (curved lines drawn above syllables) to show unstressed syllables, and vertical lines to separate each foot.

Second Person: See *Point of View*

Semiotics: The study of how literary forms and conventions affect the meaning of language.

Sestet: Any six-line poem or stanza.

Setting: The time, place, and culture in which the action of a narrative takes place. The elements of setting may include geographic location, characters' physical and mental environments, prevailing cultural attitudes, or the historical time in which the action takes place.

Shakespearean Sonnet: See *Sonnet*

Signifying Monkey: A popular trickster figure in black folklore, with hundreds of tales about this character documented since the nineteenth century.

Simile: A comparison, usually using "like" or "as," of two essentially dissimilar things, as in "coffee as cold as ice" or "He sounded like a broken record."

Slang: A type of informal verbal communication that is generally unacceptable for formal writing. Slang words and phrases are often colorful exaggerations used to emphasize the speaker's point; they may also be shortened versions of an oftenused word or phrase.

Slant Rhyme: See *Consonance*

Slave Narrative: Autobiographical accounts of American slave life as told by escaped slaves. These works first appeared during the abolition movement of the 1830s through the 1850s.

Social Realism: See *Socialist Realism*

Socialist Realism: The Socialist Realism school of literary theory was proposed by Maxim Gorky and established as a dogma by the first Soviet Congress of Writers. It demanded adherence to a communist worldview in works of literature. Its doctrines required an objective viewpoint comprehensible to the working classes and themes of social struggle featuring strong proletarian heroes.

Soliloquy: A monologue in a drama used to give the audience information and to develop the speaker's character. It is typically a projection of the speaker's innermost thoughts. Usually delivered while the speaker is alone on stage, a soliloquy is intended to present an illusion of unspoken reflection.

Sonnet: A fourteen-line poem, usually composed in iambic pentameter, employing one of several rhyme schemes. There are three major types of sonnets, upon which all other variations of the form are based: the "Petrarchan" or "Italian" sonnet, the "Shakespearean" or "English" sonnet, and the "Spenserian" sonnet. A Petrarchan sonnet consists of an octave rhymed *abbaabba* and a "sestet" rhymed either *cdecde, cdccdc,* or *cdedce.* The octave poses a question or problem, relates a narrative, or puts forth a proposition; the sestet presents a solution to the problem, comments upon the narrative, or applies the proposition put forth in the octave. The Shakespearean sonnet is divided into three quatrains and a couplet rhymed *abab cdcd efef gg.* The couplet provides an epigrammatic comment on the narrative or problem put forth in the quatrains. The Spenserian sonnet uses three quatrains and a couplet like the Shakespearean, but links their three rhyme schemes in this way: *abab bcbc cdcd ee.* The Spenserian sonnet develops its theme in two parts like the Petrarchan, its final six lines resolving a problem, analyzing a narrative, or applying a proposition put forth in its first eight lines.

Spenserian Sonnet: See *Sonnet*

Spenserian Stanza: A nine-line stanza having eight verses in iambic pentameter, its ninth verse in iambic hexameter, and the rhyme scheme *ababbcbcc.*

Spondee: In poetry meter, a foot consisting of two long or stressed syllables occurring together. This form is quite rare in English verse, and is usually composed of two monosyllabic words.

Sprung Rhythm: Versification using a specific number of accented syllables per line but disregarding the number of unaccented syllables that fall in each line, producing an irregular rhythm in the poem.

Stanza: A subdivision of a poem consisting of lines grouped together, often in recurring patterns of rhyme, line length, and meter. Stanzas may also serve as units of thought in a poem much like paragraphs in prose.

Stereotype: A stereotype was originally the name for a duplication made during the printing process; this led to its modern definition as a person or thing that is (or is assumed to be) the same as all others of its type.

Stream of Consciousness: A narrative technique for rendering the inward experience of a character. This technique is designed to give the impression of an ever-changing series of thoughts, emotions, images, and memories in the spontaneous and seemingly illogical order that they occur in life.

Structuralism: A twentieth-century movement in literary criticism that examines how literary texts arrive at their meanings, rather than the meanings themselves. There are two major types of structuralist analysis: one examines the way patterns of linguistic structures unify a specific text and emphasize certain elements of that text, and the other interprets the way literary forms and conventions affect the meaning of language itself.

Structure: The form taken by a piece of literature. The structure may be made obvious for ease of understanding, as in nonfiction works, or may be obscured for artistic purposes, as in some poetry or seemingly "unstructured" prose.

Sturm und Drang: A German term meaning "storm and stress." It refers to a German literary movement of the 1770s and 1780s that reacted against the order and rationalism of the enlightenment, focusing instead on the intense experience of extraordinary individuals.

Style: A writer's distinctive manner of arranging words to suit his or her ideas and purpose in writing. The unique imprint of the author's personality upon his or her writing, style is the product of an author's way of arranging ideas and his or her use of diction, different sentence structures, rhythm, figures of speech, rhetorical principles, and other elements of composition.

Subject: The person, event, or theme at the center of a work of literature. A work may have one or more subjects of each type, with shorter works tending to have fewer and longer works tending to have more.

Subjectivity: Writing that expresses the author's personal feelings about his subject, and which may or may not include factual information about the subject.

Surrealism: A term introduced to criticism by Guillaume Apollinaire and later adopted by Andre Breton. It refers to a French literary and artistic movement founded in the 1920s. The Surrealists sought to express unconscious thoughts and feelings in their works. The best-known technique used for achieving this aim was automatic writing—transcriptions of spontaneous outpourings from the unconscious. The Surrealists proposed to unify the contrary levels of conscious and unconscious, dream and reality, objectivity and subjectivity into a new level of "super-realism."

Suspense: A literary device in which the author maintains the audience's attention through the buildup of events, the outcome of which will soon be revealed.

Syllogism: A method of presenting a logical argument. In its most basic form, the syllogism consists of a major premise, a minor premise, and a conclusion.

Symbol: Something that suggests or stands for something else without losing its original identity. In literature, symbols combine their literal meaning with the suggestion of an abstract concept. Literary symbols are of two types: those that carry complex associations of meaning no matter what their contexts, and those that derive their suggestive meaning from their functions in specific literary works.

Symbolism: This term has two widely accepted meanings. In historical criticism, it denotes an early modernist literary movement initiated in France during the nineteenth century that reacted against the prevailing standards of realism. Writers in this movement aimed to evoke, indirectly and symbolically, an order of being beyond the material world of the five senses. Poetic expression of personal emotion figured strongly in the movement, typically by means of a private set of symbols uniquely identifiable with the individual poet. The principal aim of the Symbolists was to express in words the highly complex feelings that grew out of everyday contact with the world. In a broader sense, the term "symbolism" refers to the use of one object to represent another.

Symbolist: See *Symbolism*

Symbolist Movement: See *Symbolism*

Sympathetic Fallacy: See *Affective Fallacy*

T

Tanka: A form of Japanese poetry similar to *haiku*. A *tanka* is five lines long, with the lines containing five, seven, five, seven, and seven syllables respectively.

Terza Rima: A three-line stanza form in poetry in which the rhymes are made on the last word of each line in the following manner: the first and third lines of the first stanza, then the second line of the first stanza and the first and third lines of the second stanza, and so on with the middle line of any

stanza rhyming with the first and third lines of the following stanza.

Tetrameter: See *Meter*

Textual Criticism: A branch of literary criticism that seeks to establish the authoritative text of a literary work. Textual critics typically compare all known manuscripts or printings of a single work in order to assess the meanings of differences and revisions. This procedure allows them to arrive at a definitive version that (supposedly) corresponds to the author's original intention.

Theme: The main point of a work of literature. The term is used interchangeably with thesis.

Thesis: A thesis is both an essay and the point argued in the essay. Thesis novels and thesis plays share the quality of containing a thesis which is supported through the action of the story.

Third Person: See *Point of View*

Tone: The author's attitude toward his or her audience may be deduced from the tone of the work. A formal tone may create distance or convey politeness, while an informal tone may encourage a friendly, intimate, or intrusive feeling in the reader. The author's attitude toward his or her subject matter may also be deduced from the tone of the words he or she uses in discussing it.

Tragedy: A drama in prose or poetry about a noble, courageous hero of excellent character who, because of some tragic character flaw or *hamartia*, brings ruin upon him- or herself. Tragedy treats its subjects in a dignified and serious manner, using poetic language to help evoke pity and fear and bring about catharsis, a purging of these emotions. The tragic form was practiced extensively by the ancient Greeks. In the Middle Ages, when classical works were virtually unknown, tragedy came to denote any works about the fall of persons from exalted to low conditions due to any reason: fate, vice, weakness, etc. According to the classical definition of tragedy, such works present the "pathetic"—that which evokes pity—rather than the tragic. The classical form of tragedy was revived in the sixteenth century; it flourished especially on the Elizabethan stage. In modern times, dramatists have attempted to adapt the form to the needs of modern society by drawing their heroes from the ranks of ordinary men and women and defining the nobility of these heroes in terms of spirit rather than exalted social standing.

Tragic Flaw: In a tragedy, the quality within the hero or heroine which leads to his or her downfall.

Transcendentalism: An American philosophical and religious movement, based in New England from around 1835 until the Civil War. Transcendentalism was a form of American romanticism that had its roots abroad in the works of Thomas Carlyle, Samuel Coleridge, and Johann Wolfgang von Goethe. The Transcendentalists stressed the importance of intuition and subjective experience in communication with God. They rejected religious dogma and texts in favor of mysticism and scientific naturalism. They pursued truths that lie beyond the "colorless" realms perceived by reason and the senses and were active social reformers in public education, women's rights, and the abolition of slavery.

Trickster: A character or figure common in Native American and African literature who uses his ingenuity to defeat enemies and escape difficult situations. Tricksters are most often animals, such as the spider, hare, or coyote, although they may take the form of humans as well.

Trimeter: See *Meter*

Triple Rhyme: See *Rhyme*

Trochee: See *Foot*

U

Understatement: See *Irony*

Unities: Strict rules of dramatic structure, formulated by Italian and French critics of the Renaissance and based loosely on the principles of drama discussed by Aristotle in his *Poetics*. Foremost among these rules were the three unities of action, time, and place that compelled a dramatist to: (1) construct a single plot with a beginning, middle, and end that details the causal relationships of action and character; (2) restrict the action to the events of a single day; and (3) limit the scene to a single place or city. The unities were observed faithfully by continental European writers until the Romantic Age, but they were never regularly observed in English drama. Modern dramatists are typically more concerned with a unity of impression or emotional effect than with any of the classical unities.

Urban Realism: A branch of realist writing that attempts to accurately reflect the often harsh facts of modern urban existence.

Utopia: A fictional perfect place, such as "paradise" or "heaven."

Utopian: See *Utopia*

Utopianism: See *Utopia*

V

Verisimilitude: Literally, the appearance of truth. In literary criticism, the term refers to aspects of a work of literature that seem true to the reader.

Vers de societe: See *Occasional Verse*

Vers libre: See *Free Verse*

Verse: A line of metered language, a line of a poem, or any work written in verse.

Versification: The writing of verse. Versification may also refer to the meter, rhyme, and other mechanical components of a poem.

Victorian: Refers broadly to the reign of Queen Victoria of England (1837–1901) and to anything with qualities typical of that era. For example, the qualities of smug narrowmindedness, bourgeois materialism, faith in social progress, and priggish morality are often considered Victorian. This stereotype is contradicted by such dramatic intellectual developments as the theories of Charles Darwin, Karl Marx, and Sigmund Freud (which stirred strong debates in England) and the critical attitudes of serious Victorian writers like Charles Dickens and George Eliot. In literature, the Victorian Period was the great age of the English novel, and the latter part of the era saw the rise of movements such as decadence and symbolism.

Victorian Age: See *Victorian*

Victorian Period: See *Victorian*

W

Weltanschauung: A German term referring to a person's worldview or philosophy.

Weltschmerz: A German term meaning "world pain." It describes a sense of anguish about the nature of existence, usually associated with a melancholy, pessimistic attitude.

Z

Zarzuela: A type of Spanish operetta.

Zeitgeist: A German term meaning "spirit of the time." It refers to the moral and intellectual trends of a given era.

Cumulative
Author/Title Index

K

Keats, John
*Bright Star! Would I Were
    Steadfast as Thou Art:* V9
Ode on a Grecian Urn: V1
Ode to a Nightingale: V3
*When I Have Fears that I May
    Cease to Be:* V2
Kenyon, Jane
*"Trouble with Math in a One-
    Room Country School":* V9
King James Bible
Psalm 8: V9
Psalm 23: V4
Kinnell, Galway
Saint Francis and the Sow: V9
Kooser, Ted
The Constellation Orion: V8
Komunyakaa, Yusef
Facing It: V5
Kubla Khan (Coleridge): V5

L

l(a (cummings): V1
Lament for the Dorsets (Purdy): V5
Landscape with Tractor (Taylor):V10
Larkin, Philip
High Windows: V3
Toads: V4
Lawrence, D. H.
Piano: V6
Levertov, Denise
In the Land of Shinar: V7
Leviathan (Merwin): V5
Levine, Philip
Starlight: V8
Longfellow, Henry Wadsworth
A Psalm of Life: V7
Paul Revere's Ride: V2
Lord Randal (Anonymous): V6
Lost Sister (Song): V5
The Love Song of J. Alfred Prufrock
    (Eliot): V1
Lowell, Robert
For the Union Dead: V7
*The Quaker Graveyard in
    Nantucket:* V6

M

MacBeth, George
Bedtime Story: V8
MacLeish, Archibald
Ars Poetica: V5
Madgett, Naomi Long
*Alabama Centennial:*V10
The Man He Killed (Hardy): V3
A Martian Sends a Postcard Home
    (Raine): V7
Marvell, Andrew
To His Coy Mistress: V5

Masefield, John
Cargoes: V5
Matsuo Bashō
Falling Upon Earth: V2
The Moon Glows the Same: V7
McCrae, John
In Flanders Fields: V5
McElroy, Colleen
A Pièd: V3
McGinley, Phyllis
*Reactionary Essay on Applied
    Science:* V9
McKay, Claude
The Tropics in New York: V4
Meeting the British (Muldoon): V7
Mending Wall (Frost): V5
Merriam, Eve
Onomatopoeia: V6
Merwin, W. S.
Leviathan: V5
Midnight (Heaney): V2
Millay, Edna St. Vincent
*The Courage That My Mother
    Had:* V3
Milton, John
[On His Blindness] Sonnet 16: V3
Mirror (Plath): V1
Miss Rosie (Clifton): V1
The Missing (Gunn): V9
Momaday, N. Scott
Angle of Geese: V2
The Moon Glows the Same (Bashō):
    V7
"More Light! More Light!" (Hecht):
    V6
Mother to Son (Hughes): V3
Muldoon, Paul
Meeting the British: V7
Mueller, Lisel
The Exhibit: V9
Musée des Beaux Arts (Auden): V1
Music Lessons (Oliver): V8
My Last Duchess (Browning): V1
*My Life Closed Twice Before Its
    Close* (Dickinson): V8
My Papa's Waltz (Roethke): V3

N

Names of Horses (Hall): V8
The Negro Speaks of Rivers
    (Hughes):V10
Nemerov, Howard
*The Phoenix:*V10
Not Waving but Drowning (Smith): V3
Nothing Gold Can Stay (Frost): V3
Noyes, Alfred
The Highwayman: V4

O

O Captain! My Captain! (Whitman):
    V2

Ode on a Grecian Urn (Keats): V1
Ode to a Nightingale (Keats): V3
Ode to the West Wind (Shelley): V2
O'Hara, Frank
Why I Am Not a Painter: V8
old age sticks (cummings): V3
Old Ironsides (Holmes): V9
Oliver, Mary
Music Lessons: V8
[On His Blindness] Sonnet 16
    (Milton):V3
Ondaatje, Michael
To a Sad Daughter: V8
Onomatopoeia (Merriam): V6
On the Pulse of Morning (Angelou):
    V3
Ortiz, Simon
Hunger in New York City: V4
Out, Out— (Frost):V10
Owen, Wilfred
*Dulce et Decorum Est:*V10
Oysters (Sexton): V4

P

Pastan, Linda
Ethics: V8
Paul Revere's Ride (Longfellow): V2
The Phoenix (Nemerov):V10
Piano (Lawrence): V6
Piercy, Marge
Barbie Doll: V9
Plath, Sylvia
Mirror: V1
A Psalm of Life (Longfellow): V7
Poe, Edgar Allan
Annabel Lee: V9
The Bells: V3
The Raven: V1
Pound, Ezra
In a Station of the Metro: V2
*The River-Merchant's Wife: A
    Letter:* V8
Psalm 8 (King James Bible): V9
Psalm 23 (King James Bible): V4
Purdy, Al
Lament for the Dorsets: V5

Q

The Quaker Graveyard in Nantucket
    (Lowell): V6
Queen-Ann's-Lace (Williams): V6

R

Raine, Craig
*A Martian Sends a Postcard
    Home:* V7
Randall, Dudley
Ballad of Birmingham: V5
The Raven (Poe): V1

Cumulative Nationality/Ethnicity Index

Acoma Pueblo

Ortiz, Simon
    Hunger in New York City: V4

African American

Angelou, Maya
    Harlem Hopscotch: V2
    On the Pulse of Morning: V3
Baraka, Amiri
    In Memory of Radio: V9
Brooks, Gwendolyn
    The Bean Eaters: V2
    The Sonnet-Ballad: V1
    Strong Men, Riding Horses: V4
    We Real Cool: V6
Clifton, Lucille
    Miss Rosie: V1
Cullen, Countee
    Any Human to Another: V3
Dove, Rita
    This Life: V1
Hayden, Robert
    Those Winter Sundays: V1
Hughes, Langston
    Harlem: V1
    Mother to Son: V3
    The Negro Speaks of Rivers: V10
    Theme for English B: V6
Johnson, James Weldon
    The Creation: V1
Komunyakaa, Yusef
    Facing It: V5
Madgett, Naomi Long
    Alabama Centennial: V10
McElroy, Colleen
    A Pièd: V3

Randall, Dudley
    Ballad of Birmingham: V5
Reed, Ishmael
    Beware: Do Not Read This Poem:
      V6

American

Angelou, Maya
    Harlem Hopscotch: V2
    On the Pulse of Morning: V3
Auden, W. H.
    As I Walked Out One Evening: V4
    Musée des Beaux Arts: V1
    The Unknown Citizen: V3
Bishop, Elizabeth
    Brazil, January 1, 1502: V6
Blumenthal, Michael
    Inventors: V7
Bly, Robert
    Come with Me: V6
Bradstreet, Anne
    To My Dear and Loving Husband:
      V6
Brooks, Gwendolyn
    The Bean Eaters: V2
    The Sonnet-Ballad: V1
    Strong Men, Riding Horses: V4
    We Real Cool: V6
Clifton, Lucille
    Miss Rosie: V1
Crane, Stephen
    War Is Kind: V9
Cullen, Countee
    Any Human to Another: V3
cummings, e. e.
    l(a: V1

    old age sticks: V3
Dickey, James
    The Heaven of Animals: V6
Dickinson, Emily
    *Because I Could Not Stop for
      Death*: V2
    The Bustle in a House: V10
    *"Hope" Is the Thing with
      Feathers*: V3
    *I Heard a Fly Buzz—When I
      Died—*: V5
    *My Life Closed Twice Before Its
      Close*: V8
    *The Soul Selects Her Own
      Society*: V1
    There's a Certain Slant of Light:
      V6
    This Is My Letter to the World: V4
Dove, Rita
    This Life: V1
Dugan, Alan
    How We Heard the Name: V10
Eliot, T. S.
    Journey of the Magi: V7
    *The Love Song of J. Alfred
      Prufrock*: V1
Emerson, Ralph Waldo
    Concord Hymn: V4
Frost, Robert
    The Death of the Hired Man: V4
    Fire and Ice: V7
    Mending Wall: V5
    Nothing Gold Can Stay: V3
    Out, Out—: V10
    The Road Not Taken: V2
    *Stopping by Woods on a Snowy
      Evening*: V1
    The Wood-Pile: V6

Australian

Canadian

Canadian, Sri Lankan

Cherokee

English

Subject/Theme Index

Cumulative Index of
First Lines

Cumulative Index of
Last Lines

M

'Make a wish, Tom, make a wish.' (Drifters) V10: 98

make it seem to change (The Moon Glows the Same)
V7:152

midnight-oiled in the metric laws? (A Farewell to English)
V10:126

More dear, both for themselves and for thy sake! (Tintern
Abbey) V2:250

My love shall in my verse ever live young (Sonnet 19)
V9:211

My soul has grown deep like the rivers. (The Negro
Speaks of Rivers) V10:198

N

never to waken in that world again (Starlight) V8:213

No, she's brushing a boy's hair (Facing It) V5:110

no—tell them *no*— (The Hiding Place) V10:153

Noble six hundred! (The Charge of the Light Brigade)
V1:3

Nothing gold can stay (Nothing Gold Can Stay) V3:203

Nothing, and is nowhere, and is endless (High Windows)
V3:108

Now! (Alabama Centennial) V10:2

nursing the tough skin of figs (This Life) V1:293

O

O Death in Life, the days that are no more! (Tears, Idle
Tears) V4:220

O Lord our Lord, how excellent is thy name in all the
earth! (Psalm 8) V9:182

O Roger, Mackerel, Riley, Ned, Nellie, Chester, Lady
Ghost (Names of Horses) V8:142

of gentleness (To a Sad Daughter) V8:231

of love's austere and lonely offices? (Those Winter
Sundays) V1:300

Of the camellia (Falling Upon Earth) V2:64

Of the Creator. And he waits for the world to begin
(Leviathan) V5:204

Of what is past, or passing, or to come (Sailing to
Byzantium) V2:207

Old Ryan, not yours (The Constellation Orion) V8:53

On the dark distant flurry (Angle of Geese) V2:2

On the look of Death— (There's a Certain Slant of Light)
V6:212

On your head like a crown (Any Human to Another) V3:2

Or does it explode? (Harlem) V1:63

Or help to half-a-crown." (The Man He Killed) V3:167

or nothing (Queen-Ann's-Lace) V6:179

ORANGE forever. (Ballad of Orange and Grape) V10:18

owing old (old age sticks) V3:246

P

Petals on a wet, black bough (In a Station of the Metro)
V2:116

Plaiting a dark red love-knot into her long black hair
(The Highwayman) V4:68

Pro patria mori. (Dulce et Decorum Est) V10:110

R

Rage, rage against the dying of the light (Do Not Go
Gentle into that Good Night) V1:51

Remember the Giver fading off the lip (A Drink of Water)
V8:66

Rises toward her day after day, like a terrible fish (Mirror)
V1:116

S

Shall be lifted—nevermore! (The Raven) V1:202

Singing with open mouths their strong melodious songs (I
Hear America Singing) V3:152

slides by on grease (For the Union Dead) V7:67

Slouches towards Bethlehem to be born? (The Second
Coming) V7:179

So long lives this, and this gives life to thee (Sonnet 18)
V2:222

Stand still, yet we will make him run (To His Coy
Mistress) V5:277

startled into eternity (Four Mountain Wolves) V9:132

Still clinging to your shirt (My Papa's Waltz) V3:192

Surely goodness and mercy shall follow me all the days
of my life: and I will dwell in the house of the
Lord for ever (Psalm 23) V4:103

T

Take any streetful of people buying clothes and groceries,
cheering a hero or throwing confetti and
blowing tin horns ... tell me if the lovers are
losers ... tell me if any get more than the lovers
... in the dust ... in the cool tombs (Cool
Tombs) V6:46

That then I scorn to change my state with Kings (Sonnet
29) V8:198

That when we live no more, we may live ever (To My
Dear and Loving Husband) V6:228

That's the word. (Black Zodiac) V10:47

The bosom of his Father and his God (Elegy Written in a
Country Churchyard) V9:74

The garland briefer than a girl's (To an Athlete Dying
Young) V7:230

The hands gripped hard on the desert (At the Bomb
Testing Site) V8:3

the knife at the throat, the death in the metronome (Music
Lessons) V8:117

The lightning and the gale! (Old Ironsides) V9:172

the long, perfect loveliness of sow (Saint Francis and the
Sow) V9:222

The Lord survives the rainbow of His will (The Quaker
Graveyard in Nantucket) V6:159

The man I was when I was part of it (Beware of Ruins)
V8:43

The red rose and the brier (Barbara Allan) V7:11

The shaft we raise to them and thee (Concord Hymn)
V4:30

the unremitting space of your rebellion (Lost Sister) V5:217

The woman won (Oysters) V4:91

There is the trap that catches noblest spiritts, that
caught—they say—God, when he walked on
earth (Shine, Perishing Republic) V4:162

U

W

Y